WAGING NUCLEAR PEACE:

The Technology and Politics of Nuclear Weapons

Robert Ehrlich _____
PHYSICS DEPARTMENT GEORGE MASON UNIVERSITY

Waging Nuclear Peace: The Technology and Politics of Nuclear Weapons

State University of New York Press ▬▬▬▬ Albany

Published by
State University of New York Press, Albany

© 1985 State University of New York

All rights reserved

Printed in the United States of America

For information, address State University of New York
Press, State University Plaza, Albany, N.Y. 12246

Library of Congress Cataloging in Publication Data

Ehrlich, Robert, 1938–
   Waging nuclear peace.

   Bibliography: p. 379
   1. Atomic warfare. 2. Atomic weapons. 3. Atomic weapons and disarma-
ment. 4. Arms race—History—20th century. I. Title.
U263.E47   1984   355'.0217   84–120
ISBN 0-87395-919-1
ISBN 0-87395-920-5 (pbk.)

10 9 8 7 6 5 4 3 2 1

for David and Gary's grandchildren,
may they be allowed to exist.

CONTENTS ⎯⎯⎯⎯⎯⎯⎯⎯⎯⎯⎯⎯⎯⎯

IV   POLICY OPTIONS AND OBJECTIVES

FIGURES

TABLES

I

INTRODUCTION
TO THE ISSUES

One

THE NUCLEAR DEBATE

ARE WE DISCUSSING THE REAL ISSUE?

Ralph Swisher, director of the Civil Systems Division of the Federal Emergency Management Agency (FEMA) notes that this civil defense agency occasionally receives requests for "a guest speaker who could put nuclear war in a favorable light." This comment conveys in a nutshell much of the clouded thinking and confusion that often surround nuclear issues. For some people the nuclear issue boils down to the simple question of whether one is anti–nuclear war or pro–nuclear war. Although the Dr. Strangelove stereotype has been often invoked in fiction, in reality it is a straw man, useful for people who wish to avoid facing the really hard questions. Many people who have a deep emotional commitment to peace, which is good, find no need to think in a rational, analytical way about the frightful issues of nuclear war, which is bad. Moreover, many people have a definite revulsion to such analytical thinking in the context of nuclear issues; it reminds them of the cold calculations associated with military planners and civilian-defense analysts who are concerned with overkill, first strikes, and megadeaths.

Nuclear war is a highly emotional issue. It would be almost irrational *not* to become emotional when reflecting on the horror that a nuclear war could bring. However, the whole point of thinking analytically about nuclear war is to try to see facts objectively, not as we might wish them to be in some ideal world. It is only by

Table 1.1 The Hawk-Dove Litmus Test

Hawks	Doves
• Clearcut nuclear superiority can make us safe	• Nuclear disarmament can end the risk of nuclear war
• All Pentagon requests are justifiable	• An overzealous Pentagon has been the root cause of the arms race
• High technology is our savior	• High technology is our problem
• Arms control is a Soviet trick	• Arms control can substitute for a strong defense
• Nuclear wars can be fought and won	• Nuclear war will mean the end of life on earth
• Nuclear wars can be controlled and limited	• Nuclear war will escalate uncontrollably if even one bomb is used
• Doves are Moscow puppets	• Hawks want war

clearing away these misconceptions that we can best assess the most likely course of action to avert catastrophe.

WHAT DO HAWKS AND DOVES CONTRIBUTE TO A DEFINITION OF THE ISSUES?

To a significant degree the labels *hawk* and *dove* apply to caricatures representing extreme postions. In general, most people's views fall somewhere between these extremes, though often closer to one or the other. But a common thread links the hawks and doves; both try to promote their views through fear. The hawks dwell on fear of the Soviet Union, while the doves dwell on fear of a nuclear holocaust. Both of these fears are legitimate. It is only by dwelling on one and ignoring the other that a one-sided perspective results. Due to this limited perspective, the beliefs of both the hawks and doves are seriously flawed. Table 1.1 lists a number of paired exaggerations. Readers who wish to take a "hawk-dove litmus test" can do so by seeing which statement of each pair they consider the greater exaggeration.

One central fact of our nuclear age is that there are few hard facts about nuclear war. When we form opinions about nuclear issues, it seems likely that political values and unstated, often subconscious, assumptions play at least as great a role in influencing our thinking as those few facts that do exist. Moreover, which particular facts assume importance in our thinking is likely to depend greatly on our unstated assumptions. For example, there are any number of facts that those inclined toward the dovish or hawkish paired exaggerations in table 1.1 can cite. Concerning the first pair of entries, for example, doves are likely to note the following facts:

- Nearly all previous arms races have ended in war.
- Mankind has eventually used every weapon he has ever devised.
- Even if the risk of nuclear war in a given year is small, the probability of nuclear war becomes a mathematical certainty over a long period of time.

Alternatively, those who believe that clearcut nuclear superiority can made us safe are likely to cite another set of facts:

- There are no known wars that were avoided through disarmament following an arms race.
- There have been many wars lost by the side that had too few weapons.
- There was no nuclear war during the post–World War II period in which the United States possessed clearcut nuclear superiority.

The hawks and doves undoubtedly can each cite reasons why their set of facts is of particular importance, while those facts on the other side are of little significance. In making such arguments each side is likely to reveal something of its unstated assumptions. Doves are likely to believe that in the nuclear age, radical untried measures such as complete disarmament are made necessary by the fact that nuclear weapons are unlike anything mankind has ever faced before. Hawks, however, are more likely to base their advocacy of nuclear superiority on their belief that nuclear weapons have not changed human psychology in a world filled with evil opportunists. Both hawks and doves would probably agree with Albert Einstein's observation that the existence of nuclear weapons has changed everything with the exception of man's thinking. However, doves would urge us to change our mode of thinking if we wish to survive, while hawks would probably urge us to devise measures that do not discount the existence of evil in the world.

While the views of most people probably fall in between the hawk-dove caricatures, the adoption of a more moderate position does not exempt us from the pitfalls of basing our beliefs on unstated assumptions and selectively choosing our facts to fit those assumptions. Nor does the adoption of a "moderate" position insure that we will focus our attention on the important issues in the nuclear debate, rather than be distracted by spurious issues.

By falsely conceiving of the nuclear debate as a two-sided one between extreme hawks and doves, people may be led to believe that the debate is between those who wish to arm so as to fight and win a nuclear war and those who wish to disarm and avoid one. For example, I have been seriously asked by many persons what position I have taken in writing this book—for or against nuclear war. This book is "pronuclear" only in the sense that it views nuclear weapons as playing a vital role in deterring war. It is most certainly not pro–nuclear war!

HOW CAN NUCLEAR WAR BEST BE AVOIDED?

Any rational person must be against nuclear war, though one may not necessarily believe that being against nuclear weapons and in favor of disarmament is the best way of avoiding a nuclear war. While a "doomsday clock" may be moved forward or backward from midnight based on the collective judgment of the editors of the *Bulletin of the Atomic Scientists,* the actual closeness to the brink is not something that can be determined simply by counting the numbers of weapons, the number of articles published, the level of rhetoric of world leaders, or perhaps even the scale of the military involvement of the superpowers in parts of the Third World such as in Afghanistan or Central America. Nuclear arms control, which is not necessarily the same as disarmament, can make an essential contribution to our national security. Regardless of how one feels about the need to build new weapons, there are important mutual U.S.-Soviet interests in measures to prevent surprise attack; measures to maintain good information-gathering abilities via satellite; measures to guard against starting a war by accident; and efforts to control or eliminate the most destabilizing weapons in the arsenals—those that are simultaneously vulnerable to a first strike and threaten a first strike. It is probable that the danger the world now faces results more from these destabilizing kinds of weapons than from the sheer number of weapons.

Regardless of the perceived morality of the notion of deterrence, a plausible case can be made that it has in fact worked, which in a practical sense is the truest test of the morality of any method of avoiding nuclear annihilation. While there is no way to know whether mutual assured destruction (MAD) will continue to work, there is no way to know whether such radical untried measures, as complete disarmament will work at all. Given the ease of cheating by "storing some away just in case they are needed" and the tremendous military advantage that the side that followed this course would have in the event of hostilities, disarmament or even minimum deterrence might well have the opposite of the intended effect.

While readers may not agree with all the opinions expressed in this book, it is hoped they will be provoked and challenged to rethink some of the most important matters of life and death facing humanity. Some of these issues have been addressed since the dawn of the nuclear age, but it is essential that each generation reexamine them in the light of new knowledge and, equally important, in the light of new technology that makes possible what previously may have been only a nuclear strategist's nightmare.

Nuclear war is now a hot topic, after being a background issue since the early 1960s. While it is fortunate that people are again paying attention to the topic, so much is being said and written about nuclear war that the public will almost certainly become saturated with the issue. But the threat of nuclear war will never fade away. If we are to survive, humanity will live forever under the threat of a possible nuclear catastrophe. As the physicist J. Robert Oppenheimer noted, even if all nuclear weapons were destroyed, it would be impossible to destroy the knowledge of how to make them. Moreover, no "technical fix" could offer permanent protection against a nuclear-armed aggressor.

UNIQUE ASPECTS OF THIS BOOK

I do not believe that I have found the one answer to the nuclear dilemma. However, in contrast to other nuclear-war books written from a particular ideological perspective, this book adopts some positions that may be considered hawkish and others dovish. I firmly believe that we will avoid nuclear catastrophe only by following a narrow winding path that avoids many of the simplistic solutions advocated by the hawks or the doves. The dangers of nuclear war are very real, and the path that will enable us to avoid one is becoming increasingly narrow.

Many issues related to nuclear war depend on the answers to a number of technical questions. This book presupposes an elementary knowledge of mathematics, for example, the meaning of a cube root. However, the book is self-contained in terms of the necessary basic science on which it relies.

The wide spectrum of topics covered in this book include some not found in other books on nuclear war—topics such as how public opinion is shaped by the media, civil defense measures for the individual, long-term worldwide impact of a nuclear war, and physical principles of nuclear weapons and radiation. These and other topics are covered in a systematic organized way, with considerable attention paid to an analysis of what others have written on nuclear issues. Such a critical analysis of others' work builds on the body of studies that have been made of various technical and nontechnical issues and attempts to deflate some of the nonsense that has been written by those on all sides of the nuclear debate. While this book is most certainly not neutral on many of the perplexing nuclear issues we face, only the reader can decide how well it succeeds in its attempt to be objective. Overall, the book should anger both hawks and doves, particularly the more self-righteous of each persuasion.

Although fundamentally I believe there is no ultimate solution to the nuclear dilemma, I also believe that there are a number of measures that can reduce the risk of nuclear war. Rather than simply reversing the arms race, risk reduction must be the goal of all our efforts—a distinction that receives critical analysis here. Other analyzed assumptions include such questions as: Is nuclear disarmament desirable? Is there any relation between the perceived risk of war and the objective reality of risk? Do we really know what has so far kept us out of nuclear war?

Although this book is intended to be read by the informed layman who seeks an objective examination of nuclear-war-related issues from a balanced perspective, it may also be useful in college-level courses. I hope that colleges and universities will awaken to the great need for courses focusing on nuclear war and that this book may make a useful contribution in that regard.

Numerous individuals have made helpful suggestions for improving this manuscript. For reasons best known to them I am extremely grateful to: Tom Ackerman, David Albright, Deborah Berghoffen, Peter Black, Wayne Blanchard, Conrad Chester, Samuel Coriniti, John Evans, Howard Frost, Henry Hirsch, Dale Keller, Joseph Knox, William Lankford, Joseph Lieb, Tom Longstreth, Jeanne

Mellinger, Robert Nadeau, Hans Plendl, David Powers, Barry Schnei-der, Diana Smith, Roger Sullivan, Richard Turco, Bryant Wedge, and Peter Zimmerman. Obviously, the flaws in the manuscript are solely the responsibility of the author.

Two _____

PUBLIC OPINION AND THE MEDIA _____

▷DOES PUBLIC OPINION MATTER?

In the short run, whether or not nuclear war is averted depends greatly on actions taken by a very small group of men in the Soviet Union and the United States.[1] In the long run, however, there probably is no force more important in determining whether nuclear war will be averted than that of public opinion. This is especially true in the case of the United States and other Western democracies, where public opinion has a significant influence on the selection of government leaders and their policies. If the public is well informed and has a balanced perspective, then public opinion can be a great force for peace. An uninformed, misguided, or apathetic public may significantly increase the chances of nuclear war.

Few public issues are both as vital and as complex as the collection of issues related to nuclear weapons and nuclear war. The complexity of the nuclear dilemma should not require that its solution be left to the "experts." Indeed, the experts are just as divided on many of the most troublesome issues as the general public. In most cases, it is not necessary for an enlightened citizen to possess any "secret" information in order to make informed judgments on nuclear issues. Moreover, it is no longer realistic for political leaders to expect that the public will support on faith the government position in matters of national security simply because the leaders claim the facts are too sensitive to divulge. If government leaders withhold such facts from the public, then they are the ones endangering national security by not providing the public with the necessary information to make an informed decision. Nevertheless, there obviously do exist sensitive military and intelligence secrets whose disclosure would genuinely harm the national interest. It is unnecessary secrecy, which is the natural inclination of most governments, that should be avoided.

In order to make informed judgments about nuclear questions, it is important that we exercise our rational faculties to the maximum. It is quite proper to react emotionally to the tremendous horror that a nuclear war would bring: such a catastrophe could put an end to all our dreams for ourselves, our children, and the generations to come. Only through the cool light of reason can we hope to avoid such a horrible calamity. Voices of irrationality abound on nuclear matters from those of all shades of political opinion. For example, those who believe that there is an ultimate technical solution to the dilemma, be it a superweapon or an antiballistic missile system to protect our population, are probably deluding themselves. Moreover, the entire process of nuclear-weapons decision making is, in some eyes, largely an irrational one. Weapons decisions are generally made based on competing pressures and parochial interests within the defense establishment. Sometimes these competing pressures result in a decision or weapon that serves the national interest, but often they do not. Sometimes the weapons produced by this process are only wasteful and unnecessary, at other times they are worse— weapons it would be better not to possess.

Irrationality also abounds among those active in the antinuclear movement who seem to believe the whole nuclear problem can be made to go away if only world leaders would heed the voice of the people. These activists fail to realize that there are people in other countries who have no way at present to make their leaders heed public opinion. Many in the antinuclear movement believe that the answer to the nuclear dilemma is really quite simple, namely, to ban all nuclear weapons. However, accomplishing that worthy goal may not only be far from simple, but perhaps impossible. Moreover, attempting a total ban of nuclear weapons in our present politically volatile world could have unfortunate and even disastrous consequences, and in fact might carry a greater risk of nuclear war than other courses of action.

A U.S. public that reacts emotionally to nuclear issues is more susceptible to being manipulated by fear—a highly undesirable and dangerous situation—whether it be excessive fear of the Russians promoted by the proweapons lobby or excessive fear of a nuclear holocaust promoted by those in the antinuclear movement. Excessive fear can lead either to paralysis or to impulsive irrational actions, both of which must be avoided if we are to survive. There can be no question that a nuclear holocaust should be feared, nor should there be any doubt that Soviet military power represents a grave potential threat to the United States. However, excessive fear either of the Soviets or of the holocaust is highly dangerous. Such excessive fear is perhaps just as dangerous as the near-total lack of concern most of the public exhibited toward the risk of nuclear annihilation during most of the last three decades. We must find a middle way in which we remain alert to the grave dangers facing us, but always striving to keep them in perspective and react with reason, not emotion. It is no exaggeration to say that the fate of the world may literally depend on public opinion—particularly public opinion in the United States.

The history of the nuclear arms race justifies a certain amount of skepticism concerning the extent to which public opinion can influence nuclear policies and the risk of nuclear war. However, significant changes may have occurred in recent years. For example, U.S. congressional attitudes on the civil defense program and the nuclear-freeze proposal were undoubtedly shaped to a varying degree by public opinion on these issues. The public attitude toward the proper size of the defense budget also influences congressmen, although perhaps not as much as the presence of defense contractors or military bases in their voting districts. The U.S. Congress may soometimes seem unsynchronized with the public mood, but that is mainly due to the inertia in the political system, given six-year senatorial terms. (Inertia may, of course, have a positive aspect, especially considering the large and frequent swings in the attitude of the U.S. public toward national defense, nuclear war, and the magnitude of the Russian threat.)

Those who feel that the U.S. government in its nuclear policies is totally unresponsive to public opinion may be lamenting the extent to which their particular views have had little impact on government policy. There have been any number of presidential elections whose outcome hinged, in part, on the public perception of the winning candidate's position on defense and nuclear issues: John Kennedy in 1960 condemned the "missile gap"; Lyndon Johnson in 1964 was portrayed as being the candidate less likely to cause a nuclear war; and Ronald Reagan, in 1980 campaigned on the need to close the "window of vulnerability." Even if the public has only a limited ability to affect directly decisions on nuclear issues, it has *the* determining influence on which candidates are elected to government office. It would seem that candidates who hold naïve or ill-informed views on nuclear matters might be less likely to be elected if the public is well informed.

One indication of the influence public opinion can have on nuclear and defense issues is the manner in which the nuclear-freeze proposal became a mass movement and was then later considered by the U.S. Congress. The size of the movement is also credited with causing the Reagan administration to substantially alter its original position on arms control, although a skeptic might observe that these administration changes were only of a cosmetic nature and were designed to placate a worried public. Similarly, the House passage of a freeze resolution could be viewed merely as some representatives' opportunistic way of winning their constituents' approval without imposing any real limits on the arms race. Current public-opinion research offers further grounds for skepticism that public opinion has had a major influence on the determination of national policy to date, except in limited and indirect ways. Despite such findings, however, a gradual evolution in public opinion over time cannot help but have a profound effect on the political complexion of the elected policymakers, and it can also place constraints on their policy choices.

WHY HAS THE NUCLEAR ISSUE REEMERGED?

In view of the vital importance of the nuclear dilemma, its reemergence as a central issue on the national agenda is most welcome. There are many reasons why the issue has come, with considerable suddenness, to occupy the public's attention. These reasons would have to include actions taken by the Reagan administration to significantly expand the U.S. nuclear arsenal, careless administration talk about "limited" and "winnable" nuclear wars, and initial administration lack of action on nuclear arms control. What is not so clear is whether the vast increase in public concern over the risk of nuclear war matches a real increase in the probability of war. One cannot deny that there are both psychological and objective factors that lead many to conclude that there is such a link, for example, a belief in an increased probability of nuclear war could conceivably become a self-fulfilling prophecy. Nevertheless, we really do not know to what extent, if any, the great increase in public concern mirrors a real increase in the risk of nuclear war.

The rise in public concern over the risk of nuclear war and the need for nuclear arms control coincided with the Reagan administration's nuclear buildup and its initial disinterest in nuclear arms control. But, what of the last three decades of little public concern—is there any reason to believe that during those decades the risk of nuclear war was very low, just because it was not an issue of concern to many? There simply is no obvious connection between the level of public concern about nuclear war and the objective probability of its occurrence. Despite the assurances of some psychologists to the contrary, feeling secure and being secure may be very different matters in the nuclear age.

In examining the renewed attention paid to the nuclear issue in recent years, it is easy to read more into this phenomenon than has actually occurred. The public has not had a great change of heart about either the nature of the Soviet military threat or the desirability of controlling nuclear weapons. As we will see, public-opinion polls show that the U.S. public has always strongly favored nuclear-arms-control agreements with the Soviet Union, even at an earlier time when a sizeable fraction had reservations about the SALT II Treaty. The main change that has occurred in recent years is not the positive attitude towards nuclear arms control—which has always been present—but rather how urgent the public believes the need for a nuclear-arms-control agreement to be. The same public that a few years ago expressed somewhat negative attitudes towards the SALT II agreement to limit nuclear arms, more recently has expressed much more positive attitudes towards a proposal for a nuclear freeze. The very different public reception of those two nuclear-arms-control proposals depends on a large number of factors and is discussed at length in chapter 10. Certainly one important factor accounting for the way nuclear issues are perceived by the public is their treatment by the media.

HOW WELL HAVE THE MEDIA HANDLED THE NUCLEAR ISSUE?

On the life-and-death issue of nuclear war, the media could be a great educational force promoting rational thinking by the public.

Measured against that high standard, the media treatement of nuclear issues has with some exceptions been superficial at best. There are many reasons why the media treatment of nuclear issues has left much to be desired—some relate to the nature of the media, others to the nature of the issue itself, while still others relate to the nature of our society. Among the reasons for poor media coverage of nuclear issues are the following:

1. *Lack of knowledge.* There has been no use of nuclear weapons in war since the United States bombed Horoshima and Nagasaki in World War II, using two "small" atomic bombs. Thus, even for the experts, a large-scale war is a subject about which there are mostly speculations and few facts. People who attempt to draw conclusions about nuclear war are in a similar position to the exobiologists, whose "study" of extraterrestrial life is so far based entirely on speculation. In the area of nuclear war no one, with the exception of those Japanese who survived the bombings, has first-hand experience on which to base their conclusions.

2. *Sports mentality.* The media tends to cover many topics in the same way it covers sprorting events—there is a great emphasis on keeping score. For example, there is a tendency to portray the nuclear balance between the United States and the Soviet Union too simplistically, as hinging on numbers of warheads or numbers of megatons that give the overall "score." In reality these numbers, while not unimportant, are just one measure of the nuclear balance that depends on a great many other factors, some of which are much less susceptible to quantification, and hence they tend to get left off the scoreboard.

3. *The "trend game."* Examining trends over time is particularly susceptible to distortion, depending on the point one wishes to make. Consider, for example, defense spending under the Reagan administration. It is quite true that under the Reagan administration's five-year defense program, real annual defense expenditures were slated to increase 8.1 percent annually from 1981 to 1987 for a net increase of 59 percent. Such an increase would be the largest military buildup since the Korean War. An alternative way of describing U.S.-defense-spending trends since the Korean War, however, would be to note that as a fraction of public spending, defense took only one-third as many dollars in 1984 as it did during its Korean War peak. Thus, according to that statistic, the Reagan buildup appears to be nothing more than a relatively modest increase coming after a twenty five-year period of decline. A very different case could, of course, be made if we were to examine U.S. defense expenditures

in dollars (rather than in fraction of public spending) over the same time period, and still another perspective is gleaned if we examine tha ratio of U.S. to U.S.S.R. defense spending during that period. There are, in fact, any number of alternative trends we could cite to make one point or another and ample rationales why one statistic is better than another. It is an open question as to how much of the disinclination of the media to examine all the various alternate trends and their validity results from media bias and how much is due to the desire not to bore and confuse the public with a variety of trends that support opposing arguments.

4. *Ill-defined terms.* Discussions of nuclear war abound with ill-defined terms. For example, the term *nuclear war* itself is not well defined. Although most people using the term have in mind the all-out holocaust involving the use of a large fraction of the world's 50,000 nuclear weapons, it might also include the use of a single nuclear weapon by a Third World power.

Survivability is another ill-defined term. If in an argument one person refers to an all-out nuclear war as being survivable while another claims it is not survivable, what exactlly is being disputed? Does the claim of nonsurvivability imply that all life on earth would be extinguished, that in the directly affected countries there would be no survivors, or that the directly affected countries would not recover as modern societies? Similarly, does the claim of survivability imply that society could recover after a few years with no resulting long-term damage or that a greatly modified society might emerge after a long dark age possibly lasting many decades? With such a large range of meanings to the words survivability and unsurvivability, the argument over whether nuclear war is survivable may be more a matter of semantics than an argument over the probable effects of a nuclear war. Hearing survivors of the Hiroshima-Nagasaki bombings testify before Congress on their experiences can be a terribly moving experience that strengthens one's belief that nuclear weapons must not be used again in anger. However, when these survivors testify that there can be no survivors in a nuclear war, one senses a certain dismay at the seemingly infinite elasticity of language.

5. *Educational deficiences.* The United States, which no longer has one of the lowest rates of illiteracy among the world's developed nations, is particularly illiterate when it comes to scientific matters. Many studies have shown that compared to other technologically advanced countries such as Japan, West Germany, and the Soviet Union, the amount and quality of scientific education in U.S. schools is woefully lacking. Among the many issues related to nuclear war,

there are some that require an elementary knowledge of science which is sadly lacking in many citizens. While the amount of scientific knowledge required may be small, its lack among a substantial fraction of the U.S. public limits the kinds of programs a ratings-conscious TV network would be prepared to broadcast. Can a citizen with only a small knowledge of science understand that:

- Even though we may have a new generation of video-game addicts who have great skill in shooting down enemy missiles on a video screen, the ability to protect the population against a real missile attack is currently nonexistent for very many technical reasons.

- Even though a thickness of three feet of dirt is sufficient to shield oneself against the harmful effects of nuclear-fallout radiation, an effective civil defense is very much more complicated than digging a hole and climbing in, and it may be totally ineffective under certain conditions.

- Even though sheltering may make short-term survival possible following a large-scale nuclear attack, there are a number of long-term worldwide impacts that could possibly turn our earth into a most inhospitable environment.

Conversely, can a citizen with only an elementary science education understand that:

- Even though there is the equivalent of three tons of TNT in the nuclear arsenals for every person on earth, that particular fact does not imply that "we could kill the world's population many times over" in a large nuclear war.

- Even though nuclear weapons are the most destructive kind of weapons ever devised, it is possible to measurably increase our chances of survival through civil defense under certain circumstances.

- Even though scientists have identified many worldwide environmental impacts resulting from a large-scale nuclear war that could conceivably make the earth unlivable, there is no general consensus among scientists that this ultimate catastrophe would be likely to occur.

Regrettably, science is just one of many areas in which a lack of knowledge on the part of the U.S. public contributes to a low level of sophistication in the nuclear debate. Other significant educational deficiencies would have to include:

- A lack of appreciation for U.S. and world history, including a general understanding of the causes of conflict between nations as well as a good comprehension of the historical roots of tensions between the superpowers that goes beyond slogans such as "the cold war."

- A very poor knowledge of the nature of contemporary Soviet society, including both its shortcomings and positive features. Our profound ignorance of Soviet society can be measured in terms of the very small number of American experts in this field, as well as the near-total lack of instruction most students receive in high school or college. This state of affairs is in sharp contrast with the extensive factual knowledge of the United States by Soviet citizens—both experts as well as average citizens.[2]

6. *Contamination by association.* Those in the media who have very definite views on the solution to the nuclear dilemma often find it easier to attack opposing views by undermining the credibility of the most extreme supporters of such views rather than by analyzing the arguments objectively. We shall consider two very different examples to illustrate the point.

Reader's Digest, one of the most widely read publications in America, in a 1982 article described in considerable detail how Moscow has had a behind-the-scenes influence on the peace movement in the West.[3] In particular, the article discussed how various covert agencies of the Kremlin have allegedly given considerable support to the nuclear-freeze movement and gotten very large numbers of well-meaning Americans to support a position actively and secretly promoted by the Soviet Union. Is there anything irresponsible about such reporting? Surely, such allegations of a behind-the-scenes orchestration by Moscow are worthy of discussion, even if the vast majority of those supporting disarmament proposals are doing so for the most idealistic of motives.

A report such as this one is not so much irresponsible journalism as it is an example of highly selective journalism. If a journalist believes the nuclear freeze is a bad proposal, it is much more important for him or her to explain why it is bad than to try to taint the proposal by exposing Soviet covert support for it, even if that support could be clearly documented to exist. The Soviet Union's support for a proposal does not necessarily mean that the proposal is against American interests. Thus, the fact of Soviet support, even covert support, while worthy of our attention, should not obviate the need for a substantive analysis of the proposal on its merits.

A second example of contamination by association may be found in the way that many in the press have treated the issue of civil defense. Many journalists regard civil defense as an issue only suited for ridicule and cartoons, but not serious analysis. Some in the press take great pleasure, for example, in quoting civil defense overenthusiasts such as T. K. Jones, a Reagan-administration assistant undersecretary for defense, to the effect that we can all be saved following a nuclear war, "if there are enough shovels to go around." [4] As in the previous example, this also does not constitute irresponsible journalism. It is important for the public to be made aware that there may be some members of the defense establishment who hold grotesquely simplistic views as to what is necessary to mount an effective civil defense or that there may be some in government who view nuclear war as something that would not interfere with the regular government business of tax collection and mail delivery. However, to hold up to ridicule the whole idea of civil defense on the basis of such misguided beliefs is another example of selective journalism and contamination by association.

Moreover, media accounts of government civil defense plans are sometimes caricatures rather than honest reports. For example, the proposal to use the U.S. postal service to distribute address cards in the event of an evacuation was not made with the intention of insuring mail deliveries following a nuclear attack. The purpose was instead to allow surviving relatives to contact one another following an attack. Most media accounts of this postal-service plan failed to mention the stated purpose of the plan, instead opting for the more "interesting" caricature.

7. *False dichotomies.* The notion that there are two sides to the nuclear debate rather than many sides certainly did not originate with the media, but the notion is one the media tends to perpetuate. Portrayal of the nuclear dilemma as strictly a two-sided debate occurs, in part, because of constraints imposed on the media. For example, in a TV news program covering many topics, only a very brief time will be devoted to each one. Often in the case of a complex topic such as the nuclear question, there is no way to convey the various

shadings of opinion and explore positions in depth. Even when ample time is devoted to such an in-depth exploration, there is sometimes a tendency to invite panelists representing diametrically opposing views, e.g., an administration spokesman and an antiadministration critic, rather than panelists whose exploration of the issues knows no political allegiance.

The biggest constraint imposed on the media is that imposed by ratings. Many people seem impatient with in-depth explorations of issues that do not result in definitve answers to questions. There seems to be a relatively low public tolerance for ambiguity, particularly on nuclear issues. Questions such as: Is the Soviet Union ahead of the United States in nuclear weapons? Does it matter who is ahead in nuclear weapons? Can an arms-control treaty be completely verified? Can civil defense do any good? seem to cry out for unambiguous answers. Many in the public would much prefer to resolve such life-and-death issues one way or the other than to hear such ambigious answers as:

- In some respects the United States leads the Soviets in nuclear weapons, while in other respects the Soviets lead. The overall balance depends on how much weight is given to different factors.

- Who is "ahead" could matter under certain kinds of scenarios of uncertain likelihood.

- Certain aspects of arms-control treaties can be verified to a high degree, while others cannot be verified at all.

- Civil defense could result in the saving of many lives only in certain kinds of attacks of unknown likelihood.

Even though such ambigious answers may be closer to the truth than more definitive answers, ambiguous answers are less pscyhologically satisfying; nor do they offer clearcut prescriptions to action or support our preconceived positions as well. Many people, therefore, have a strong psychological need for clearcut solutions that can serve to calm their fears. However, the nature of the simple solution depends greatly on whether it is a fear of the Russians or of nuclear war that is aroused. Thus it is not uncommon to find a tendency for the media to conform to the belief of many people that there are essentially two sides to the nuclear debate.

Probably the most pernicous false dichotomy that exists is that the nuclear debate is between those who wish to fight and win a nuclear war and those who wish to avoid one. Thus, supporters of civil defense and increased U.S. nuclear strength are believed by many to favor fighting and winning a nuclear war, while supporters of the nuclear freeze proposal are believed by many to wish to avoid one. There are conceivably some crazy people, perhaps even some in positions of power, who do wish to fight and win a nuclear war. However, the overwhelming majority of those who support civil defense and nuclear rearmament, including the overwhelming majority of those in power, almost certainly have no such desire. In fact, it seems highly likely that the majority of those supporting so-called militaristic policies do so with precisely the same motivation as those who oppose them, i.e., they want to make nuclear war less likely. To characterize those who favor civil defense and nuclear rearmament as desiring to fight and win a nuclear war is just as incorrect and unfair as characterizing those who favor disarmament and nuclear-freeze proposals as being Soviet puppets. In many circles, however, the latter characterization would be considered slanderous, while the former would be deemed quite respectable.

HOW FAIRLY ARE ADMINISTRATION POSITIONS REPORTED?

Much of the new public concern about "winnable" or "limited" nuclear wars has originated from statements and policies made by members of the Reagan administration. How can the public not be greatly alarmed to learn about administration contingency plans to fight and win a nuclear war? [5] Many people find such contingency planning extremely frightening, even though it may have gone on unreported under all U.S. administrations. Such nuclear-war-fighting planning is believed by many to foster the illusion that nuclear war is manageable and perhaps not to be greatly feared. However, it is at least a debatable point whether such exercises make nuclear war more likely through creating the illusion or manageability or less likely by convincing the adversary that we would have the means to retaliate under all conceivable circumstances. As we shall see later, the common notion that a nuclear war would necessarily involve one awful spasm, initiated simply by someone pushing the red button, may not be correct. If without contingency nuclear-war-fighting planning, the United States were to leave itself only that option, we would in effect be attempting to prevent the unthinkable by refusing to think about it. In our present world, that policy might actually have the result of making nuclear war more likely, and it could guarantee escalation to the all-out catastrophe. To portray administration nuclear-war-fighting contingency planning as a desire to fight and win a nuclear war is a large step that many in the media have no hesitation in making. A desire to develop a capability to fight an extended nuclear war, to match a perceived capability of the Soviet Union, is not de facto evidence of a belief in a winnable nuclear war. Rather, the more charitable (and hopefully correct) interpretation is that it reflects a U.S. adminstration's desire to prevent a reckless Soviet leader from every coming to believe that he had any hope of initiating a winnable nuclear war.

The treatment by the U.S. media of nuclear issues has undergone a considerable shift over time. Greater skepticism is now voiced by the media concerning government claims and proposals than, say, twenty years ago. At one time when a U.S. president could put forth an arms-control proposal and find it promptly rejected by the Soviet Union, the press would invariably report this action as clear evidence that "our side" favored peace. Presumably, it was only due to Soviet intrasigence that the nuclear-arms-control proposal (which we knew was fair to both sides), was not instantly signed. Consider, however, the very different press reception of a 1982 Reagan-administration proposal to make sizable mutual cuts in the nuclear arsenals. Some newspaper reports grudgingly praised the proposal. Many others noted that it was largely a way of relieving the public pressure on the administration for its previous lack of action on arms control. Still others criticized the proposal as being either one-sided in favor of the United States, probably unattainable, or not in the interests of slowing the arms race. Much of the criticism on this proposal came even before the Soviet Union had an opportunity to give its considered response. The Soviets, in expressing negative views on the U.S. proposal, were not seen by the media as obstructionists, but rather as reacting in the only way they could to a proposal that was clearly biased and quite probably insincere. The actual merits of the administration proposal were certainly quite debatable, and they are discussed later. Here we simply wish to note how different was the media response to this proposal and to the Soviet rejection compared to those U.S. arms proposals of an earlier time.

For another example of greatly increased press skepticism on nuclear issues during the last twenty years, we need only compare the press handling of the 1962 Cuban missile crisis with comparable crises today. Before that earlier crisis was over, the press had co-operated with the government in ways that would be unthinkable today, short of an actual nuclear war. Specifically, in the Cuban missile crisis the press withheld news developments at the request of the government, turned over radio facilities at the request of the government, and, in general, relayed the administration's view of events without dissent.[6] Moreover, after the crisis was over, the press shared the view generally held by the public that the outcome was a great victory for "our side." In our post-Watergate, post-Vietnam era, U.S. government allegations are no longer accepted at face value—be they allegations of Libyan hit squads or Soviet nuclear superiority. The label of national security, abused as it was during Watergate, is no longer sufficient to elicit press cooperation on sensitive matters or to prevent government claims and actions from being skeptically scrutinized.

Public skepticism toward government is, of course, warranted in many instances. The U.S. government and the Pentagon have on more than one occasion been known to resort to public relations campaigns to promote the cause of an increased defense budget. The increased skeptism of the U.S. public towards government often shows itself in media portrayals of such efforts strictly in terms of government propaganda offensives. In other words, such government efforts are understood as attempts to manipulate rather than educate the public. It should be clear, however, that manipulation is most effective when those being manipulated are not made aware of this fact. The effect of such media coverage is therefore to engender still more public skepticism about government and make it more difficult for government propaganda offensives to succeed—even when the merits of the case might justify a less skeptical hearing.

By and large, such increased press skepticism towards government is a healthy thing. Some analysts of the media, however, believe we may have gone too far in the direction of cynicism, to the point where many citizens expect the government to lie to them, even concerning issues of national survival. Moreover, as a people we in the United States like to think of ourselves as fair and always capable of seeing the other side's point of view. For some, an increased skepticism of U.S.-government actions and proposals seems to have accompanied a less skeptical acceptance of claims and proposals made by others whose motives should also be suspect. One can only hope that healthy skepticism is applied equally to claims made on all sides in the tricky nuclear debate. The stakes are too high to

assume that anyone has a monopoly on virtue and good intentions—
or the reverse.

WHAT IS THE NATURE OF THE ANTINUCLEAR MOVEMENT?

There has long been an antinuclear movement in the United
States, which for many years involved groups on the left of the
political spectrum. Today, the antinuclear movement has considerably broadened its political base of support to the point where being
against all things nuclear is as American as Mom and apple pie.
Being antinuclear to some now embraces being against nuclear war
as well as being against nuclear power and nuclear weapons. It is
hard to see how anyone cannot be antinuclear in the antiwar sense.
By blurring the distinction between being against nuclear war, nuclear
weapons, and nuclear power, the notion is created that being against
one is somehow the same as being against all three. One can, of
course, be fervently against nuclear war, but not necessarily against
nuclear weapons and nuclear power—a distinction many in the
antinuclear movement would much prefer not to recognize.

No movement as large and diverse as the antinuclear movement
can be easily characterized in a simple way. One issue on which the
movement appears divided is the desirability of acts of civil disobedience, such as blockades of weapons laboratories or new U.S.
Trident submarines, or other such dramatic and largely symbolic
acts. Those who favor such acts of mass civil disobedience argue
that people will have to be arrested in large numbers before the
desired changes can be brought about. They believe that such acts
of civil disobedience will cause the conscience of the public to
recognize the innate justice of the protesters' cause, just as in the
case of the civil rights movement. Others in the antinuclear movement, while feeling just as strongly about the need for disarmament,
view civil disobedience as a tactical error. This group believes that
the large majority of the U.S. public subscribes to the basic goals
of the movement and might be alienated by such tactics. Many in
the antinuclear movement believe that the basic problem in the
world is not East versus West, but rather people versus governments.
Therefore, the maintenance of the large reservoir of public support
for the movement is of crucial importance in promoting the necessary
political changes to promote disarmament. There is little point in
resorting to acts that may make one feel better, if the net effect is

to alienate a large conservative, but prodisarmament, segment of the public.

The antinuclear movement, like any other mass movement, undoubtedly contains some very thoughtful people, a small percentage of whom have ulterior motives and very many of whom are somewhat naïve and romantic. Some in the movement seem to believe that the nuclear problem can somehow be wished away, if only the people can make their voices heard and alter the policies of a militaristic government. While many recognize that the so-called militaristic government may have been freely chosen by the people, they attribute this to the manipulation of the voters by a powerful military-industrial complex—the mirror image of the charge that those in the antinuclear movement are puppets of the Soviet Union.

Even when idealistic outsiders such as Jimmy Carter gain the most powerful office in the land with the intention of making drastic reductions in the U.S. nuclear arsenal, the allure of power or the influence of the military-industrial complex caused the outsider, in the eyes of some in the antinuclear movement, to back away from his worthy goal. A more charitable view would be that the realities of power have a way of making prodisarmament idealists more aware of the need to keep U.S. defenses strong, just as anticommunist conservatives often seem to learn to appreciate better the need for nuclear arms control, even if only for political reasons, once they are elected.

Ever since World War II, thinking about the unthinkable has been the province of the U.S. government, as well as a group of think tanks such as the Rand Corporation. A more recent development has been the growth of a large number of public-interest research groups devoted to an examination of defense, nuclear, and environmental issues. Many of these organizations are not simply engaged in a dispassionate examination of policy alternatives, but in the promotion of particular proposals. Although these groups include some with a hawkish viewpoint, e.g. the American Security Council, the majority tend to be dovish and, as such, generally espouse policy alternatives with which the antinuclear movement often finds itself in harmony. Although these groups are not often part of the antinuclear movement per se, they in a sense serve as its intellectual foundation, and they often find themselves allied with single-issue antinuclear groups such as those in favor of a nuclear freeze. These organizations have been a major factor in raising the general level of public concern on nuclear matters, particularly among the intellectual elite.

DOES THE SOVIET UNION MANIPULATE WESTERN PUBLIC OPINION?

To what extent is the Soviet Union able to manipulate Western public opinion on nuclear issues and is that something to be concerned about? It is important to stress that the overwhelming majority of those in the disarmament movement are acting out of the most idealistic of motives and would deeply resent being viewed as manipulated by anyone. Their fears of nuclear war are very legitimate ones and so is their concern over a measurable increase in tensions between East and West. Moreover, it is probably also legitimate to be concerned about an objective rise in the risk of nuclear war resulting from the new weapons added to the superpowers' arsenals. Such factors as these are almost certainly much more responsible for the dramatic growth of the antinuclear movement than any brilliant Kremlin master plan.

Nevertheless, it also true that the Soviets have mounted a massive campaign over the years to promote disarmament movements in the West, seeing in them a way to constrain the Western nuclear arsenals. There is in fact a department of the Soviet KGB specifically charged with subversion of Western media—an effort on which the Soviets spend an estimated 3 to 4 billion dollars.[7] In fact, one would need to believe the Soviet government to be quite stupid not to undertake an effort of this kind. Contrary to mythology, the Soviets have tended to be rather cautious militarily, acting only when the risks are low. The Soviet government would much prefer to accomplish its political objectives by winning the battle for public opinion than by resorting to military means. Given the nature of open Western societies, Moscow would have to be extremely lacking in intelligence to bypass the opportunity to covertly and overtly attempt to influence Western public opinion on nuclear issues.

The Soviets, however, also realize that different settings call for different tactics. In Europe many citizens would like to stay out of any U.S.-Soviet nuclear conflict, and they view new U.S. missile deployment in their countries only as an action that makes them targets. Thus, Soviet-sponsored peace efforts can focus largely on the threat posed only by new U.S. missiles. Although the Western European peace groups are united in their desire to be pro-European rather than anti-American, they do include some groups that are known to be influenced by pro-Soviet Communist parties.[8] Thus, while all Western European peace groups are opposed to new U.S. missiles, some are silent about the Soviet missiles aimed at them.

That silence in some cases is rationalized on the grounds that the U.S. missiles are extremely provocative to Moscow and increase the chances of nuclear war, whereas the Soviet SS-20s were merely an upgrading of an existing threat.

In the United States, where the pro-Soviet constituency is very small, Moscow realizes that its goals can be better served by proposals to end the arms race and to portray the problem in the world as between good people and militaristic governments. Quite apart from any alleged Soviet support of disarmament groups in the United States, Moscow also has many direct channels for influencing U.S. public opinion on nuclear matters. For example, in 1981 and 1983 the Pentagon published and widely distributed a booklet entitled *Soviet Military Power,*[9] to support the U.S.-administration claim of a military imbalance in favor of the Soviet Union. In a classic "battle of the booklets," the Soviet ministry of defense then put out its own booklet, *Whence the Threat to Peace?*[10] which attempted to rebut all the Pentagon claims and to show that it was the U.S. military buildup that represented the real threat to world peace. The Soviet booklet attracted considerable attention in the U.S. media, and it was freely distributed by at least three U.S. publishers.[11] The reverse situation would very likely not occur given the nature of Soviet society. It is hard to imagine Pentagon-prepared booklets being freely distributed to Soviet citizens to counter the Soviet government's views on an issue involving national security. The Soviet government also has other direct avenues to influence U.S. public opinion on nuclear issues. For example, Soviet leaders' statements about what actions they would be forced to undertake in response to new "provocative" U.S. weapons are prominently reported by the American media.

The matter of direct Soviet access to U.S. public opinion, as illustrated in the preceding two examples, is not something to be particularly concerned about. In fact, it is probably highly desirable that such channels exist. It is, however, a matter of considerable concern that reciprocal channels by which the Soviet people can hear undistorted U.S.-government positions are much more limited.

How effective is the Soviet effort in its goal of influencing the U.S. public? According to the F.B.I., "We do not see Soviet active measures in the United States as having a significant impact on U.S. decision makers. . . . The American media is sophisticated, and generally recognizes Soviet influence attempts."[12] While the Soviet Union may have had only a limited success in direct efforts at influencing the U.S. public and the media, its indirect efforts may have borne more fruit. For example, in contrast to an earlier era, many media commentators now feel no stigma whatsoever attached to opposing U.S.-administration positions and supporting positions that happen to be favored by the Soviet Union. The Soviet government cannot be unaware of the important psychological impact of inducing people to support Soviet positions, while opposing those of the U.S. administration. Therefore, Soviet-government proposals are usually presented in a seemingly balanced form that serves the cause of peace in order to maximize their chance of support. All Soviet proposals usually share these characteristics: they seem reasonably balanced, they slow or reverse the arms race, and they tend marginally to favor the Soviet Union strategically in one way or another. By putting forth only reasonable-sounding proposals, the Soviets stand to gain in a number of ways:

- They enhance their Western public image as peacemakers and establish themselves as a voice for moderation.

- They make the U.S. administration appear intransigent and against peace if it rejects the reasonable-sounding proposal.

- They make it increasingly respectable for U.S. opinion leaders to support Soviet positions and oppose U.S. administration positions.

- They gain strategically in some marginal way if the U.S. government should agree with the proposal.

The last point is probably the least important one, since the reasonable-sounding proposal is generally made with the expectation that it will be rejected, and indeed it is that rejection that gives the Soviets one more propaganda victory. The days when a Soviet leader would say to the West, "We will bury you," [13] as Nikita Khrushchev is reported to have said, are long gone. Whatever the Soviet Union's ultimate intentions are, the Soviets have learned very well the need for sophistication in their attempt to manipulate Western public opinion. The U.S. government has, of course, also been guilty of making one-sided the insincere arms-control proposals to the Soviets. However it is important to realize that given the closed nature of Soviet society, all the posturing on both sides represents an effort to manipulate Western public opinion. It would be naïve to view only one side's disarmament proposals as representing a sincere desire to promote peace.

HOW IMPORTANT IS SOVIET PUBLIC OPINION?

In contrast to the many ways the Soviet Union can influence U.S. public opinion, there is much less the United States can do to influence Soviet public opinion. Equally important, there is at present very little opportunity for dissident voices in the U.S.S.R. to alter their government's policies. As most U.S. citizens are aware, the Soviet news media are under firm government control; in the treatment of nuclear matters as well as all other matters, dissenting voices are not tolerated.

Is there hope for signs of liberalization of tight government control of the Soviet news media? Some Western analysts might find encouragement in such things as Soviet media stories about misconduct of government officials. However, these attempts to reform the bureaucracy are certainly not exposés in the sense of unauthorized stories about government malfeasance. Similarly, Soviet press coverage of Afghanistan is strictly in accordance with the government position on that war.

Recalling the important role that Western media coverage played in changing the U.S. public's perception of the Vietnam war, many may hold a similar hope in the case of Afghanistan. However, that hope may be illusory. Soviet media coverage through its government-controlled press is unlikely to depict that conflict by showing brutality against innocent civilians, a corrupt puppet government, or courageous guerillas fighting for their freedom—as was done by the U.S. media in the case of Vietnam. It is conceivable that if greatly increased numbers of Soviet troops were to return home in coffins, this would have an effect on the Soviet populace, but it must be remembered that there are no statistics on such things published in the news media, nor would mothers of killed or missing soldiers be likely to have access to the media. If the Soviet government ever should decide to depart Afghanistan "with honor," public opinion could be a factor—but it would probably be Western public opinion rather than Soviet public opinion. Afghanistan represents, for Western public opinion, a continuing reminder of Soviet expansionism.

As long as the Soviet news media remains under tight government control there are many stories and points of view, regularly reported by the Western press, that will never appear in the Soviet media—for example, challenges to the Soviet government on the topics of unnecessary new weapons systems, too high a level of defense spending, military involvement in another country, or hard-line governmental positions on arms control. The Soviet news media may on occasion depict Western groups and individuals in positive terms, however, the Western groups or individuals so portrayed are those who support positions that the Soviet Union favors, in opposition to the official positions of their own governments. Thus, favorable portrayal of U.S. protest groups or groups favoring a nuclear freeze is a way of showing the Soviet people that the U.S. government is out of touch with its own people.

One area in which there has been considerable evolution is in the Soviet media's treatment of nuclear weapons. In the years immediately following World War II, when the U.S. nuclear monopoly posed a severe risk to the physical survival of the U.S.S.R., it was important that the Soviet people not be frightened by the new U.S. superweapon. Accordingly, the controlled Soviet press rarely ever referred to the bomb. On those very few occasions when the U.S. bomb was referred to, it was termed a weapon of no military significance and only useful for frightening faint-hearted people.

Nowadays, the Soviet press, while acknowledging the horror of nuclear warfare, portrays the threat of a nuclear holocaust as coming exclusively from other countries, primarily the United States. Soviet nuclear weapons are depicted by the Soviet media as being strictly for defensive purposes and are not viewed as threatening to anyone. In other words, the Soviet-media portrayal of the risks of nuclear war is similar to that in the United States twenty and thirty years ago when this country also had a very clear consensus as to where the threat to peace came from. The Soviet press widely reports antinuclear demonstrations in capitalist countries as evidence that the people in the West oppose the provocative weapons and policies of their own governments, rather than nuclear weapons generally. There are, of course, no Soviet press reports of non-government-controlled peace demonstrations in the Soviet Union because such demonstrations don't exist. In the Soviet Government's view, it is not necessary to have such demonstrations, since everyone in the Soviet Union is opposed to war. In fact, war propaganda is forbidden by the Soviet Constitution. Those few dissenters brave enough to put on small and extremely rare peace demonstrations in the U.S.S.R. are dealt with very harshly under the Soviet system, which has little use for spontaneous demonstrations of any kind—particularly those dealing with disarmament. While Moscow apparently welcomes pacifism in the West as a means of blocking new weapons, it has made very clear to its own citizenry that similar actions, even those of a nonpolitical nature, will not be tolerated. The great Soviet fear is that spontaneous demonstrations could easily become a habit that citizens might use to challenge government policies and the system itself.

For example, after the mass demonstrations in Western Europe and the United States, a young Soviet artist tried to form a small peace group modeled on those in the West. Although the small group was not opposing any Soviet government policy, it was quickly suppressed by the government. The members of the group were arrested and its leader, Sergei Batovrin, was placed in a psychiatric hospital—a common Soviet treatment for political dissidents.[14] Batovrin's small group had, in the view of the Soviet authorities, represented a real challenge to a system in which peace committees, like most other things, are a monopoloy of the state.

Another vast difference between the Soviet- and U.S.-press treatment of nuclear weapons concerns the silence of the Soviet press on new Soviet weapons systems. While there is much secrecy in both the Soviet Union and the U.S. concerning new weapons, in the case of the United States the secrecy concerns the technical details of the proposed systems, not their existence. Since the U.S. Congress must approve funds for major weapons programs, there is a good deal of discussion and lobbying by the military-industrial complex to convince Congress and the public that the proposed weapons should be built. The Soviet government makes its decisions on new weapons in a manner that does not require public involvement, and, therefore, there is no need to discuss such things in the media. It seems difficult to imagine a discussion of alternative basing modes for the Soviet equivalent of the MX missile in the Soviet press. It seems equally hard to imagine that Soviet leaders might decide not to deploy the equivalent of the MX due to protests of Ukranian environmentalists and ranchers. Soviet citizens who might suffer an "environmental impact" due to the placement of missiles in their region would not be likely to know that their area was to receive new missiles, nor would they be likely to consider protesting the missiles' placement if they somehow were to learn of it. Quite apart from any direct suppression of such a protest, it probably would not occur to the average Soviet citizen to question a government assertion that Soviet missiles were strictly for the defense of the motherland and not "provocative" in any way.

Many in the Western antinuclear movement would agree with all these assertions of the present impotence of Soviet citizens to affect their government's policies. In fact, they would probably cite such impotence as an important reason why free citizens in the West who can affect their governments' policies need to work all the harder to end the arms race. However, this view fails to consider that if all the public pressure comes from only one side, the end result may be a very lopsided kind of arms control. Since the Soviet government is under no constraint to placate public opinion in order to achieve reelection, it has a very significant arms negotiating advantage over the United States, particularly when a very large majority of the U.S. public strongly favors an agreement with the Soviet Union to limit nuclear weapons. Thus, if a U.S.-administration position on limiting nuclear arms is not to the Soviet government's liking, the Soviets may find it advantageous to portray the U.S. administration as intransigent, in the belief that a U.S. public, yearning for a permanent solution to our nuclear predicament, will replace the administration by one that is more forthcoming on arms control.

Some who favor disarmament believe that a U.S. administration that proposes a significant increase in the nuclear arsenal as a means of including Soviet willingness to reduce nuclear weapons is engaging in "voodoo arms control." However, an alternative view is that given the lack of domestic pressure on the Soviet Union to constrain its arms expenditures, the West would have no bargaining leverage in arms control unless it exhibits a willingness to match Soviet arms efforts. If there is a sharp division in U.S. public opinion on this score, the U.S.S.R. may prefer to outwait the administration, anticipating that the U.S. public will elect a more reasonable one. It would be naïve to think that the Reagan administration proposed a major expansion in the U.S. nuclear arsenal solely to induce Soviet willlngness on meaningful reductions, but it is perhaps equally naïve to dismiss that motivation.

Are there prospects for a liberalization of the tight government control that might make Soviet policies more responsive to the wishes of its people? According to Hedrick Smith, an American correspondent and long-term resident of the Soviet Union:

> The longer I lived in Soviet Russia, the more Russian it seem to me and hence the less likely to undergo fundamental change. Whenever I would see signs of change, Russian intellectuals would disabuse me. Gradually, it came through to me that Russians—unlike Westerners—do not take it for granted that Russian dictatorship must inevitably evolve into democracy for they know its power and its permanence; they recognize its ability to adapt without surrendering its essence; they find comfort in the stability and order that it

provides. Fearing what seems to them the chaotic turbulence of Western liberal democracies, most of them do not want democracy for Russia. Even those intellectuals who long for it will say their society is not ready for the give-and-take, the political tolerance and compromise, the self-restraint that democracy requires even they draw back from it or say that it must take generations to evolve.[15]

Even in the absence of internal public-opinion pressures on Soviet leaders, economic and social constraints do place limits on policy, much as in the United States. In a society such as the U.S.S.R. in which all planning hinges on economics, leaders are well aware that every ruble spent on new nuclear missiles is one less ruble that can be spent on other items. Moreover, if the Soviet leadership felt that the security of their nation would benefit (or at least not be harmed) by a particular arms-control agreement with the United States, there would seem to be every reason for them to seek such an agreement. There is, however, no evidence for the existence any Soviet leadership faction interested in seeking arms agreements for their own sake or for putting Soviet security interests in second place to more universal concerns.

WHAT ARE U.S. PUBLIC ATTITUDES TOWARD NUCLEAR ARMS CONTROL?

Many public-opinion polls confirm the strong desire of the U.S. public to reach a nuclear-arms agreement with the Soviet Union. For example, one national survey found 80 percent in favor of negotiating such an agreement, while only 13 percent were opposed.[16] On the specific question of freezing nuclear weapons at their present levels, 70 percent of those surveyed favored such a proposal, while only 20 percent were opposed. These large majorities favoring nuclear arms control show little variations with the respondent's gender, educational level, political affiliation, and geographic region. Only those survey respondents from the South showed slightly smaller majorities in favor of negotiating an arms-control agreement with the Soviets (63 percent favored and 26 percent opposed). These large U.S. majorities favoring a negotiated nuclear-arms agreement do not reflect any kindly U.S. public attitude toward the Soviet government. In fact, according to the pollster Louis Harris:

- A large majority of the American people (84 percent) see the Soviet Union as a threat to the security of the United States.

- Two-to-one majority (63 percent to 23 percent) think there is a likelihood that over the next forty years the Soviet Union will attack the United States.

- A substantial majority (69 percent to 24 percent) think the Soviet leaders would not hesitate to use nuclear arms, if they were desperate enough.

- Fully 49 percent of the American people view the Soviet Union as an outright "enemy," while another 31 percent think the Soviet Union is unfriendly to the United States even if not our enemy.[17]

These findings clearly show that the U.S. public greatly distrusts the Soviet government even though it strongly favors reaching a nuclear-arms-control agreement between the U.S. and U.S.S.R. In fact, a large majority (73 percent) of those surveyed believe that it would be "not at all likely" that the Soviets would abide by a nuclear-arms agreement. Apparently, many people consider the risks of nuclear war to be so great that they want a nuclear-arms agreement, despite their great misgivings about the Soviets. Nevertheless, polls also show that the public has little interest in unilateral disarmament. For example, among those who favor a nuclear freeze, only 15 percent also favored "the United States deciding to gradually dismantle our nuclear weapons before getting an agreement from other countries to do the same," while 82 percent of freeze supporters were opposed.

The public desire to avoid unilateral moves while strongly supporting mutual nuclear-arms-control agreements explains why the public and Congress has been willing to support expanding the U.S. nuclear arsenal while disarmament agreements are being pursued. In some cases the funding for new weapons is closely linked to specific arms-control initiatives. President Carter's support for the MX missile was, in part, an effort to win conservative votes for the SALT II Treaty. The MX was also closely linked to arms-control efforts under Carter's successor. President Reagan was able to win congressional support for MX only after embracing several specific arms-control initiatives, including the "build down" idea under which two old warheads would be dismantled for every new one deployed.

Most U.S. presidents have come to understand that the best way to maintain public support for a strong defense is to evince a genuine interest in peace and a desire for arms control.

Does the simultaneous public support for a strong defense and nuclear arms control demonstrate that the public is gullible and inconsistent? Or, alternatively, does the apparent contradiction show that much of the public views nuclear weapons as a necessary evil it is prepared to accept as long as the U.S. president is perceived to be trustworthy and responsible? Whatever the answer to these questions, Reagan, like many presidents before him, has learned an important lesson of U.S. presidential politics: a challenger who gains office by portraying his predecessor as soft on defense needs to moderate his position once he is in office so as to convince the public that he is a peacemaker.

In view of the strong public support for arms control, some believe that "softness" or lack of vigor in pursuing arms agreements could become a greater political liability that softness on defense. Some have argued that the tremendous upsurge in public support for nuclear arms control makes that switch a distinct possibility. Although no one can predict the future evolution of public opinion, it is important to note that no such dramatic change in public support for nuclear arms control has in fact occurred. The U.S. public has always strongly supported nuclear arms control. For example, in 1979 at a time when the U.S. public was expressing significant wariness towards the SALT II nuclear-arms-control treaty, the public also strongly supported the need to reach an arms-control agreement with the Soviet Union. In one 1979 poll, 86 percent of those surveyed favored trying to reach a nuclear arms agreement with the Soviets, while in contrast 58 percent believed that the SALT II Treaty "does not adequately protect U.S. security." [18] The change in public attitudes since 1979 does not reflect an increased public approval towards nuclear arms control, but rather an increased interest in the subject due to a greater concern over the risk of nuclear war.

The great change in public attitudes on specific arms-control measures (SALT II versus the nuclear freeze) is one indication that nuclear arms control is a rather volatile issue that depends greatly on how particular proposals are perceived. Another indication of the volatility of the issue is the great upsurge in the level of public concern that can result largely from careless administration statements, and, alternately, the decrease in public concern that accompanies soothing administration statements. The volatility of the issue

Table 2.1 Volatile Public Reactions to Arms Control

	Agree	Disagree	Uncertain
"At a time when it's possible for the U.S. and Russia to blow each other up with nuclear weapons, it is vital for the two countries to reach an agreement to limit nuclear arms."	83%	14%	3%
"Because the chances are that we will keep our end of the bargain while the Russians will not, we should not sign any agreement limiting nuclear weapons."	47%	48%	5%

Source: E. Hastings and P. Hastings, eds., Index to International Public Opinion 1979–1980, (Westport: Greenwood, 1981), P. 222.

of nuclear arms control can also be illustrated by the responses to two questions from a 1980 survey listed in table 2.1. Based on the responses to these two questions, there seems to be a sizable fraction of the public that subscribes to a belief in the need for an arms-control agreement until they are reminded that the Russians are untrustworthy.

A shift in response based on the wording of the question might be expected on any controversial issue included in a survey. However, I believe that the magnitude of the shift is likely to be far greater on the question of nuclear arms control than on most other questions such as capital punishment, gun control, or abortion. It seems highly unlikely, for example, that a substantial fraction of those on either side of the gun-control debate would change their stance depending on whether or not they are reminded of the other side's arguments. It is not so much that the nuclear debate is less polarized or emotional than the abortion or gun-control debate. Rather there is a more substantial group of undecided and poorly informed people in the middle who could swing either way, depending on which of their fears are aroused: fear of the Russians or fear of nuclear war.

WHERE DO WE GO FROM HERE?

The magnitude of the upsurge of public attention to the nuclear dilemma has surprised most observers, although the justification for a high level of public concern about nuclear war has been with us ever since the dawn of the nuclear age. However, a peculiar combination of circumstances seems to have been required to bring the issue to a central place on the national agenda after it had faded into the background following an earlier period of concern in the early 1960s. Will the nuclear issue once again fade rapidly into the background? The public and the media seem to have a way of focusing on one issue of the moment (or the year) and then allowing it to resubmerge into a general sea of concerns. Thus, we have seen the energy crisis, nuclear-reactor safety, crime, inflation, race relations, and the environment each in turn occupy center stage in the minds of the public and the media. Despite the fact that nuclear war represents the greatest threat to our survival, many people may find it too horrible to contemplate for any length of time, and they will gladly move on to other topics and once again suppress such concerns. It seems possible that this psychic numbing will, after a time, again take hold, and we will revert to the disinterest of the last forty years.

The possible resubmergence of the nuclear issue would be most unfortunate. The nuclear dilemma will not solve itself, and the risk of nuclear war may be lessened if the public is informed and attentive. In fact, as we noted in the beginning of this chapter, in the long run there may be no more important factor than public opinion in determining whether nuclear war is averted. For now, the hope of averting a nuclear catastrophe rests primarily with public opinion in the United States and Western Europe. The opinions of the Soviet people could also be crucial if they ever achieve a comparable degree of influence over their government's policies. In fact, being aware of the Soviet people's great desire to avoid war, I would gladly trade half the U.S. nuclear arsenal if that act could magically give the Soviet people a major influence on their government's policies.

It is possible that the Soviet political system could change over time to permit its citizens a greater voice, but the political changes that have occurred since the founding of that nation do not offer great reason to hope that this will happen very soon. Our nuclear problem is too pressing to await such hoped-for possible changes in the Soviet system. We must deal with the Soviet system as it now exists. This requires us simultaneously to be vigilant against possible Soviet military threats, while attempting to reach an accord on nuclear arms that can promote mutual security. We must not be unnecessarily bellicose and provocative, thereby causing a possibly uncontrolled escalation leading to war. Nor must we be soft on defense and regard arms control as a substitute for a strong U.S. defense. Even though no nuclear weapons have been used against another nation since

World War II, to what degree this non-use proves that the "balance of terror" can be counted on the deter war really cannot be known.

With the great dangers of either overreacting or underreacting to the Soviet military threat, we are in the same position as a blind man groping his way along a narrow winding path with precipitous cliffs falling away on either side. As we grope along, we realize that one misstep off the path, on either side, could be fatal. We hear the voices of three other blind men behind us, urging us with great assurance that the path ahead veers off in different directions. One voice continually urges that we veer to the left. This voice points out that the Soviet people have no desire for war and that they are our friends. It also notes that the Soviet government is not aggressive and that the U.S.S.R. maintains its large military machine strictly for defensive purposes, in light of past acts of aggression committed against the Soviet Union. This voice blames the Pentagon and the U.S. military-industrial complex as the root cause of the arms race and the main obstacle to peace. According to this voice, we need to have general and complete disarmament, both nuclear and conventional, and that we should not be so suspicious as to worry about whether treaties are completely verifiable.

A second blind man behind us urges that the true path ahead of us lies always to the right. According to this second voice, the Soviet Union is an aggressive expansionist power that has demonstrated its ruthlessness both internally and externally on numerous occasions. This voice notes that it would be folly to trust the Soviets to keep any arms-control agreement and that any pact the Soviets would agree to could not possibly be in the U.S. interest. According to this second voice, the only way to prevent nuclear war is to be so strong that no would would ever dare attack us.

A third blind man's voice urges us to always proceed directly straight ahead. The third voice explains that the root cause of the nuclear dilemma lies with the arms race itself rather than with either one of the superpowers. According to this voice, our own nuclear weapons represent just as great a danger to our security as those of the Soviet Union. It notes that as we build new weapons, we induce the Soviet Union to do likewise in kind of an action-reaction phenomenon. This third voice notes that we will never solve the nuclear problem until we change our way of thinking to avoid the false dichotomy of "we" and "they." In our nuclear age, the only kind of security possible is mutual security.

We listen to the three voices and we are truly perplexed. We know that each speaker is as blind as we are, and we marvel at the great assurance with which each urges us on to the true path. We also recognize that there is some element of truth in what each of the voices says. Yet we also know that since the path ahead is a winding one, it is not clear which of the three voices we must heed at any given point. To listen exclusively to any one is bound to insure disaster since the path ahead has many turns. We grope along, inch by painful inch, hoping for the best, and we are unsure as to whether the path will ever end. We have just outgrown our nuclear adolescence.

STUDY QUESTIONS

1. How great an influence do you think public opinion has, in the short run, on the likelihood of a nuclear war? In the long run? Is that influence always to the good?

2. What factors contributed to the reemergence of the nuclear-war issue as a topic of great public concern? To what extent does that increased public concern reflect a real increase in the probability of nuclear war?

3. What factors prevent the media from doing a better job in dealing with issues related to nuclear war?

4. How has the medial portrayal of U.S.-administration pronouncements and policies varied over time?

5. How much of a Soviet effort is made to influence the Western media on nuclear issues? How successful does that effort appear to be?

6. What role does public opinion play in the Soviet Union in affecting nuclear-weapons policy? What is the likelihood of that situation changing in the future? Is that something to worry about? Why?

7. What are U.S. public attitudes on arms control? How have these attitudes varied over time? What accounts for the different public reception of the SALT II agreement and the nuclear-freeze proposal?

II

NUCLEAR ARMS
AND NUCLEAR WAR

Three

NUCLEAR WEAPONS AND NUCLEAR STRATEGY

HOW DID U.S. NUCLEAR STRATEGY EVOLVE?

Carl von Clausewitz, the nineteenth-century philosopher of war, viewed war not as an aberration but as "the continuation of politics by other means." In Clausewitz's view, war must be evaluated as a means towards certain political ends. In the absence of such ends, war loses all meaning and reduces to senseless violence. The central Clausewitzian question that relates to nuclear weapons is what purpose, if any, their use in war could be expected to achieve. Nuclear strategists generally assume that nuclear weapons have such a purpose or that ends exist that would justify their threatened or actual use. An alternative view would be that nuclear weapons are so different from other means of destruction that it is misleading even to use the term "weapons," as it presupposes a military utility.

Efforts to control the bomb and prevent its further use in war were begun even before the end of World War II. In contrast, efforts to develop a nuclear strategy in the Clauswitzian sense did not begin until some years later. Military strategy prior to the nuclear age tended to be an obscure topic primarily of interest to a segment of the military establishment. Nuclear strategy had a different genesis, and it was largely developed both within academic circles and the numerous think tanks that were created in the post–World War II

43

era. Such people as Bernard Brodie, Henry Kissinger, Herman Kahn, and Albert Wohlstetter are among those who have made major contributions to nuclear strategic doctrine.

There are four areas with which military strategists have traditionally concerned themselves: objectives, procurement, deployment, and employment. In the context of nuclear weapons, the question raised about these four areas are:

1. *Objectives.* What goals do we attempt to achieve by possessing nuclear weapons?
2. *Procurement.* How many and what kinds of nuclear weapons would best achieve those goals?
3. *Deployment.* How should the weapons be deployed to best achieve those goals?
4. *Employment.* How should the weapons actually be used in war, if that should become necessary?

The first question concerning objectives was answered by strategists very early, and the answer is one that most people still consider valid today: the purpose of nuclear weapons should be to prevent war. The procurement, deployment, and employment questions initially received much less attention, and their answers tend to be much more controversial.

Military strategy formulated prior to the nuclear age was, like scientific hypotheses, testable in terms of actual consequences. The unfeasibility of strategies was sometimes not obvious in advance, but unworkable strategies often became very evident when they were tested in war. In some cases, the effectiveness of particular weapons or tactics was grossly underestimated or overestimated prior to their use. For example, in World War II the strategic bombing of civilian populations was found to produce far less strategic (war-winning) results in terms of destroying the war economy and the enemy's will to resist than was originally thought.

There is no reason to believe that strategies concerning the use of nuclear weapons have any closer relation to reality than was the case for other weapons prior to their large-scale use in war. Despite the great amount of thought given to the subject of nuclear strategy, it is possible that the subject has as little relation to an actual nuclear war as would nuclear etiquette.

There are other reasons to be modest in any pretension that nuclear strategy has applicability to a real nuclear war. A nuclear war might unfold in a way that would make all previous strategy irrelevant. Moreover, the strategy of one country may depend on false assumptions about strategies held by the adversary, assumptions that only become evident when it is too late. Our ability to fully appreciate Soviet nuclear strategy is somewhat limited, as will be discussed at the end of this chapter.

A long-standing debate exists over the relationship between nuclear strategy and nuclear weapons. On one side are the "technological determinists" who believe that weapons designers devise whatever man's inventiveness will allow, and strategy is then determined by the weapon's capabilities. On the other side are those who believe that we design weapons to suit a particular strategy, even if that strategy has not been explicitly enunciated. The difference between the two positions is not just a matter of academic interest. For those who believe that strategy drives technology, man is basically in control of his fate. For the technological determinists, however, technological progress may dictate certain strategies, whatever our intentions. Whichever position is more nearly correct, it is important to consider the development of nuclear weapons in the context of the evolution of nuclear strategic doctrine. While it may not have been true that particular nuclear weapons were built in accordance with any grand strategy in mind, strategic doctrine and weapons have had a mutually reinforcing parallel evolution. Moreover, in order to form a clear idea of the balance of nuclear forces, one must understand the strategic purpose of those forces.

Following the use against Japan of the only two nuclear weapons the United States possessed, America did not immediately begin to amass a large arsenal. In 1947, for example, two years after World War II, the United States had an arsenal of only thirteen A-bombs. The great expansion in the United States arsenal largely began in 1949 when the Soviet Union exploded its first nuclear weapon many years earlier than most U.S. observers thought possible. The discovery that some workers who developed the first U.S. bomb in the World War II Manhattan project acted as spies for the Soviet Union was probably a factor in deepening the U.S. distrust of the Soviet Union and promoting the development of a large U.S. nuclear stockpile. Another factor in the increasing U.S. reliance on nuclear weapons was economics. Following the U.S. demobilization in World War II, nuclear weapons offered a cheap substitute for a conventional defense that was particularly attractive to the fiscally conservative Republican administration under President Eisenhower in the early 1950s.

The United States had massive nuclear superiority over the Soviet Union throughout this early phase of the nuclear era. The destructive power of the U.S. arsenal increased dramatically when America tested the first thermonuclear (hydrogen) bomb in 1952, a move some U.S. scientists, most notably J. Robert Oppenheimer, regarded as unwise. Even though Oppenheimer had led the effort to develop the atomic bomb, he felt that the H-bomb was too destructive to have any military significance and that it was unnecessary in view of the growing U.S. arsenal of fission bombs. Edward Teller, often called the father of the H-bomb, felt otherwise. According to Teller, the United States needed to maintain its nuclear advantage over the Soviet Union, which would certainly seek to develop the H-bomb regardless of what the United States did. Although it took the Soviet Union a full four years after the first U.S. A-bomb test to duplicate that feat, its first H-bomb test came only one year after the U.S. H-bomb test. While the Soviet Union was only one year behind the United States in that sense, its much smaller arsenal, lack of inter-continental bombers, and lack of overseas bases left the United States not seriously threatened by a Soviet nuclear attack at that time.

Following the Yalta and Potsdam agreements concluded at the end of World War II between the United States, England, and the Soviet Union, the major victorious allies, Europe was divided into two spheres of influence. The countries of Eastern Europe and the eastern part of a divided Germany came within the Soviet sphere and as a result came to be dominated by the Soviet Union. Because of its fear of further Soviet expansion, the U.S. government adopted a policy of containment of communism and used its nuclear su-periority to threaten the Soviet Union with massive retaliation if it committed unspecified aggressive actions anywhere in the world. During this early cold war period, the U.S. would have been able to carry out its threatened massive retaliation using its forward-based bombers in Europe and, after 1948, using its U.S.-based in-tercontinental bombers. The Soviet Union was not able to begin to pose a serious nuclear threat to the United States until 1955 when it deployed its first intercontinental bombers.

The U.S. policy of massive nuclear retaliation against the Soviet Union for any misdeeds gradually became untenable. Without a clear indication by the United States of what specific Soviet actions would trigger a massive retaliation, the Soviet Union was not deterred from actions that probed the limits of U.S. policy. More importantly, the U.S. policy became increasingly untenable as the Soviet Union began to accumulate its own nuclear arsenal that could seriously threaten the United States. Even though the Soviet Union's arsenal in the early 1960s was a very small fraction of that of the United States, it was large enough to be able to inflict a devastating level of damage. It would only take one large nuclear weapon whose yield or destructive power is measured in millions of tons of TNT (megatons) to destroy a city.

Once the Soviet Union accumulated a sufficient number of nuclear weapons, the U.S. policy of massive retaliation for Soviet misdeeds gave way to the doctrine of mutual assured destruction (MAD). The idea of MAD is that each side is deterred from attacking the other by the realization that its own destruction would be assured in retaliation. For that reason, MAD is now also understood to stand for mutual assured deterrence. Unlike the earlier era in which the United States assumed it could deter any Soviet aggression, it now recognized that the increasing size of the Soviet arsenal severely limited what Soviet actions could be deterred. According to the doctrine of mutual assured destruction, it did not matter which side had more nuclear weapons, as long as each had enough to assure the destruction of the aggressor in retaliation.

In the early 1960s, Robert McNamara, secretary of defense in the Kennedy administration, brought in a team of "whiz kids" to try to bring some coherence to nuclear-weapons strategy as a basis for policy decisions on weapons programs. To quote two of McNamara's analysts:

U.S. weapons should be measured against U.S. objectives. . . . The most important question is not total megatons or numbers of delivery systems or any other single measure of strategic nuclear capability, but whether U.S. forces can effectively carry out their missions. Once, we are sure that, in retaliation, we can destroy the Soviet Union and other potential attackers as modern societies, we cannot increase our security or power against them by threatening to destroy more.[1]

That is the essence of MAD. Although some may regard it as bizzare that one's security should depend, in effect, on a mutual suicide pact, MAD is not as insane a policy as some of its detractors have claimed. The policy does, for example, offer a number of important advantages:

- There is no need to build more weapons than necessary to assure the destruction of potential attackers in retaliation.

- There is no need to worry if an adversary should choose to waste his money building more weapons than needed.

- There is no need to worry about a surprise attack, as long as the capacity to retaliate cannot be destroyed by such an attack.

- There is little likelihood that a nuclear war would occur at all if potential attackers could be assured that the result would be mutual suicide.

- There is considerable reluctance to get involved in any kind of direct military confrontation with the adversary, since it could escalate unpredictably.

In view of these considerable advantages to the policy of mutual assured destruction, why have the superpowers' arsenals continued to grow, and why have more dangerous nuclear strategies evolved? The answers to both questions have a great deal to do with a particular technological development, the intercontinental ballistic missile (ICBM).

WHAT CHANGES IN NUCLEAR STRATEGY DID THE ICBM BRING ABOUT?

The ICBM is the decendant of the V-2 rocket used with terrifying effect by Germany against England in World War II. German scientists, in fact, played a major role in the development of rocketry in both the United States and the Soviet Union after World War II. The only important respect in which an ICBM differs from a rocket used for space exploration is its more deadly payload, the nuclear warhead. An ICBM is ballistic in the sense that after the missile consumes its fuel, it follows a ballistic trajectory similar to a thrown stone. The powerful rocket thrust causes the ICBM to travel high above the atmosphere and then descend toward targets thousands of miles away at over ten times the speed of sound. The only part of the missile to reenter the atmosphere and approach the target is the reentry vehicle (RV), which contains the nuclear warhead.

ICBMs and bombers are both nuclear-weapons delivery systems. However, the ICBM is a much more threatening delivery system than the bomber:

- ICBMs take thirty minutes or less to reach their target, compared to ten to fifteen hours for intercontinental bombers.

- ICBMs, once launched, cannot be recalled.

- No successful defense against ICBMs yet exists.

The thirty-minute flight time of ICBMs means that even if there is continuous satellite surveillance over an attacker's ICBMs, one can have at most thirty-minutes warning of an impending attack. The warning time could be even less if the victim's spy satellites were to suddenly stop working or if the attacker used missiles launched from nearby submarines (seven- to fifteen-minutes warning time).

Since bombers are recallable, they can easily be "scrambled" in case it is believed an attack might be imminent. The nonrecallability of ICBMs is particularly worrisome considering the possibility of a false alarm. The policy choices open to the victim of an ICBM attack regarding launching of his ICBMs would seem to be limited to three unattractive alternatives:

- Launching ICBMs on warning of an attack, hoping that it is not a false alarm

- Launching ICBMs while they are under attack, hoping that the decision could be made in time and that communications would still be working

- Launching ICBMs after the attack, hoping that they will have survived

In view of the problems presented by each of these choices, some have occasionally suggested that it might be desirable to be able to arm or disarm ICBMs in flight by coded radio signal. However, it seems unlikely that such a proposal would be adopted, since that would leave open the possibility that an adversary could discover the proper code signal to disarm ICBMs. In addition, if either sides' ICBMs were launched due to a false alarm and then disarmed in flight, it seems unlikely that the other side would refrain from launching its own missiles based on hot-line assurances that it was only a computer error.

The lack of any defense also makes ICBMs a very threatening weapon. Surface-to-air missiles (SAMs) can be effective against bombers, but to date they have had much less success against the higher-velocity ICBMs. Over the years, extensive amounts of research have been devoted to an antiballistic-missile (ABM) defense, but most experts believe we are still a long way from being able to build a successful ABM system, notwithstanding the existence of a Soviet ABM system around Moscow. The existence of the Galosh ABM system around Moscow would probably cause the United States to "waste" warheads by attacking the city with a large enough number that some would be sure to get through the defenses. However, a defense that fails to prevent the destruction of the city can hardly be considered effective simply because it causes the United States to expend extra missiles.

The three properties of ICBMs just discussed, i.e., short flight time, nonrecallability, and no defense, are not their most destabilizing characteristics. The refinements in ICBM technology that have made them especially destabilizing and have most undermined the doctrine of mutual assured destruction are improvements in ICBM accuracy and the use of multiple warheads. Initially, ICBMs were rather inaccurate, suitable only for attacking large "soft" targets such as cities, where a miss by a mile is just as likely to cause immense destruction. As greater accuracy began to be achieved, it became feasible to aim one's missiles at small, hardened targets such as underground bunkers and the adversary's ICBMs. This ability, though destabilizing, was not unwelcome to military planners, since the most basic principle of military doctrine is to aim primarily to destroy the military capability of the opponent, not his society. Attacks directed against military targets, particularly the adversary's nuclear deterrent, are known as counterforce attacks, as distinct from so-called countervalue attacks directed at his economy and population.

Once the technology began to make counterforce attacks feasible, counterforce strategy became self-reinforcing. Thus, for example, ICBMs initially above ground were placed in hardened underground silos to make them less vulnerable to attack by the adversary's increasingly accurate ICBMs, only to stimulate the adversary to achieve greater ICBM accuracy. As counterforce attacks became increasingly feasible, the doctrine of flexible response gradually came to replace that of mutual assured destruction. Flexible response meant that the United States had to be able to respond to a range of possible attacks with a range of possible retaliations, commensurate with the scope of the attack. Flexible response was adopted in the belief that it was neither sound policy nor a credible deterrent to the Soviet Union to pretend that any kind of attack, even a limited one, would lead the United States to push the red button and commit mutual suicide by unleashing everything.

However, believing that a limited nuclear war could occur and adopting contingency plans based on that belief are absolutely not the same as planning to start a nuclear war. The belief that a limited nuclear war could never occur would apparently obviate the need to make any contingency plans for a flexible response. Presumably, someone holding that belief would advocate responding massively to even a limited nuclear attack, thereby insuring our own destruction in retaliation. In an age where counterforce attacks are technologically possible, a policy based solely on the impossibility of a limited nuclear war would seem likely to both increase the probability of such a war (since it is not a credible deterrent) and increase the probability that if a nuclear war did start that it would lead to the ultimate holocaust.

Flexible response is, however, a rather disturbing policy. Nuclear war is now no longer unthinkable when one can imagine a whole spectrum of possible nuclear wars ranging from a exchange of single bombs to an all-out nuclear war. In addition, flexible response is disturbing because one is compelled to consider how one would actually go about fighting a nuclear war, rather than count on simply letting everything go in one terrible spasm. Such war-fighting contingency planning by the U.S. government makes some people extremely nervous, since it may be seen as planning to start a war. A related fear, though still we hope an unfounded one, is that such war-fighting planning could develop into a belief that the contingency plans might actually work and that a war could successfully be fought and won. These are real dangers, but the alternative of adopting U.S. policies based on the belief that limited nuclear war is not possible, may be worse.

It is worth noting that the shift from the doctrine of mutual assured destruction to that of flexible response was actually a less pronounced shift than it might seem. According to Harold Brown, secretary of defense in the Carter administration:

It has never been U.S. policy to limit ourselves to massive counter-city operations in retaliation, nor have our plans been so circumscribed. For nearly 20 years, we have explicitly included a range of employment options—against military as well as non-military targets—in our strategic nuclear employment planning. . . . In particular, we have always considered it important in the event of war to be

able to attack the forces that could do damage to the United
States and its allies.[2]

In other words, counterforce attacks and flexible response were really
considered all along by U.S. planners. It was the technology that
made them increasingly feasible.

According to some observers, for exactly the opposite reason
there is little difference between MAD and flexible response: we
never gave up the idea of massive retaliation. In this view, our
vulnerability to a sudden surprise "decapitating" attack that would
result in the severing of command, control, and communications
links requires that we predetermine the nature of our retaliatory
response. Thus, many observers believe that the U.S. single integrated
operations plan (SIOP), which is the highly secret U.S. contingency
plan for the use of its nuclear forces, is "loaded for the big one"
and would go into operation barring last minute orders to the
contrary.

Under the doctrine of mutual assured destruction, there was no
need to add more weapons to the arsenal beyond a level that could
assuredly destroy the aggressor. In the early 1960s, then Secretary
of Defense McNamara calculated that 25 percent of the population
and 60 percent of the industry of the Soviet Union could be destroyed
with 400 one-megaton bombs.[3] He considered that this level of
damage would effectively destroy the Soviet Union as a modern
society. Whether or not McNamara was correct in gauging what level
of damage would be sufficient to deter the Soviet Union, there is
under the doctrine of MAD some approximate way to answer the
question: How much is enough? Unfortunately, that is no longer the
case under the flexible response doctrine. When your weapons are
aimed at your adversary's weapons, then any expansion in the
number of his weapons provides more targets and, therefore, an
incentive for you to add more weapons, leading to a vicious circle.

Many people calculate the amount of overkill in the U.S. and
Soviet arsenals by referring to McNamara's criterion of 25-percent
fatalities and 60-percent industry destroyed. Estimates of the percentage of fatalities versus the number of weapons delivered against
either the United States or the Soviet Union generally look like the
graph in figure 3.1. The shaded area between the two curves is
intended to convey the large degree of uncertainty in the percentage
of fatalities for any given number of delivered weapons. In view of
this large uncertainty, McNamara's criterion for MAD (25 percent
fatalities), could be achieved by anything between 100 and 400

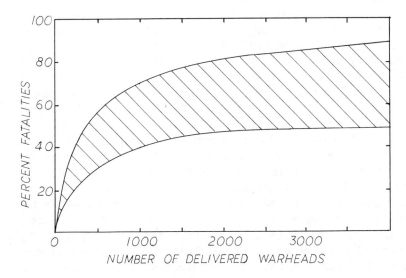

Figure 3.1   Estimated percentage of fatalities.
Source: G. W. Rathjens and G. B. Kistiakowsky, "The Limitations of Strategic Arms," *Scientific American,* January 1970.
Notes: Percentage of fatalities estimated as a function of number of one-megaton warheads delivered against population concentrations. The shaded area indicates approximate range of uncertainty in estimate.

megatons, as seen by the two curves in figure 3.1. The most striking feature of these curves is the manner in which they level off above about a thousand weapons delivered. The plateaus on the curves suggests another way to measure overkill. Beyond about a thousand weapons delivered, a nuclear-weapons targeteer trying to kill as many people as possible simply runs out of significant population concentrations. The actual number of weapons in the U.S. strategic arsenal is roughly ten thousand, leading many people to conclude that the overkill in the U.S. arsenal is roughly ten times what is needed to destroy the Soviet Union, a contention that we will later critically examine.

WHY WAS MIRV A PARTICULARLY DESTABILIZING DEVELOPMENT?

The one technical development that more than any other is responsible for the present era of mutual assured *anxiety* is the multiple warhead ICBM. When first introduced by the United States in 1966 as a multiple reentry vehicle (MRV), it consisted of three separate warheads, or reentry vehicles (RVs), mounted on a single ICBM. The main reason that MRVs were developed was so that in a retaliatory attack on the Soviet Union, the United States could more easily penetrate an ABM defense that it was believed the Soviets would soon deploy. However, no feared massive Soviet ABM deployment actually took place, and both sides later agreed to limit ABM deployment to one system with no more than a hundred launchers. Nevertheless, the refinements in multiple-warhead technology continued, and MRV soon gave rise to the still more threatening MIRV (multiple independently targeted reentry vehicle). The multiple warheads on the original MRV simply scatter like the pellets in a shotgun shell and thereby increase the area of damage. In the MIRV, the separate warheads can be individually aimed at widely separate targets hundreds of miles apart. This is accomplished by using as the ICBM nose cone a "bus" carrying a number of warheads. After a MIRVed ICBM is launched, the bus has a separate rocket engine enabling it to alter its direction and speed, so as to send its deadly "passengers" one by one on their separate destinations.

If unMIRVed (single warhead) ICBMs are used to attack enemy ICBMs, the attacker would expend at least one missile for every enemy missile destroyed, assuming the target missiles are widely dispersed. In the real world of less than 100-percent accuracy, more missiles would be expended by the attacker than would be destroyed in the attack, offering no advantage to the aggressor. MIRVed ICBMs can change the situation drastically. As an example, let us suppose that each side had a thousand ICBMs, each MIRVed with ten warheads. Let us further suppose that the warheads have sufficient accuracy that they would fail to destroy the target ICBMs only 10 percent of the time. In that case, the probability of a miss with two warheads aimed at a target ICBM would be only one percent, assuming both warheads detonate independently. Thus, only ten of the victim's original one thousand warheads would survive. The attacker, using two warheads to attack each of the enemy's thousand ICBMs, can carry out the attack using two hundred missiles (two thousand warheads). So following the attack, the aggressor would be left with eight hundred missiles and the victim would only have ten. This bit of arithmetic shows how MIRVing of ICBMs can theoretically give a significant advantage to the side that strikes first. The technical feasibility of a successful first strike will be considered later.

In hindsight, many strategic thinkers believe that the United States erred in not pressing harder for an agreement with the Soviet Union to ban multiple-warhead ICBMs while the technology was in its infancy. The United States had at the time many reasons for wishing to pursue the new MIRV technology:

- It was an area in which the United States had a clear advantage over the Soviet Union.

- It allowed the United States to keep up with the rapidly increasingly number of Soviet warheads at less expense than building new single-warheads ICBMs.

- It would have allowed a U.S. retaliatory strike to penetrate any Soviet ABM defense more easily.

- It might complicate the job of the defender sufficiently to deter the Soviet Union from ever building an ABM defense.

- It was an irresistably clever bit of technology.

It is worth noting, however, that the U.S. reasons for developing MIRV apparently did not include a desire to seek a first-strike capability against Soviet ICBMs. In fact, in the late 1960s and early 1970s the Congress, apparently out of a desire to avoid threatening the Soviet ability to retaliate, consistently denied requests to fund accuracy improvements in Minuteman and Poseidon missiles. Unfortunately, after catching up to the United States in MIRV technology, the Soviet Union appears to have been less concerned about the destabilizing effect of a reciprocal threat to U.S. land-based ICBMs, judging from the Soviet deployment of large-warhead MIRVed ICBMs, although that may not have been their intention.

ARE THERE SOME NEW WEAPONS THAT MAKE FOR GREATER STABILITY?

Not all advances in nuclear-weapons technology have been destabilizing. One development that has definitely stabilized the balance of terror has been the nuclear-powered submarine and its cargo of sea-launched ballistic missiles (SLBMs). In 1960, the United States launched its first Polaris submarine, and the Soviet Union launched its first nuclear submarine eight years later. The nuclear-reactor-powered submarines, in contrast to the older diesel-powered submarines, are able to stay submerged for months at a time. This is an important feature in making the nuclear submarine fleet exceedingly difficult to locate by the enemy and, therefore, a secure deterrent in case of a surprise attack on the more vulnerable strategic nuclear forces, the ICBMs and bombers.

The three strategic nuclear-weapons delivery systems—the nuclear submarines, the land-based ICBMs, and the bombers—are collectively known as the triad. The United States did not initially set out to structure its nuclear forces according to the triad concept, but the idea is sound enough that something similar might well have resulted from any such long-range plan. The primary advantage of the triad is that each of its three legs has different vulnerabilities and strengths, so it would be impossible for all three legs of the triad to be simultaneously eliminated in a surprise attack. A second important advantage is that if one of the three legs of the triad should become vulnerable to a surprise attack, the relative security of the other two legs allows time to remedy the problem with the vulnerable leg. Other choices might be to "amputate" that leg, to replace it by another one, or to choose not to worry about it.

At present, the nuclear-submarine leg of the triad is said to be virtually invulnerable, despite the fact that individual submarines can be located and destroyed using current anti-submarine-warfare (ASW) techniques. However, to make a surprise attack feasible, most of the U.S. nuclear submarine fleet would need to be destroyed nearly simultaneously. Approximately one-third of the fleet of thirty-four U.S. submarines are in port at any one time, so that an attacker would need to destroy the bulk of the ships at sea. If only seven or eight of these submarines survived the attack on the fleet, their combined SLBMs could devastate all 247 Soviet cities with 1982 populations exceeding 100,000. Some observers, President Carter included, have noted that such devastation could be inflicted by as few as one or two Polaris submarines, since each is capable of launching 160 separate warheads. We have used the higher figure of seven or eight submarines to allow for the fact that perhaps as many as 10 "small" warheads carried by some U.S. SLBMs would be needed to destroy the larger Soviet cities.

The submarine leg of the triad is not without some drawbacks—secure communications being a large potential problem. Even with redundant channels of ship-to-shore communication, it is conceivable that no orders would reach the fleet in the event of a surprise attack on the United States. In the event of a loss of communications, it is unlikely that a submarine commander would wish to compromise the security of the vessel by broadcasting a message to learn whether war had started. One can only speculate what his standing orders might be under such circumstances.

It could happen that the submarine leg of the U.S. triad might become vulnerable in the future. There are conceivable technologies that might one day allow an attacker to destroy the bulk of the U.S. submarine fleet virtually simultaneously. The fact that many articles in the open literature conclude that an ASW effort capable of eliminating the bulk of the fleet is unfeasible may lead to too sanguine a view of the long-term invulnerability of the nuclear submarine fleet.

It is tempting perhaps to conclude that perhaps we should refrain from vigorous ASW efforts so that the fleet would stay relatively invulnerable. However, Soviet efforts in this area would not cease just because U.S. efforts did. Moreover, unlike the case of ABM or MIRV technology where the other side's testing can be easily monitored, there are few ways, apart from espionage, that each side can find out what the other is doing. Unfortunately, it may be true that by keeping up our efforts in this vital area, the result may be that we end up considerably less secure than before if the United States and the Soviet Union both achieve ASW breakthroughs. However, the real issue is not whether we might be less secure afterwards than before, but whether we might be less secure if we do not proceed with ASW research.

Most U.S. observers consider the United States to be well ahead of the Soviet Union in anti-submarine-warfare capability. Submarine expert Owen Wilkes has reported that the United States is, in fact, now capable of detecting all Soviet ballistic-missile submarines.[4] The method of detection uses hidden hydrophones and other acoustic sensors capable of distinguishing submarine noises from all other sounds. Whether the United States could actually use this capability to destroy Soviet submarines in wartime would, of course, depend on whether the secret locations of these U.S. sensors became known to the Soviets, in which case they could easily be destroyed.

The ships in the U.S. submarine fleet are acknowledged to be quieter than Soviet submarines, making the U.S. ships harder to detect. In fact some observers, such as Joel Wit, believe that the present U.S. ability to destroy Soviet submarines "is unlikely to be matched by the Soviet Union in the forseeable future."[5] However, that assessment may be overly sanguine if Soviet submarines have, in fact, been vulnerable for several years.[6]

Table 3.1   U.S. and Soviet Nuclear Arsenals

	Year	U.S.	U.S.S.R.
ICBMs	1962	294	75
	1972	1,054	1,500
	1984	1,040	1,398
SLBMs	1962	144	20
	1972	656	450
	1984	568	950
Long-range bombers	1962	1,650	200
	1972	520	156
	1984	325	156
Strategic nuclear weapons	1962	7,400	400
	1972	5,800	2,100
	1984	10,000	8,000

Source: Tom Longstreth, The Arms Control Association, March 1984.
Note: Different sources report somewhat different numbers. Variations in number of warheads by as much as 20 to 30 percent are not uncommon. Some quantities such as total megatonnage and missile accuracy are subject to much larger variations, depending on the source. The figure listed for Soviet long-range bombers does not include 115 Backfire bombers.

HOW DO THE U.S. AND SOVIET TRIADS COMPARE?

The Soviet Union, like the United States, has a triad of strategic nuclear forces. The relative strengths of the different legs of the U.S. and Soviet triads are indicated in table 3.1 for the years 1962, 1972, and 1984. Also, see figure 3.2 for 1984 arsenals. Several observations may be made concerning these figures:

- Both the U.S. and the Soviet Union have increased their arsenals significantly during the last twenty years, the Soviet Union very much more so than the United States.

- By some measures, e.g., numbers of ICBMs and SLBMs, the Soviets are now ahead, while by others, e.g., numbers of bombers, the United States leads.

- According to the single measure some observers claim to be the best overall indicator of strategic nuclear strength, i.e. numbers of warheads, the United States holds a small lead in 1984.

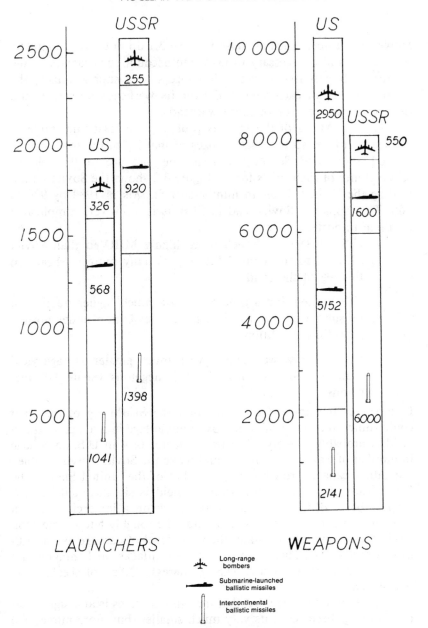

Figure 3.2   Strategic arsenals of the superpowers.
Source: Tom Longstreth, Arms Control Association, January 1984.
Note: The relative numbers of strategic nuclear delivery systems (launchers) are shown on the left, and the relative numbers of strategic nuclear weapons (bombs and reentry vehicles) are shown on the right.

However, numbers such as those in table 3.1 do not give a complete picture. It is also necessary to take into account such factors as the relative vulnerability of each side's forces to a suprise attack, the relative ability of each side to deliver its warheads on target, and the yield and accuracy of those warheads.

The SLBM leg of the triad is probably the least vulnerable to a surprise attack, so the relative sizes of that leg of the triad for the United States and Soviet Union is one measure of the relative survivability of each side's forces. Figure 3.2 shows the Soviet Union leading the United States in numbers of SLBMs in 1984 by 920 to 568. This apparent Soviet lead in SLBMs is, however, complicated by three important factors:

- U.S. SLBMs are much more highly MIRVed than Soviet SLBMs, so the United States has many more warheads in this leg of the triad.

- The United States generally has a much higher fraction of its submarines at sea than the Soviet Union under normal peacetime conditions.

- Soviet SLBM warheads have a much greater average yield than U.S. SLBM warheads—0.6 megatons versus 0.06 megatons.

In terms of the amount of destruction the SLBM leg of the triad could inflict, the factor of 10 in Soviet advantage in average warhead yield is probably roughly offset by the factor of 4 in U.S. advantage in number of warheads, which would make the Soviet "invulnerable" retaliatory capacity roughly equal to that of the United States. The U.S. disadvantage in SLBM warhead yield is significant if, for example, the SLBMs were used in an attack on a large city. As can be seen in figures 3.3 and 3.4, it would take roughly ten .04-megaton (40-kiloton) warheads to inflict the same level of damage as one 1.0-megaton warhead. These two hypothetical attacks on Leningrad are from a study done by the U.S. Congress, Office of Technology Assessment.[7]

It should not be concluded that the United States is at a significant disadvantage because of its very much smaller (but more numerous) SLBM warheads. A 40-kiloton bomb is more than twice the size of the bomb used against Hiroshima, and it would be more than adequate to destroy most medium-size cities, airports, oil refineries, and many other military and economic targets. It is, however, neither a silo-buster nor, if used singly, is it a big city–killer.

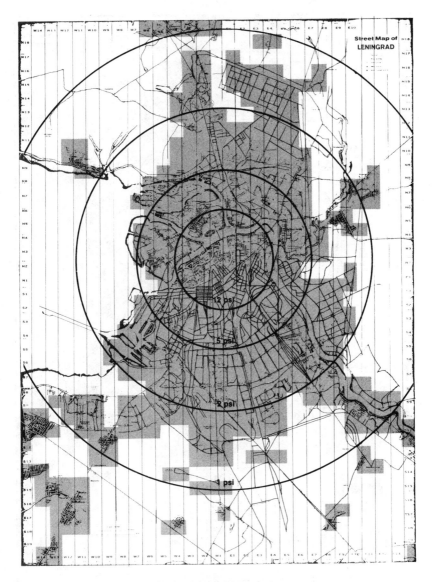

Figure 3.3   One-megaton airburst over Leningrad.
Source: Office of Technology Assessment, *Effects of Nuclear War,* p. 42.
Note: Estimated number of casualties includes 890,000 fatalities and 1,260,000 injured.

The fact that a greater fraction of U.S. submarines are continuously on patrol compared to the Soviet fleet gives the United States a significant second-strike (retaliatory) advantage, given the vulner-

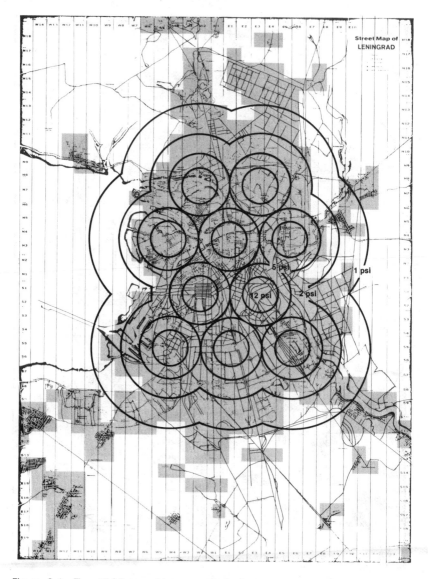

Figure 3.4   Ten 40-kiloton airbursts over Leningrad.
Source: Office of Technology Assessment, Effects of Nuclear War, p. 44.
Note: Estimated number of casualties includes 1,020,000 fatalities and
1,000,000 injured.

ability of submarines in port. However, the Soviet submarine fleet
may have a greater first-strike advantage since some Soviet SLBMs,

unlike their U.S. counterparts, are capable of reaching their targets even though the submarines are in port.

HOW IMPORTANT IS MISSILE ACCURACY?

The accuracy of each sides' warheads is another important factor in assessing U.S. and Soviet capabilities. Accuracy is usually expressed in terms of the CEP which, according to some, stands for "circle of equal probability," and according to others, the "circular-error probable." The CEP is the radius of a circle that would contain 50 percent of the landing points when a large number of warheads are aimed at a target. If, for example, you were to play a game of darts, and you found that when aiming for the bullseye, the darts landed inside a six-inch-radius circle 50 percent of the time, the CEP would be six inches.

Although the exact CEP of U.S. warheads is classified information, one of the most accurate deployed ICBM warheads, the Mark 12A on the Minuteman III, is claimed to have a CEP of approximately 0.1 miles. This means that it would land within roughly 500 feet of its target half the time. No statistics or any aspect of Soviet nuclear weaponry are made publicly available by the Soviet Union. However, information has been pieced together from a variety of sources, and it is publicly disseminated on an annual basis by the London-based International Institute for Strategic Studies (IISS) in its annual publication *The Military Balance*. This publication, and a similar one published by the Stockholm International Peace Research Institute (SIPRI), *The SIPRI Yearbook,* are two widely consulted sources of statistics on the military forces of various countries.

Although some kinds of information such as the number of missile silos in the Soviet Union can be obtained quite easily from satellite photographs (apparently even if they are camouflaged), other kinds of information are much less reliable. One less reliable piece of information is the accuracy (CEP) of Soviet missiles. The CEP of a Soviet warhead must be determined by eavesdropping on Soviet missile tests. However, inferring the CEP by observing a test is a very indirect procedure, since warheads are not aimed at a publicly announced bullseye. For example, suppose you were to observe ten warheads landing at the positions indicated by the dots in figure 3.5.

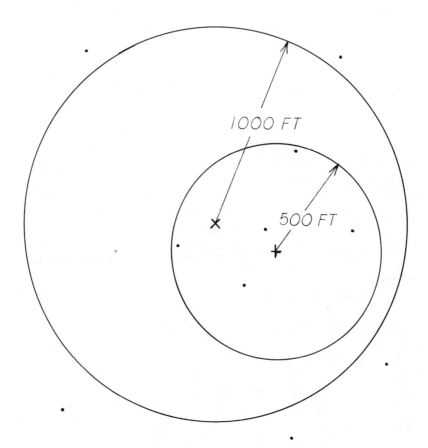

Figure 3.5   Determination of CEP from warhead landing points.
Notes: The CEP is the radius of a circle including half the warhead landing points. Its value depends on a knowledge of the aim point. A CEP of 500 feet is obtained if the plus is assumed to be the aim point, while twice that value is obtained when the cross is assumed to be the aim point.

Assuming that the warheads were aimed at the cross, the CEP measured in this test would be approximately 500 feet. However. an eavesdropping observer who believed that that ten warheads were actually aimed at the plus sign would falsely conclude that their CEP was 1000 feet. To make matters even more confusing to potential eavesdroppers, the individual warheads could be deviously aimed at a series of different unannounced targets, which would make the missiles appear less accurate than they actually are.

According to another definition of the CEP, it is not relevant where the warheads are aimed; the CEP is determined simply by drawing the smallest circle that includes half the hits. However, this definition of the CEP measures only the scatter of warheads and not their accuracy. That would make it a somewhat useless quantity for computing the probability of hitting a target, unless further information is known on the so-called bias of the warheads—the distance from the center of the cluster of hits to the aim point.

The accuracy of a warhead, as noted earlier, is somewhat unimportant if it is used to attack a soft target such as a city. For a hard target such as a missile silo, the probability of a "kill" depends on a combination of three factors: the warhead yield, the warhead accuracy (CEP), and the hardness of the target, measured in terms of the pressure in pounds per square inch (psi) it can withstand. There are some self-evident propositions concerning the relationship of these factors:

- The more accurate a warhead is, the smaller its yield has to be to destroy a particular hard target.

- The harder a target, the greater the yield or accuracy of the attacking warhead needs to be in order to destroy it, accuracy being the more important of the two factors.

- The hardest target conceivable could not survive an attack by ground-burst warheads of sufficient yield and accuracy to place the target within the bomb crater, assuming that the target is not buried deeply beneath the earth.

These relationships can also be expressed in more quantitative terms. The mathematical relationship that gives the kill probability P, for the target of hardness H (in psi) attacked by a missile of yield Y (in megatons), and CEP (in miles) is given by

$$P = 1 - e - \frac{k}{(0.22 \ H^{2/3})},$$

where the "lethality," k, is given by $k = Y^{2/3}/CEP^2$.

This formula can be applied to each of the warheads in the U.S. and Soviet arsenals to find the kill probability against the other side's missile silos. However, due to the fact that the yield and accuracy (CEP) appear in an exponent in the formula for P, the value obtained for the kill probability depends very sensitively on these quantities, particularly on accuracy. The relative importance of accuracy and yield can be seen by observing that a warhead that has half the CEP of a second one needs only one-eighth the yeild to have the same kill probability. Different judgments on the vulnerability of land-based missiles, dependent on calculations of kill-probability, can usually be traced to different assumptions of the yield, and particularly the accuracy, of the other side's warheads. Because of the exponential dependence of kill probability on CEP, it is not surprising to sometimes find that a factor of 2 difference in the value assumed for CEP results in a factor of 20 difference in the number of missiles predicted to survive an attack.

Tables 3.2 and 3.3 give information on each of the warheads in the U.S. and Soviet arsenals. Other sources report different values for these data, particularly the CEP. Columns (7) and (8) in both tables show the kill probability against the other side's missile silos, assuming one and two warheads aimed at each target respectively. The following facts may be gleaned from table 3.2 and 3.3:

- Both the United States and Soviet Union now have ICBMs with warheads having a high probability of knocking out the other's ICBMs.

- The Soviet Union has far more ICBM warheads having a high two-shot kill probability than the United States, making the theoretical Soviet threat to the U.S. ICBM force much greater than the converse U.S. threat at present. (This point will be further discussed in the next chapter.)

- The high kill probability of warheads carried by bombers is not particularly relevant to the possibility of a surprise attack on ICBM silos, given their relatively long flight time.

HOW IMPORTANT ARE THE AREAS OF U.S. ADVANTAGE?

There are many factors that must be assessed in considering the relative strengths of U.S. and Soviet military forces. Some of these are listed in table 3.4, based on which side they favor. It is certainly not true that all factors are equally important, and some may not be very meaningful. For example, the U.S. advantage in having quieter submarines only becomes a meaningful advantage if ASW efforts should advance to the point where either side's fleet can be

Table 3.2 1984 U.S.S.R. Strategic Nuclear Forces

| | | Warheads Carried | | Deployed Warheads | CEP (miles) | Silo Kill Probability | |
| | | | | | | 1-Shot | 2-Shot |
Number (1)	Name (2)	Number (3)	Yield and Type (4)	(5)	(6)	(7)	(8)
Intercontinental ballistic missiles							
550	SS-11	1	(450-kt. (or 3 MRV)	550	.7	.06	.12
60	SS-13	1	(450-kt. warhead	60	.7	.06	.12
150	SS-17	4	(200-kt. MIRV warhead	600	.25	.3–.6	.6–.8
50	SS-18	1	(10,000-kt. warhead	50	.25	.97	.99
258	SS-18	8–10	(450-kt. MIRV warhead	2,580	.15	.59	.83
330	SS-19	6	(450-kt. warhead	1,980	.15–.25	.60	.85
Submarine-launched ballistic missiles							
45	SS-N-5	1	(1,000-kt. warhead	45	1.5	.01	.02
368	SS-N-6	1	(1,000-kt. (or 3 MRV)	368	1.5	.01	.02
292	SS-N-8	1	(1,000-kt. warhead	292	.8	.05	.10
12	SS-N-17	1	(1,000-kt. warhead	12	.5	.10	.19
224	SS-N-18	3	(200-kt. MIRV warhead	672	.5	.16	.29
32	SS-N-18	7	(200-kt. MIRV warhead	224	.5	.16	.29
40	SS-NX-20	1–9	(?) MIRV warhead	—			
Intercontinental bombers							
30	Tu-95 (Bear)	2	1,000-kt. bomb	60	.2	.52–.83	.77–.97
75	Tu-95 (Bear)	1	1,000-kt. bomb	75	.2	.52–.83	.77–.97
		+1	(500-kt. AS-3 Kangaroo	75	.2	.52–.83	.77–.97
49	Mya-4 (Bison)	1	1,000-kt. bomb	49	.2	.52–.83	.77–.97
				7,692			

Sources: Figures for columns (1)–(5) from Tom Longstreth. The Arms Control Association, March 1984. Columns (6)–(8) from F. Kaplan, *Dubious Specter: A Skeptical Look at the Soviet Nuclear Threat* (Washington, DC: Institute for Policy Studies, 1980). pp. 88–91.
Note: Warhead yields in parenthesis are less well-known.

Table 3.3 1984 U.S. Strategic Nuclear Forces

Number (1)	Name (2)	Number (3)	Yield and Type (4)	Deployed Warheads (5)	CEP (miles) (6)	Silo Kill Probability	
			Warheads Carried			1-Shot (7)	2-Shot (8)
Intercontinental ballistic missiles							
550	Minuteman 3	3	335-kt. MIRV warhead	1,650	.1	.70	.91
450	Minuteman 2	1–2	1,500-kt. warhead	450	.3	.27	.31
40	Titan 2	1	9,000-kt. warhead	40	.7	.11	.21
Submarine-launched ballistic missiles							
304	Poseidon	10–14	40-kt. MIRV warhead	3,040	.25	.05	.10
264	Trident	8	100-kt. MIRV warhead	2,112	.25	.10	.19
Intercontinental bombers							
264	B-52GH	4	100–1,000 kt.ᵃ	1,020	.1	.94	.99
		+4	170-kt. SRAM missile	1,020	.1	.94	.99
		+20	200-kt. ALCMs	600	.05	.99	.99
60	FB-111	2	100–1,000 kt.	120	.1	.94	.99
		+2	170-kt. SRAM missile	120	.1	.94	.99
				10,472			

Sources: See Table 3.2
ᵃ Bomb has variable yield.

Table 3.4   Relative U.S.-U.S.S.R Nuclear Strength

Factors Favoring U.S.	Factors Favoring Soviet Union
• marginally more warheads	• more ICBMs
• more warheads on submarines	• greater threat to adversary's ICBMs
• quieter submarines	• bigger missiles (megatonnage)
• more advanced ASW capability	• greater MIRV capacity (fractionation)
• more submarines on station	• more submarines
• greater general readiness	• more SLBMs
• nuclear allies	• better civil defense program
• forward-based nuclear forces	• more air defense (against bombers)
• better technology	• larger conventional forces
• cruise missile technology	• greater access to adversary's technology
• more intercontinental bombers	• better post-attack survivability
• better access to the seas	• more cruise missile launch platforms

easily located and destroyed in wartime. Moreover, if an ASW breakthrough should occur in a nonacoustic area, quieter submarines might prove to be of no significant advantage. Although acoustic techniques would seem to offer the most promising possibility of a breakthrough, other methods such as maintaining continuous tails on all the adversary's ships are also conceivable. Other U.S. advantages could prove ephemeral as well. For example, the fact that there are a greater number of U.S. submarines on station or that it has greater readiness generally are factors that the Soviet Union could apparently compensate for by putting its own forces in a greater state of readiness. For still another example, although the United States holds a slight lead in number of warheads, the Soviet Union could dramatically increase the number of its warheads much easier than the United States and in much shorter time, because the larger Soviet missiles could carry many more multiple warheads on each ICBM than could the U.S. missiles.

Finally, whether a factor is considered an advantage or a disadvantage depends on which side would be the attacker. The United States does have a second-strike retaliatory advantage by virtue of the fact that its submarine fleet is quieter and spends less time in port than the Soviet fleet. The Soviets, however, would not have a first-strike disadvantage because of noisier submarines which are more often in port. Precisely the same point can be made about the greater diversity of the U.S. arsenal among all three legs of the triad, compared to the Soviet arsenal which disproportionately emphasizes ICBMs. Thus, quite apart from each side's intentions, the U.S. arsenal seems the one better suited for a second-strike retaliatory mission. It is probably for this reason that U.S. military leaders have consistently indicated no wish to trade arsenals with the Soviet Union, despite Soviet nuclear superiority in some areas.

One very important area in which the United States holds a lead over the Soviet Union is in overall technological quality. However, here also there are offsetting factors. While the United States is believed to be ahead in overall military technology by about five years, there are specific areas such as ICBM cold-launch capability and high-pressure physics in which the United States does not lead.

Moreover, the future of technology depends crucially on the quantity and quality of people devoting themselves to the enterprise. The number of Soviet engineering graduates has increased fourfold since 1955 while the number of U.S. engineering graduates has shown little growth during this same period. These trends could in the future have a profound effect on the U.S. technological leadership in both the military and civilian areas. In addition, the Soviet Union is catching up to the level of U.S. technology, in no small measure due to extensive Soviet efforts to acquire Western technology of military relevance through various open and clandestine means. According to a 1982 Central Intelligence Agency report: "Today, this Soviet effort is massive, well planned and well managed—a national-level program approved at the highest party and government levels." [8]

One major area of Soviet interest is the microelectronics technology crucial to many military applications. The CIA report notes that

over the past 10 years, the Soviets legally and illegally purchased large quantities of Western high-technology microelectronics equipment that has enabled them to build their own microelectronics industry in short time. This acquired capability in microelectronics is the critical basis for the present wide-ranging enhancements of Soviet military systems and for their continuing sophistication.

The highly successful Soviet efforts in acquiring Western technology means that the United States is, in more ways than one, in a technological race with itself. However, to abandon the technological race, in view of major Soviet advantages in other areas, could have unfortunate consequences.

One example of a major technology in which the United States until recent years appeared to be ahead is the cruise missile. Cruise missiles are air-breathing, pilotless drones that have a range of up to 1500 miles and can be launched from platforms in the air, on the sea, or on the ground. They are so small that perhaps twenty could be loaded onboard a B-52 bomber. It is planned to put over three thousand cruise missiles on the B-52s in the U.S. fleet. The cruise missiles' maximum speed of Mach .95 makes them much slower than ICBMs, but their small size and the fact that they can fly at extremely low altitudes (150 feet over land), following the contours of the terrain, makes them nearly invisible on ground-based radar. Cruise missiles are equipped with television cameras that can "see" the terrain over which they fly and navigate by a terrain-contour-matching technique (TERCOM). The cruise missile has stored in its computer memory a map of the terrain elevation contours over which it will fly. It is able to continually measure terrain elevation and correct its course after periodically finding out where it is by a comparison with the computer-stored maps, thereby achieving extremely high accuracy. Despite their numerous advantages, cruise missiles may be considerably easier to detect with the advent of look-down radar such as that on an AWAC-type plane. This fact was undoubtedly responsible for President Reagan's 1983 decision to suspend deployment of air-launched cruise missiles until a more advanced version incorporating "stealth" technology is built.

Until recent years it was believed that the United States was far ahead in cruise-missile technology. The Soviets, however, have successfully obtained this technology from the West by clandestine means, and they will have begun to deploy cruise missiles by 1985.[9] As a result an area formerly thought to be a U.S. advantage (better cruise-missile technology), has become a Soviet advantage (more cruise-missile launch platforms), once the Soviet Union has acquired the necessary technology from the West. The cruise missile is, accordingly, an excellent example of how the United States, in effect, is in a technological race with itself.

HOW IMPORTANT ARE THE AREAS OF SOVIET ADVANTAGE?

In another chapter we will discuss the Soviet advantage in the area of civil defense and its significance. The fact that the Soviets possess an extensive air defense system against bombers, while the United States does not, may also be of significance. The Soviets, for example, have deployed ten thousand surface-to-air missile (SAM) launchers while the United States has none. The dramatic failure of Soviet SAM missiles employed by the Syrians during the 1982 Israeli invasion of Lebanon may say very little about the probable performance of the Soviet air defense system. The defensive missiles destroyed by the Israelis were not the most modern Soviet missiles; they were not operated by Soviets; the operators may have been caught by surprise; and they were not part of a massive well-integrated Soviet defense system.

Although some analysts have claimed that the U.S. B-52 bombers are no longer capable of penetrating Soviet air defenses, many other analysts would violently disagree, and they would point out that the B-52 fleet, in reality, is not homogeneous in its capabilities. According to Pentagon estimates, the newer B-52s, which have been continuously upgraded with electronic countermeasures to foil enemy radar, should continue to be able to penetrate Soviet air defenses until 1990.[10] Furthermore, the condition of Soviet air defenses following a U.S. ICBM strike might bear little resemblance to their prewar state. Finally, while Soviet air defense may be somewhat effective against penetrating bombers, it would be less effective against bombers armed with cruise missiles that could be fired from outside Soviet air space.

In chapter 7, we will discuss the historical, geographical, political, and socioeconomic factors that could affect the relative probabilities of the United States and the Soviet Union being able to survive a nuclear war. On balance, there may be a greater probability of eventual Soviet postattack survival—another factor that must be weighed in assessing the U.S.-Soviet nuclear balance. Other factors listed in table 3.4 are indirectly related to the nuclear balance, i.e., the Soviet lead in conventional forces, and the U.S. lead in nuclear allies and forward-based nuclear forces in Europe. These will be discussed in chapter 5.

Two of the more controversial Soviet advantages are the larger size and younger age of Soviet missiles. Figure 3.6 shows the relative sizes of weapons in the U.S. and Soviet strategic missile forces and the dates they were first deployed. This chart, and charts like it, have often been used to argue for the need for U.S.-strategic-force modernization based on the relative pace of U.S. and Soviet weapons programs during the past twenty years. Although U.S. strategic forces may need modernizing, the stark comparison made in figure 3.6 is misleading on all the following counts:

- The relative age of U.S. and Soviet forces is not truly depicted by showing only the date of initial deployment. The Minutemen III ICBM, for example, which was initially deployed in 1970, was deployed during the entire period 1970–75, and some were deployed as late as 1978.

- The relative number of different models of missiles in each arsenal is much less important than the number deployed for each model and their capabilities. The Soviet Union, which deploys many different models (produced by several competing rocket bureaus), may simply be hedging its bets in case one missile maker's product is not as good as another.

- The fact that the Soviet Union has many more very large missiles than the United States is not as significant an advantage as it might seem.

Missile size or "throw weight" is of some significance in that it can determine how many warheads missiles can carry. However, apart from that factor, sheer missile size is not a very good measure of anything. The Reagan administration, which has not been accused of being soft on defense, in 1982 began retiring the Titans, the only very large missiles in the U.S. arsenal. Warhead yield is a much more significant factor than throw weight, although the two are not completely unrelated.

HOW SIGNIFICANT A FACTOR IS EQUIVALENT MEGATONNAGE?

Equivalent megatonnage is a measure of the area of blast damage which weapons can inflict. For soft targets such as cities, the circular area of destruction is approximately proportional to the square of the "lethal radius" or the two-thirds power of the yield, $Y^{2/3}$ (see chapter 6). Thus, for a number of warheads, N, the total area of destruction is proportional to $NY^{2/3}$, assuming nonoverlapping areas. This is the basis of the definition of equivalent megatonnage, EMT $= NY^{2/3}$. Equivalent megatonnage is perhaps the best single indicator of the level of damage that each side could inflict on the other side's territory, population, and environment. Given roughly equal numbers of warheads in the U.S. and Soviet arsenals and the larger yield of Soviet warheads, it is not surprising that the Soviet arsenal exceeds the U.S. arsenal in equivalent megatonnage by 7100 to 4100. The value of 4100 equivalent megatons for the U.S. arsenal in 1982 corresponds to a level of damage that could be inflicted by 4100 one-megaton bombs. Of this total, approximately 900 equivalent

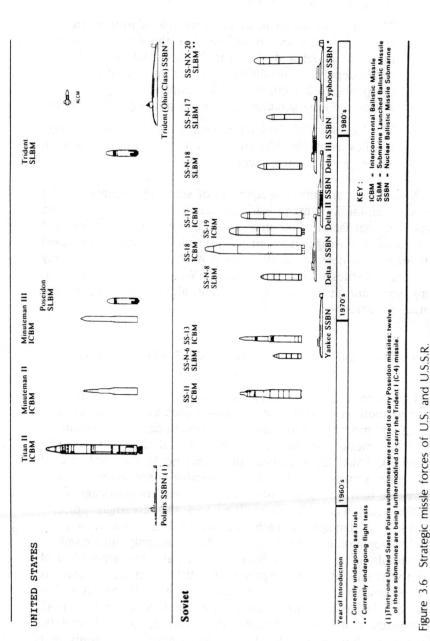

Figure 3.6 Strategic missile forces of U.S. and U.S.S.R.
Source: U.S. Department of State, 1982; reprinted in *Armed Forces Journal,* August 1982, p. 50.
Note: Intercontinental ballistic missles (ICBMs), submarine-launched ballistic missles (SLBMs), and nuclear ballistic-missle submarines (SSBNs), showing the year each was introduced and the relative sizes of each model.

megatons, or 22 percent, is carried on submarines on station and is, for now, relatively invulnerable to a surprise attack.

In figures 3.7 and 3.8 we illustrate how the levels of U.S. and Soviet nuclear forces have varied over time for the last twenty years. Two somewhat different views are obtained depending on whether we give emphasis to the number of warheads or to equivalent megatonnage. In figure 3.7, we see that during the decade of the 1960s the United States decreased the number of warheads in its arsenal from 6,500 to 3,900, while Soviet warheads increased from 300 to 1,800. During the entire period 1962 to 1984 the great expansion in the Soviet arsenal brought them to approximate parity with a much more modestly increasing U.S. arsenal that started from a much higher base.

A somewhat more sobering view of the overall U.S.-Soviet nuclear balance is indicated by a comparison of the equivalent megatonnage in the two arsenals. From 1962 to 1982 the Soviet Union has increased its equivalent megatonnage from 800 to 7,100. During the same period the U.S. has *decreased* its equivalent megatonnage from 8,000 to 4,000. The twenty-year decrease in U.S. equivalent megatonnage was not the result of a deliberate unilateral disarmament, but rather resulted from the MIRVing of U.S. missiles to carry more numerous but smaller warheads. The total EMT for a MIRVed missile is inevitably less than that of a single warhead missile of the same throw weight, since the "bus" that carries the individual warheads has a nonnegligible weight. From a military point of view this means that the MIRVed missile poses a threat to a greater number of separate targets, but to a smaller total land area.

A one-megaton air-burst bomb would create lethal (5 psi) blast effects over a circular area 4.5 miles in radius. We can get an upper limit to the total land area of each country that the adversary could destroy by blast by taking a number of nonoverlapping circles of radius 4.5 miles equal to the number of equivalent megatons in the adversary's arsenal. If these numbers are divided by the land area of each country, we then obtain the maximum percentage of land area subject to lethal blast damage. Figure 3.8 shows the trends for the United States and the Soviet Union over time. The fact that the percentage of U.S. land area subject to lethal-blast pressures is shown to be five times greater than that of the Soviet Union in 1984 is due both to the larger Soviet equivalent megatonnage (twice the U.S. megatonnage) and to the larger Soviet land area (2.5 times the U.S. land area). Figure 3.8 shows that in 1960 the ratio was also

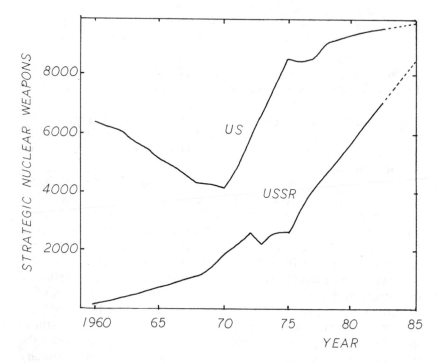

Figure 3.7   Strategic nuclear warheads of U.S. and U.S.S.R.
Source: The Defense Monitor, Volume XI, Number 6, 1982, Published by the Center for Defense Information.
Note: Total number of strategic nuclear warheads deployed as a function of time. The extrapolations for 1982 to 1984 are based on data supplied by CDI in January 1984.

five to one, but the threatened damage to the Soviet Union was then five times that to the United States. The relative Soviet advantage depicted in figure 3.8 would not have been quite so dramatic had we plotted the absolute area of each nation that could be devastated rather than the percentage. In that case, the curve labelled U.S.S.R. would need to have been multiplied by 2.5 relative to the U.S. curve in order to account for the difference in land areas of the two nations.

The curves in figure 3.8 could be misleading in at least two other respects. First, the fact that the percentage of each country's land area subject to lethal blast damage is very small should not

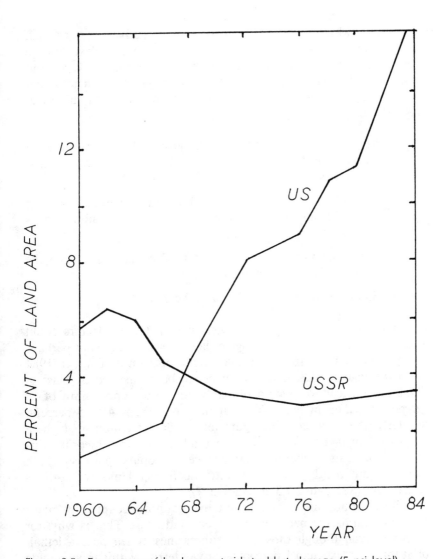

Figure 3.8   Percentage of land area at risk to blast damage (5 psi level).
Notes: Figure shows percentage of land area in the U.S. and the U.S.S.R. that
would be subject to lethal blast damage at the 5-psi level, if the adversary's
entire arsenal were air burst. The curves are calculated based on the amount
of equivalent megatonnage in each superpower's arsenal and assuming nonoverlapping circles of radius 4.4 miles.

imply that people residing outside these small areas would be spared
the effects of a nuclear war. Second, although the curves in figure
3.8 give an idea of the relative percentage of each country's land

area that could be devastated by blast from the adversary's arsenal, they probably do not give a realistic portrayal of the blast damage likely to occur in an all-out nuclear war. According to U.S. (and presumably Soviet) targeting strategy, there are four factors that would probably greatly lower the percentage of land area subject to blast damage:

- Many weapons are likely to be ground burst—resulting in an area of blast damage about half that of an air-burst weapon (see chapter 6).

- Multiple weapons are likely to be used on key military and industrial targets, causing many of the lethal-radius circles to overlap.

- Some weapons are likely to be used on targets outside the adversary's home territory.

- Some weapons are likely to be held in reserve.

It would not be unreasonable to estimate that these factors could lead to a more realistic percentage of land area devastated of perhaps one-quarter to one-third of the calculated upper limit. Thus, in 1984 the percentage of U.S. land area likely to be devastated by blast in an all-out nuclear war would probably not be the upper limit of 16 percent indicated in figure 3.8, but instead perhaps 4 to 5 percent. Similarly, the corresponding figure for the Soviet Union might be a bit less than 1 percent. The Soviet advantage indicated by this comparison is somewhat overstated since the populated areas of both countries are roughly equal, despite the Soviet Union's 2.5-times larger size. (See figure 7.3 in chapter 7.)

Furthermore, the total area of either country occupied by major cities is a miniscule percentage of their land areas. That is why, for example, even though those U.S. submarines at sea pose a lethal-blast threat to less than 1 percent of Soviet territory, this invulnerable deterrent can hold hostage a majority of the Soviet population— assuming, of course, that the cities have not been evacuated.

In addition to blast, thermal radiation and fallout would also create a lethal environment over much of the land area of a country attacked with nuclear weapons. However, the effect of including thermal radiation and fallout as well as blast would be to widen further the gap in relative damage to the United States and the Soviet Union because of the larger average yield of weapons in the

Soviet arsenal.[11] The sizable gap in relative damage done to both countries in an all-out attack could be further accentuated both by defensive measures (civil defense and air defense) and by the destruction of retaliatory forces by the side that strikes first.

In summary, one comes to rather different conclusions concerning the U.S.-Soviet arms competition depending on whether number of warheads (figure 3.7) or equivalent megatonnage (figure 3.8) is viewed as the more important measure. Those who believe the Soviet lead in EMT to be unimportant note that it does nothing to prevent U.S. nuclear forces from carrying out their dual mission of deterring war by threatening an unacceptable level of damage against the aggressor and carrying out that retaliatory threat should deterrence fail. If the threatened retaliation is against military and other "point" targets (though not ICBM silos), then the observation is certainly a valid one. However, if deterrence is strengthened when the United States has the capability of inflicting a comparable level of damage to the territory, population, and environment of the Soviet Union, then EMT (and especially survivable EMT) does matter.

WHAT IS THE PRESENT STATE OF THE U.S.-SOVIET NUCLEAR BALANCE?

In the preceding pages we have discussed many factors, some of which favor the United States and some of which favor the Soviet Union. Readers ultimately will have to decide for themselves, based on all these factors (and others), how they would answer the question Who's ahead?, or whether this question has any meaning.

In a controversial statement, President Ronald Reagan has indicated that the Soviet Union has "a definite margin of superiority" over the U.S. nuclear arsenal. While Reagan is the first American president to have made such a claim, it is also true that the relative trends according to some of the indicators, e.g., equivalent megatonnage, have increasingly over time favored the Soviet Union. Thus, President Reagan's statement, while contestable, was certainly not blatantly incorrect.

Nevertheless, even if President Reagan's allegation of U.S. nuclear inferiority were true, some observers have been dismayed that a U.S. administration would inform the Soviet Union of this fact in such strong terms. The fear is less one of a Soviet nuclear attack than of Soviet adventurism based on the belief that a United States that considers itself inferior is unlikely to respond to subnuclear challenges. Soviet leaders, however, are not completely naïve concerning the workings of U.S. domestic politics. They are certainly aware that U.S. administrations often need to resort to "the Russians are coming" rhetoric in order to scare the U.S. public into supporting defense buildups. The Kremlin is perfectly capable of making its own assessment of the military balance, and they have no more reason to take U.S. official statements of nuclear inferiority at face value than we have for trusting statements by Soviet leaders. Moreover, any president who genuinely believes that the U.S. nuclear arsenal is deficient in ways that make the country vulnerable would be duty bound to present his case to the Congress and the people, regardless of the possible Soviet reaction.

Whatever is the state of the current U.S.-Soviet nuclear balance, it certainly would be a distortion of recent history to claim that the superpower arsenals have expanded comparably over the last twenty years—at least in terms of the devastation they could inflict on the other's society. Many observers' comments often convey a much more symmetrical view of the nature of the arms race than has actually been the case. For example, according to Edward Kennedy and Mark Hatfield: "If nuclear war broke out now, the U.S. and the Soviet Union would suffer more destruction than they would have 10 years ago and far, far more than 20 years ago." [12] And similarly, according to Strobe Talbott: "In the '60s and '70s both sides increased their nuclear firepower by several orders of magnitude. It was a classic vicious spiral. Neither nation wanted to be on the losing side of an overkill gap." [13] Given the actual trends in equivalent megatonnage over the last twenty years, it is blatantly false that the United States has increased its "firepower" by several orders of magnitude. It is also equally false that the United States could inflict "far far more" damage against Soviet society than twenty years ago.

Of course it would be equally false to portray the United States as not making significant qualitative and quantitative changes to its nuclear arsenal—at least during the decade of the 1970s. These additions include MIRVing of five hundred Minuteman III missiles with three warheads, MIRVing of most of the submarine missiles to carry ten warheads each, and adding short-range attack missiles (SRAMS) to the B-52 bomber fleet. Nevertheless, while the number of U.S. warheads has increased somewhat during the last twenty years, the 49-percent decline in U.S.-equivalent megatonnage makes it unclear whether the United States could inflict more or less damage against the Soviets as a society than twenty years ago. Moreover, if we are primarily interested in a second retaliatory strike, there is no question that the level of damage the United States could inflict against the Soviet Union is much less than twenty years ago, given the greater capability the Soviet Union now has for destroying a larger fraction of the U.S. arsenal and its more extensive air defense and civil defense than twenty years ago. The important question about which we can only speculate is what impact these changes will have on the thinking of U.S. and Soviet government leaders and on the risks they are willing to run.

In view of the size of the U.S. and Soviet arsenals, many people take the point of view that it really does not matter who is ahead, as long as both the United States and the Soviet Union have enough nuclear weapons to destroy the other many times over. Even without ascribing total insignificance, however, to the who's-ahead question, we may find that there are more important questions from the standpoint of U.S. and world security.

Our main focus in this chapter has been on strategic nuclear weapons, i.e. those weapons capable of being delivered directly against the other country. Such weapons are termed "strategic" because they can produce results that can affect the course of a war at its onset. Both superpowers also possess tactical nuclear weapons intended for battlefield use. By definition, tactical nuclear weapons have a range that prevent their being delivered against the home territory of the adversary. Theatre nuclear weapons represent a category that is intermediate between tactical and strategic weapons; their range lies between that of the short-range tactical weapons and the long-range strategic weapons. For example, theatre nuclear forces based in the Soviet Union would be capable of reaching Western Europe, but not the United States. On the other hand, intermediate-range U.S. missiles stationed in Western Europe are considered to be strategic weapons by the Soviet Union. A complete assessment of the overall military balance between the United States and the Soviet Union needs to involve many factors besides strategic nuclear weapons. These factors, such as tactical nuclear weapons, conventional forces, and allied military strength will be considered in a subsequent chapter.

WHY IS SOVIET NUCLEAR STRATEGY HARD TO DISCERN?

In some respects it is as important to be cognizant of Soviet nuclear strategies as it is to be aware of Soviet weaponry. The viability of U.S. nuclear strategies may critically hinge on whether our assessment of the Soviet strategy is accurate. Moreover, incorrect assessments of Soviet strategy can have unwanted effects in creating crises or causing them to escalate. Such incorrect assessments can also make arms-control accords unattainable. Despite the importance of assessing Soviet strategy correctly, the undertaking is fraught with pitfalls, and it may never be possible to have great confidence in our assessment.

There are four principle sources of information on Soviet nuclear strategy:

- Public statements or writings by Soviet leaders or official commentators

- Written Soviet literature intended for the Soviet military establishment

- Information provided by Soviet defectors and that obtained through espionage

- Inferences made based on Soviet-weapons procurement and other areas, e.g., civil defense preparations

Statements made by Soviet leaders are often intended for their propaganda value in influencing Western public opinion and may reveal little about Soviet nuclear strategy. Statements that are completely unenforceable, such as the Soviet unilateral declaration of "no first use" of nuclear weapons, are found nevertheless to be reassuring to some Westerners. We need not inpute any sinister intent to the Soviet leadership in such cases, only a moderate degree of intelligence in their understanding of American psychology. Moreover, we must remember that the meaning of words and phrases in two cultures may be very different. Even if by some miracle a country could bind itself to "no first use" by a simple pledge, it is not clear what that would mean. If, for example, a country had what it believed to be unambiguous evidence that its adversary was about to attack, it might well launch its missiles preemptively, regarding its attack as "second use." An even more sophistic argument could be made by the U.S.S.R. that any Soviet use of nuclear weapons would be second use, since the United States had already committed first use of nuclear weapons against Japan and that those two weapons were indirectly intended as a warning to the Soviet Union.

The greatest single source of information on Soviet nuclear strategy is from the books and periodicals written primarily for their military establishment rather than for Western consumption. The problem, of course, is that now that the Soviets are keenly aware of the attention given to these writings by Western strategists, these writings may no more reflect what they really believe than do statements made for Western media consumption. Moreover, a further problem is that Soviet military journals such as *Voyennaya mysl'* (Strategic thought) often describe the great value of certain strategies, such as surprise attacks, by attributing the strategies to the United States. We can read into this use of the Aesopic voice either an offensive or defensive connotation, depending on our assumptions about the Soviet Union's ultimate intentions.

Information provided by Soviet defectors is also of limited value. Information is tightly compartmentalized in the U.S.S.R., and key bits of strategic information are probably known to far fewer people than in the United States. Moreover, given the scope of the Soviet intelligence system, there are undoubtedly defectors who are, in fact, double agents whose job it is to convey false information and confuse the adversary. (It is clear that the United States would gladly resort to such devious tactics if it were possible.)

Finally, we can draw inferences about Soviet nuclear strategy based on their actions in procuring and deploying weapons. This represents in some ways both the best and the worst source of such information. Inferences drawn from weapon deployments are always indirect and subject to alternative interpretations. Moreover, such inferences may reveal more about what the strategy was five years ago when the weapons were planned than about the present strategy. Another possibility is that Soviet weapons decisions are driven by their view of U.S. weapons and strategy, or possibly by their view of the "objective realities" of nuclear weaponry. Those who subscribe to this view often speak of inevitable convergence of U.S. and Soviet nuclear strategies. Generally, the convergence is believed to be such that the Soviet view will, over time, inevitably move toward the American view, which is considered the more highly developed one, having evolved over a longer time span. This view would seem to suffer from extreme ethnocentrism; it also seems to ignore the possibility that a nation's views on nuclear strategy, of necessity, are influenced by its unique history, geography, politics, economics, and culture.

In some respects, however, inferences about Soviet nuclear strategy drawn from weapons deployment offer the greatest amount of information of all the sources mentioned. Deployed weapons can be directly observed in many cases, and, therefore, they do not offer the same kinds of opportunities for disinformation as would propagandistic statements of policy. Moreover, according to the technological determinists, there really is no fundamental strategy driving weapons decisions—rather, the weapons capabilities will dictate strategy. Finally, since a leader's intentions and strategies can change much more quickly than the weaponry in the nation's arsenal, it is more relevant to pay attention to the adversary's capabilities than his ephemeral intentions or strategies.

Given the many reasons to be suspicious that our knowledge of Soviet nuclear strategy is reliable, we must recognize the strong possibility of error in any such assessment. Despite these strong caveats we nevertheless shall attempt in what follows to give a brief description of the evolution of Soviet nuclear strategy.

HOW DO U.S. AND SOVIET NUCLEAR STRATEGIES COMPARE?

Joseph Stalin appears not to have understood the revolutionary implications of the atomic bomb, viewing the weapon in the hands of his principal adversary as useful only for frightening faint-hearted people. Stalin's successor, Nikita Khrushchev, on the other hand, seems to have been well aware of the new level of destructiveness such weapons made possible. Krushchev in a 1959 speech noted that

> much would perish in this [world] war. It would be too late to discuss what peaceful coexistence means when the talking will be done by such frightful means of destruction as atomic and hydrogen bombs, as ballistic rockets which are practically impossible to locate and which are capable of delivering nuclear warheads to any part of the globe.[14]

All subsequent Soviet leaders also have evinced an awareness of the enormous levels of destruction a nuclear war would inflict. Soviet nuclear strategy, first formulated under Khrushchev, appears in some eyes to have undergone comparatively little evolution since the early 1960s. The main departure from Western nuclear strategy is that Soviet strategy appears closer to a traditional Clausewitzian view— that nuclear weapons are not fundamentally different from other weapons and do have a war-fighting role. The Western notion of deterrence is considered, by some analysts, not to play a role in Soviet thinking. That does not mean that the Soviets do not wish to prevent nuclear war by posing an unacceptable level of damage to the adversary. The difference with the Western notion of deterrence lies in the fact that some Western strategists see little purpose for nuclear weapons if deterrence should fail, while the Soviets, according to some analysts, believe that they should press for a clear-cut military victory. Other analysts view the Soviet's professed belief in the need to strive for victory in a nuclear war as nothing more than a ritual incantation that socialism, being superior to imperialism, must in the end prevail.

The extent to which the Soviets have thought through the implications of using nuclear weapons for war-fighting purposes is claimed by some Western strategists to be far greater than is the case of the United States. The Soviet readiness to think through the implications of war-fighting strategies and to structure its military posture accordingly, of course, does not imply that they would willingly undertake a nuclear war with the West. Exactly the opposite course is advocated in Marxist-Leninist theory, according to which the initiation of war as an instrument of policy can only be justified if (1) victory is virtually certain, and (2) the gains clearly outweigh the costs. Whether the first condition could be satisfied for the forseeable future is in considerable doubt and depends in large measure upon how one defines victory. The second condition is more problematical since Westerners may have a very different view of the "gains" and "costs" than that held by the Soviets. Many wars have been started because both sides lacked an appreciation of how much or how little value the adversary attached to a particular threat.

The Soviets do not appear to have wavered in their belief that a strong military capability is the surest way to prevent war and to prevail if one should occur. This view need not be in conflict with a desire to promote arms control, particularly if arms-control measures can be achieved that allow certain Soviet advantages to be established and that place limits on areas in which the United States leads, e.g. high technology and new kinds of weaponry. Whether arms control is seen by the Soviets as primarily a strategic tool for constraining the West or alternatively as a means of actually reducing the risk of war is not clear, whatever Soviet leaders may profess in statements intended for Western consumption.

The Soviet nuclear strategy also differs in some respects from that in the West concerning the possibility of short and long nuclear wars. Soviet military writings indicate that a nuclear war could be very short, particularly if surprise is successfully achieved and if the enemy's forces are caught in a low state of readiness, of course attributing such a sneak attack to the West. However, it is also admitted that the war could be of extended duration if victory should not be achieved in the initial attack. Concern over the possibility of extended nuclear wars has been a much more recent one on the part of the United States. The greater Soviet awareness of the possibility of extended nuclear war may, in part, explain their civil defense measures which become more feasible if a nuclear war is extended in time. This may also account for their somewhat different view toward various weapons systems. Unlike the United States, the Soviets can cold launch their land-based missiles, allowing for the possibility of reload missiles that could greatly expand the number of warheads attacking an enemy, if a substantial reserve supply of missiles exists. Whether such a reserve supply exists and how great it is we can only speculate. The fact that Soviet missiles have a cold-launch reload capability does, however, imply that (1) the possibility of having a reserve force of missiles is something that interests the Soviets, and (2) they believe such reload missiles may have military utility, i.e., that a nuclear war might not be decided by an initial massive exchange.

The Soviet view of the possibility of extended nuclear war also affects their attitude towards ballistic-missile submarines, which includes 50 percent of U.S. warheads. While the United States may view this force as insurance in providing a secure second-strike deterrent, the Soviets apparently see this force as a U.S determination to fight and win a prolonged nuclear war.

In many respects U.S. and Soviet nuclear strategies appear to be more similar now than in the past, with both sides paying more attention to war-fighting strategies and the possibility of extended nuclear wars. This convergence appears to be a kind of "reverse convergence", with the U.S. attitude moving closer to the Soviet position, rather than the reverse. It is, of course, a matter of some speculation why this apparent shift has occurred, or even if it has occurred. A technological determinist might suggest that new destabilizing kinds of weapons have made war-fighting scenarios more feasible. A dove might suggest that the changes in U.S. strategy have come about due to an overly aggressive hawkish administration. Finally, a hawk might suggest that the change in U.S. strategy reflects an acknowledgment of the greater "realism" implicit in the Soviet position.

Whichever position is most nearly correct, it is perhaps worthwhile to conclude this discussion of relative Soviet and U.S. nuclear strategy by recalling how little there is that we can know with confidence, and, moreover, how little nuclear strategy may ultimately have to do with the course of an actual nuclear conflict.

STUDY QUESTIONS

1. Why did the United States amass a huge arsenal a few years after World War II?

2. Why did the U.S. policy of massive retaliation gradually change to mutual assured destruction (MAD)? Is MAD a mad policy?

3. What impact did the introduction of the ICBM and MIRV have on MAD?

4. Have some technological advances had a stabilizing effect on the nuclear balance? Which ones?

5. What is the qualitative relationship between missile accuracy, warhead yield, target hardness, and kill probability?

6. What are all the ways in which the United States leads the U.S.S.R. in nuclear weaponry and all the ways the Soviet Union leads the United States? What is the relative importance of each factor? Overall do you think one side is ahead?

7. How important do you think equivalent megatonnage (EMT) is in assessing the strategic balance?

8. Why is it hard to discern Soviet nuclear strategy? How do U.S. and Soviet nuclear strategies compare?

9. Do you believe strategy drives decisions on weapons or that the characteristics of weapons determines strategy? What support can you give for your belief?

10. Why is the United States, in a sense, in a technological race with itself?

Four _____

THE CONTINUING
ARMS RACE _____

WHAT IS THE RELATIONSHIP BETWEEN ARMS RACES AND WARS?

There have been at least twenty-five distinct arms races in modern history, and they have usually lasted thirty to forty years—approximately the amount of time since World War II.[1] The arms races of the past were often characterized by an increasing frequency of small wars and culminated in one big balance-of-power war. The driving force behind an arms race appears to be mutual fear. A state feels threatened by increased defense expenditures or new weapons developed by another and reacts by similarly developing its own weapons, which causes a further reaction by the other state. In order for this action-reaction mechanism to work, the political relations between the states must be such that they see themselves as adversaries within a balance-of-power system.

An especially troublesome aspect of an arms race is that each state sees a very clear basis for its own fears and is led to take actions that it views as strictly defensive, but which are seen by the other state as being very provocative and aggressive. In past arms races, as each state increased its armaments in reaction to the other's provocation, the level of tension and "moral armament" also increased. Moral armament refers to the willingness to go to war for a case that is increasingly perceived to be right and just. There can

89

be little question that a belief in the inevitability of war has often become a self-fulfilling prophecy. During an arms race, one state may come to feel that its relative pace of acquiring weapons will put it in a less competitive position at some future time. In that event, the state may believe that as long as war is probably inevitable over the long term, the preferable tactic might be to initiate war before the state's relative military position deteriorates. There have been many examples of nations engaging in such "preventive" wars or in using their temporary military advantage to political effect, e.g., the United States threatening the Soviet Union with massive retaliation for any Soviet aggression during the period of U.S. nuclear monopoly.

The reason that arms races are dangerous is because they can raise the level of fear and suspicion each side has of the other. Thus, what one side considers a simple modernization of its arsenal in replacing old weapons with new versions may be seen by the other side as a qualitatively new escalation threatening its vital interests. If the weapons advances are particularly threatening, the end result may be confrontation and war. These points are made very well in a 1961 address by General Douglas MacArthur.

> Present world tensions are fostered by two great illusions. The one is complete belief on the part of the Soviet world that capitalist countries are preparing to attack them: that sooner or later we intend to strike. And the other, a complete belief on the part of the capitalistic countries that the Soviets are preparing to attack us: that sooner or later they intend to strike. Both are wrong. Each is desirous of peace. Both dread war. But the constant acceleration of preparation may, without specific intent, ultimately precipitate a kind of spontaneous combustion.[2]

Some researchers, most notably Lewis Richardson, have even developed complex mathematical models demonstrating the statistical link between arms races and wars.[3] One study, for example, showed that in twenty-eight serious international disputes since 1816 involving arms races, all but five resulted in war, while in seventy-one disputes not involving arms races only three resulted in a war.[4] Statistical correlations, however, cannot demonstrate a cause and effect relationship. Rather than concluding that arms races cause wars, it would seem that all that can be said is that arms races can exacerbate existing tensions, and in certain circumstances they may make wars more likely. In other instances, it is possible that the decision not to have an arms race made unilaterally by one of the nations may cause a war through the process of appeasement. In still other cases, it is possible that some arms races have no effect on the probability of war. One study by W. Ladd Hollist, for example, showed that arms races can be one of two types—either stable or unstable—and that it is only the unstable variety that leads to war.[5]

Political science probably will never attain the predictive value of a hard science, notwithstanding its sophisticated mathematical models. The causal links if any between arms races and wars will, of necessity, remain a matter of conjecture. Our primary interest in this chapter concerns the nuclear arms race, particularly the U.S.-Soviet competition. It is conceivable that the unique nature of nuclear weapons makes comparisons with past arms races especially hazardous, although this is a matter of conjecture. As has been noted earlier, there is no way to clearly establish that the world is either "close to the brink" or further away, based solely on the numerical growth in the nuclear arsenals, and our intuitive perceptions in this regard may have little to do with reality.

WHAT HAS BEEN THE NATURE OF THE U.S.-SOVIET ARMS COMPETITION?

Some analysts in examining the post-World War II nuclear-arms competition clearly identify one side as initiating the arms race and the other side as simply responding. The United States was obviously the leader in developing nuclear weapons during the early postwar years. America was also the first to develop a number of new weapons—particularly the H-bomb and the MIRVed ICBM, an especially destabilizing weapon. It would be misleading, however, to portray the United States always as the actor and the U.S.S.R. always as the re-actor, as some analysts do, since there have been numerous developments in which the Soviet Union led the way. Some of those developments include:

- First ICBM tests (1957)
- First ABM deployment (1968)
- First antisatellite (ASAT) system
- First "super" (58-megaton) H-bomb test (1961)

- First fractional orbital bombardment system (FOBS, 1967)

- First "heavy" ICBMs

- First reloadable ICBMs

In the early years of the U.S.-Soviet arms competition (up to the early 1960s), the United States clearly was leading the arms race. The Soviet Union's "restraint" during that early period may have been more a lack of technical prowess than any desire not to develop weapons that would be considered too provocative.

In the years since the early 1960s both the U.S. and Soviet arsenals have continued to expand, the Soviet arsenal very much more so than the U.S. one, largely because the U.S.S.R. was trying to catch up to (some would say overtake) the United States. Thus, the U.S.-Soviet arms competition, if it is to be termed a race, is a rather peculiar tortoise-and-hare kind of race with one competitor doing most of his racing during the first twenty-year phase of the race and the other during the second twenty-year phase, while the first one permits him to catch up. In fact, as can be seen in figure 3.7, there actually was a ten-year period (1960–70) during which the U.S. arsenal shrank significantly.

It is probably no accident that the large-scale twenty-year Soviet nuclear buildup began around the time of the 1962 Cuban missile crisis, an event that no doubt had a great effect on Soviet thinking. It is clear that American nuclear superiority at the time was a factor, although not the only one, in the Soviet decision to withdraw its offensive nuclear missiles it had secretly placed in Cuba. The Soviet Deputy Foreign Minister Vasily Kuznetsov is reported to have remarked to an American negotiator at the time, "You'll never be able to do this to us again." [6]

It would be a great overstatement to attribute the Soviet backdown in the Cuban missile crisis entirely to American nuclear superiority at that time. Certainly the Soviets were also deterred by the thought of fighting a conventional battle very far from their shores. Nevertheless, Kuznetsov's candid statement cannot be anything but an acknowledgment that U.S. massive nuclear superiority was a major factor in Soviet thinking.

It appears that the forced Soviet withdrawal in the Cuban missile crisis seems to have taught its leaders a number of important lessons:

- Despite the prevailing mutual-assured-destruction capability, a preponderance of nuclear power can have its psychological and political uses for intimidation.

- The United States, possibly because of its Pearl Harbor experience in World War II, is especially alarmed by sudden moves that upset the military balance or threaten surprise attack, such as the placement of missiles in Cuba.

- The United States is much less alarmed by a gradual military buildup, which if sustained over a long period of time can pose a much greater threat.

- There is no need for the Soviet Union to be secretive or deceptive about its buildup, as was done in Cuba. As long as Soviet leaders refrain from provocative rhetoric such as Nikita Khrushchev's famed remark, "We will bury you," the U.S. public will not become overly concerned by the buildup.

- Even if the United States becomes alarmed at the size of a Soviet buildup, public anxieties about nuclear war and the dangers of the arms race generally can be stimulated to deflect public support for U.S. moves to match the Soviet effort.

It should certainly not be inferred that the extensive media coverage of the horrors of nuclear war is all part of some communist conspiracy. These remarks also should not be misconstrued to mean that we can blame only the Soviet Union for the arms race. The Soviet desire to remedy their earlier position of pronounced nuclear inferiority is quite understandable, particularly in light of their experience in the Cuban missile crisis. That event may in fact largely account for their massive buildup since the early 1960s.

It would be silly to deny that there has been an arms competition between the United States and the Soviet Union,—but the tortoise-and-hare nature of that competition may not be fully understood by Western public opinion. Moreover, we cannot deny that some aspects of the competition should be a cause for grave concern. However, the concern should be primarily focused on the particularly desta-bilizing technologies rather than simply on numbers of weapons. It seems unlikely that nuclear war is made more probable if each side has too many weapons. However, the possession of the wrong kinds of weapons, especially those that threaten a significant first-strike advantage, is a real threat to world peace.

A plausible case can even be made that the possession of massive overkill by each side is actually a stabilizing factor in the balance of terror. Massive overkill assures each side that retaliation is possible even if a very large faction of its forces are destroyed in a surprise attack, and it is therefore a strong disincentive to the attacker to commit mutual suicide. It continues to be true that both the United States and the Soviet Union possess substantial overkill. Nevertheless, that possessed by the Soviet Union is considerably more massive than twenty years ago, and that possessed by the United States, in its forces that would likely survive a surprise first strike, is considerably less massive.

It was noted earlier that the three legs of the triad insure against any unfavorable technological developments affecting any one leg. The possession of overkill capacity by each side constitutes a similar kind of insurance. For example, if each side had only a minimum deterrent instead of overkill, then a technological breakthrough in ABM, ASW, or some other vital area could transform that minimum deterrent into no deterrent at all.

Many find the concept of minimum deterrence highly appealing since it would move the United States and U.S.S.R. away from considerations of war-fighting strategies and back to the notion of mutual assured destruction. However, with a minimum deterrent there might be considerably less assurance that the destruction would indeed be mutual, independent of future technological developments. Moreover, with a minimum deterrent, a nation is in effect stating that its policy would be to respond massively to any form of nuclear attack, however limited. To the extent that this is not a credible policy, a minimum deterrent may not deter. Lord Solly Zuckerman in *Nuclear Illusion and Reality* notes that the British and French governments have, by virtue of the size of their independent nuclear forces, given their seals of approval to the concept of minimum deterrence.[7] However, that position, while credible for "supporting players" in a potential nuclear conflict, is not supportable for the superpowers. The level of damage that England or France could inflict on the Soviet Union almost certainly would deter the Soviets from attacking either of these countries with nuclear weapons in the absence of any U.S.-Soviet nuclear exchange. It is precisely because the United States does possess massive overkill that France and England need not worry about their minimal deterrents being insufficient.

ARE U.S. LAND-BASED MISSILES VULNERABLE?

Most people would probably agree that fear is the driving force behind the arms race. Some analysts might put the blame on a generalized mutual fear that each superpower has developed of the other's intentions, while others would point to specific fears, such as the fear that one's nuclear forces might be vulnerable to attack. Each side, of course, believes that it has good grounds for its fears of the other side's intentions, and the continuing development of nuclear weapons by each side may serve to reinforce those fears. What is seen by one side as remedying a vulnerability in its weaponry can be seen by the other side as an increasing threat to its survival to which it must respond. Nevertheless, it does not follow logically that each side should refrain from remedying vulnerabilities because its actions may be viewed as provocative by the other side. It is of prime importance, therefore, to determine whether alleged vulnerabilities are real or merely offered as a rationale to achieve the necessary degree of public support for another spiral in an endless arms race.

Most defense analysts believe that the question of vulnerability is a much more crucial one than the simplistic inquiry as to who is "ahead" in weaponry. One area that has received much attention is the vulnerability to attack of the land-based leg of the triad, since both the United States and the Soviet Union now possess warheads having sufficient accuracy and yield to destroy the other's hardened missile silos.

Various theoretical calculations have been made of the fraction of U.S. land-based missiles that would survive a Soviet surprise attack. The results of these paper calculations depend crucially on what figures are assumed for Soviet missile accuracy (CEP), which can only be roughly estimated. According to one Defense Department calculation, 20 percent of U.S. ICBMs would survive an attack in 1984 but only 8 percent in 1986, in light of continued improvements in Soviet missile accuracy. In view of the considerable uncertainty in our knowledge of the accuracy of Soviet missiles, it is probably more realistic to express the calculated results as a range of values: 8- to 46-percent surviving ICBMs in 1984, 2 to 16 percent in 1986, and 0 to 6 percent in 1988.[8] The calculated ranges correspond to intelligence estimates on the smallest and largest Soviet missile CEPs considered likely and their anticipated rate of improvement over time.

Of course a vast difference exists between such paper calculations and the real world. In the real world, an attacker would face a great many uncertainties in a surprise attack on a victim's ICBM silos. Four uncertainties cited most often are noted below.

1. *Reliability.* In any complex system, a certain fraction of its components will be defective. We can only get a fragmentary indication of the overall reliability of the Soviet missile force by making observations on Soviet missile tests. The true overall reliability of the Soviet (or U.S.) missile force would only become apparent in a nuclear war. Whatever their overall reliability, the fact that a certain percentage of Soviet missiles would not work raises the estimated fraction of U.S. missiles that would survive a surprise first strike by some unknown amount. That fact could make a very considerable difference in the number of missiles surviving a surprise attack, thereby making it a much riskier gamble for the attacker.

2. *Fratricide.* One important reason why the number of ICBMs calculated to survive an attack is so small is because it is assumed that each ICBM silo is attacked by two warheads, and the kill probability for two warheads is often considerably greater than it is for one. It is possible, however, that the second warhead could be destroyed when the first one detonates (fratricide). In that case, the kill probability for two warheads would then be no greater than for one. On the other hand, the fratricide effect may be of little value in deterring the attacker, since even if it occurred 100 percent of the time, some Soviet warheads have an extremely high one-shot kill probability of 95 percent.

3. *Gravitational anomalies.* Another uncertainty facing an attacker would be the fact that local gravitational anomalies can cause small variations in a missile's flight path. It is often noted, for example, that since no ICBMs have ever been fired over the North Pole, the presumed path of U.S. or Soviet missiles, an attacker cannot be sure what the exact effect of the gravitational anomalies would be on the accuracy of his missiles. However, this uncertainty may be of dubious significance. Polar gravitational anomalies can be measured by space satellites launched in a variety of orbits without having fired missiles over the North Pole.

4. *Launch on warning.* The ultimate uncertainty facing the attacker is whether the victim might choose to launch his missiles on warning of an attack or while an attack is underway. In the former event, the preemptive attack would be worse than useless. The attacker's missiles would land on empty silos and accomplish nothing, and he might suffer devastating damage in retaliation. The

United States and Soviet Union have not publicly stated whether they would launch on warning, launch under attack, or launch after the attack. Moreover, even if there were a publicly stated policy, the attacker cannot know in advance what launch policy the victim would actually follow. According to this reasoning, with so much riding on one "cosmic throw of the dice," the attacker would not dare take the chance that the victim would in fact launch on warning.

It is unclear, however, how much deterrent value the possibility of a launch on warning has if the aggressor concludes that the potential victim is highly unlikely to be able to carry it out. Moreover, if the United States should ever want to deter an attack through a launch-on-warning posture, it would seem necessary to actually have a command and communications structure that could, and actually did, incorporate that policy. A pretend launch-on-warning policy would seem unlikely to be mistaken for the real thing by an adversary skilled in intelligence-collection methods, and therefore such a policy would have little deterrent value.

The four uncertainties considered in the preceding discussion certainly would indicate that the purely theoretical calculations on U.S. ICBM vulnerability are unduly pessimistic and should not be taken literally. Nevertheless, it would not be correct to conclude that these uncertainties, in any sense, demonstrate the converse, namely that land-based missiles are not vulnerable to a surprise attack. They only show that the vulnerability is not as great as worst-case estimates would indicate. There is, however, a more important question to address than whether land-based missiles are vulnerable.

DOES ICBM VULNERABILITY MATTER?

The question of the vulnerability of land-based missiles started out as an interesting theoretical exercise for defense analysts. It now seems to have evolved into the primary rationale for a new generation of U.S. weaponry. Even if we grant that there is, at least theoretically, a vulnerability problem, the more interesting question is whether that vulnerability matters. The main argument put forth by those who say it does not is that the extensive U.S. nuclear forces that would survive a successful attack on U.S. ICBMs, particularly those on the nuclear submarine fleet, are quite sufficient to carry out any retaliatory mission. This knowledge should, therefore, deter any potential attacker. Moreover, the retaliatory attack with surviving

U.S. SLBM forces need not necessarily be delivered against Soviet cities, which would be an act of mutual suicide in view of the probable large Soviet reserve force not used in its initial attack. This reasoning is nicely summarized by former Defense Secretary Harold Brown:

> Even after a total loss of Minuteman missiles, we would *not* face the dilemma of surrender by inaction or mutual suicide by an all-out attack on Soviet cities and industry, provoking an equal attack on ours. We would instead have surviving bomber and submarine forces fully capable of selectively attacking military, economic, and control targets, thus negating any gain the Soviets might imagine they could attain by an attack on our ICBM force.[9]

Barring some Soviet technological ABM or ASW breakthrough, Brown is certainly correct that surviving U.S. forces would have the capability of selectively attacking a wide range of targets. His assertion that this U.S. capability would negate any gain the Soviets could attain by a preemptive attack is less clear. Following a Soviet preemptive counterforce attack and a U.S. retaliatory attack, the Soviets could have a sizable nuclear-force advantage. Moreover, the Soviet advantage needs to be judged by what forces would survive on each side in the event that the Soviets did not launch a surprise attack and the United States did. As long as a very sizable military advantage exists for the side that strikes first, then there could be a considerable gain in attacking the enemy's ICBM force. This destabilizing factor undermines deterrence and makes ICBM vulnerability a cause for concern.

Despite Soviet leaders' disavowals of nuclear wars being winnable, Soviet military strategists writing for internal consumption appear to be cognizant of the military advantage gained by the side that strikes the first blow.

> In view of the immense destructive force of nuclear weapons and the extremely limited time available to take effective countermeasures after an enemy launches its missiles, the launching of the first massed attack acquires decisive importance for achieving the objectives of war.[10]

Moreover, Soviet military strategists also appear to have considerable concern about not being "beaten to the draw" by the United States.

Mass nuclear missile strikes at the armed forces of the opponent and at his key economic and political objectives can determine the victory of one side and the defeat of the other at the very beginning of the war. Therefore, a correct estimate of the elements of the supremacy over the opponent and the *ability to use them before the opponent does,* are the key to victory in such a war. (Emphasis added.) [11]

Such statements as these, of course, no more demonstrate that the Soviet Union plans to undertake a surprise attack on the United States than do the Soviet leaders' public statements about nuclear wars being unwinnable demonstrate the converse. Rather, these statements indicate that Soviet strategists are aware of the large military advantage that the attacker might have in a surprise nuclear attack.

But would a Soviet surprise attack on U.S. land-based missiles really represent a military advantage to the attacker? The average Minuteman missile is MIRVed with only two warheads. Therefore, the Soviets in targeting each Minuteman silo with two warheads would destroy fewer land-based missile warheads than they would have expended, assuming less than 100-percent kills. Unfortunately, that analysis overlooks the fact that a counterforce attack could also destroy about one-third of U.S. submarine warheads and a sizable fraction of bomber-based warheads with a much smaller number of attacking warheads. Overall, therefore, very many more warheads would be destroyed than expended. In addition, the severe damage done to command, control, and communication links in a surprise attack could also give the attacker a very significant military advantage.

Those who question the importance of U.S. ICBM vulnerability sometimes cite other reasons for believing that a Soviet counterforce attack would be implausible. One line of reasoning is based on the thinking of the nineteenth-century philosopher of war, Carl von Clausewitz.

Since war is not an act of senseless passion but is controlled by its political object, the value of this object must determine the sacrifices to be made for it in magnitude and also in duration. Once the expenditure of effort exceeds the value of the political object, the object must be renounced and peace must follow.[12]

Fred Kaplan uses Clausewitz's idea in discussing the implausibility of a Soviet counterforce attack, and he notes that

> nobody . . . has conceived of a credible scenario in which the Soviet leadership would risk a chance of nuclear attack on the Motherland; no one has thought of a political goal whose gain would be worth the possible sacrifice of possible American nuclear retaliation.[13]

Kaplan, however, has misapplied Clausewitz's theory of how wars stop and has used it to show why a nuclear war could not start. Prior to a war's beginning the Soviets (or the Americans) might be comparing two risks to the survival of the motherland: the risk of waiting for the expected enemy attack versus the risk of launching a preemptive attack. The preemptive attack would be seen as the far lesser of two evils, despite the grave risk it posed to survival, which is the "political goal" in this case.

Those who dismiss the importance of ICBM vulnerability sometimes invoke questionable propositions. For example according to Bruce Russett and Bruce Blair:

> The threat of a disarming first strike was and still remains— nonexistent. Moreover, even in the extreme hypothetical case of a disarming first strike, not only the attacked nation but also the aggressor could expect to suffer from the disastrous aftereffects of a nuclear war.[14]

A "disarming" first strike may be understood as one in which the victim is unable to retaliate to any significant degree. In that hypothetical event, the "disastrous aftereffects" suffered by the aggressor would be comparable to the level of worldwide damage in the aftermath of a nuclear war. Russett and Blair's statement seems to carry the implication that the worldwide aftereffects of a limited counterforce attack may be so disastrous as to deter the disarming first strike. However, as we shall see in chapter 8, the worldwide effects in remote lands of an all-out nuclear war would likely be very much less severe than the effects in the attacked countries. It strains credulity to believe that the possibility of a worldwide climatic catastrophe would deter the Soviet Union, or perhaps the United States, from a disarming first strike that it believed could succeed.

For the Soviet Union, environmental issues, public opinion, and public health issues have a definite second priority compared to issues of national security. It is noteworthy, for example, that during the last decade, Soviet citizens have paid a very high price in terms of inadequate health care to finance their government's large military buildup. In the decade 1972–82:

- Soviet infant mortality has nearly doubled (from 23 to 40 deaths per 1000 live births)

- Soviet men have had their life expectancy fall from 66 to 62, with a smaller decrease for women.[15]

By way of contrast, these very severe negative effects on the health of Soviet citizens are, in fact, probably greater than the worldwide impact of an all-out nuclear war on an untargeted country.

If a disarming first strike were possible, then the threat of some degree of worldwide environmental damage and a statistically small increase in cancer rates in their own country are unlikely to deter the Soviets from such a move. Moreover, the United States would probably also consider the possibility of worldwide environmental damage an acceptable price to pay if the political objective were great enough. It should be recalled that during World War II, U.S. scientists did proceed with their work on the bomb, even after having determined that there was an exceedingly small but nonzero risk that the first nuclear detonation could incinerate the atmosphere and end all life on earth.

The key point in the preceding discussion is not that the worldwide damage following a nuclear war will necessarily be less than catastrophic, which we cannot know. Rather, the point is that by falsely believing that the worldwide impact will likely be catastrophic, we can easily be led to draw unwarranted inferences about the inconceivability of a disarming first strike.

At no point in the discussion on U.S. ICBM vulnerability has it been claimed that a Soviet preemptive counterforce attack is a likely occurrence. Hopefully, any kind of U.S.-Soviet nuclear conflict is unlikely. However, within the spectrum of possible U.S.-Soviet nuclear wars, those starting with a counterforce attack by either side are perhaps the least unlikely. Such an attack might well follow a chain of escalations in a conventional war, rather than simply be a bolt-out-of-the-blue (BOOB) attack. Consider, for example, that the Soviet Union, for whatever reason, were to decide to attack the United States. In that event it is very hard to see why the Soviets would attack U.S. cities in a first strike. By sparing most U.S. cities without military value in the first attack and striking only military targets, the Soviets lose nothing, since they would not give up the capability to hit U.S. cities with their reserve nuclear forces should the U.S. retaliate against Soviet cities. Moreover, the Soviets could gain a great deal by their initial restraint, if the end result is that their population survives. Hence, sparing cities in an initial attack is simply a matter of self-preservation, not humanitarian concern for the victim. A U.S. retaliatory strike could not be more formidable in any way due to the initial survival of its cities. Thus, the Soviets have everything to gain and nothing to lose if, once having decided on a surprise nuclear attack, they spare most cities in the initial strike while keeping a large nuclear force in reserve. The same reasoning would, of course, apply should the United States ever decide to launch a surprise attack on the Soviet Union.

If the preceding analysis is correct, than an attack that starts out as a counterforce attack on ICBM silos and other military targets is considerably more likely than the all-out nuclear holocaust invariably associated with the popular notion of a nuclear war. It has already been conceded that a counterforce attack might not stay limited after an escalating series of attacks and counterattacks. However, the fact that such a conflict is likely to start out as a limited counterforce attack is very important when considering measures that have value in deterring that kind of conflict. Reducing U.S. ICBM vulnerability could have exactly that effect.

One can find all kinds of psychological reasons why U.S. or Soviet military planners would take or refrain from taking certain actions. However, we cannot discount the possibility that a real or potential weakness of the adversary will be perceived as a decisive factor in a moment of extreme crisis. It is unfortunately the case that technology has advanced so far that the doctrine of mutual assured destruction and the unthinkability of nuclear war can no longer be counted on to deter nuclear war. In view of what is now technologically possible, counterforce attacks can be ignored only at our peril.

One often-heard criticism of the "window of vulnerability" is that many past threats later turned out to be nonexistent and were originally claimed only for political reasons or because of faulty intelligence. For example, the missile gap that was a factor in the 1960 presidential election turned out to have little basis in fact. While politics assuredly played a role in the manner the 1960 missile gap was presented to the public, the perception of a real threat was not a matter of deliberate exaggeration. The U-2 reconnaisance plane used for surveillance prior to the use of satellites was simply unable to cover enough Soviet territory to reveal the extent of Soviet ICBM deployment. Extensive Soviet ICBM testing had been observed, leading some intelligence analysts to assume the worst. The first satellite photographs of the Soviet Union taken in 1960–61 showed that the U.S.S.R. had in fact deployed only a handful of ICBMs, and the missile gap turned out to be in the United States's favor.

Erroneous intelligence estimates of Soviet capabilities have not always been overestimates. One notable example is the significant CIA underestimate of the projected numbers of Soviet ICBMs in the late 1960s. A second example of a significant underestimate would be the 1975 CIA conclusion that Soviet SS-18 and SS-19 missiles were less than half as accurate as they now appear to have been.[16] Thus, erring on the side of caution seems warranted in a world where one serious underestimation of a threat posed by a nuclear-armed adversary could spell disaster.

To some extent, vulnerabilities are a matter of perception rather than fact. Those who believe that vulnerabilities are wholly a matter of perception claim that the problem of ICBM vulnerability is a concoction of alarmist hawks wishing to scare the U.S. public into increasing U.S. defense expenditures. It is further claimed that the hawks themselves have actually jeopardized U.S. security by creating a belief in the minds of allies and adversaries that the United States is militarily vulnerable. Vulnerabilities are not, however, solely a matter of perception. While perceptions are important, so are quantitative and qualitative analyses, which also include guesses as to how human beings might act under various circumstances. Putting the blame on the hawks for raising the vulnerability issue may be blaming the messenger for the bad news. Obviously, there are dangers in overstating the magnitude of U.S. nuclear vulnerabilities. Such overstatements by U.S. officials undermine their own case for modernizing the nuclear arsenal, and raise questions about the officials' strategic understanding. Moreover, the myth of America as a second-rate nuclear power could demoralize our allies and encourage the Soviet Union to test U.S. power. However, such considerations, while important, should not prevent the United States from remedying any vulnerabilities or imbalances that do exist—even if there are many who believe it is unlikely that the Soviets would ever take advantage of them.

Our main focus so far has been on the Soviet threat to U.S. land-based ICBMs. There are some who view the present U.S. threat to Soviet ICBMs as being of greater magnitude, although that would hardly seem to be a reason to be complacent about any vulnerability in the U.S. arsenal. For example, according to Herbert Scoville:

> The United States with its advanced Minuteman III ICBMs can threaten to destroy about 50 percent of the Soviet strategic force (3,000 warheads), while the Soviet Union can threaten to destroy less than one-quarter of the U.S. force (2,150 warheads) even if its ICBMs could destroy all U.S. land-based missiles.[17]

Whether or not Scoville is correct depends on the hardness of Soviet missile silos. If they are as hard as some U.S. experts say (4500 psi), then they are not seriously threatened by Minuteman III. If, however, a more realistic value for Soviet-missile-silo hardness is 2000 psi, then Minuteman III is definitely a silo-killer. Moreover, even if the Minuteman IIIs could be used in a preemptive attack against the Soviet ICBM force, such an attack would require virtually the entire U.S. ICBM force, and it would only destroy about one-third of the Soviet force. In contrast, the Soviets, following a successful attack on U.S. ICBMs, would have expended only a fraction of their ICBMs.

Finally, we note that Scoville is correct that a successful U.S. first strike on Soviet ICBMs would leave the Soviets with a smaller fraction of their total warheads (50 percent) than would a corresponding Soviet attack on U.S. ICBMs (75 percent). However, we must remember that a real attack would probably be against ICBMs, bombers, and submarines in port. If left with only its SLBMs, the United States would still have a greater fraction of its warheads than would the Soviets under a comparable attack, but U.S. SLBM warheads have five to ten-times-smaller average yields. Thus, the assured destruction capability the Soviets would have following a successful surprise first strike by the United States probably would be comparable or marginally greater than that possessed by the United States if it was similarly attacked.

Another kind of vulnerability now receiving increasing attention may be much more serious than that of land-based missiles, namely the vulnerability of command, control, and communications. For example, John Steinbruner has written that

> fewer than 100 judiciously targeted nuclear weapons could so severely damage U.S. communications facilities that form the military chain of command, that the actions of individual

weapons commanders could no longer be controlled or coordinated. Some bomber crews, submarine officers, and ICBM silo launch officers could undertake very damaging retaliation and hence continue to pose a deterrence threat. Nonetheless, even 50 nuclear weapons are probably sufficient to eliminate the ability to direct U.S. strategic forces to coherent purposes.[18]

It may be argued by some that the vulnerability of command, control, and communication links make thoughts of war-winning counterforce attacks even more tempting to military planners. However, others have argued that such a "decapitating" attack would result in an uncontrolled and uncontrollable retaliation and that this knowledge should have significant deterrent value.

Another factor deterring an attacker is the fact that with present-day intelligence capabilities, the very act of bringing one's strategic nuclear forces to full readiness would almost certainly not go unnoticed by the victim. A period of strategic warning would probably result and make the decapitation unlikely to succeed. Furthermore, according to John Steinbrunner, "U.S. forces have always been seriously vulnerable to an initial attack and the 1980s will not produce unusual dangers in this regard, as is often alleged." [19]

A basic point to bear in mind, however, is that it does not greatly matter whose nuclear arsenal and whose command, control, and, communications are marginally more vulnerable. Both arsenals are, at present, comparably vulnerable, and it would be desirable to eliminate that vulnerability on both sides, if possible. It is just as dangerous for the United States to face a paranoid adversary who believes its nuclear retaliatory forces are highly vulnerable to surprise attack as it is for U.S. forces to be so vulnerable. The real problem, however, is that actions taken by one side to remove a perceived vulnerability may often be seen in a very different light by the adversary. What one side may view as strictly a defensive measure may, in fact, appear to the other as further preparation to achieve a surprise first strike. The particular choice of new weapons and strategies, therefore, assumes great importance. The wrong choices can definitely decrease a nation's security by being unduly provocative to the adversary.

NEW U.S. OFFENSIVE WEAPONS – ARE THEY THE BEST CHOICES?

It must be remembered continually that nuclear weapons are different from other kinds of weapons. The main purpose of nuclear weapons should be to deter war, thereby insuring that they will not be used. In view of this unique role, many believe that decisions involving nuclear weapons must be made on a different basis from decisions involving conventional war-fighting weapons. A reflexive reliance on a policy of matching the Soviet Union in all aspects of nuclear weapons is perhaps both unnecessary and unwise. Deterrence may be enhanced by matching the Soviets in some areas. However, there are also areas where the United States may undermine deterrence by attempting to match the Soviet Union.

It is appropriate that details about nuclear weaponry be a subject of debate in Congress and among the general public, given the unique role of nuclear weapons in deterring rather than fighting war. It is lamentable, however, that all too often the nuclear debate reduces to one between antinuclear doves and anti-Soviet hardliners. In the nuclear debate a very constructive role can be played by those who, while believing in the need for a strong defense, critically examine specific proposed weapons systems as well as overlooked alternatives. With this idea in mind, we shall now examine some of the weapons that the United States has added and plans to add to its arsenal in the mid-1980s and beyond.

President Ronald Reagan has initiated an unprecedented program to modernize simultaneously all three legs of the U.S. strategic nuclear triad. Serious questions have been raised by critics about each of the weapons programs, and the long-term funding of particular programs will largely be determined by domestic and international political and economic developments.

The bomber leg of the U.S. triad is a crucial one as it carries 26 percent of the nuclear warheads and 42 percent of the megatonnage. More importantly, the features of recallability and survivability make bombers ideal second-strike weapons and hence a stabilizing factor in the U.S.-Soviet balance of terror. The Reagan administration has announced that it intends to build a hundred B-1 bombers, thus reversing an earlier Carter-administration cancellation of the program. Many B-1 critics concede that it is not unreasonable to replace a portion of the aging B-52 fleet since some of the planes are of 1950 vintage. What is more open to question, however, is whether the B-1 is the right bomber and whether both the B-1 and the follow-on Stealth bombers are needed. The main objection to the B-1 bomber is that by the time it is built, it will have a useful life as a penetrating bomber of at most a few years, based on a Defense Department assessment of the rate of improvement in Soviet air defenses. After that time a new bomber using stealth technology would be needed to penetrate Soviet air space. The B-1 would, of course, still be usable as a stand-off bomber used to launch cruise missiles 1500 miles away from their targets. However, B-1 critics argue that until Stealth is built, the placement of advanced avionics on board the B-52 fleet could allow it to be just as good a penetrating bomber as the B-1 at a small fraction of the cost. B-1 proponents, on the other hand, note that the plane is capable of a faster takeoff than the B-52 and is more hardened against the electrical disturbance known as EMP, making it significantly more survivable in the event of a surprise attack.

The sea leg of the U.S. Triad is being upgraded with the addition of thousands of sea-launched cruise missiles (SLCMs) to both surface ships and attack submarines. Although the United States has lead the Soviet Union in cruise-missile technology, it may find itself in a less secure position now that the U.S.S.R. has followed the U.S. lead in this area. Cruise missiles can be stored in large numbers on ships, and, unlike ballistic missiles, their presence can be easily hidden. (Ballistic missiles require silos or launch tubes that can be more easily detected.) The U.S.S.R. has many more surface ships and attack submarines which can be made into cruise-missile carriers than the United States does, giving the Soviet Union a relative advantage in the number of potential cruise-missile platforms. It is conceivable that at some time the United States might find off its coasts Soviet trawlers carrying large numbers of cruise missiles. Many observers, therefore, have argued for unilateral U.S. restraint in deploying SLCMs. The past history of the arms race, however, does not offer much encouragement for the belief that unilateral restraint will usually be reciprocated.

In another major enhancement of the sea leg of the triad, the present fleet of Poseidon and Polaris submarines is scheduled for eventual retirement, to be replaced by a smaller number of Trident submarines now being built at a rate of one every eight months. The Trident submarine primarily differs from the older Poseidon and Polaris in that the much larger Trident is capable of carrying bigger missiles. The C-4 (Trident I) missile presently used in the Trident submarine, although larger than those in the Poseidon, does not have sufficient accuracy and yield to threaten Soviet missile silos. That will not be the case for the higher-yield silo-busting D-5 (Trident II) missile due to be ready for deployment around 1989. The sea leg of the triad, being relatively invulnerable, constitutes a secure second-strike deterrent. Therefore, most observers agree that it enhances deterrence to replace the Poseidon-Polaris fleet as these ships reach the end of their useful life. As in the case of the B-1 bomber, many critics of the Trident submarine have focused primarily on the nature of the ship rather than on the need for some kind of submarine replacement. One criticism concerns Trident's huge size. By replacing the Poseidon-Polaris fleet with a smaller number of more powerful Trident submarines, the United States in effect will be putting a greater fraction of its retaliatory force in a smaller number of ships, making each one a more tempting target. At present it is planned to build a fleet of about twenty Tridents. Both the smaller number and greater size of the ships in the Trident fleet may be factors that make them more vulnerable to Soviet ASW efforts. Some critics have therefore argued that the United States might have been better off with a larger number of submarines of smaller size. Moreover, with the shift from Poseidon-Polaris to Trident, the present imbalance between the number of U.S. and Soviet ballistic-missile submarines (thirty-six U.S. versus eighty-four Soviet) will shift still more in favor of the Soviet Union. Another controversy concerning the Trident submarine concerns the countersilo capability of its D-5 warhead now under development. This important question of whether the United States should match the Soviet Union in its countersilo capability will be discussed in the context of the MX missile—the third and probably most controversial of the Reagan additions to the U.S. triad.

WHAT IS THE CASE FOR THE MX MISSILE?

The MX missile had its genesis in 1974 design studies for a mobile ICBM to replace the Minuteman and Titan missiles. Prior to 1972 the United States had been opposed to mobile ICBMs, based on the belief that any Soviet mobile ICBM would be difficult to monitor through satellite surveillance. But the United States gradually began to view mobile missiles more favorably because they offered a possible solution to ICBM vulnerability.

The MX missile is two-and-a-half-times heavier than the Minuteman III. It can carry ten warheads of up to 475-kiloton yield.

The yield and accuracy of these warheads would be sufficient to give them a one-shot kill probability of 99 percent against Soviet ICBM silos.[20] The planned one hundred MX missiles would therefore pose a significant threat to the Soviet ICBM force. The original justification advanced for MX was its role in remedying the problem of U.S. ICBM vulnerability. However, the question of whether MX is invulnerable to attack depends entirely on how the missile is to be based. Many factors need to be considered in evaluating particular MX basing modes, but unless a mode can insure survivability, the original justification for the MX missile would seem to be called into question. There has, for this reason, probably been more controversy surrounding the method for basing the MX missile than there has over the missile itself.

One of several Carter-administration proposals involved an arrangement of multiple protective shelters (MPS), between which missiles could be shuttled—the so-called racetrack mode. These various MPS proposals called for shuttling two hundred MX missiles between forty-six hundred shelters, or one missile for every twenty-three shelters. The whole idea was to keep a potential attacker guessing as to which shelters contained the missiles, so that an attack to knock out the two hundred missiles would require at least forty-six hundred warheads. By raising the price to the aggressor this high, an attack, even if successful, would be essentially a self-disarming move, assuming that the arsenals were constrained by the SALT II Treaty. President Reagan decided, probably for political reasons, to shelve the Carter racetrack plan and initiate several additional studies to come up with a basing plan. A partial list of the over thirty MX basing modes considered would include:

- Minisubmarine basing
- Wide-bodied-aircraft basing
- Single silos or MPS defended by ABM
- Launch under attack
- Densepack

A number of the most outspoken critics of the racetrack basing mode have favored placing the MX missile aboard a fleet of minisubmarines. For example, fifty such boats might each carry four MX missiles in watertight cannisters attached to the exterior of the hulls. The advantage of placing the MX aboard submarines is that they are the least vulnerable leg of the triad, although this basing mode would do nothing to remedy the vulnerability of the land-based leg. Moreover, the percentage of U.S. nuclear warheads aboard submarines is already quite high (50 percent). If that percentage were further increased by minisubmarine basing of MX, any Soviet ASW breakthrough could have very serious consequences.

The proposal to put the MX missiles on board a fleet of wide-bodied aircraft is also not without drawbacks. In common with the minisubmarine proposal, the air-mobile MX basing mode also would do nothing to remedy the vulnerability in the land-based leg of the triad, and the proposal would take some time to implement. In addition, putting the MX aboard aircraft would mean that they would have a common failure mode with bombers, that is, an attack successful against one would also be successful against the other. An air-mobile MX would be considerably less vulnerable if a sizable fraction of the aircraft were kept continuously airborne, but that would be very expensive and likely to generate public fears about crashes of planes carrying nuclear weapons.

Various proposals to use an antiballistic-missile (ABM) defense of MX silos have been made to assure MX-missile survivability. That action might be in violation of the 1972 ABM Treaty, although the treaty does specifically call for five-year reviews. The technical feasibility of defending ICBM silos using a ground-based-point defense is considerably greater than would be required for a population defense. The hardness of an ICBM silo means that a defender must protect a relatively small "keep-out zone" centered on the target. Thus an ABM system designed to protect missile silos hardened to thousands of psi can have considerably shorter "reach" than one designed to protect cities which are much larger and softer targets. Even more importantly, the fact that all ABM systems must be assumed to "leak" would pose much less of a problem for a defense of missile silos than for population defense. For example, an ABM defense of missile silos could be considered a success if more missiles were expended by the attacker than were destroyed, since in that case, there would seem to be little incentive to the first strike in the first place. There are, however, many additional important questions concerning the desirability of ABM systems, and these will be deferred to a subsequent section on ABM defense of populations.

All the MX basing modes so far considered share a number of serious drawbacks:

- They are very expensive.

- They would take a long time to implement.

- They don't clearly solve the vulnerability problem.

One proposal that might avoid these three drawbacks would be for the United States to adopt a launch-under-attack (LUA) policy.

WHAT ARE THE MERITS OF A LAUNCH-UNDER-ATTACK POLICY?

A policy of launch under attack is not the same as the much more risky launch on warning of an attack. It is also a much more difficult policy to carry out, since an attacker could be expected to try to disrupt all command, control, and communications (C^3), so as to minimize the scope of the victim's retaliatory capability. The United States would need to greatly upgrade its C^3 to insure that a determined enemy could not eliminate the whole top U.S. command structure in a decapitating attack or, alternatively, sever all communication links, making a prompt retaliatory strike unfeasible. Such a C^3 upgrading was also one of the Reagan-administration initiatives for the U.S. strategic nuclear arsenal. It is unclear whether the C^3 upgrades are preparatory to a launch-under-attack policy, but a strengthening of command, control, and communications would seem to be a wise policy in any case. There are those, however, who see a more sinister side to the upgrade in C^3, despite its evident impact on reducing the risk of accidental war and removing any temptation for an aggressor to launch a decapitating attack against the United States. Given the suggestions by some members of the Reagan administration that a nuclear war might be protracted, there are those who see the C^3 upgrades as a matter of intention to fight and win an extended nuclear war.

Even if no such war-winning intention exists on the part of the administration, some C^3 upgrades can have a destabilizing effect. For example, some satellite communication and navigation systems to be used for submarines will give them a counterforce capability. That capability, however, would probably be severely degraded in the early phases of a nuclear war in which vulnerable communication systems would be destroyed. Therefore, the ironic effect of adding communication and navigation systems such as the NAVSTAR satellite could be to transform the submarine fleet from an invulnerable second-strike force to one with a counterforce capability that if not used in an early phase, could be lost later on.

Accidental nuclear war is a serious concern for many people. In the past there have been several widely reported incidents in which the United States came close to a mistaken belief that it was under a nuclear attack. In one such case, the rising moon is reported to have been mistaken for a group of Soviet missiles by a newly installed warning system. In another case, a simulated Soviet attack recorded on tape was loaded into a computer and thought to be a real attack. Given the likelihood that such events will continue to occur, a launch-on-warning policy would seem to be an invitation to disaster. A launch-under-attack policy, for which no response would occur until enemy missiles actually start landing, is certainly less likely to start World War III based on a false alarm. Moreover, LUA does offer some important advantages over other proposals so far considered for reducing ICBM vulnerability.

- It would remedy the problem without requiring a new MX missile, and it does so much sooner and at much lower cost than MX.

- It would increase the survivability of the entire ICBM force, not just the new MX missiles for which no invulnerable basing mode has been proposed anyway.

- It greatly reduces the incentive for a surprise strike against U.S. ICBMs since there would be little point in attacking missile silos, many of which would be empty by the time enemy missiles arrived.

However, despite the merits of a launch-under-attack policy as a solution to the problem of ICBM vulnerability, it is unlikely that it could be more than an interim solution. Over the long term LUA is risky for several reasons.

- The very small risk of a nuclear war starting by accident due to a false alarm under a LUA policy may not be so small over an extended period of time.

- The possibility of third parties acquiring ICBMs in the future might allow them to initiate a U.S.-Soviet nuclear war under a LUA policy.

- The possibility also exists that any C^3 system, no matter how sophisticated, could be disrupted by a determined enemy.

The last point is sometimes overlooked by those who describe C^3 vulnerabilities purely in technical terms and who stress exclusively technical solutions to such vulnerabilities, e.g., hardening against EMP. An examination of Soviet strategic literature shows that great attention is given to the value of sabotage and disinformation as tools in achieving a surprise attack and in blunting any possible retaliation. Strategic results could be obtained at the start of a nuclear war if such tactics were to confuse the enemy for only twenty minutes. The idea of sabotage teams now in place in the United States would not seem to be totally farfetched based on the stress on such actions in Soviet military literature and, equally importantly, on the 1970 defection of a Soviet KGB agent who had been in charge of supervising just such a secret sabotage network in Great Britain.[21]

While the U.S.S.R. is, in principle, also susceptible to sabotage from in-place Western agents, in practice it would seem that this particular U.S. vulnerability is virtually unmatched for several reasons: (1) There are far fewer Americans than Russians whose knowledge of the adversary's society and language would allow them to pose as citizens, and (2) there are very great barriers to foreigners surreptitiously posing as citizens over an extended period of time in the tightly controlled Soviet society.

In view of the possibility of in-place sabotage teams disrupting communications on the eve of a nuclear war, scheduled C^3 upgrades can only make it harder, but not impossible, for a determined attacker to cripple a defender's command, control, and communications. This fact makes it unclear whether launch under attack (LUA) is feasible as a long-range solution to the vulnerability of land-based missiles.

WHAT IS THE REAL RATIONALE FOR MX?

After considering any number of possible MX missile basing modes, the Reagan administration, at the urging of yet another commission, finally proposed the one that clearly does nothing to remedy the problem of ICBM vulnerability, namely placing the missiles in existing Minuteman silos. There are at least two inferences that can be drawn from that proposal: (1) after studying any number of alternative basing modes, there appears to be no way that is technically and politically feasible to base MX missiles in a way that "closes the window of vulnerability"; (2) the Reagan administration's strong support for the MX missiles is based on reasons other than a desire to remedy the vulnerability of land-based missiles, despite the fact that this was the stated rationale.

The entire debate over what to do about U.S. land-based missiles is filled with many ironies. Those who have argued most strenuously that the Soviets would never dare undertake such an unpromising venture as attacking U.S. ICBMs have later found themselves arguing against specific remedies to the vulnerability problem, such as the densepack scheme, on the grounds that the Soviets would probably find some way to successfully attack it. President Carter, who came into office with the hope of ridding the world of nuclear weapons entirely, left it after recommending a complex racetrack basing mode for two hundred MX missiles. President Reagan, after gaining office by attacking Carter for being soft on defense and allowing a window of vulnerability to open, eventually recommended deploying only a hundred MX missiles in the most vulnerable basing mode possible.

If the MX missile is not intended to close a vulnerability gap, what is its rationale? According to Air Force Brigadier General J. P. McCarthy in testimony on the MX to the House Appropriations Committee: "We put Soviet hard targets at risk, which is the principal reason we need the MX missile." [22] In all probability, those attempting to justify the need for a new land-based missile may have believed all along that making the case for a hard-target killer was not as easy as making the case for remedying land-based-missile vulnerability. Now that the feasibility of closing the window of vulnerability seems questionable, a different rationale therefore assumes greater importance. How valid is that rationale?

SHOULD THE U.S. BUILD FIRST-STRIKE WEAPONS?

The prolonged debate over the MX missile has only in part been a debate over a particular weapons system. While it may not be explicitly recognized, the debate has been intimately tied to a broader debate over the future strategic posture of the United States. The MX missile has forced us to reexamine the purposes for which it is necessary to build new weapons and the kinds of weapons needed to achieve those purposes.

Weapons capable of a surprise counterforce attack are often called first-strike weapons. Both the United States and Soviet Union already have first-strike weapons in their arsenals, although the number of Soviet silo-killers significantly exceeds the number of such weapons in the U.S. arsenal. Among new U.S. weapons, the MX, Pershing II, and Trident II missiles would all be considered first-strike weapons. The question we wish to consider here is whether the United States should build additional first-strike weapons independent of what the Soviet Union does. In other words, is this an area in which it is wise to match Soviet capabilities? This is not an easy question to answer, since there are some very good reasons for either course of action.

It should be stressed that it would be highly desirable if neither the Soviet nor the American arsenals had first-strike weapons. Weapons of this kind promote a use-them-or-lose-them psychology in a crisis, and therefore they put a hair trigger on the nuclear arsenals. They also further stimulate the adversary's paranoia. Having granted that such weapons are highly destabilizing and should be eliminated, the more difficult question to answer is whether the United States should continue to build them if the Soviet arsenal has a significantly greater counterforce capability and, moreover, one that continues to grow. To put the question another way, Is it in the interest of the United States to build weapons that might be perceived by the Soviets as threatening a surprise first-strike even though that may not be our intention? That threat, incidentally, appears to be highly plausible according to a secret Defense Department study that found, under favorable assumptions, that a hypothetical U.S. first strike in 1993 could virtually eliminate all Soviet missile silos.[23]

One of the main justifications for the MX has been that only by matching the Soviet Union in counterforce weaponry would the Soviet Union be willing to agree to reductions in such highly destabilizing weapons. That argument is based on the plausible proposition that the Soviet Union is unlikely to agree to actual reductions in a category of weaponry in which it holds a commanding lead in exchange for U.S. promises not to build such weapons. Unfortunately, both the Soviet Union and the United States have shown a tendency to lack an appreciation for the seriousness of threats perceived by the other party. It is, therefore, not unreasonable that the Soviet Union might better appreciate the desirability of reducing its land-based missiles if their ICBMs were to become vulnerable to the same degree as U.S. missiles.

However, other Soviet reactions to the deployment of a new generation of U.S. counterforce weapons are also possible. Some observers worry that an economically hard-pressed Soviet Union might resort to the least costly countermeasure and adopt a launch-on-warning policy, in fact some observers suspect that the Soviets may already have such a policy. If the Soviets should opt for such a risky policy, the fate of the world could well hinge on the reliability of Soviet computers and warning systems. The fact that suggestions of a possible Soviet launch-on warning policy in response to new U.S. weapons have come from Soviet sources does, however, make them suspect as possible disinformation designed to stir fears of war starting by accident.

The Soviet Union, unlike the United States, appears to place greater weight on intelligence gathered through espionage rather than by technical means such as spy satellites, which are, of course, also available. In the unlikely event that the United States should ever decide to launch a surprise attack against the Soviet Union, the Soviet Union very probably has numerous highly placed agents who would become aware of this fact long before the U.S.S.R. would need to rely on the very brief warning time furnished by their spy satellites. In this sense, the Soviet need for a launch-on-warning policy is probably less than the United States need, no matter how suspicious they may be of U.S. intentions.

Other more plausible Soviet reactions to the U.S. development of counterforce weapons are possible, including the deployment of land-mobile missiles that could not be easily targeted. Reportedly the Soviets have such a missile in the SS-16 which they temporarily stopped work on in 1977 during the SALT II negotiations. Soviet testing of their SS-16 missile in 1982–83 may be a prelude to its deployment. Such land-mobile missiles could be put in place long before new U.S. counterforce weapons posed a serious first-strike threat. Mobile missiles could, however, pose serious arms-control problems since they can be moved around and hidden and are therefore difficult to count.

Another possible Soviet response to new U.S. first-strike missiles would be to deploy an ABM system to defend their missile silos, although that might require a modification or withdrawal from the ABM Treaty. Alternately, the Soviets could opt to keep a larger fraction of their submarine fleet at sea at all times, since their fleet outnumbers the U.S. fleet by two to one. A fourth possibility would be for the Soviets to expand the bomber leg of their triad. Given all the options available to the Soviet Union in response to an increased U.S. counterforce threat, it does not seem likely that they would feel compelled to opt for a highly risky launch-on-warning policy.

Apart from the bargaining-chip argument, what other arguments are there for building new U.S. counterforce weapons? Although the

United States does possess such weapons in its sixteen hundred Minuteman III warheads, it is feared that too few of these would be left after a Soviet surprise attack to strike at Soviet targets such as hardened command and control sites, ICBM silos, and the shelters where senior Soviet officials would relocate. It is important to have the ability to retaliate against these targets that would pose a grave continuing threat to the United States even after the first Soviet attack. Thus, a U.S. counterforce capability could serve to limit damage to the United States during a nuclear war, and it could also convince the Soviet leadership that a surprise counterforce attack against the United States would serve no military purpose because we could retaliate in kind.

Nevertheless, even if we grant that counterforce weapons are necessary on such a basis, the U.S. arsenal does already contain a large number of counterforce weapons in its B-52 bomber fleet which are capable of highly accurate strikes with large-yield weapons. Those who argue for new counterforce missiles, however, believe that the uncertain option of waiting ten to fifteen hours for bombers to arrive on target is not adequate for a counterforce mission against Soviet missile silos. The logic of that argument is, however, unclear. Once the Soviet Union has attacked the United States, a U.S. retaliatory attack using counterforce missiles instead of bombers would not seem to be a more promising military action. While the Soviets might consider it risky to put their ICBMs under a launch-on-warning posture in peacetime, they would surely do so after they had just initiated a nuclear war. It would seem implausible to expect that the Soviets would be unable to launch a second wave of ICBMs upon detecting American missiles thirty minutes from their targets. The fact that the U.S. missiles could reach their targets much faster than bombers would not, therefore, prevent them from destroying empty silos. This would seem to imply that U.S. retaliation against Soviet missile silos is not a wise course of action in any case. The situation is further complicated, however, by the reload capability of Soviet missile silos which could make their prompt destruction a way of limiting damage to the United States.

It could be an important factor psychologically if Soviet leaders knew that their retreats would be assuredly destroyed in an American retaliatory attack, but having counterforce missiles capable of retaliating in thirty minutes rather than ten to fifteen hours needed for bombers seems to do little to increase the U.S. capability in that regard. While Soviet leaders might relocate in the ten to fifteen hours it takes bombers to arrive, it is also possible they would not go to the expected retreats in the first place.

Another argument against the need for more counterforce missiles said to possess "time-urgent hard-target kill capability," in Pentagon jargon, is that such missiles, if land based, would be a magnet for a Soviet attack. These weapons threaten Soviet land-based missiles with a surprise first strike, and they are simultaneously vulnerable to such an attack by the U.S.S.R. Weapons such as the MX missile based in a vulnerable mode make a surprise attack a more attractive option to the Soviets as a way of limiting their own damage. This argument has some validity, especially to the degree that Soviet planners conclude that the overall U.S. nuclear arsenal is beginning to pose a real first-strike threat. Nevertheless, it is disturbing to find that those who believe a Soviet attack on U.S. ICBMs is only a fantasy of alarmist hawks, then go on to describe the likely Soviet reaction to an increase in American ICBM capability in such apocalyptic terms. It is, of course, important that the United States consider how the Soviets will view U.S. actions and refrain from actions that may be viewed as extremely threatening to the Soviets. However, it is also unreasonable to believe that improbable actions on the part of the Soviets might suddenly become highly probable as a result of some U.S. "provocation"—particularly an increase in U.S. counterforce capabilities that would still be less than that of the Soviet arsenal, even with MX.

Opponents of the MX missile note that even if some increase in U.S. counterforce capability is considered desirable, the D-5 (Trident II) missile will also be capable of destroying hard targets by the end of the 1980s, so there is no need for an MX in addition. Furthermore, the Trident II, unlike the MX, would be relatively invulnerable to attack, making it not nearly as destabilizing a weapon. Another alternative would be to MIRV the entire Minuteman force to carry three Mk 12A warheads, as one-half of the Minuteman force does at present. On the other hand, that action suffers from the same drawback as deploying MX missiles in vulnerable Minuteman silos, namely, it makes U.S. land-based missiles a more tempting target for a Soviet surprise attack.

A number of observers have suggested that the real problem is not with counterforce weapons per se, but rather with multiple warheads, which is a major source of the first-strike advantage. It appears inevitable that the gradual evolution of improved guidance systems will lead to further increases in counterforce capability. However, a return to single-warhead land-based missiles would yield weapons that, even though they may be silo-killers, would no longer give a first-strike advantage to the attacker. This would be the case even if only one side were to decide to return to single-warhead missiles and even if they were placed in vulnerable fixed silos, as long as the total number of warheads on each side was comparable. A return to single-warhead missiles seems, therefore, the ideal way to preserve the land-based leg of the triad and create a more stable deterrent. Why has it taken nuclear strategists so long to come up with this solution? Unfortunately, we have been asking the wrong question. Instead of asking how land-based missiles could be made less vulnerable to attack, the more important question should have been how can the military advantage to the attacker in a surprise first strike be reduced.

A commission, headed by Brent Scowcroft and reporting to President Reagan, has urged that the United States simultaneously pursue a small single-warhead "Midgetman" missile and, for the nearer term, deploy the ten-warhead MX in fixed (vulnerable) Minuteman silos. Opponents of the MX believe the two commission recommendations to be mutually contradictory, while supporters claim that over the near term the MX is the most feasible way to upgrade U.S. land-based missiles, despite their continuing vulnerability. MX supporters suspect that the main lure the Midgetman may have for MX critics is that it does not exist and that its flaws too will be discovered once its deployment nears.

Land-based missiles in any form may continue to present serious vulnerability problems, as well as being to some degree a magnet for a first strike. Nevertheless, they will probably continue to be regarded as an important element of the triad in view of the following needs:

- Have highly accurate, reliable weapons that are easily and quickly retargetable

- Have diversified strategic forces in case a vulnerability should develop in the sea-based leg

- Make a simultaneous enemy attack on all three legs of the triad impossible to execute

- Have strategic forces that do not have the command and communication problems of bombers and submarines

- Have homeland-based forces to guard against a war of attrition against submarines, whose loss might be tolerated in preference to initiating World War III

- Present the U.S.S.R. with a sufficient counterforce threat to serve as an incentive to reach agreement on the mutual reduction of these destabilizing weapons.

The Scowcroft Commission report supporting the MX in effect closed the window of vulnerability by saying that land-based missiles are a sufficiently important component of the triad that we need to retain and modernize them, even if they are vulnerable. The report also noted that the extent of that vulnerability has probably been exaggerated, especially considering the much larger vulnerability of C^3 to a decapitating attack.

Until now we have focused largely on the continuing arms race in offensive weapons. There is some evidence we may be on the verge of a new defensive arms race as well.

SHOULD THE UNITED STATES BUILD A BALLISTIC-MISSILE DEFENSE?

The defense of ICBM silos against nuclear attack is probably both feasible and desirable in terms of reducing their vulnerability to a surprise attack, hence removing any advantage to the attacker. Richard Garwin, a long-time critic of administration defense policies, believes that relatively low-cost, nonnuclear options exist to defend ICBM silos that might well make the MX unnecessary. One such option involves the Swarmjet concept in which thousands of small projectiles are simultaneously fired at an incoming warhead when it is one to two miles from its target. Garwin is sufficiently suspicious of the nature of the military beauracracy that he believes the low cost of Swarmjet and the fact that it could make the MX unnecessary are precisely the reasons that there has been little official interest in the concept to date.[24]

While ICBMs may be defendable using current technology, defending populations against a missile attack is quite a different matter. Nevertheless, recent advances in using lasers in ABM research have given rise to the belief in some quarters that such a defense may be feasible within one or two decades if a number of complex technical questions can be resolved. One concept said to have promise would involve three components: (1) a ground-based laser of extraordinarily high power, (2) a large number of mirrors in satellite orbits, and (3) a ground-based system to track missiles and orient the mirrors to reflect the laser beam toward missile targets thousands of miles away. Hundreds of orbiting mirrors, each perhaps a hundred feet in diameter, might be necessary to deal with a large Soviet attack. Infrared sensors on satellites would detect a Soviet missile attack based on the heat generated by Soviet rockets during launch; then signals would be sent to the ground-based tracking system to allow it to compute the orientation needed for the mirrors.

The feasibility of such a system, referred to as "the high frontier" by proponents, and "star wars" by detractors, remains unclear. Some of the uncertainties include:

- Whether it is possible to build lasers of sufficient power

- Whether laser beams can somehow be transmitted through rain and clouds

- Whether computers could be built that could cope with the enormous data-handling capacity needed to track and shoot down thousands of missiles during a time span of a few minutes.

According to a classified 1981 study by the Government Accounting Office, an ABM system using ground-based lasers could be ready for testing by 1993, with a total-system price tag of $30 billion. Other knowledgeable experts, including William Perry, undersecretary of defense in the Carter administration, estimate that a more likely initial operating date would be sometime in the next century at the earliest and that the price tag would be in excess of $100 billion.

Although we shall consider a range of arguments for and against ABM, the question of technical feasibility does not seem to be the most compelling argument on either side. It simply is not possible to know whether or not formidable technical obstacles can be overcome in the case of a system that even its proponents acknowledge is two decades away. Any number of examples can be given of new weapons originally said to be impossible by knowledgeable scientists, in some cases just on the eve of the weapons' development. The atomic bomb and the intercontinental ballistic missile were both considered impossible by some very knowledgeable experts. There is, however, something different about a complex system such as ABM and a specific device such as the atomic bomb. The real issue for an ABM system is not whether or not it would work, but rather how well it could be made to work and at what cost. We also need to know what countermeasures might defeat the system and what they might cost.

It is very clear that in the case of a system two decades away, the Russians would have ample time to develop possible countermeasures that might render a U.S. ABM system impotent. Many countermeasures have already been suggested. Moreover, most of the countermeasures are far less expensive than the likely cost of the ABM system. Some simple, presently available countermeasures would include:

- Setting tens of thousands of small fires at the same time as a surprise missile attack, thereby confusing the infrared sensors

- Coating ICBMs with heat-absorbent materials or rotating them in flight so as to spread the laser-heat energy over the surface and not allow the beam to penetrate the skin of the missile

- Placing a large number of nuclear weapons in permanent satellite orbits (in violation of the 1967 Outerspace Treaty), and firing them all by coded radio signal at a predetermined time

- Attacking by means of air-breathing cruise missiles and bombers, which might circumvent a system designed to work against missiles above the atmosphere

- Building a large enough arsenal to overwhelm any ABM defense

- Destroying the ground-based laser or tracking system prior to an attack using teams of well-armed saboteurs

- Infiltrating the design team building the ABM system and implanting some very hard to notice flaw, for example, a small change in the computer program that would direct the angle of the mirrors to be slightly off

- Stationing killer satellites or space mines in orbit to attack the orbiting mirrors

Space mines represent a threat that is particularly difficult to cope with. Small satellites containing nuclear or conventional weapons could be made to follow all the orbiting mirrors and could be detonated on radio command. As Richard Garwin has noted:

Even on the sea, it is certainly hallowed by international law and customs that every nation has the right to maintain the vessels of another nation within range of its guns (except in domestic waters). To attempt to establish the opposite in space will lead to war in space—and that is a prelude to war on earth, not a substitute for it.[25]

In addition, a highly complex ABM system is bound to have vulnerabilities that may not initially be evident to its builders. Given the possibility that a large number of Soviet agents might infiltrate the American effort during its twenty-year development, the Soviets might discover defects in the U.S. system even before it is deployed. Moreover, vulnerabilities in an ABM system would allow the possibility of catastrophic failure rather than simply a degraded performance under a surprise attack.

Quite apart from all countermeasures and vulnerabilities, no ABM system could do better than offer partial protection against a massive nuclear attack. Even if by a truly remarkable degree of technological progress it proved possible to design a system that was 95-percent effective, the Soviet Union could still deliver three hundred ICBM warheads on U.S. targets given its present arsenal. If three hundred weapons of megaton yields were used in a surprise attack against U.S. cities, a large fraction of the population would be killed. Thus, even a near-perfect ABM defense would not exorcise the threat of nuclear holocaust. If the United States were ever to build such a system, it would also be necessary to build a separate air defense against bombers and cruise missiles, as well as an extensive civil defense to cope with ABM "leakage." In fact, it would make little sense to build an expensive and exotic ABM system of uncertain feasibility without first investing in a much cheaper civil defense system. Such a course of action would be akin to installing an expensive photovoltaic solar-energy collection system on your roof and not bothering first to add insulation in your ceiling—a much more cost-effective measure.

Even though the protection gained per dollar spent is probably much greater for civil defense than ABM defense, it seems very likely that the American passion for high-technology solutions will result in the United States continuing to slight the former in favor of the latter. The thought of possessing an exotic "star wars" system to zap attacking missiles and keep us secure probably appeals much more to the American psyche than the idea of needing to dig a backyard shelter and spending a few days or weeks in a hole in the ground. Of course, as we have already noted, even a near-perfect ABM defense would not be a substitute for civil defense, which would be required in any case.

There are other reasons why Americans, by nature an optimistic people, find ABM defense appealing. For many people, the thought of forever living under the threat of a nuclear holocaust is intolerable. While some may see an eventual way out in terms of complete disarmament and world government, others prefer to believe that there is some ultimate technical solution. The policy of mutual assured destruction with its emphasis on killing millions of innocent civilians in retaliation is morally repugnant to many people. Fred Iklé, a Reagan undersecretary of defense, compares the policy of mutual assured destruction with the policy of looking for a defensive alternative: "The first view [MAD] is like a permanent nightmare; the second view is a vision of the future that offers hope." [26] That vision, however, may turn out to be a dangerous fantasy.

A third reason that an ABM system may hold special appeal to Americans is that some citizens may be tiring of the U.S. role as the defender of allies who do not always show the degree of gratitude that some U.S. citizens may feel is warranted. An ABM system that protected America from nuclear attack might leave Western Europe and Japan unprotected from Soviet medium-range missiles or from a conventional assault. Under these circumstances the United States might consider that it no longer needed its allies to provide for its own security, thus defending Europe with American forces would become much harder to justify. In addition, the allies, realizing that America's survival was now decoupled from their own, might well choose to seek a neutral course and come to terms with the Soviet Union. America has often demonstrated isolationist tendencies, and some U.S. citizens might welcome a policy whereby the United States no longer risked its own destruction by defending its allies.

The 1972 ABM Treaty is the only major bilateral U.S.-Soviet treaty officially in force as of 1984. If either country were unilaterally to abrogate the treaty or announce its intention to do so, the achievement of future arms-control treaties would probably become much more difficult. The extensive ABM research going on in both the United States and the U.S.S.R. is not forbidden by the treaty, but testing or development of a weapons system would be forbidden.

Reagan administration allegations that the Soviet deployment of large phased array radars represent a "probable" ABM treaty violation are of uncertain validity in light of ambiguities in the treaty, and the administration's apparent desire to find grounds for the U.S. to back away from the ABM treaty without blame.

It seems unlikely that the Soviet Union would agree to renegotiate the ABM Treaty just because a U.S. administration has made an about-face on ABM defenses, now viewing them as offering "a new hope for our children in the 21st century," in President Reagan's words from his March 23, 1983 "Star Wars" speech. Chairman Yuri Andropov's reaction to President Reagan's ABM proposal was not unlike the previous U.S. government position. Andropov has noted that the development of ABM would: "open the floodgates to a runaway race involving all kinds of strategic weapons, both offensive and defensive." [27] As has happened on a number of occasions, the United States and the Soviet Union have reversed their positions, each taking the position formerly held by the other.

For many years prior to the 1972 treaty, the Soviets believed that antimissile systems were strictly defense and not "a cause of the arms race, but designed instead to prevent the death of people." [28] Why did the U.S.S.R. change its mind and agree with the United States to restrict ABMs? Some analysts believe that Washington convinced Moscow through the logic of its argument. There are, however, other more pragmatic reasons that may have accounted for the Soviet reversal. Moscow may have feared that the United States was on the verge of deploying an ABM system, which the Senate had just approved in the early 1970s, and wished to forestall that possibility. It may be reading too much into Soviet motives to claim that the ABM Treaty demonstrates on their part "a tacit acceptance that all-out thermonuclear war would mean the end of the U.S.S.R. as well as the U.S.," as former Defense Secretary Harold Brown has claimed.[29] It seems far more likely that the Soviets pragmatically decided to invest their efforts in defensive measures of more proven feasibility, i.e. air defenses and civil defense, and to wait until it became clearer whether ABM defense was feasible before engaging in an all-out ABM effort. Moreover, given America's high-technology advantage it was in the interests of the U.S.S.R. not to engage the United States prematurely in a long-term ABM development race that it could well lose.

Proponents of ABM say that even if such systems should initiate a new dimension to the arms race, a defensive race is preferable to an offensive one. That position, however, overlooks the close linkage between offensive and defensive weapons. Even if both sides had ABM systems, that alone would not be seen as a reason for giving up offensive weapons. Quite the contrary, both sides probably would want to be sure that they continued to have sufficient offensive weapons to do an unacceptable level of damage to the adversary in retaliation, and they might therefore want to substantially increase their offensive weaponry. Additionally, both sides would probably seek to develop new types of offensive countermeasures, e.g., space mines capable of destroying the other side's ABM system. Some observers have even suggested that the laser ABM system itself might be capable of offensive action against a wide range of military and economic targets.

There can be little question that ABM systems could be highly destabilizing in a crisis, even if both sides had them. A clever military briefer might persuade a political leader that a vulnerability had been discovered in the other side's ABM defense that would allow a reasonable chance for a disarming attack. Alternatively, one side might become worried that a real or perceived vulnerability in its own system had been discovered by the adversary, thus it might be tempted to strike first while it still had enough offensive forces to saturate the enemy's defenses.

The destabilizing consequences could be even more grave if one side were to develop a "working" ABM defense before the other. Should the Soviets, who already have massive air defenses and a civil defense system in place, be able to develop an ABM system that they *believed* could protect their population, they could be greatly tempted to resort to nuclear blackmail against the United States if it had no similar protection. The results might be equally catastrophic if the United States were the winner of an ABM race. Many Americans believe that a U.S. ABM monopoly would not cause the United States to attack the U.S.S.R. or resort to nuclear blackmail. The Soviet Union, however, could not afford to allow itself to be put into a position where it was effectively disarmed. Given the extreme threat that a U.S. ABM system would pose to the Soviet Union, their only recourse would be to destroy the ABM system before it could be completely deployed. That action would lead to a war in space—a prelude to one on earth, in Richard Garwin's words.

Some proponents of ABM systems suggest that perhaps their provocative aspect could be mitigated by offering to develop such a system jointly with the Russians. Such a joint effort, however, would not prevent each side from secretly searching for vulnerabilities and countermeasures. Any mutual U.S.-Soviet development effort would probably become something of a charade, with each side keeping to itself various key bits of technical information. A U.S.-Soviet joint ABM effort would seem as implausible as a joint effort to develop better espionage techniques. The United States might alternatively choose to develop an ABM system and then give it to the Soviet Union, but many of the same problems would exist in this case. The United States might decide to give a different (more vulnerable) version of the system to the Soviets. Also the Soviets could not be sure that we did not have some countermeasures secretly developed to defeat the system.

In the view of the considerable problems with ABM, some people believe it is unwise even to pursue ABM research. For example, according to Solly Zuckerman, "even if such systems never prove significant in the reduction of unacceptable destruction, suspicion is generated by the fact that R and D to devise such systems and counter-systems continues." [30] The problem with this reasoning is that it is vital that political leaders be given accurate and up-to-date information on the technical feasibility of proposed weapons systems. The nuclear balance would probably be less stable if, having forsworn ABM research, U.S. scientists were to come upon seemingly promising ideas that could not be tested beyond the paper and pencil stage. Moreover, there would be continual doubts that research was secretly being conducted by the U.S.S.R., despite the existence of any agreement, which would be exceedingly difficult to verify. Rumors of secret Soviet programs would certainly materialize, prompting the United States to start its own secret research programs. Thus, despite the serious problems with ABM systems, it seems unlikely that both sides would agree to discontinue their research efforts. Many analysts, therefore, while they hope that ABM defenses prove unfeasible, recognize the need to continue research in this area.

The continued threat of mutual assured destruction is certainly not a desirable state of affairs, but it appears that there is no way to exorcise the spectre of retaliation from deterrence. As Winston Churchill expressed in three decades ago: "Safety will be the sturdy child of terror and survival the twin brother of annihilation." [31] MAD may often be subject to criticism on moral grounds, but surely it is less moral to hold forth a technical "solution" to the nuclear dilemma that may have great popular appeal, but that most of its proponents understand cannot literally keep us safe and could increase the risk of war.

Many people believe that the same disadvantages to ABM defenses also apply in the case of civil defense. However, I believe they are mistaken. There are many defects that a U.S. civil defense effort would not share with an ABM defense.

- Civil defense is a low-technology effort whose main components are not of uncertain technological feasibility. These components include shelter construction, stockpiling, industrial dispersal and hardening, and public education.

- A civil defense system would not need to wait twenty years for development but could be put in place quickly.

- Civil defense is potentially much less costly than ABM defense and offers much more protection per dollar spent.

- A breakdown on vulnerability in an ABM defense might lead to total catastrophe, whereas a breakdown in a civil defense system is more likely simply to degrade its performance.

- Civil defense, unlike ABM, could offer protection against any kind of nuclear attack: bombers and cruise missiles as well as ICBMs.

- The adversary is unlikely to seek to develop countermeasures to defeat a civil defense program, which would not be so likely to be viewed as provocative.

- Civil defense does not offer the kind of offensive capability that might be inherent in a ground- or space-based laser ABM system.

- A U.S. civil defense effort would restore a balance rather than upset it, since the Soviets already have a large-scale civil defense effort.

- A U.S. civil defense effort would not violate any U.S.-Soviet treaty, unlike an ABM system.

- Civil defense, unlike ABM defense, would not promote any false sense of security, since people can understand that even with civil defense the United States could not escape a devastating level of destruction in a nuclear war.

- Civil defense would not set off an all-out arms race in offensive and defensive weapons and countermeasures.

- Civil defense would not be so destabilizing in a crisis, as an ABM defense would. Leaders in either the United States or the Soviet Union would probably be unlikely to come under the illusion that civil defense offered the possibility of a disarming attack against the adversary.

While civil defense may not appeal to the American desire for a permanent, high-technology solution to the nuclear dilemma, it is feasible using today's technology. ABM, on the other hand, seems to be a trap for the unwary, which, even if it could be made to work, would probably lead to disaster. It seems unwise to allow a desperate wish to be permanently free of the nuclear spectre to undertake a solution that is worse than the problem. It has happened before in the nuclear age that today's panacea becomes tomorrow's nightmare.

STUDY QUESTIONS

1. Are U.S. land-based ICBMs really vulnerable? How confident are you in that assessment?

2. How important is knowledge of Soviet missile accuracy in determining ICBM vulnerability? How well can Soviet missile accuracy be determined?

3. Does it matter if U.S. ICBMs are vulnerable?

4. How vulnerable are Soviet ICBMs? Should that be of concern to the United States?

5. In what ways is the U.S.-Soviet arms competition a "race"? What have been the separate phases of that race?

6. What are the advantages and disadvantages of massive overkill versus minimum deterrence?

7. Are there ways in which it is best for the United States not to try to match the Soviet Union in nuclear weaponry?

8. Which of the new U.S. nuclear weaponry being built or scheduled to be built are particularly destabilizing?

9. Why is the MX in some basing modes a more destabilizing weapon than in others? Which are the least objectionable basing modes?

10. What would be the probable effect of the United States abrogating the 1972 ABM Treaty and building an ABM defense of MX?

11. What are the difficulties in building a successful ABM to defend missile silos? To defend cities?

12. Why is an ABM that protects missiles much less destabilizing than one that protects people?

13. How vulnerable is the U.S. and Soviet missile submarine fleet?

14. Should we seek a treaty forbidding ABM research and development?

Five _____

LIMITED NUCLEAR WAR _____

HOW DID WE GET WHERE WE ARE?

In October 1981 President Ronald Reagan, in response to a reporter's question about the possibility of a nuclear war remaining limited, offered this observation: "It could be where you could have the exchange of tactical nuclear weapons in the field without it bringing either one of the big powers to pushing the button." [1] That apparently offhand comment by an American president caused a firestorm of protest and concern, especially in Western Europe, which is after all the "field" where the tactical nuclear weapons would likely be used.

Americans referring to limited nuclear war usually have in mind one that is limited to the European continent, the repository of roughly half of America's tactical nuclear weapons. Such a nuclear war is unlikely to be a limited one from the perspective of Europeans, who according to some studies could suffer levels of damage as great as those resulting from an all-out U.S.-Soviet nuclear exchange. The tactical and theatre nuclear weapons with which such a limited nuclear war would be fought have yields that, in some cases, are as great as or greater than strategic nuclear weapons, particularly in the case of Soviet tactical nuclear weapons.

Two other kinds of limited nuclear wars include the counterforce nuclear exchange discussed in the previous chapter and a nuclear war involving Third World countries which will be discussed in chapter 11. It is commonly believed, however, that if a limited nuclear war is possible, it most likely would happen in Europe where most of the world's tactical nuclear weapons are stored and where two vast armies of NATO and the Warsaw Pact tensely face each other along the "fault line" that divides Europe.

To better understand the extreme level of anxiety voiced among Europeans about President Reagan's remarks about a limited nuclear war, it is necessary to appreciate the delicate balance on which NATO strategy for the defense of Europe rests and how easily that balance can be upset, thereby pushing Europeans to one or the other of their opposite anxieties: being abandoned by America in a confrontation with the Soviets or being destroyed in a nuclear war between the superpowers in a conflict not of their making.

Soviet actions following World War II, including Stalin's repression of Eastern Europe, the takeover of Czechoslovakia, and the Berlin blockade, caused the nations of Western Europe to develop a profound distrust of the Soviet Union. In view of their relative military weakness compared to Russia, the Western European powers were eager to accept United States guarantees of protection in case of attack by the Soviet Union. This, in fact, was the primary purpose of the NATO alliance. The United States, as concrete evidence of its commitment to the defense of Europe, placed five divisions of troops on European soil as part of a joint NATO military command headed by an American. The strategy was to use the U.S. troops as a "tripwire" which, in the event of a Soviet invasion, would have resulted in a massive retaliation by U.S. nuclear forces against the Soviet Union.

During the height of the cold war in the early 1950s, events such as the Korean War and the Soviet suppression of the Hungarian revolt deepened U.S. concern about the need to contain communism and led the United States to reinforce the strength of NATO by rearming the Federal Republic of Germany (West Germany), a highly controversial move at the time among other Europeans. Lacking intercontinental bombers, the United States also stationed forward-based aircraft in Europe capable of nuclear strikes against the Soviet Union. Needless to say, the rearming of the Germans, whose aggression during World War II cost the Soviet Union very dearly, was also a matter of great concern to the Soviets and their East European allies and led to the continued buildup of Soviet and Warsaw Pact conventional military strength.

Once the Soviet Union, already a formidable power in conventional military strength, developed its own nuclear weapons and began to amass a large arsenal, West Europeans increasingly questioned the whole premise of the U.S. "nuclear umbrella" on which the defense of Western Europe was based. Would a U.S. president really risk New York in order to defend Hamburg or Paris, many Europeans wondered? These concerns became more pressing as the growth of the Soviet nuclear arsenal continued and as NATO countries proved unwilling to provide the money, people, and commitment necessary to counter growing Soviet conventional military strength. Because of these NATO concerns, in the early 1950s the United States proposed, and European governments accepted, the deployment of tactical nuclear weapons (TNWs) in Europe as a quick and inexpensive way of countering the perceived growing Soviet threat.

Aside from the political attractiveness to Europeans of a defense strategy that put the primary burden of defending Europe on a rich and powerful ally, another appeal of TNWs to many European governments was that TNWs formed a link between the U.S. conventional forces in Europe and the U.S. strategic nuclear deterrent. Thus, the possibility appeared to lessen that the United States, rather than risk its own destruction, might abandon Europe after losing a conventional war with the Soviet Union. Tactical nuclear weapons and the doctrine of a "flexible response" to Soviet aggression seemed at the time a good way to deter attack and to fight a war if necessary. However, the TNW solution to the problem of the defense of Western Europe also unfortunately seems to have allowed "official strategic thought in Western Europe to sleep comfortably during a quarter century under the U.S. nuclear umbrella," in the words of Marc Geneste.[2]

In recent years, the earlier doubts of West Europeans about the credibility of the U.S. nuclear umbrella have resurfaced with a vengeance. There are many reasons that numerous Europeans (and Americans) are now questioning the value of American nuclear guarantees to defend Europe. Despite the fact that the U.S. government has never wavered from its assurance that it would defend Europe with nuclear weapons if necessary, only 37 percent of U.S. citizens agreed with that course of action in a 1981 Gallup poll.[3] Furthermore, most people realize that brave statements made in peacetime in an effort to deter war may not be a good guide to what actions a country would actually take if war comes. If only a little over a third of U.S. citizens now favor using nuclear weapons to "save" Europe, it would seem to require a peculiar view of human nature to imagine that the United States would become more resolved to save Europe if the outbreak of war made the possibility of the destruction of the United States by Soviet nuclear weapons a real possibility.

It is more likely that if a war in Europe broke out, everyone would suddenly become very sober and greatly reluctant to take even that first step up the ladder of nuclear escalation. Alternatively, if tactical nuclear weapons were used and Europe were turned into a radioactive wasteland, it would seem that America would be especially eager to avoid the same fate and would very likely to come to terms with the Soviet Union. It seems unlikely that the United States would deliberately retaliate against the Soviet Union after the destruction of Western Europe, knowing that the United States would then also be destroyed. The probable reason that the nuclear umbrella can work at all in deterring Soviet aggression is that there is a distinct possibility that a conventional war could escalate to a nuclear war involving the superpowers, regardless of each side's intentions.

Americans are not the only ones to question the wisdom of a nuclear response to a conventional attack. In a 1980 poll, only 7 percent of French citizens favored using their own nuclear weapons to repel a hypothetical Soviet invasion of France.[4] (Sixty-three percent favored negotiating peace, and only 21 percent favored defending themselves using conventional weapons.) It is interesting to note, however, that while the French may be highly dubious about the utility of nuclear weapons in case of a conventional invasion, they clearly recognize the deterrent value of such weapons against nuclear attack. In another 1980 poll, 64 percent of those French citizens surveyed believed their country's nuclear arsenal to be indispensible to France's defense. Only 20 percent of those surveyed responded that nuclear arms were "not at all" indispensible.[5] Likewise in a poll of British citizens conducted in 1979, a similar margin (65 percent) agreed on the value of their nation's nuclear deterrent.[6] The views of citizens in those European nations not possessing their own independent nuclear arsenals are quite another matter and will be considered later.

HOW DO THE FORCES OF NATO AND THE WARSAW PACT COMPARE?

Why has the credibility of the American nuclear umbrella deteriorated so greatly? Aside from the fact that it may not have been very credible to begin with, the principal reason is the decline in military power of NATO relative to the Warsaw Pact, and more specifically the decline in U.S. military power relative to that of the Soviet Union. An equally important (some would say more important) factor in undermining credibility of the U.S. nuclear umbrella has been the perception of such a relative decline in NATO military strength.

For example, in a 1980 poll, 59 percent of British citizens considered the Warsaw Pact forces ahead in conventional strength and 50 percent believed the Pact to lead in nuclear strength.[7] Much smaller percentages of Britains surveyed believed NATO forces to lead in conventional and nuclear strength (13 percent and 15 percent respectively). A 1979 poll of Dutch citizens yielded similar results: 44 percent of those surveyed believed the Warsaw Pact nations to be more strongly armed, while only 13 percent believed NATO to be more strongly armed.[8]

A clear trend may be seen when such polls are examined over a long period of time, indicating a growing belief that the military balance is shifting against NATO. The results from polls of West Germans on the question of which side they consider to be the stronger is very instructive in this regard (see table 5.1).

From 1954 to 1976 it may be seen that a gradual shift took place in German public opinion on the relative strength of the East and the West. The large jump in the 1980 percentage who believe the West to be stronger is only a result of the fact that the "Both Equal" category was not included in the 1980 poll. It may be noted that the percentages of Germans answering "both equal" was quite sizable in prior years. From such polls it may be inferred that, even though there has been a decline in the perceived strength of the West, the perceived difference in strength is not enormous.

To what extent do perceptions of a military balance shifting against NATO forces mirror reality? For a variety of reasons, comparisons of NATO and Warsaw Pact military strength are subject to greater uncertainties than similar comparisons of U.S and Soviet strategic nuclear strength. In the case of the strategic arsenals, while there may be uncertainties on the yield and accuracy of each side's ICBM warheads, there is no uncertainty over the number of fixed ICBM silos or ballistic-missile submarines. The large uncertainties in the case of NATO and Warsaw Pact forces can best be illustrated by comparing each side's assessment of the military balance using a variety of static indicators (see table 5.2). The Soviet figures in every category listed, except bombers, show both sides to have

Table 5.1. West German Views of the Comparative Strength of East and West (percentage)

Year of Poll	West Stronger	East Stronger	Both Equal
1954	40	23	33
1960	32	22	38
1964	54	7	29
1968	34	21	35
1974	23	24	43
1976	16	35	47
1980	42	53	—

Source: C. deBoer, "The Polls: Our Commitment to World War III," Public Opinion Quarterly 45 (1981): pp. 126–34.

Table 5.2 Two Views of the NATO–Warsaw Pact Military Balance Using Selected Static Indicators

		Soviet Count	NATO Count
Tanks in Europe	NATO	24,000	13,000
	Pact	25,000	42,500
Soldiers in Europe (millions)	NATO	2.1	2.6
	Pact	1.7	4.0
Medium-range bombers	NATO	700	377
	Pact	410	880
Chemical-munitions stockpiles (tons)	NATO	?	42,000
	Pact	?	350,000
Intermediate-range nuclear launchers	NATO	986	800
	Pact	975	3,100

Sources: U.S.S.R. Ministry of Defense, Whence the Threat to Peace? (Moscow, 1982), pp. 65–70; Anthony Cordesman, NATO's Estimate of the Balance, Armed Forces Journal, August 1982, p. 54.

comparable strength, both in conventional and intermediate-range (theatre) nuclear forces. In fact, the Soviets, in an overall assessment of the military balance between NATO and Warsaw Pact forces, state that parity exists in both conventional and intermediate-range nuclear forces.[9]

The official NATO view is quite different, based on a very different set of figures.[10] According to NATO, the Soviets have sizable advantages in nearly all measures of conventional military strength and intermediate-range nuclear strength. In the category of chemical-warfare capability, no comparison can be made since, while NATO figures show a vast disparity in favor of the Warsaw Pact in the size of the stockpiles of nerve gas and other chemical agents, the

Soviets have made no direct public reference to their possession of such weapons since 1938. Table 5.2 does not include every static indicator used in making such comparisons since our main purpose here has been only to illustrate the vast difference in the two side's assessments in selected categories.

To better understand how it is possible for NATO and Soviet figures to differ so widely, it is instructive to compare one particular category in detail, namely the intermediate-range nuclear forces. Unlike short-range tactical nuclear weapons intended for battlefield use, the intermediate-range weapons are capable of offensive action against enemy territory. Intermediate-range nuclear weapons based in Western Europe are capable of reaching the Soviet Union and vice versa. It may be seen in table 5.3 that for a particular category of missile or aircraft, say the number of Soviet SS-20s, both sides' numbers do not greatly differ. Much larger differences, however, result from which particular weapon systems each side chooses to include in the comparison.

For example, the Soviets count the nuclear weapons in the independent British and French arsenals, while NATO does not since these arsenals are not under NATO control. In fact, France has withdrawn all its military forces from NATO control. While the Soviets may believe they have a fairly good rationale for including French and British nuclear weapons, a good case can also be made for not counting them. Despite their governments' assurances to the contrary, it is very possible that the British and French would reserve their nuclear weapons only for the defense of their own countries (and as we have seen, French public opinion overwhelmingly does not even favor that use!). Thus, while the Soviets are justified in worrying about all nuclear weapons pointing in their direction (including Chinese missiles), it is highly questionable whether the British and French would use their nuclear arsenals to repel a Soviet attack on, say, Germany.

The Soviet claim of parity in intermediate-range nuclear weapons in 1983 mirrors a similar claim by Leonid Brezhnev in 1979, even though at that time the Soviet SS-20 force was only one-third as large as in 1983. Evidently, the Soviets in their public assessments of the military balance do not wish ever to be seen as either weaker or stronger than the West.

The Soviet count of intermediate-range nuclear forces in table 5.3 also includes all U.S. tactical aircraft (A-6s and A-7s), based on all U.S. aircraft carriers available to Europe, as well as all NATO short-range land-based tactical aircraft. The Soviets, however, in their

Table 5.3 Two Views of the NATO–Warsaw Pact Balance of Intermediate-Range Nuclear Forces

NATO Intermediate-Range Nuclear Forces

	Soviet Count		NATO Count	
Missiles	French IRBM	18		
	French SLBM	80	None	
	U.K. Polaris	64		
Bombers	F-111	172	F-111	164
	FB-111	65	FB-111	63
	F-4	246	F-4	265
	A-6 and A-7	240	A-6 and A-768	—
	French Mirage	46		
	U.K. Vulcan	55		
TOTAL		986		560

Warsaw Pact Intermediate-Range Nuclear Forces

	Soviet Count		NATO Count	
Missiles	SS-20	243	SS-20	250[a]
	SS-4 + 5	253	SS-4 + 5	350
	SS-N-5	18	SS-N-5	30
			SS-12/22	100
Bombers	Backfire Tu-26		Backfire Tu-26	
	Blinder Tu-16		Blinder Tu-16	
	Badger Tu-22		Badger Tu-22	
		461	Su-17	395
			Su-24	
			Mig-27	2,700
TOTAL		975		3,825

Source: Four Approaches to an INF Agreement, Jane Sharp, *Arms Control Today* 12 (March 1982) p. 2.
[a] Increased to about 378 by March 1984.

assessment of the balance, have absentmindedly neglected to count their own 2,700 tactical aircraft capable of delivering nuclear weapons on Western Europe. It should be clear from this analysis that there is some tendency for each side to understate its own strength and overstate that of the other.

WHAT INTANGIBLES ARE THERE IN ASSESSING THE MILITARY BALANCE?

There are other factors besides such static indicators in table 5.2 that could greatly affect the military balance in an actual conflict.

One such intangible factor concerns the reliability of allies, which on the basis of conventional wisdom favors the West. Fully 45 percent of Warsaw Pact standing ground forces in Europe are East European, and the Soviet Union cannot be sure whether in wartime the Poles and Czechs will fight with them or against them. On the other hand, it is quite possible that if a war actually started, both alliances would rapidly crumble as individual countries tried to keep outside their borders the enormous levels of devastation inherent in either nuclear or all-out conventional war. To the extent that the countries of NATO are more autonomous than those of the Warsaw Pact, such a disintegration might even be a greater probability in the case of NATO. The autonomy of NATO countries is, in part, also responsible for the lack of standardization in their armies' weaponry and communications gear. This serious disadvantage would prevent a sharing of supplies and spare parts and would greatly undercut wartime flexibility.

The quality of weaponry is another important factor in assessing the military balance. Although the best NATO weapons remain superior to the best Warsaw Pact weapons, far more Pact forces are equipped with the most advanced weapons. In fact, the only NATO forces believed to have clearly better equipment that the Pact forces they face is the limited number of NATO M-day divisions in West Germany. Moreover, there are limits to tradeoffs between quality and quantity in weaponry. According to Lanchester in his famous treatise on military combat, there is a square-law relationship between quality and quantity. Thus, NATO tanks, if outnumbered three to one, would need to be nine times more effective to offset that advantage. There is, of course, no need for NATO to try to match Pact forces in every weapons category. For example, as long as NATO has a sufficient arsenal of antitank weapons, (about half the number possessed by Pact armies), this can somewhat offset the large Warsaw Pact advantage in tanks.

One major factor in assessing the NATO-Pact military balance is the People's Republic of China. China is usually cited as a factor of strategic importance to the West since, as a result of Soviet-Chinese hostility, Moscow feels it necessary to station fifty Soviet divisions (a half million men) on the Chinese border. However, a sudden Soviet-Chinese rapprochement, while perhaps not likely, is not particularly unlikely either at some future time. Moreover, in a war in Europe the Soviets might feel no hesitation in transferring their fifty divisions on the Chinese border to the European front, threatening the Chinese with massive nuclear retaliation if one Chinese soldier stepped across the Soviet border. Thus, even without any Sino-Soviet rapprochement, the Soviets may not be hindered from transferring large numbers of their troops to the European theatre at the outbreak of a war. Some Western experts on Soviet studies point out that the Soviets are probably not as fearful of the Chinese as they would have the West believe and that they view the Chinese only as a potential power to be reckoned with in the future.[11]

Another intangible affecting the NATO-Pact military balance is that NATO is preparing for a defensive action, and, according to conventional military theory, less forces are needed for a defensive action than for an offensive one. On the other hand, this judgment greatly depends on the particular weaponry and tactics used. A substantial fraction of both NATO and Warsaw Pact conventional forces achieve battle readiness only after several days of preparation. Should NATO forces fail to detect or respond to Pact mobilization measures, an early Pact force advantage could lead to a decisive breakthrough against NATO.

It is difficult to find completely objective assessments of the military balance between NATO and the Warsaw Pact, since each side has reason to distort the facts. Government and military leaders in the Western democracies often feel it necessary to portray an exaggerated view of the "Russian menace" in order to generate public support for increased defense expenditures. The Soviet Union has no similar need domestically since there is no Soviet public debate about their defense expenditures. However, the Soviets have a great stake in trying to influence the public debate in Western countries and if possible deflect Western attempts to bolster their own defenses. Although there may not be much of a pro-Soviet constituency in the West, the Soviets are able to portray those in the West who are defense minded as being alarmist hawks who threaten the cause of peace by pursuing an endless and useless arms race. Those in the West who exaggerate Soviet military strength and unnecessarily deprecate NATO strength can only give credibility to such Soviet claims, and therefore they undermine the very cause they espouse. Moreover, an exaggerated view of Soviet military strength could conceivably cause hysterical reactions either in the direction of appeasement and a collapse of morale or, alternatively, in the direction of an attempt to achieve clear-cut military superiority, regardless of how provocative that may be to the Soviet Union.

It seems probable that an objective assessment of the military balance is somewhere between the Soviet claim of parity and the official NATO claim of a sizable imbalance in favor of the Pact. It must be remembered, however, that in the highly unstable situation involving the outbreak of hostilities, it might not take a very large imbalance to result in a total collapse of morale as countries desperately try to avoid their own devastation. The view that the actual military balance is between the NATO and Soviet assessments, i.e. marginally, but not decisively, in favor of the Warsaw Pact, would seem to be in reasonable agreement then with Western public opinion as measured by polls. The fact that these polls also show a gradual loss over time in perceived military power of NATO relative to the Pact is also probably an accurate reflection of the shift that has in fact occurred.

At the end of World War II the United States was the preeminent power in the world: its land had not been invaded, its losses were proportionately small compared to many other countries, it produced a GNP equal to half that of the entire world, and it had a monopoly on the atomic bomb. Since that time, U.S. economic and military power relative to the rest of the world has significantly declined. In part, this relative decline has been due to the post-World War II recovery of the devastated countries of Europe and Asia and in part to the continued growth of Soviet military power relative to that of the United States. While America could at one time be considered the protector of its allies, in today's world America needs them as badly as they need it.

Although the United States may not now be clearly in second place to the Soviet Union militarily, there are enough questions about American power, her commitment, and her leaders' political acumen to fully justify European concerns over American nuclear guarantees. In fact, it was precisely such concerns that led the British and French many years ago to build their own independent nuclear arsenals (much to the U.S. chagrin at the time), in case the day should ever come when America lost either the will or the ability to defend Europe at the risk of its own destruction. As we have previously noted, the U.S. nuclear umbrella may have been a gigantic bluff all along, and the British and French simply realized that some day someone might recognize that fact.

HOW SERIOUS IS THE SOVIET-THEATRE NUCLEAR THREAT?

The nervousness among NATO governments about U.S. nuclear guarantees has been accentuated in recent years as the spectre of

Soviet superiority in the area of intermediate-range nuclear weapons began to loom on the horizon. The one development that particularly alarmed West European leaders was the Soviet deployment of SS-20 missiles begun in 1977. These missiles replaced, on a one-for-one basis, the older SS-4s and SS-5s which were also capable of striking targets deep in Western Europe. Why then the concern? Two important features distinguish the SS-20s from the older missiles they replaced: They are MIRVed and hence carry three times as many warheads, and much more importantly, they are extremely accurate, supposedly threatening Western Europe for the first time with a sudden disarming first strike against U.S. nuclear forces based in Western Europe. The fact that the SS-20s are solid fueled and can be readied for firing very quickly, in contrast to the liquid fueled SS-4s and SS-5s, accentuates that concern.

After a counterforce strike by the Soviet Union against U.S.-based nuclear forces, America would almost certainly retaliate. But, would the United States really respond to a disarming Soviet first-strike against U.S. missiles based in Europe, knowing that the United States might be annihilated in return? What purpose would that retaliation serve? The existence of the Soviet SS-20s raised such disturbing questions as these and, therefore, further undermined the American nuclear umbrella.

In order to counter the threat posed by the Soviet SS-20 deployment, and also the deployment of large number of Soviet backfire bombers, the NATO governments agreed in 1979 to upgrade NATO intermediate-range nuclear forces under U.S. control. It was at that time agreed to deploy 108 Pershing II missiles and 464 cruise missiles starting by the end of 1983. Simultaneously, the NATO governments agreed to try to seek an agreement with the Soviet Union to dismantle its SS-20s in exchange for the nondeployment of the Pershing II and cruise missiles—the so-called zero option.

The NATO decision to follow a two-track approach was virtually a political necessity for many West European governments whose liberal wings made their initial support for the new U.S. missiles contingent on talks to obviate the need for their deployment by dismantling the Soviet SS-20s. The NATO military justification for the planned deployment of Pershing II and cruise missiles was threefold. Firstly, the deployment posed a threat of attack against Soviet military targets similar to the threat posed by the SS-20s against NATO military targets. Secondly, it would add 572 new nuclear targets on European soil, greatly complicating the task of a Soviet disarming first strike against NATO military targets and thereby deterring one. Thirdly, and perhaps most important, it would add what had been a missing link to the chain of nuclear escalation between tactical nuclear weapons intended to be used for defensive purposes on West European soil and the American strategic arsenal that many West Europeans feared might not be used except for a direct attack on the U.S. itself. The strengthening of the link between tactical and strategic nuclear weapons made nuclear escalation more likely, and therefore it presumably made U.S. guarantees more plausible.

Does the installation of U.S. intermediate range missiles in Europe under U.S. control really strengthen these links or not? Soviet spokesmen, in their effort to prevent deployment of the new U.S. missiles, presented an interesting argument that the new missiles do not really strengthen the U.S. nuclear guarantee:

> Let us assume . . . that the American nuclear guarantees are now undependable in the sense that America will not want to sacrifice Chicago for Hamburg. Would they be more dependable in the presence of Euromissiles? In that case, too, the American sense of self-preservation may turn out to be just as strong.[12]

The Soviets, in other words, regard the U.S. commitment to defend Europe with nuclear weapons, at the risk of its own destruction, as quite possibly a bluff, and one that is not made any more believable by the stationing of U.S. intermediate-range missiles in Europe. According to this Soviet argument, the United States would be just as reluctant to use those so-called Euromissiles as they would be to use the U.S.-based strategic arsenal against the Soviet Union, since it knows the result would be Soviet retaliation against American cities. Of course, that Soviet threat might also be a bluff—but one that the United States, considering the risks, might not with to call.

The 1979 NATO decision to deploy intermediate-range U.S. missiles if the Soviets refused to dismantle their SS-20s was a political decision at least as much as a military one. As already noted, the move was intended, in part, to reassure its nervous European allies that American would stand by them by putting its own survival at risk. Since the 1979 NATO decision, however, the main focus of European anxiety has shifted from fear of abandonment by the United States to fear of annihilation in a U.S.-Soviet nuclear war fought to "save" Europe. The massive antinuclear public demonstrations in Europe are a clear indication of this fear. It is in this context that one must understand European sensitivities over an American president's casual reference to limited nuclear wars. On the other hand, it would be naïve to assume that all the uproar in Western European countries has had a completely spontaneous origin. Given the distinctly anti-American tone of some of the protests and their focus on U.S. missiles rather than on Soviet missiles, it is certain that some of the protests in Europe were actively promoted and stimulated by the Soviet Union in an attempt to forestall the U.S. missile deployment.

It seems likely that the Soviet Union had primarily a political rather than a military motivation for deploying the SS-20 missiles. It is well known that a major political objective of the Soviet Union is to separate the United States from its NATO allies. From the Soviet vantage point virtually any Western reaction to the original placement of SS-20 missiles would seem to rebound to the Soviet advantage.

- NATO countries might have done nothing. Inaction in the face of intimidation would have been seen by many as a sign of weakness and might permit further probes of NATO's resolve.

- A European request for U.S. missiles to counter the SS-20s might have been turned down (as it nearly was orginally). President Carter acceded reluctantly to then Chancellor Schmidt's 1979 request for U.S. missiles. The missiles were Carter's way of obtaining Schmidt's support for the SALT II Treaty and making amends for some earlier U.S. bungles. Had Carter turned down Schmidt's request, Germany might well have felt isolated and sought a greater rapprochement with the Soviet Union.

- After agreeing to accept U.S. missiles, some NATO countries might have developed second thoughts because of a serious degree of domestic unrest that could have threatened the cohesion of the alliance.

- The degree of political unrest within one or more NATO countries might have been sufficient to bring to power left-wing governments that would seek to either leave the alliance or remove all U.S. nuclear weapons from its territory.

- There might have been sufficient domestic unrest to prevent any agreed-upon NATO deployment of U.S. missiles. In that case NATO would have demonstrated its impotence to carry out an important collective decision.

- The United States might have become increasingly isolationist as a result of being rebuffed on the missile deployment by its NATO allies or from witnessing numerous anti-U.S. peace demonstrations in Europe. In the end, there might be increased U.S. domestic support to bring the troops home from Western Europe.

- Even if the political strains in the NATO alliance were not sufficient to prevent the U.S. deployment of missiles in Europe, there would still be several advantages to the Soviet Union. Firstly, the NATO countries would have paid a very high price in terms of political upheaval and domestic unrest. Secondly, the Soviet Union could, if it wished, either offer to eliminate its SS-20s in return for the U.S. missiles' removal or, alternatively, use the U.S. missiles as an excuse to take some other action it otherwise might have been deterred from taking. The Soviet placement of missiles in Latin America, for example, would pose precisely the same threat to the United States that U.S. missiles stationed in Europe pose to the Soviet Union. Unlike the case of the 1962 Cuban missile crisis where the Soviets were believed to be secretly trying to change the military balance, they might, in this case, be seen as merely responding to an American challenge.

Given the forgoing analysis, which one can almost imagine being carefully thought out in advance by the Soviet leadership, it seems quite likely that the SS-20s were deployed largely for political reasons. Had the Soviet Union sought a specific military capability against Western Europe, it could have merely designated a small fraction of its ICBM force for use against European targets, rather than build intermediate-range missiles only capable of hitting these targets. In fact, it is believed that prior to deploying its SS-20s, the USSR did aim a portion of its ICBMs at Western Europe. Even now the Soviet Union, if it wished, could eliminate all intermediate-range weapons simply by adding a third stage to the rockets, thereby converting them into ICBMs capable of reaching targets anywhere in the world.

The fact that American missiles placed in Europe represent a new military threat may be less of a source of Soviet consternation than the fact that events subsequent to the SS-20 deployment did not follow any of the expected scenarios. The Soviet Union's rage and frustration over its inability to prevent the U.S. missile deployments may be akin to that of the professional chess player whose brilliant plan is upset by a lucky amateur.

It is not clear whether the deployment of U.S. Pershing and cruise missiles makes war more or less likely. It can be argued, for example, that they increase the risk of nuclear war by causing the Soviets to put a "hair trigger" on their arsenal. Alternatively, the missiles could decrease the risk of war, either by making it unfeasible for the Soviets to launch a disarming first strike or by becoming more willing to give up their own SS-20 missiles as part of a deal. Likewise, it is not clear whether deploying the U.S. missiles acts to keep a nuclear war limited or to insure its escalation. For example, adding an intermediate link between tactical and strategic nuclear weapons would seem to make escalation of a conventional war more likely. On the other hand, the Soviet Union, knowing that the United States has credible options to match each level of escalation, might be more reluctant to initiate the conflict.

In the complex nuclear age, the effects of certain actions may not be known even long afterwards. For example, did the forced withdrawal of Soviet missiles from Cuba under U.S. pressure in 1962 remove a threat to the United States and, therefore, reduce the risk of nuclear war in the future? Or, did the increased Soviet resolve to engage in a massive nuclear buildup, in part as a result of that case of American nuclear blackmail, fuel the arms race and increase the risk of nuclear war? The business of trying to figure out the other side's psychology has probably gotten so convoluted that it is no longer possible to know with any confidence which is the prudent course of action and which the risky one in a given circumstance. That is particularly true in regard to the European deployment of U.S. Pershing II and cruise missiles. The Soviets have argued that such missiles pose a qualitatively new threat against the Soviet Union: European-based missiles capable of destroying hard targets in the Soviet Union. However, the number of missiles eventually scheduled for deployment and their limited range should not allow them to pose any disarming first-strike threat. Moreover, it is only the Pershing IIs, not the much slower cruise missiles, that pose any real threat in that regard. The range of the Pershing II missiles is short enough that fully 90 percent of Soviet strategic targets, as well as the vital command and communication links in Moscow, could not be targeted, although Soviet planners dispute this contention. In addition, while the 108 Pershing II missiles could strike at most 4 percent of Soviet strategic targets, the approximately one thousand SS-20 warheads could strike the bulk of NATO strategic targets. In both range of missiles, and number and size of warheads, the Soviet SS-20s pose a much more serious counterforce threat against NATO nuclear targets than the Pershing II and cruise missiles pose against the U.S.S.R. However, the relative military capabilities of the SS-20s and the Euromissiles are almost beside the point since both were probably deployed primarily for their political impact. A counterforce threat existed before these missiles were deployed, and they only add to it in a marginal way.

Nevertheless, those old enough to remember the 1962 Cuban missile crisis can easily recall the sense of danger when the Soviets placed their offensive missiles in Cuba and the extremely serious American reaction that this act provoked. The emplacement of Pershing II and cruise missiles in Western Europe is claimed by the Soviets to pose a new direct threat to their security, which they have promised to counter in some appropriate manner by a reciprocal threat to U.S. security. Whatever action the U.S.S.R. undertakes in response, the possibility exists of a confrontation arising out of a series of moves and countermoves, in which each side fails to appreciate the magnitude of a threat perceived by the other.

COULD A NUCLEAR WAR STAY LIMITED?

The question of whether a nuclear war could stay limited has been discussed extensively. By a limited nuclear war we mean one limited either by geography to specific countries, limited by types of weapons employed, e.g., tactical nuclear weapons only, or one limited according to targets, e.g., no strikes against cities. In his 1957 book *Nuclear Weapons and Foreign Policy,* Henry Kissinger gave this succinct argument for the plausibility of a limited nuclear war:

> The argument that neither side will accept a defeat, however limited, without utilizing every weapon in its arsenal is contradicted both by psychology and by experience. There would seem to be no sense in seeking to escape a limited defeat through bringing on the cataclysm of an all-out war, particularly if an all-out war threatens a calamity for transcending the penalties of losing a limited war.[13]

The logic of that argument seems compelling, even though Kissinger himself, in a 1960 reappraisal, indicated he was less sure that a nuclear war could stay limited.[14] It is, of course, quite possible that a nuclear war that began as limited could escalate out of control, especially given that weapons systems on each side call for faster and faster reaction times. However, it is also possible that each side's instinct for self-preservation would prevent escalation to the ultimate holocaust—a thought of little consolation to the people of Europe who might be annihilated before the United States and the Soviet Union had sufficient fear struck in their hearts for them to desist.

Quite apart from whether a limited nuclear war is possible, there are two opposing views on whether it is even desirable to make efforts that reduce the probability of escalation. There are many who oppose any such efforts that are seen as making nuclear war more "practical," and therefore more likely. These efforts might include such things as developing low-yield "clean" bombs or trying to establish a set of rules that the United States and the Soviet Union might agree to in advance of any conflict—as Henry Kissinger actually suggested at one time.[15] Those against all such attempts at trying to keep nuclear war limited think that such attempts will delude people into believing nuclear wars can in fact be kept limited, encourage the development of new war-fighting weapons and strategies, and thereby bring about nuclear catastrophe.

The opposing view, that it is desirable to make advance efforts to control the level of escalation, is based on the reasoning that if the United States adopts a defense posture that relies solely on massive retaliation against the Soviet Union, such a posture would not be a believable response to a Soviet conventional invasion of Western Europe, and hence it would not deter Soviet conventional aggression. The threat to use tactical nuclear weapons is in this view much more believable than massive retaliation and, therefore, a better deterrent against a conventional attack.

Finally, it may be argued that an American policy that agrees (or pretends to agree) to commit suicide through the only option of massive retaliation against the Soviets to "save" Europe is an immoral policy: firstly, because it is clearly a lie, since no American president would be likely to carry it out; and secondly, because no nation should be asked to commit suicide to save another or to avenge it after it has been annihilated. It is only fair that if Europe is unwilling to make the sacrifices needed to build a sufficiently strong conventional force, then Europe should continue to run the risk that it will become the battlefield for a limited nuclear war.

The main way in which attempts have been made to control the level of escalation in a nuclear war is through the creation of "firebreaks" between different levels of escalation. The idea is that if there is a big enough difference between the consequences of conventional weapons, tactical nuclear weapons, and strategic nuclear weapons, the both sides will hesitate before climbing to the next rung of the escalation ladder. This goal of creating firebreaks is precisely the opposite of that of many of America's West European allies who would prefer that a more credible deterrent be created by making it appear that uncontrolled escalation is more likely. With clearly defined firebreaks, many Europeans fear the United States will abandon Europe when the risk (to the United States) becomes too high. As long as Europe is going to be devastated anyway at the lowest level of the nuclear escalation ladder, many Europeans would prefer to tie the fate of America to that of Europe.

Some observers believe that the only real firebreak is between conventional weapons and nuclear weapons, and that a nuclear weapon is a nuclear weapon, no matter how "clean" or how small. It must be realized, however, that it is now technologically possible to make miniaturized nuclear bombs smaller than the largest conventional bombs (e.g. "Tallboy"), used in World War II. Therefore, there is now a continuum of bomb yields running all the way from conventional bombs to the largest nuclear bombs; thus the firebreak between conventional and nuclear weapons is now primarily of a psychological nature. Nevertheless, that psychological barrier could be a very significant one, since once it is crossed, a continuous chain connects mininukes capable of destroying a few tanks to twenty-megaton city-killers.

Obviously, the possibility of a nuclear war with the Soviet Union staying limited depends crucially on Soviet military strategies and doctrines. The Soviets have consistently maintained that there is no such thing as limited nuclear war. Nothing in Soviet military doctrine suggests that having once invaded Western Europe with conventional forces, the Soviets would abandon the invasion after NATO used tactical nuclear weapons on a limited basis as a show of strength. Quite the contrary, Soviet military doctrine calls for massive retaliation with nuclear weapons against all military forces with their own nuclear weapons. Moreover, Soviet tactical nuclear weapons have megaton yields, in contrast to the U.S. tactical nuclear weapons, the majority of which have yields under ten kilotons.[16] While the relatively small U.S. tactical nuclear weapons were designed to reduce collateral civilian casualties, the Soviets apparently feel no need to design small, clean bombs intended for use on enemy territory. Clearly, the Soviet Union, both through its doctrine and choice of weapons, fully intends to make any limited nuclear war fought in Europe a very messy affair. Indeed, why should the Soviets agree in advance to fight a war according to NATO rules? Why should the Soviets agree to a plan that would, in effect, permit NATO forces to use clean surgical nuclear strikes that would not cause serious civilian casualties to West Europeans but that would hold back superior conventional Pact forces.

On the other hand one should not conclude that the repeated Soviet assertion that there is no such thing as a limited nuclear war, means that they intend to escalate any nuclear war into all-out war between the United States and the Soviet Union. The Soviets would almost certainly wish to avoid that ultimate calamity.

How might a limited nuclear war start? Escalation from a conventional conflict is usually thought to be the most likely possibility. Another possibility, considered less likely but certainly not to be dismissed, would be a Soviet surprise first strike intended to disarm NATO's nuclear forces. The Soviets might conclude that they could destroy a very substantial fraction of NATO's nuclear (and conventional) retaliatory capacity in one surprise blow. As the Soviets demonstrated in their 1968 invasion of Czechoslovakia, final preparations for an attack might be concealed from NATO, even in a period of growing international tensions.

It is generally conceded that preparations for the invasion of Czechoslovakia were not detected by Western intelligence, in part because that Soviet move was so unexpected. A Soviet surprise missile attack certainly seems much less expected—making it that much more likely that an ambiguous intelligence warning of such an attack would be interpreted in a less ominous light. The Soviets might well choose to forgo a conventional-force mobilization prior to the missile attack in order to further insure the element of surprise.

The importance of surprise is clear in much Soviet military writing.[17] Because nuclear weapons can achieve strategic results at the outset of a war, the Soviet military understands the need to prevent NATO from striking first by administering the first telling blow themselves.[18] Underlying the desire for a surprise first strike would be the need to destroy NATO nuclear forces before they could be used in a coordinated retaliatory attack. The Soviets have estimated that over 70 percent of NATO targets would be "lost" if NATO were forewarned of the attack and had time to go on alert and disperse its forces.

In launching a surprise counterforce attack, the Soviets would very likely spare European cities, in effect holding them hostage to attack if NATO attempts to retaliate. There might well be a sudden collapse of will to resist following the massive military setback that a successful first strike would entail. The United States in particular, not harmed directly in the attack, might conclude that giving up Western Europe would be far preferable to risking all-out war with the Soviets and having the United States destroyed—a conclusion that the Soviets would certainly emphasize by providing a variety of rationalizations for U.S. inaction. Moreover, realizing these things, European leaders would probably see resistance as serving no purpose, and they might simply surrender.

Is this scenario of a Soviet surprise attack on NATO nuclear and conventional forces improbable? History is filled with improbable surprises. To be effective, a surprise attack, by definition, must come when it is not expected. The existence of nuclear weapons, particularly counterforce weapons, does not negate the military advantages of a surprise attack, rather it tremendously accentuates the advantages by threatening a level of damage at one blow that may completely eliminate the will or ability to resist.

However, it must also be remembered that the Soviets have shown themselves to be cautious in their military undertakings in the past. They are not likely to risk the motherland in one gigantic gamble unless they can be quite certain of the outcome. It is not likely they would conclude that the correlation of forces is yet sufficiently in their favor to seriously consider a counterforce attack on Western Europe. However, if the military balance ever should tip decisively in the Soviet Union's favor, it seems most unlikely that they would not press their advantage to achieve their political goals.

WHY ARE THERE DIFFERENT PERCEPTIONS OF THE "SOVIET THREAT"?

Many Western observers feel that the most likely danger of a nuclear and conventional military balance favoring the Warsaw Pact is not an actual attack, but instead the gradual undermining of NATO and the "Finlandization" of Europe. The government of Finland, while not in any way repressive, has felt it necessary to carefully adjust its foreign policies so as not to give offense to its powerful neighbor.

It is possible for Finlandization to occur so gradually that even without thinking about it, West European governments begin to bend their decisions to please, or at least not to offend, the Soviet Union. There is, of course, considerable disagreement over how far the Finlandization process has already gone. There are, for example, a number of illustrations in recent years that might point to the process as already at work, although we shall see that there are also very plausible alternative explanations in each case.

- West European governments were not eager to follow the U.S. lead in taking a hard line in reaction to the Soviet invasion of Afghanistan.

- West European governments, in agreeing to finance the gas pipeline to the Soviet Union, may be giving the Soviets the ability to threaten turning off the tap in the future. That ability would certainly make Europeans even less likely to take action the Soviets might find offensive, and it indicates their relative unconcern about having to make accommodations with the Soviet Union.

- West European governments experienced great domestic political pressures to change the 1979 NATO decision on deployment of U.S. Pershing II and cruise missiles.

There are, of course, very different interpretations of each of the three instances just discussed. It can be argued that they are not examples of Findlandization at all, but rather a combination of genuine differences of opinion between sovereign allies over the best course of action and Washington's ineptness in dealing with its allies. The Soviet invasion of Afghanistan, for example, was not seen by many Europeans in terms quite as stark as those of the United States, given that Afghanistan had had a Soviet puppet regime for some prior years. Moreover, many European governments resented the lack of consultation on the U.S. Olympic boycott decision and the U.S. expectation that its allies would simply follow the U.S. lead.

The decision to finance a gas pipeline to the Soviet was seen by many Europeans on a par with the U.S. decision to resume grain sales to the Soviet Union while Soviet troops remained in Afghanistan. On what basis could the United States justify its own action on grain sales, while at the same time trying to dictate a reversal of the European-gas-pipeline decision to which Europeans had firmly committed themselves? Moreover, how could the United States blame Europeans for trying to provide for their own energy future, when it was to no small extent an energy-profligate United States, unable to take serious steps to solve its own energy problem, that exacerbated the energy problem for the rest of the world?

Many Europeans would probably put the third alleged example of Finlandization in a different light as well. How can the American government blame some Europeans for having second thoughts about the wisdom of deploying U.S. missiles to counter Soviet SS-20s, when the U.S. government created needless anxiety among Europeans with its loose talk about the possibility of a limited nuclear war and with overly bellicose presidential statements and actions? Moreover, Europeans would also note that many Americans themselves are unsure about the need for a new generation of counterforce weapons.

Some sophisticated Europeans realize that the Soviet Union, through political manipulation, is doing all it can to break the NATO alliance. Due to American ineptness, the Soviets are often quite successful at putting the United States into the position of a disruptive power that is threatening both European interests and world peace. This American-government ineptness is in large measure due to a U.S. political system in which each administration must begin anew and has to learn "on the job." Moreover, the cyclical swings in American public opinion between excessive fear of the Soviet Union and unconcern about the need for a strong defense often cause America's European allies to oscillate between their twin fears of obliteration in a limited war among the superpowers and abandonment by America in a moment of crisis. As Henry Kissinger has observed, it remains to be seen whether we are doomed to oscillate erratically between excessive conciliation and excessive bellicosity.

These oscillations that periodically occur in U.S. and Western public opinion often are triggered by particular events. Two such events would include the 1979 Soviet invasion of Afghanistan and the 1983 Soviet downing of a Korean airliner, both of which had a significant effect on shaping Western attitudes toward the Soviet Union and on the proper level of defense spending. The disproportionate importance of such events is probably due both to the public's short-term perspective and its need to continue to need new evidence on which to form its opinion of the Soviet Union. The Soviet Union, in its turn, often seems surprised by Western reactions to such events. In the case of Afghanistan, it appears that the U.S.S.R. viewed its action as just another defensive move that a superpower might be expected to undertake in its own backyard, and certainly not something that should cause great alarm in the West. The Western reaction to the 1983 downing of a Korean airliner was, in Soviet eyes, also quite unexpected. In the Soviet view, the extent of the U.S. effort to lead in condemning the U.S.S.R. for this action and its use in squelching domestic opposition to the U.S. defense buildup was proof that the entire event was orchestrated by the United States to manipulate world public opinion against Russia. To most Westerners that Soviet interpretation, if genuinely believed, would indicate extreme paranoia.

Those wishing to claim that Soviet behavior does not show any aggressive intent often point to Russia's insecurity and paranoia—the result of no less than fourteen separate invasions since 1800. The shock of World War II, in particular, which Russia scraped through by the barest of margins, has left an indelible imprint on the Russian psyche. After World War II, the encirclement of the U.S.S.R. by unfriendly powers wishing to contain communism fed Soviet paranoia and was responsible for the Soviets building a massive military machine—at least according to the more benign interpretation of Soviet intentions.

There are, however, those who note that while Russia may have suffered many invasions in the past, she has also many times invaded and inflicted comparable traumas on her neighbors. The very fact that the Soviet Union has steadily grown in size, since the seventeenth century, to what is now the world's largest country is not simply the result of repelling invasions by others. Russians may not be uniquely aggressive and expansionist, but neither should they be thought of only as victims of other's aggression.

Obviously, the Soviets claim that their massive military buildup is solely for defensive purposes. However, while the Soviets may have some reason for their paranoia, prudent planners in the West must take into account the possibility that an unprovoked Soviet invasion of Europe could occur. The West needs to be militarily strong, whether the threat comes from a country dedicated to conquering the world or one whose aggression is the result of a fear that it is about to be attacked. Clearly, however, these contrasting views of Soviet intentions have great relevance to the wisdom of NATO taking specific defensive measures that could be unduly provocative and misinterpreted by the Soviet Union.

One particular fear of the Soviet Union is the possible loss of its Eastern European satellites, due to Western pressures and threats that might spark popular uprisings. Some Western analysts believe that in order to prevent that loss from happening, the Soviet military posture has an "offensive" appearance, thus making it indistinguishable from one designed to conquer Western Europe. Soviet military doctrine, in fact, calls for massive and swift offensive movements into Western Europe, including the heavy use of large tactical nuclear weapons in case of NATO attack. If they are attacked, the Soviets clearly intend that the battle be waged on NATO soil, not that of Eastern Europe, where popular uprisings might help the NATO invaders and overthrow continued Soviet rule.

The nub of the issue then is that what appears to the Soviets to be a commonsense defensive military posture, appears rather menacing to the West. The same comment applies, incidently, to Soviet doctrine concerning their strategic nuclear posture. There are those who see an extensive Soviet air defense and civil defense, and the possible first-strike threat against U.S. land-based missiles as clear evidence that the Soviet Union intends to fight and win a nuclear war with the United States, if necessary. Other observers dismiss such thoughts as overly alarmist and attribute Soviet actions to bureaucracy, defense-mindedness, and a defense establishment and government not constrained by the force of public opinion. The disagreement over the Soviet Union's true intentions could continue indefinitely. Whatever the Soviet's intentions, their sizable military force represents a serious potential threat in Western eyes which it would be imprudent to ignore.

HOW CAN NATO BEST DEFEND ITSELF?

The countries of Western Europe fall in vastly different nuclear categories. At one extreme, there are Britain and France who possess their own nuclear arsenals and who, therefore, are not dependent on American nuclear guarantees. At the other extreme is West Germany which borders Warsaw Pact nations and has the greatest number of U.S. nuclear weapons on its soil, thereby taking the greatest risk on behalf of NATO. West Germany's special status as a defeated aggressor in World War II, its great geographic vulnerability, and its renunciation of the development of its own nuclear arsenal, place Germany in a nuclear category all by itself among NATO countries. Germany has, in the past, been extremely sensitive to any NATO policies singling it out for special treatment on nuclear matters. For example, Germany only agreed to the placement of

U.S. intermediate-range missiles on its soil if at least one other NATO country would do likewise.

Among the other countries of Western Europe, five also have U.S. nuclear weapons on their soil: Belgium, The Netherlands, Luxembourg, Greece, and Italy, and one (Greece) has indicated that it wishes to have them removed. The other states of Western Europe have no U.S. nuclear weapons and two (Norway and Denmark) have explicitly rejected the idea.

The attitude of those NATO countries that have nuclear weapons appears to be that nuclear weapons are a necessary evil—needed for their deterrent value, but greatly feared in actual use, even in a limited war. For example, many Europeans believe it would be a mistake for NATO to agree to a Soviet proposal to forswear first use of nuclear weapons, as attractive as that proposal might seem. Without a conventional force strong enough to repel a Soviet conventional invasion, however, forswearing first use constitutes a prior agreement to surrender if the West loses a conventional war. That proposition seems every bit as unreasonable as it would be to expect the Soviets to agree in advance not to escalate further if the Western use of tactical nuclear weapons successfully repelled a Soviet conventional assault on Western Europe.

A refusal to agree to "no first use" does not necessarily imply that NATO would in fact resort to first use, even though NATO doctrine calls for just such an eventuality. However, keeping the option of first use would seem to complicate things for Soviet military planners. The no-first-use position can be more easily supported as a goal toward which NATO should strive, by making its conventional forces sufficiently strong enough to make first use unnecessary. Regardless of the unenforceable, largely symbolic no-first-use pledge, many Western observers agree that it would be desirable for NATO to have sufficiently strong conventional forces to make first use unnecessary in case of a conventional Soviet attack—a view espoused by Solly Zuckerman[19] and Irving Kristol,[20] among many others. There are, however, contrasting opinions. For example, Admiral Gene La Rocque sees no utility for large conventional forces on each side, believing that the countries of Western Europe should have confidence in the U.S. nuclear umbrella.[21] Senators Edward Kennedy and Mark Hatfield also consider the U.S. nuclear umbrella to be in fine shape and perfectly adequate to guarantee the security of Western Europe.[22]

There are other very different proposals that have been advanced for the defense of Europe, including one by Laurence Beilenson who believes that the United States should heavily arm all the countries of Western Europe and China with nuclear weapons and bring U.S. soldiers home[23]—a proposal that in some eyes might seem a sure prescription for World War III. In its impatience to relieve itself of the primary burden for the common defense of NATO and turn over a greater share of that burden to its European allies and Japan, the United States must be careful not to take precipitous actions such as sending all its soldiers home, which would be viewed as abandoning Europe, or alternatively arming Germany with its own nuclear arsenal. Not only do the Germans claim not to want their own nuclear weapons, but such an action, if taken, would probably be extremely provocative to the Russians and might well lead to war.

How then to defend Europe? The neutron bomb at one time had been touted by some as a kind of wonder weapon that would be able to stop a Soviet tank attack without harming civilian populations. However, the neutron bomb, or more properly the enhanced radiation weapon (ERW), does not seem to hold great promise for a defense that would not destroy Europe. ERWs are tactical nuclear bombs designed to produce a smaller area of blast for a given yield and to kill primarily by radiation capable of penetrating armor. Thus, in principle, a massed tank attack could be stopped using a relatively small number of ERWs, which would do less damage to civilian areas than other kinds of nuclear weapons. Of course, if the Soviets retaliate with their big messy nuclear weapons, it would not matter a great deal to the civilians by exactly whose weapons they are killed—so why bother making U.S. weapons so clean?

There is an even more fundamental reason neutron bombs cannot successfully defend Europe, namely the tactic can be easily countered by the U.S.S.R. The Soviets would be able to disperse their tanks making it possible for the defenders to knock out only a few at a time. Moreover, the radiation dose received by many Soviet tank crews might not be sufficient to kill them immediately. In some cases, tank crews receiving lethal radiation doses would be incapacitated, but in many other cases they might become reckless kamakazis who would fight with greater fury, knowing they would be dead in a matter of days or weeks. On the other hand, as weapons, neutron bombs are not totally useless either, and they are certainly no more immoral than any other nuclear weapon, despite propaganda about their being the ultimate capitalist weapon—bombs that kill people without destroying property.

What about the possibility of a defense of Europe by conventional means? A strong conventional defense is generally believed to be much more costly, both in money and personnel, than a nuclear defense. Many observers believe that Europe has rested too long under the U.S. nuclear umbrella and is reluctant to undertake any serious effort in its own defense. According to that view, it now would be politically impossible for Western Europe to marshall the necessary degree of commitment and resources to provide its own defense by conventional means, short of some unambiguous threat by the Soviets. Of course, as Henry Kissinger has observed, in the nuclear age by the time a threat is unambiguous it may be too late.

The imbalances between the defense efforts of the United States and those of its allies is shown by the fact that while the United States spends 7 percent to 8 percent of its GNP on defense, Western Europe spends 2 percent to 4 percent, and Japan spends only 1 percent. The question then is can NATO mount a conventional defense that is both credible, i.e., stands a good chance of working without destroying Europe in order to save it, and not exhorbitant in terms of cost or personnel? Only then can NATO rely less on its nuclear crutch, and only then will doubts about whether the United States will risk New York to save Hamburg be quieted.

One radical solution to the problem of a credible conventional defense of Europe has been suggested by Peter Zimmerman and G. Allen Greb, among others.[24] The proposal suggests building a non-nuclear defense of Europe on the basis of precision-guided munitions (PGMs) or "smart bombs." PGMs are descended from the U.S.-supplied TOW and Maverick missiles used by the Israelis with great effectiveness against the Egyptians in the Yom Kippur War. In that war, fifty-two Egyptian tanks were destroyed by only fifty-eight launched Mavericks. PGMs have proven many hundreds of times more effective against tanks than unguided munitions. Using self-contained minicomputers and precision guidance systems, PGMs have a very high probability of stopping a tank on the first shot. The original TOW missiles had the disadvantage that their wire guidance required a soldier to stand exposed, guiding the missile to its target while holding a pair of trailing wires. More modern PGMs use optical or infrared sensors that allow the missiles to home in on their target, while the person who launches them need not stand exposed during their flight. There are considerable advantages that PGMs might offer over tactical nuclear weapons in a defense of Europe. As Peter Zimmerman notes:

The new generation of precisely delivered munitions can accomplish virtually any mission ascribed to small nuclear weapons in the defense of Europe. New conventional weapons should, therefore, replace nuclear warheads. Conventional explosives do not require Presidential authority for their use, nor do they require the involvement of the NATO Nuclear Planning Group. The cumbersome procedures to request a nuclear strike . . . are not required before the launching of a TOW or Assault Breaker. PGMs can be used instantly when and where needed and *per tank destroyed,* PGMs may actually cost less than artillery fired nuclear rounds, including neutron bombs. Lastly, the fallout, political and radiological, from a PGM is far less than that of a mini-nuke.[25]

Zimmerman's case seems to be fairly convincing. Moreover, he has neglected to mention another great advantage of PGMs, namely that they can be widely dispersed rather than stored in a number of tightly guarded storage depots, as is the case of nuclear weapons. This much greater dispersal means that a disarming first strike by the Soviets would not be feasible, and hence PGMs would greatly enhance deterrence. If NATO were to build a conventional defense around a sufficient number of PGMs to counter a Soviet conventional attack, it could then afford to cut off the bottom rung of the ladder of nuclear escalation and dispense with tactical nuclear weapons. For deterrence purposes, NATO might choose to keep intermediate-range nuclear weapons, which are a much better deterrent than TNWs anyway, since they would land on Soviet, not NATO, territory. But with a conventional defense built around PGMs, NATO would no longer suffer from the self-deterrence implicit in its reliance on tactical nuclear weapons that it greatly feared to use.

PGMs may not offer a permanent solution to the problem of a nonnuclear defense of Europe. Any solution that relies on purely technological means may later prove to be obsolete in the light of further technological developments. However, permanent or not, PGMs seem now to offer great advantages over TNWs in virtually all respects for a viable defense of Europe.

Lastly, we shall conclude this chapter by considering why the United States should be so concerned about the fate of Western Europe. There are many who believe that since Western Europe and Japan have recovered from the devastation of World War II, they ought to be able to look after themselves. If that should mean the

Finlandization of Europe and Japan, or possibly their outright domination by an expanded Soviet empire without a shot being fired, why should that overly concern the United States? The United States, in light of its history as a nation of immigrants, has strong social and cultural ties to Europe. There are, however, two very practical reasons for not abandoning Europe that go beyond such intangibles. Firstly, the abandonment of Europe and Japan by the United States could lead to war rather than to their quiet submission, and the war ultimately would involve the United States. Secondly, if Europe and Japan came under Soviet domination, the balance of world power would shift drastically against the United States. It seems highly unlikely that, in the face of U.S. abandonment, Europe and Japan could for long maintain a neutral position between the superpowers. With such a drastic global shift of power, the standard of living in the United States would probably drop severely. The United States, not self-sufficient in petroleum as well as a large number of other resources, would probably find many of these resources much more expensive in unfriendly hands. The present competitive economic contest between the United States and its Japanese ally would take on a much more destructive character if Japan came under Soviet influence.

The domestic political consequences in the United States could be even greater than the economic ones. With a drop in its standard of living and a search for scapegoats over who "lost" Europe and Japan to the communists, the right-wing backlash would probably dwarf anything America has ever seen. The United States would probably become an isolated, beleaguered, fortress-state, seeing itself alone in the world, allied perhaps with a few other equally isolated compatriots such as South Africa, Israel, and Taiwan. America's huge nuclear arsenal could perhaps still keep the rest of the world at bay, but the United States would never again be the same country—economically, politically, or spiritually.

Seeing enemies everywhere, the United States would likely develop the kind of paranoia many now ascribe to the Russians. The decisive global power shift against the United States would probably make it into a much more meanspirited, selfish country, not caring a great deal for world public opinion, which would simply be dismissed as being under the influence of the communists. Finally, because of such an attitude, the United States might be much more likely to take vindictive belligerent actions that could in the end precipitate a catastrophe.

An American abandonment of its allies would, therefore, be a self-destructive move of incalculable proportions. Many citizens in allied countries, however, now seem to regard neutrality between America and the Soviet Union as a realistic alternative, and certainly a preferable one to being either Red or dead. Moscow obviously will encourage such sentiments as a means of severing U.S.-European ties. Is neutrality, on the Austrian model, a viable alternative for Western Europe and Japan? Although one or two states might opt out of the Western alliance without consequence, once a clear trend was established and America felt it was unwelcome, it would surely turn its back on its former allies. There would be little U.S. public support to keep troops in Europe or Japan as an occupying force protecting countries who feared their protector more than their potential adversary.

The process of intimidation is a subtle and often gradual one. Once American security guarantees were withdrawn, it is possible that the Soviet Union would resort to considerably cruder methods of intimidation to bring Western Europe and Japan into its orbit. Neutrality is much easier to preserve in a bipolar world in which neutral countries can maintain their equidistance between the superpowers by trading one off against the other. Neutrality may be far more difficult to preserve when one superpower has written off the rest of the world during a periodic return to isolationism and when the balance of global power has been substantially altered as a result.

STUDY QUESTIONS

1. Why were tactical nuclear weapons originally developed by the United States?

2. How plausible are American nuclear guarantees to defend Europe?

3. Why do the United States and its European allies have very different perspectives on the need to have firebreaks between different levels of escalation?

4. What is the state of the NATO–Warsaw Pact military balance, including intangible factors? In what respects do the NATO and Soviet assessments vary?

5. What were the political and military reasons the Soviet Union might have had for deploying its SS-20 missiles?

6. What were the political and military reasons that NATO had for adopting its decision to deploy U.S. Pershing II and cruise missiles? Was that decision a wise one?

7. Do you think a nuclear war could be limited? Why?

8. How serious is the possibility of a Soviet surprise counterforce attack against Western Europe?

9. Why are there different perceptions of the Soviet threat?

10. To what extent has "Finlandization" of Western Europe already occurred?

11. What advantages do precision-guided munitions (PGMs) offer as a means for mounting a nonnuclear defense of Europe?

12. Would it be a good idea for NATO to adopt a policy of no first use? Why?

13. Why should the United States care about defending Europe and Japan?

III

THE EFFECTS OF NUCLEAR WAR

Six

NUCLEAR-WEAPONS EFFECTS

INTRODUCTION

7 December 1941 is a date familiar to most Americans. The date 6ᵛ August 1945 is probably familiar only to a small percentage, although its significance in the history of the world is enormous, representing as it does the first use of a nuclear weapon in war. On that day the city of Hiroshima was in an instant turned into hell, and 70,000 people perished immediately or during the ensuing thirty days. Three days later a second bomb annihilated the city of Nagasaki killing 40,000 people. In addition, by the end of 1945 another 100,000 Japanese died of their injuries sustained in the two bombings. The suffering and death of civilian populations during World War II was also horrendous due to conventional bombings: 84,000 died in one night during the great fire raid on Tokyo, and in excess of 100,000 are believed to have been killed in the bombing raid on Dresden. The special horror of nuclear weapons consists in how much easier it is to kill in an instant huge numbers of people as compared to conventional weapons. Moreover, the potential for death and sickness continues long after the attack owing to the harmful effects of radiation. Even today the survivors of Hiroshima and Nagasaki still suffer the effects. These *hibakusha* are seen by many other Japanese to have a kind of invisible contamination, making them and their

descendants poor candidates for marriage, jobs, or living generally. Whether it is more immoral to kill people by nuclear weapons than conventional weapons is, however, not the real issue. What is of much greater significance is that because of increases in the number and size of nuclear weapons since World War II, there exists the potential for mass destruction on a scale never before imaginable.

All the issues surrounding nuclear war, e.g., whether it is winnable or survivable, whether it can be limited, etc., cannot be intelligently discussed without a clear understanding of the effects of a nuclear war. The logical place to begin is with the effects of one nuclear weapon, the subject of this chapter. Before reading this chapter, however, it may be helpful to read appendix A which deals with the physical principles of nuclear energy and radiation.

The basic nature of the effects of a nuclear weapon is the same for nuclear weapons of all sizes or yields, although the magnitude of the effects obviously depends on the weapon's yield. Nuclear weapons kill people and do other damage through a number of means including:

- *Blast*—the explosive force of the bomb and the primary killer

- *Thermal radiation*—the very intense heat created by a nuclear detonation which takes place at enormously higher temperatures than conventional explosions

- *Prompt radiation*—the intense burst of ionizing radiation, mainly neutrons and gamma rays, produced in the nuclear reactions at the time of detonation

- *Electromagnetic pulse (EMP)*—the sudden electromagnetic disturbance created at the time of detonation

In addition to these prompt effects there are also a number of delayed effects, including:

- *Fires*—the ignition of combustible material by the thermal radiation

- *Fallout*—the wide dispersal of large amounts of dirt and other material, vaporized and made radioactive in the detonation, which falls back to earth after being thrown up by the blast

- *Other effects*—the numerous other indirect ways nuclear bombs kill people, including the creation of an environment generally inhospitable to life

WHAT ARE THE IMMEDIATE EFFECTS OF A NUCLEAR DETONATION?

All the facts and figures that appear without specific references in this chapter have been taken from two basic reference works: *The Effects of Nuclear Weapons* by Glasstone and Dolan[1] and *The Effects of Nuclear War* by the U.S. Congress, Office of Technology Assessment (OTA).[2]

Thermal Radiation

Your first awareness of a nuclear detonation, assuming you were not close enough to be instantly vaporized or killed by prompt radiation, would be of the nuclear fireball created by the explosion. The intensity of light and heat (thermal radiation) from the fireball from a one-megaton bomb would be thousands of times greater than from the sun. The thermal radiation from such a bomb would cause third degree burns to all exposed skin at distances up to 5 miles. A reflex glance at such a fireball could cause temporary vision loss ("flash blindness") at distances up to 13 miles on a clear day or 53 miles on a clear night. Vision usually returns after around twenty minutes, and permanent retinal burns are rare. (Only one case of permanent retinal burns among survivors was reported at Hiroshima and Nagasaki.) [3] Nevertheless, the temporary loss of sight might well have fatal consequences under certain circumstances, e.g., while driving a car. The distance at which thermal radiation can cause burns is considerably dependent on the size of the weapon and also on weather conditions. Thermal radiation behaves similar to light, so that a heavy smog, for example, would drastically reduce visibility and reduce the range of thermal radiation, while the presence of reflecting clouds or snow on the ground would, to a lesser degree, increase the danger. The thermal radiation from the fireball would not be over in a flash like a flashbulb, but would last for what would undoubtedly seem an eternity to survivors: ten seconds for a one-megaton bomb. However, of all the effects of a nuclear weapon, thermal radiation is in principle the easiest one to protect oneself against. Being indoors away from windows, or being behind anything that casts a shadow (including some clothing) offers protection against severe burns. At Hiroshima, for example, among those survivors who were outdoors and unshielded, 90 percent of those within a 2.5-mile radius received burn injuries, while only 13 percent of those who were indoors received such injuries. Burns would represent the most serious problem among the kinds of injuries incurred by survivors in terms of the unavailability of medical treatment. Even a single one-megaton nuclear weapon could produce more than 10,000 severe burn injuries which is five to ten times the total available burn-treatment capacity in the United States. Moreover, severe burns, unlike many other types of injuries, are usually fatal unless treated promptly using such highly specialized facilities.

Blast

The greatest number of deaths and injuries from a nuclear explosion would be caused by the blast, which is similar to that from a conventional explosion of the same size. The term blast includes both the sudden change in pressure (static overpressure) created by the rapidly expanding fireball, as well as the extremely high-velocity winds that immediately follow. The harm done by the blast depends on the static overpressure measured in pounds per square inch (psi) and the speed of the winds, both of which decrease with distance from ground zero. For example, the static overpressure usually considered sufficient to knock down a typical two-story house is 5 psi. It has also been determined that on the average there is a 50 percent chance of being killed inside a house subject to this overpressure. The effect of a 5-psi overpressure on a wooden-frame house of typical construction is indicated by the pictures in figures 6.1 and 6.2 taken before and after a nuclear test explosion. It is remarkable that as many as half the people whose houses would collapse on top of them would probably survive, although probably not without injuries. Although 5 psi is enough to knock down a typical house, it is not enough to directly crush someone standing in the open. Such a person is more likely to be killed by the winds of perhaps 180 mph, expected to accompany a 5-psi overpressure, which would likely cause fatal collisions between people and objects. (See table 6.1 for the effects of various overpressures.) Nevertheless, the chance of being injured by the blast would be less for someone

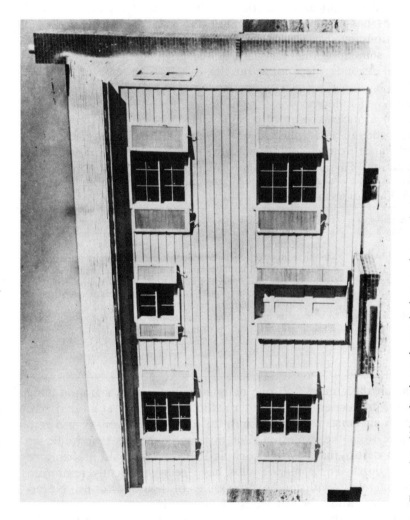

Figure 6.1 Wooden-frame house before nuclear explosion, Nevada test site.
Source: Defense Nuclear Agency.

who is outdoors than for someone who is indoors—just the reverse of the situation for burn injuries.

The blast wave travels in excess of the speed of sound, or about one mile every five seconds, while the thermal radiation travels at the speed of light and essentially arrives instantly. Thus, someone who has had the presence of mind and good luck to have taken precautions against the thermal radiation, e.g., by quickly getting behind something that casts a shadow, might then have many additional seconds (depending on the distance) to take precautions against blast, e.g. by laying down and covering one's face away from windows, if indoors.

For a nuclear bomb of specific yield, the static overpressure in psi depends in a complicated way on the altitude of detonation and the distance from ground zero, which is the point directly below the detonation. There are important differences between a bomb deto-

Table 6.1   Blast Overpressure Effects

½ to 1 psi	breakage of window glass
3 to 4 psi	severe damage to wooden frame or brick homes (homes could be made habitable only after extensive reapir)
5 psi	complete destruction of wooden frame or brick homes; severe battering of automobiles and trucks (tops and sides caved in, but engines still operable) 200 to 600 bits of debris, shards of glass, and so on, per square yard, flying through the air at speeds of 40 to 180 miles per hour
6 to 7 psi	moderate damage to massive, wall-bearing, multistory buildings
7 psi	possible internal injuries to human beings
8 psi	people standing will be picked up and thrown.
12 psi	people lying flat on the ground will be picked up and hurled about
20 to 30 psi	50 percent probability of ear drum rupture.

nated on the ground and one detonated in the air. A ground-burst weapon produces a much greater static overpressure at ground zero than an air-burst weapon, since in this case ground zero is also zero distance from the explosion. For this reason bombs that would be used to destroy hard targets such as ICBM silos would probably be ground burst. These missile silos have been sufficiently reinforced with concrete to withstand overpressures of thousands of psi. Nevertheless they would be vaporized if directly hit with a ground-burst weapon. For an air-burst weapon, as the altitude of detonation increases from zero, the circular area centered on ground zero subject to an overpressure exceeding some value, say 5 psi, first increases, then reaches a maximum, and finally decreases. Therefore, an optimum height of detonation exists that yields the greatest area of blast damage for a bomb of specific yield and targets of specific

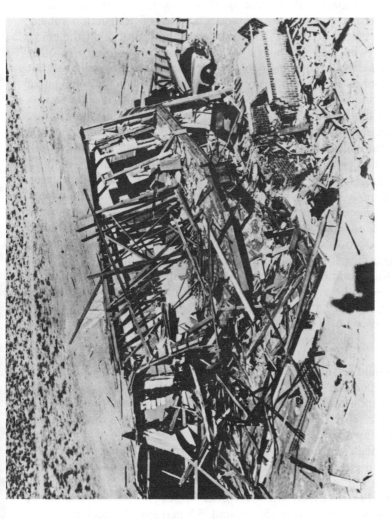

Figure 6.2   Wooden-frame house after nuclear explosion.
Source: See figure 6.1.
Note: Distance from ground zero corresponded to a peak overpressure of 5 psi.

hardness. The optimum height of detonation can be determined from the curves in figure 6.3, which show the peak overpressures that would occur at different distances from ground zero for different altitude detonations of a one-kiloton bomb.

As an example of the use of these curves, let us suppose an attacker wished to maximize the circular area of destruction subject to overpressures of 10 psi. It may be seen that point P on the curve labelled 10 psi has the largest distance from ground zero (plotted on the x-axis) for any height of burst (plotted on the y-axis). Point P corresponds to a height of burst of about 750 feet. This height of burst therefore would give the largest area of 10-psi or more overpressures for a one-kiloton bomb. For yields other than one kiloton, it is necessary to scale both axes of figure 6.3 according to the cube root of the bomb yield, $y^{1/3}$. For example, for a one-megaton bomb (1000 times greater yield), the optimum height of burst would be $1000^{1/3}$ times greater than 750 feet, or 7500 feet. It may also be seen from figure 6.3 that a bomb set to go off at this optimum height would produce a peak overpressure at ground zero slightly in excess of 30 psi, enough to demolish a reinforced concrete structure, though not enough to destroy a well-constructed blast shelter which might withstand 50 psi or more. Finally, we may see from figure 6.3 that detonating a bomb at its optimum height can result in a considerable difference in the area of destruction, but only for "soft" targets. For example, a glance at the two contours labelled 50 and 200 psi shows that there is not a great difference between the distance to ground zero for a ground-burst detonation versus the distance for one detonated at optimum altitude. However, in the case of a soft target, which could easily be destroyed by 10-psi overpressure, there is a sizable difference between the distance to ground zero for a groundburst weapon and for an optimum-altitude air-burst weapon (1430 feet versus 1015 feet), that results in the air-burst weapon having twice the area of destruction.

Although the 5-psi contour is not shown in figure 6.3, it has a distance to ground zero of 0.44 miles for an optimum-altitude one-kiloton bomb, or therefore 4.4 miles for a one-megaton bomb. As noted earlier, 5 psi is the overpressure for which the chance of surviving the blast becomes around 50 percent. Thus, for an airburst one-megaton bomb, you would have roughly a 50-percent chance of being killed immediately from blast at a distance of 4.4 miles. At greater distances the chances of being killed or injured decrease, although even at 11.6 miles where the overpressure has dropped to 1 psi there would be some injuries due to flying glass

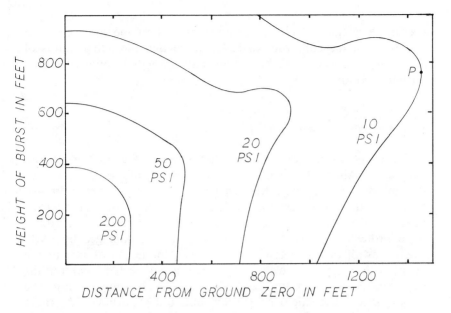

Figure 6.3   Peak overpressures on the ground for a one-kiloton detonation.
Source: Glasstone and Dolan, *Effects of Nuclear Weapons,* p. 113.
Notes: Contours show different peak overpressures. There is a point for any peak overpressure for which the largest area of that overpressure is created on the ground. *P* indicates that point for the 10-psi overpressure contour.

and other debris. The area of the 5-psi circle is sometimes called the "lethal area" of the bomb, even though there will be some survivors inside this circle and some fatalities outside. To calculate in a very approximate way the immediate fatalities from a nuclear explosion, it is sometimes assumed that the number of survivors inside the 5-psi circle equals the number of immediate fatalities outside, which means that the total fatalities equals the number of people inside the 5-psi circle.

The radius of the 5-psi circle for an air-burst weapon of any yield can be found in terms of that of a one-megaton weapon, which is 4.4 miles. Since the total energy of a bomb is distributed into a sphere, and since the volume of a sphere is proportional to the cube of its radius, this means that the cube of the lethal radius of a bomb is proportional to its yield. Thus, the yield of bomb that has two, three, or four times the lethal radius of a one-megaton bomb would be 8, 27, or 64 megatons respectively. Alternatively, if we wished to find the lethal radius of a bomb of specific yield, say 167 kilotons = 1/6 megaton, then we need to take the cube root of 6. Without needing a pocket calculator we know that the cube root of 6 is a bit less than the cube root of 8, i.e. 2, so that the lethal radius of a 1/6-megaton bomb will be around half the lethal radius of a one-megaton bomb.

Electromagnetic Pulse (EMP)

EMP is another of the immediate effects of a nuclear-weapon detonation. Although it is not believed to be harmful to living things, the intense burst of radio-frequency electromagnetic energy, known as EMP, can induce very high voltages in the antenna or the wiring of electrical equipment. The voltage rise is so rapid that even equipment protected against lightning strikes may be damaged by EMP. The extent of the damage is dependent on the length of an antenna or wire to which the electrical device is connected, and on the electrical shielding of the device. Thus, a radio plugged into the wiring of a house might be shorted out, but a portable AM radio without an extended antenna should not be damaged,[4] particularly if it is electrically shielded by putting it in a metal box or wrapping it in aluminum foil. Over a hundred broadcast stations have protection against EMP, and one might surmise that military communication channels also have protection against EMP, although the subject is a sensitive one for obvious reasons. The strength of the EMP from nuclear weapons is so great that a single large megaton warhead detonated two hundred miles above Nebraska could potentially blanket the United States with a sufficiently great electromagnetic pulse to shut down the power grid, perform a lobotomy on computer memories, and knock out unprotected communication systems all across the country.[5] It is difficult to enumerate all the areas of everyday life that would be affected, but electronic watches, television sets, and cars with electronic ignitions might all stop functioning if the EMP pulse were sizable enough. It is somewhat startling to realize how much damage this could cause to a high-technology country like the United States.

Prompt Radiation

The last of the four immediate nuclear-weapon effects consists of the intense burst of ionizing radiation, mainly neutrons and gamma rays, produced at the instant of detonation. At Hiroshima and

Nagasaki this radiation caused many deaths, injuries, and long-term health effects. For the much larger weapons now in the U.S. and Soviet arsenals, prompt radiation is not a matter for concern. In such large weapons the lethal range of prompt radiation is much less than that of the blast, so there would be no one killed or injured by prompt radiation who would not be killed by the blast. A survivor located at the 5 psi distances from two detonations of 1 kt and 100 kt, for example, would receive a lethal dose of prompt radiation in the former case, and an insignificant dose (1/500 the lethal value), in the latter case. The effects of prompt radiation, of particular concern when smaller weapons are used—especially the enhanced-radiation or neutron bomb—are similar to those produced by the delayed radiation present in fallout. However, there are also some important differences, e.g., fallout can be ingested with food, leading to internal radiation exposures.

WHAT ARE THE DELAYED EFFECTS OF A NUCLEAR DETONATION?

Fallout

All nuclear detonations produce radioactive aerosols from the debris of fission reactions. Fallout occurs when these aerosols are deposited on the ground. In the case of a detonation low enough in height to produce a crater or cause surface dust to be swept up into the mushroom cloud, the aerosols will attach to the dust which itself becomes radioactive. The larger size particles, and hence the most highly radioactive ones, are carried just a short distance up into the mushroom stem and come down within the first hour not too far from ground zero. The smaller dust-size radioactive particles are carried by the winds and deposited in the ensuing hours and days. This so-called local fallout is not that local, and, depending on the speed of the wind, may be deposited hundreds of miles downwind. Finally, there is a third type of worldwide fallout consisting of still finer radioactive particles that may take weeks, months, and even years, to fall back to earth. The greatest danger created by fallout is from the highly radioactive early and local fallout which under the idealized atmospheric condition of a constant wind speed is deposited in a long cigar-shaped pattern downwind of the detonation.

The fallout pattern gradually spreads downwind, as fallout reaches more and more distant points. The progressive spread of fallout is

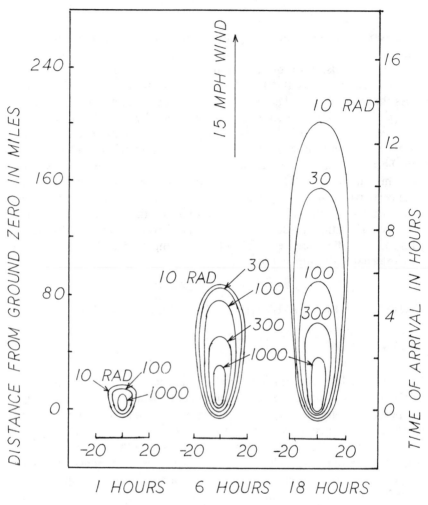

Figure 6.4   Radiation-dose buildup from fallout.
Source: Glasstone and Dolan, *Effects of Nuclear Weapons,* p. 426.
Notes: Total-dose contours from early fallout at 1, 6, and 18 hours after the surface burst with a total yield of two-megaton and one-megaton fission yield (15 mph effective wind speed).

indicated in figure 6.4 showing three idealized patterns corresponding to 1 hour, 6 hours, and 18 hours following the detonation of a two-megaton ground-burst bomb. Two units used to measure radiation dose are the rad and the rem which are discussed in appendix A. The rad and the rem are essentially equivalent for the radiation present in fallout. The contours in figure 6.4 show different cumulative radiation doses in rads. To convey a better sense of scale,

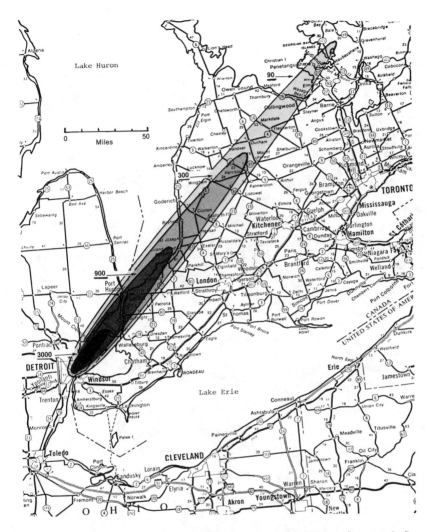

Figure 6.5   Dose contours for one-megaton ground burst (southwest wind).
Source: Office of Technology Assessment, *Effects of Nuclear War*, p. 24.
Notes: Contours for seven-day accumulated dose (without shielding) for a
one-megaton ground burst in Detroit, in the presence of a 15 mph southwest wind. Contours show total doses of 3000, 900, 300, and 90 rems.

figure 6.5 gives contours for the one-week accumulated dose in rems,
in the case of a one-megaton bomb ground burst on Detroit. It is
clear from this figure that the impact of fallout from a single weapon
can depend crucially on which way the wind is blowing. For example,
a northwest wind (figure 6.6) would result in heavy fallout on much

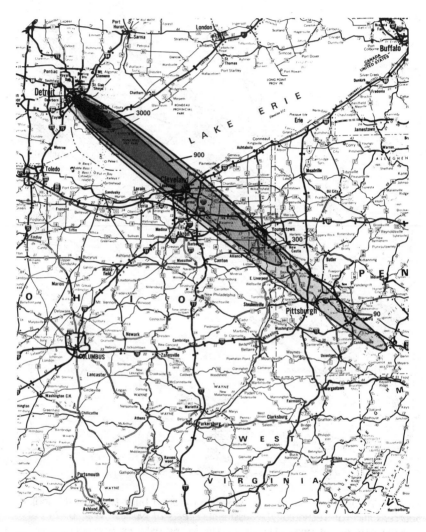

Figure 6.6   Dose contours for one-megaton ground burst (northwest wind).
Source: Office of Technology Assessment, *Effects of Nuclear War,* p. 25.
Notes: Contours for seven-day accumulated dose (without shielding) for a
one-megaton ground burst in Detroit in the presence of a 15 mph northwest
wind. A northwest wind would deposit heavy fallout over more heavily populated areas than would a southwest wind.

larger population concentrations than would a southwest wind (figure
6.5). These fallout patterns are, as already noted, extremely idealized,

and they show none of the irregularities and "hot spots" one would likely find in an actual case.

In examining the levels of cumulative radiation dose in figures 6.5 and 6.6, it should be kept in mind that the dose fatal to humans ranges between 200 rem and 700 rem. The dose at the midpoint of this range, i.e. 450 rem, is lethal to approximately half the exposed population. However, this dose, the so-called LD-50 dose, is found to be greater if it is delivered over a longer period of time, due to bodily radiation repair mechanisms. For example, while half the exposed population would survive a dose of 450 rem delivered over one week, they would be able to survive as much as 1000 rem delivered over one year. (We are only considering fatalities due to radiation and have ignored the ways that high radiation doses can increase the probability of death due to other causes, such as, for example, increased susceptibility to infection.)

Death from radiation sickness can be particularly unpleasant. According to Glasstone and Dolan, the initial symptoms are "nausea, vomiting, diarrhea, loss of appetite and malaise." There is then a remission period in which recovery seems to occur, giving the victim false hope. However, two or three weeks after the exposure "there is a tendency to bleed into various organs and small hemorrhages under the skin . . . are observed," including bleeding from the mouth and intestinal tract. "Loss of hair . . . also starts after about two weeks . . . ulceration about the lips may . . . spread from the mouth through the entire gastrointestinal tract." Eventually "the decrease in the white cells of the blood and injury to other immune mechanisms of the body . . . allow an overwhelming infection to develop."

Less-than-lethal radiation levels can also have very serious human health effects, which are discussed in chapter 8 on the long-term worldwide effects of a nuclear war.

It should be clear from the preceding discussion that for a single nuclear detonation, the number of casualties resulting from fallout can depend crucially on:

- Size of weapon

- Height of burst (ground or air burst)

- Weather conditions

- Speed and direction of the wind

- Efforts made by the population to evacuate or seek shelter

The effect of these factors on the number of casualties can be better described for an attack involving a large number of nuclear weapons, and therefore a more complete discussion of the effects of fallout is given in subsequent chapters.

Fires

The thermal radiation from a nuclear explosion travels in straight lines and may be sufficiently intense to directly ignite combustible material exposed to it. House fires will be caused primarily by thermal radiation coming through open or closed windows, igniting curtains, beds, and over-stuffed furniture inside. (Thermal radiation is like light and will not enter blackened windows.) Estimates are that at the edge of the lethal radius circle, where the overpressure is 5 psi, about 10 percent of buildings would sustain a serious fire due to all causes. One matter of serious concern is the possibility that a number of separate small fires could coalesce into one enormous fire or "firestorm" in which winds rush inward from all directions and form an extremely hot updraft at the center. It is widely believed that inside the area of a firestorm, such as those that occurred during the World War II Dresden and Hamburg bombings, there are virtually no survivors. For example, according to H. Jack Geiger in recent congressional testimony: "The only people who survived [the Hamburg and Dresden firestorms] were those who fled the shelters early because otherwise, even with independent atmospheric supplies, which most of them did not have, they simply became crematoria for those who were in them." [6] These assertions do not appear to be supported by the facts. At the time of the World War II Hamburg bombing, 280,000 people are reported to have lived in the five-square-mile area of firestorm. "Of these, an estimated 40,000, or 14 percent, who were either in poor basement shelter or outside, were killed by blast or fire. . . . Some 142,000 people survived in basement shelters or escaped by their own initiative, and 45,000 were rescued, in addition to an estimated 53,000 who survived in blast protection shelters." [7] It is also important to note that many unique physical conditions of the target and the weather are required to produce a firestorm. In particular, it is believed that the density of combustible materials in U.S. and Soviet cities is too low to result in a firestorm.[8] The density needed for a firestorm to occur is believed to be around 8 lb/ft^2, which may be compared to 2 lb/ft^2 for a typical suburban U.S. neighborhood and 32 lb/ft^2 in the Hamburg firestorm.

Mass fires can also occur in the form of a "conflagration," consisting of a slowly advancing wall of fire along a broad front. Escape from a conflagration is possible for those not injured too badly to walk. The likelihood of a conflagration such as the Great Chicago Fire depends on many factors including the geography of the area, the speed of the wind, and the type of building construction. It is, therefore, definitely an overstatement to say that "the majority of shelters would become crematoria," as some wishing to portray the totality of devastation have claimed. Those who survived the blast in a blast shelter (even inside the lethal area), might suffer such a fate only in the event of a mass fire, although it is possible that they would perish from any number of other causes. (The effectiveness of blast shelters is discussed at greater length in chapter 9.) Outside the area of direct bomb effects, the likelihood of such a mass fire would be very remote.

Other Effects

There are many other indirect ways that nuclear weapons might kill people—starvation, disease, and exposure are a few (see chapters 7 and 8). In addition, while the individual effects might not in themselves be enough to kill, they might act together synergistically to bring about death. For example, burn injuries would make injuries sustained in the blast more susceptible to infection, and radiation sickness would lower one's resistance to such infection. Alternatively, injuries sustained in the blast might make someone physically and psychologically more prone to death from starvation and cold, avoidance of which might require considerable movement or effort. The possibilities and combinations are endless, and they include suicide as a "rational" response to one's environment.

WHAT WOULD BE THE LIKELY IMPACT OF ONE NUCLEAR WEAPON ON A CITY?

Studies have been made of the effects that nuclear weapons of various sizes would have on each of the major cities in the United States. To get a rough estimate of prompt fatalities, you need only draw a circle whose radius corresponds to the lethal (5 psi) radius for the particular yield bomb centered on some hypothetical ground zero and estimate the number of people inside that circle. Generally, most studies, such as that done by the Office of Technology Assessment (OTA), *The Effects of Nuclear War,* take a more careful approach by allowing for the probability of death and injury due to various causes at different distances from ground zero. However, all such calculations are subject to considerable uncertainty because they depend on the following circumstances:

- Whether the attack occurs during the day or at night, which would determine both were people are and whether they are likely to be standing up or laying down (the chances of being killed by blast overpressures of 5 psi are significantly less in the latter case)

- The altitude of detonation, which would determine the area of blast damage

- The weather, which might have a significant effect on the extent of burn injuries and deaths

- Whether a mass fire occurs

- Whether there is any warning prior to the attack that would allow some attempt at protective measures

- What the highly wind-dependent effects of fallout would be

The OTA study included estimates for the effects of a one-megaton detonation on the city of Detroit. The study made some assumptions that would tend to increase casualties (clear weather and no warning) and other assumptions that would tend to reduce casualties (attack at night and no mass fire). Detroit is a typical large American city in terms of area and population density.

A one-megaton bomb ground burst on downtown Detroit would leave a 200-foot-deep, 1000-foot-diameter crater. No significant structure would remain standing within 1.7 miles from ground zero, except possibly some bridge abutments. There would be virtually no survivors inside this 1.7-mile-radius circular region. The total levelling of tall buildings in the downtown area might well result in debris cluttering the street to a depth of some tens of feet. The extent of devastation would decrease moving outward from ground zero. The area of blast damage for a ground-burst bomb would be about half that of an air-burst weapon. It therefore would seem unlikely that a bomb intended for a city would be ground burst,

Table 6.2 Estimated Number of Casualties following a Nuclear Attack on Detroit (thousands)

	1 Mt Ground Burst	1 Mt Air Burst	25 Mt Air Burst
Fatalities	220 (5%)	470 (10%)	1,360 (30%)
Injuries	420 (9%)	630 (10%)	1,840 (41%)
Uninjured	3,860 (86%)	3,400 (76%)	1,300 (29%)

unless it was meant to destroy a particular hard target such as an underground blast shelter.

Fallout from the ground-burst weapon would cause life-threatening radiation exposures to some survivors within the first hour (see fig. 6.4). However, the total area covered by this early radiation would be relatively small compared to the lethal-blast area. The fallout drifting to earth at later times would cover a much larger area as seen in figures 6.5 and 6.6. This "local" fallout could cause many deaths if it came down over populated areas at lethal levels and if the population neither evacuated nor took shelter. The many uncertainties, including wind direction and speed, make reliable estimates of fallout deaths impossible. However, the fallout deaths are likely to be a small fraction of total deaths under "average" circumstances.

The damage done to the population of the Detroit metropolitan area by a one-megaton weapon would be dwarfed by that inflicted by a 25-megaton weapon.[9] Such a huge weapon, air burst over downtown Detroit, would be expected to heavily damage the entire metropolitan area, and it would result in many more casualties. The results of the OTA study summarized in table 6.2 include both air-burst and ground-burst detonations for the one-megaton weapon. The larger number of casualties for the air-burst case are a consequence of the more extensive area of blast damage. It may seem that some of the fatality estimates in table 6.2 are surprisingly "low". For example, considering that 70,000 were killed in Hiroshima with a weapon sixty-seven times smaller than a one-megaton bomb, it may seem strange that "only" seven times as many people would be killed if a one-megaton bomb were air burst over Detroit. However, it must be remembered that the lethal radius of a bomb varies as the cube root of its yield, $Y^{1/3}$, so that a one-megaton bomb would have roughly four times (not sixty-seven times) the lethal radius of a Hiroshima bomb.

These sanitized numbers and percentages cannot convey the horror that the detonation of a large nuclear weapon would bring to a city. Many of the injured would not be expected to survive owing to the near total unavailability of medical care—a particular problem for serious burn victims who might number as many as 18 percent of the injured. There undoubtedly would be many additional thousands of people who would perish in the ensuing weeks, months, and even years from disease, hunger, exposure, and other causes, particularly if a hypothesized "nuclear winter" should occur (see chapter 8).

Nevertheless, we do not have to believe nuclear weapons are "benign" to find many examples of overstatement concerning nuclear-weapons effects. For example, Jonathan Schell in *The Fate of the Earth* gives a very vivid description of the death and destruction resulting from a one-megaton ground burst on New York City. Although Schell gives no numbers in his discussion, he concludes by observing that "it is difficult to believe that there would be appreciable survival of the city after a one megaton ground burst." [10] This extremely pessimistic assessment, unsupported by any calculation, may be compared to the OTA estimate for a one-megaton ground burst on Detroit which estimated that 220,000, or 5 percent of the metropolitan area, would be killed. (Since New York City has a larger area than Detroit, the percentage killed might be expected to be smaller than 5 percent under the assumptions made in the OTA calculation.)

As in the case of many such pessimistic estimates as Schell's, it is possible to imagine circumstances under which they might be true. One need not go so far as to imagine all of New York City in the Times Square area on New Year's Eve. It would be sufficient to postulate the highly unlikely absence of any wind (even at higher altitudes), which would result in the local fallout descending to blanket the entire city. If one further assumes that the uninjured population made no attempt to evacuate or seek shelter, then there would indeed be "no appreciable survival of the city." The effects of one nuclear weapon on a city would seem to be terrible enough without any need to exaggerate them. However, it should also be clear that the nuclear-weapons effects likely to be experienced by a city in wartime are, in fact, probably severely understated in our hypothetical example of *one* bomb hitting one city. Given the size of the U.S. and Soviet strategic nuclear arsenals, it is likely that if a city the size of Detroit is attacked, it would be hit by many bombs in an all-out nuclear war. Moreover, in such an event there might well be no outside assistance on which the surviving residents of the devastated city could rely.

In the next two chapters we shall consider the effects of a nuclear war—both on the targeted countries and worldwide. We shall then consider what impact civil defense efforts might have in mitigating the effects of such a catastrophe.

STUDY QUESTIONS

1. What are all the prompt and delayed effects of a nuclear-weapon detonation?

2. How does the relative range of each of the effects vary with distance from ground zero?

3. Why would a bomb targeted on a city probably be airburst?

4. Why would a bomb targeted on a hardened missile silo probably be ground burst?

5. What action (if any) would you take if you saw an immensely bright flash of light while outside? While inside?

6. How far would you have to be from ground zero to have a 50 percent chance of surviving a 20-megaton-bomb blast? A one-megaton-bomb blast?

7. Under which conditions would a bomb detonated over a city be likely to cause the greatest number of prompt casualties: night/day, fair weather/smoggy, summer/winter, airburst/ground burst?

8. Why is it difficult to predict the effects of fallout?

9. Why are the number of fatalities estimated by the OTA report likely to be underestimates?

Seven _____

THE EFFECTS OF NUCLEAR WAR ON THE UNITED STATES AND THE SOVIET UNION _____

WHAT LIMITS ARE THERE TO OUR KNOWLEDGE OF THE EFFECTS OF A NUCLEAR WAR?

Much has been written on the effects of a nuclear war between the United States and the Soviet Union. The fact is, however, that no one really knows what the results of such a horrendous catastrophe would be despite the numerous detailed studies that have been made. A typical view is that expressed in a speech by Senator Alan Cranston: "Total U.S.-U.S.S.R. nuclear war could mean the death of everyone inhabiting the Northern Hemisphere." [1] The key word in this sentence is "could." In light of the vast uncertainties as to what an all-out nuclear war might involve, only a rash optimist would assert the opposite, i.e., that a large-scale nuclear war could not mean the death of everyone inhabiting the Northern Hemisphere. Of greater concern than whether such a catastrophe is theoretically possible, however, is some estimate of its likelihood.

Before the very first nuclear explosion was detonated on the sands of Alamagordo, New Mexico, scientists recognized the theoretical possibility that mankind's first nuclear detonation could be its last. There was a nonzero probability that the explosion could set off a chain reaction that would incinerate the atmosphere. One can only imagine the thoughts going through physicist Hans Bethe's mind while he attempted to calculate the odds against such an event. He found incineration of the atmosphere to be exceedingly improbable, since it would require, among other things, that natural laws be at variance with what physicists had found to be true. It is not particularly reassuring to learn that the fate of the world may have rested on a few scientists' judgment that their understanding of the universe was sufficiently complete that the incineration of the atmosphere was an extremely unlikely eventuality. However, my main point is that we must make such estimates of the probability of events that have never occurred and not simply be satisfied by statements that some particular eventuality "could" occur.

Nuclear war aside, the fact that we literally could die in the next moment should certainly have an impact on the manner in which we conduct our lives. However, the fact that our death in the next moment is unlikely should also effect the way we conduct our lives. Jonathan Schell's central thesis, that "once we learn that a holocaust *might* lead to extinction we have no right to gamble, because if we lose, the game will be over, and neither we nor anyone else will get another chance," [2] is fatally flawed since any action we take to avoid the nuclear holocaust (including Schell's recommendation of disarmament and world government) is a gamble that may not work. While we have no choice but to gamble on some course of action, hopefully we will choose the one that minimizes the probability of catastrophe. We shall consider at another time why Schell's suggested course of action may in fact be more of a gamble than some others.

There are many reasons for our lack of knowledge about the consequences of a nuclear war. The following list is only meant to be illustrative.

- It is unknown what fraction of the 50,000 nuclear weapons in the world would be used, or how they would be detonated.

- It is unknown what the targets of these weapons would be.

- It is unknown what actions would be taken by governments or individuals before the attack or survivors after the attack.

- It is not known what actions would be taken by untargeted countries following the attack.

- Our knowledge of atmospheric processes is not sufficient to predict long-term worldwide effects with great confidence (see next chapter).

- There is a possibility that a nuclear attack would be combined with a biological and chemical attack as well.

- There is no way to reliably estimate the probability of catastrophic epidemics or severe ecological or environmental imbalances arising from the attack.

- Other incalculable or totally unknown factors might greatly alter any estimates of damage.

The last two points are especially important ones that may be generally summarized by one of the major conclusions of the previously mentioned OTA study: "The effects of a nuclear war that cannot be calculated are at least as important as those for which calculations are attempted. Moreover, even these limited calculations are subject to very large uncertainties." [3] For this reason we should be wary of any pronouncements, even by supposed experts, that are categorical statements about the effects of a nuclear war. One type of statement, made by a few misguided civil defense supporters, is that our society would be able to recover from the effects of an all-out nuclear war in only a few years. Such optimistic statements reflect an ignorance of the enormous degree of devastation that nuclear weapons are capable of inflicting; a neglect of incalculable or unpredictable physical, environmental, and psychological effects; and an assumption that after an all-out nuclear war there will be a continuing federal government in charge of some kind of recovery effort. Perhaps for those who make such statements, the nonexistence of a federal bureaucracy following a nuclear holocaust is just as unthinkable as nuclear war itself.

A related view, that nuclear war can be thought of as an extension of conventional war with a clear-cut winner and loser, is also held by some people in both the United States and U.S.S.R. The belief that nuclear war might be winnable, expressed in the past writings of a number of Soviet leaders, have not appeared in recent Soviet writings or pronouncements. However, that may or may not say anything about what the Soviets actually think about this matter. Certainly if the Soviet military did believe nuclear war to be winnable, it would be in the interest of the Soviet government to profess the contrary, thereby giving no ammunition to an American administration that maintains the Soviets have nuclear superiority. The Soviet government is sufficiently sophisticated to understand how public pronouncements on certain nuclear issues may have a desirable impact, from their perspective, on American public opinion, and hence on military-deployment actions approved by the Congress. The need to not speak carelessly about nuclear matters may not have been as well appreciated by some U.S. administrations.

Related to the winnable-nuclear-war school of thought is the idea that a nuclear war can be fought in a carefully controlled manner. Reportedly it is more often some civilian defense analysts who believe such absurd ideas, rather than the more "conservative" military people who have had no experience fighting a nuclear war and do not know what would happen. Those believing that nuclear war is likely to be winnable or controllable would almost certainly be psychologically predisposed to play down the effects of a nuclear war.

WHY IS IT UNDESIRABLE TO UNDERSTATE OR OVERSTATE THE EFFECTS OF A NUCLEAR WAR?

Just as there are those whose outlook may predispose them to be optimists or understaters of the effects of a nuclear war, so also there are those predisposed to be pessimists. Consider, for example the statement made by Jonathan Schell in *The Fate of the Earth:* "It has sometimes been claimed that the United States could survive a nuclear attack by the Soviet Union, but the bare figures on the extent of the blast waves, the thermal pulses, and the accumulated local fallout dash this hope irrevocably." [4] As we shall see, the "bare figures" show no such thing. Moreover, to refute Schell's assertion one need not believe that nuclear war is certainly survivable—only that it might be survivable. The kind of uncertainties referred to earlier inherent in estimates of what a nuclear war might involve are so great that they refute categorical statements either of survivability or nonsurvivability.

Our discussion on the effects of a nuclear war will be largely based on material contained in the previously mentioned OTA study, *The Effects of Nuclear War.* An examination of the possible long-term worldwide effects discussed in the next chapter is at least as important to examine as the effects on the countries directly involved. If a significant probability of a long-term, worldwide ecological, climatological, or other catastrophe actually exists, then of course the effects on the directly involved countries are almost irrelevant.

As we examine the probable effects of a nuclear war, we shall also examine what others have written on this matter. We shall find considerable examples of both overstatement and understatement, even when others refer to the conclusions from the same study. Although we shall point out examples of both overstatement and understatement, it is not unreasonable to pay a bit more attention to the former, which seem to occur in the media with much greater frequency. Moreover, surveys of popular beliefs about nuclear war would seem to indicate that such overstatements are widely believed. One example of this should be illustrative. In a recent poll, 91 percent of Americans surveyed expressed a belief that they would personally not have a "good" chance to survive a limited nuclear war involving strikes against military targets.[5] This finding may be contrasted with the OTA study estimate that between 1 and 20 million Americans might be killed in an attack limited to military targets, the so-called counterforce attack. The "most likely" fatality figure was reported to be 10 million or 5 percent of the population. Thus, quite apart from what the likelihood of a nuclear war remaining "limited" might be, there is a considerable variance between the public perception of probable casualties in a limited nuclear war and the results of a detailed analysis. There may be those who believe it is best to overstate the horrors of nuclear war in order to help insure that such a war remains in the domain of the unthinkable. Perhaps the analogy might be that overstatement of the effects psychologically deters nuclear war in much the same way that the nuclear-overkill capacity deters one. With such a high-minded justification, the need for objectivity and critical analysis based on facts may easily be dismissed as an obstacle in the way of a larger political good.

The political importance of dwelling on apocalyptic imagery to further the cause of peace is made quite explicit, for example, by Louis René Beres: "We must come to understand that the growing number of formulations of livable post-apocalypse worlds are both nonsense and dangerous. *This is the case because they interfere with the essential task of cultivating end of the world imagery—imagery that must preclude a durable peace*" (emphasis added).[6]

A common method of overstatement involves always assuming the worst when confronting uncertain predictions. Thus, for example, the OTA study, which found that a Soviet counterforce attack on the United States would probably lead to between 1 and 20 million U.S. fatalities, is summarized in that report by noting that such an attack might result in as many as 20 million fatalities. This is almost invariably the way the results of the study are reported by others. An "overstater" very likely would find nothing wrong with such a statement, but would almost certainly conclude that someone reporting the equally correct statement that a counterforce attack might result in as few as 1 million fatalities was deliberately playing down the probable effects of nuclear war for some sinister purpose. If one is sincerely interested in conveying the great extent of our uncertainty in such things, is it not best to quote the 1-to-20-million result rather than simply an upper limit? However, there may be another reason for such overstatement in this case. By ignoring the extremely wide range of estimated fatalities, the overstater is able to conveniently ignore the fundamental reason for the wide range, i.e., the likely effectiveness of civil defense in the case of a limited nuclear war.

There have also been many examples of understatement on the effects of a nuclear war, not infrequently from government sources. For example, the reason that the OTA study was done in the first place was because several U.S. senators were highly skeptical of estimates presented to Congress by James Schlesinger, former secretary of defense, on the likely casualties following a Soviet counterforce attack on U.S. ICBM silos. Schlesinger's estimate was "only" 800,000 civilian deaths.[7] The OTA study was then commissioned by Congress to check on this figure. The higher estimate in the OTA study was arrived at because it assumed a more probable counterforce-attack scenario that included attacks on bomber bases and submarines in port—targets often near population concentrations. The Schlesinger study also assumed a lower-than-normal wind velocity that produced less fallout than expected. Studies based on such optimistic assumptions have little credibility, and they raise questions about the optimist's motives. But exactly the same can be said about the pessimists, who always obtain results by making worst-case assumptions. Of course there is nothing wrong with making worst-case assumptions, as long as it is explicitly recognized that the underlying premises are probably extremely unlikely, a subtlety often lost when such results are presented to the public.

For too long we have been living in a dream, suppressing the knowledge that a nuclear holocaust could suddenly turn everyday existence into a hell. Our reawakening to the potential horrors of nuclear war is a healthy thing. Nuclear war certainly must be avoided, and it should indeed be greatly feared. However, an objective assessment of the facts (with all the uncertainties) will better serve us than will an overly optimistic or pessimistic portrayal. It is essential for our psychological health that we look into the face of the nuclear war "monster" and see it for what it is or is likely to be (as far as it is knowable)—not for what it could conceivably be if our worst fantasies came true.

It is also highly undesirable for government leaders and others to suffer from illusions that lead them to understate the probability of nuclear war and make it seem manageable. However, while the great danger of such illusions of understatement should be obvious to anyone, the dangers of overstating the consequences of a nuclear war may not be as well appreciated. Nevertheless, the danger of overstatement, if it should lead the public to support unwise policies, may conceivably be just as important in terms of its effect on the probability of a nuclear war.

WHAT ARE THE PROBABLE EFFECTS OF AN ATTACK LIMITED TO MILITARY TARGETS?

A nuclear attack on the United States that was limited to strategic military targets, i.e., ICBM silos, bomber bases, and submarines in port, would necessarily also involve targeting a number of civilian areas—it would certainly not be a neat "surgical" strike. As we have already noted, the OTA study estimated that such a strike would result in 1 to 20 million deaths, depending on the wind and on the actions taken by the population such as seeking shelter or evacuating from areas downwind of the directly targeted areas. During a period following the attack, medical care would probably be unavailable in many areas, particularly those directly hit or those where the fallout was especially intense. Although most productive resources would survive a counterforce attack,[8] the economy would be effectively shut down until people were sure the war was over. The greatest degree of damage to the economy would result from lost production time and from deaths and injuries to the workers. According to the OTA study: "Economic viability would not be at issue following a counterforce attack. . . . The Nation would be able to restore production and maintain self sufficiency. The attack would cause enormous economic loss, *but the Nation's capacity for growth would be at worst only slightly impaired*" (emphasis added).[9] A counterforce attack would necessarily involve ground bursts on ICBM silos which would create a significant amount of fallout. Although most of those civilians taking appropriate evacuation or shelter precautions could survive following a period of considerable hardship, many farm animals in the heavier fallout areas would be killed. Crops would be less effected as they are more radiation resistant than animals. Meat would probably be scarce for a number of years while the livestock supply was being rebuilt. There would be some long-term public health problems when the present peacetime "negligible risk" criteria for setting permitted radiation levels would be changed to "acceptable risk," in order to avoid greater dangers, e.g., starvation.

The greatest uncertainty in the event of a counterforce attack would be whether the war would escalate to all-out catastrophe. It would be of little value to speculate about the consequences of an attack that has no probability of occurrence. Those who are predisposed to the view that the United States needs to modernize its nuclear arsenal worry that the United States could lose such a limited nuclear war. However, their belief that nuclear war would probably stay limited may place too much confidence in the role of rational calculation during a period in which there would be enormous pressures on political and military leaders to make literally earth-shattering decisions in a very short time and when an adversary will undoubtedly be doing everything possible to disrupt such planning. No American president is likely to fail to retaliate with all means at his disposal after a "limited" counterforce attack involving the loss of 1 to 20 million citizens. On the other hand, those who dismiss the possibility that a counterforce attack could remain limited, believing it would inevitably lead to all-out war, are also probably mistaken. It is possible, for example, that our instinct for self-preservation might assert itself to prevent the ultimate catastrophe, even after a limited nuclear war had begun. But there is no way to know in advance what would happen. Those who believe in the impossibility of a nuclear war remaining limited may wish to dismiss counterforce scenarios because such people assume that to discuss such possibilities and to make contingency plans only makes them more thinkable and, therefore, more likely. They may also believe that if one grants the possibility of a nuclear war remaining limited, such an admission may give ammunition to those who argue that the U.S. nuclear forces are vulnerable and need modernizing.

If the United States were to launch a comparable counterforce attack on the Soviet Union, the OTA study projects a similar result though with somewhat fewer estimated fatalities: 1 to 5 percent of the Soviet population.[10] The biggest imponderable following a counterforce attack (aside from what further military action would follow), would be the psychological effect of the attack—particularly in the case of the U.S. population, which has never suffered anything like the number of casualties that a counterforce attack might cause. Such an attack on the U.S.S.R. would also be an enormous psychological blow, but perhaps comparable to some that country has borne in the past. (However, this statement does not imply that such a loss would be considered "acceptable" by the U.S.S.R.) Other important differences between the impact of a nuclear attack on the United States and Soviet Union will be discussed in the next section.

WHAT ARE THE PROBABLE EFFECTS OF A LARGE NUCLEAR ATTACK?

A massive nuclear attack on the United States by the Soviet Union, usually associated with an all-out nuclear war, would involve a large fraction of the Soviet strategic nuclear arsenal delivered against a wide range of urban and industrial targets, strategic targets, and other military targets. It is possible that every major and medium-size U.S. city would be hit, some with many weapons. The heaviest-hit targets would undoubtedly be those military targets hit in the hypothetical counterforce attack in an attempt to minimize damage done by a U.S. retaliatory attack. Those weapons targeted on the midwestern ICBM fields would probably be ground burst, in which case they would generate great amounts of fallout. Other weapons might be either airburst or ground burst. The OTA report presents the results of three different studies of such a large scale attack on the United States; the studies were completed by the Department of Defense (DOD) in 1977, the Arms Control and Disarmament Agency (ACDA) in 1978, and the Defense Civil Preparedness Agency (DCPA) in 1978. The three studies assume Soviet nuclear-force-level growth to the mid-1980s, but constrained by SALT II ceilings. The ACDA study assumed, however, that 60 percent of the weapons would be ground burst, while the other two studies assumed that all weapons would be ground burst for maximum fallout. The three studies calculated different numbers of fatalities for such an attack; figures in each category given below represent the extreme ranges based on all three studies:

Percent U.S. Fatalities in Large Soviet Attack

No civil defense measures taken   48–75 percent fatalities

Available nearby shelter used   35–66 percent fatalities

Relocation and sheltering of population   10–26 percent fatalities

The percentages given above are of the entire U.S. population, and they account for fatalities during the first thirty days, including those due to fallout. The percentages do not count subsequent deaths among the injured or deaths due to economic disruption, epidemics, or deprivation.

To better understand how a relocation and sheltering of the population can make so much difference in the preceding fatality estimates, it is helpful to examine figure 7.1 which shows the areas of the United States that might be directly affected by blast and thermal damage in a hypothetical attack involving 6,559 megatons. The circles show areas covered by 2-psi or greater overpressure. As previously pointed out, the total area affected by blast and thermal damage is a relatively small fraction of the total U.S. land area. The map in figure 7.2 shows the extent of fallout resulting from this attack. The contours show different levels of two-week cumulative dose under the idealized, but not atypical, condition of a constant 20 mph westerly wind. It will be seen that over more than half the United States, the two-week cumulative dose exceeds the LD-50 dose of 450 rem (lethal to half the exposed unprotected population).

The factor by which the dose to the occupant is reduced measures a shelter's protection factor. For a population sheltered in home basements (typical protection factor of 10 to 20), or in fallout shelters (typical protection factor of perhaps 100), lethal levels of the two-week cumulative dose would be present over a very small fraction of the U.S. land area. For example, if it were possible to shelter the entire population at a protection factor of 22, the two-week dose to shelter occupants would exceed LD-50 only for the one-percent of the land area lying inside the 10,000 rem contours of figure 7.2. Moreover, after two weeks the radiation intensity will have dropped to one-thousandth the intensity at one hour after the detonation (see appendix A). A much smaller fraction of the population is likely to be in areas of extremely high fallout levels if the population were dispersed over the countryside rather than if it remained in place near likely targets. This conclusion is not highly dependent on which particular areas might be targeted.

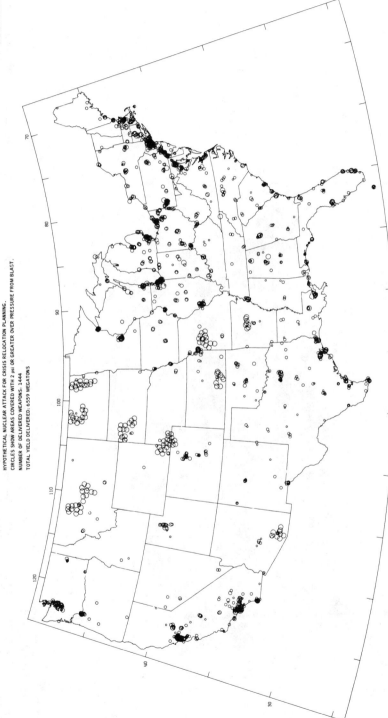

HYPOTHETICAL NUCLEAR ATTACK FOR CRISIS RELOCATION PLANNING.

CIRCLES SHOW AREAS COVERED WITH 2 psi OR GREATER OVER PRESSURE FROM BLAST.

NUMBER OF DELIVERED WEAPONS: 1444

TOTAL YIELD DELIVERED: 6559 MEGATONS

Figure 7.1   Blast damage from large-scale nuclear attack (2 psi or more).
Source: "Survival of the Relocated Population of the U.S. after a Nuclear Attack," Oak Ridge National Laboratory, p. 22.
Note: Circles show areas covered with 2 psi or greater overpressure from blast in a hypothetical nuclear attack against the U.S. in which 6,559 megatons are delivered.

FOURTEEN–DAY RADIATION EXPOSURE DOSES
EFFECTIVE WIND: 20 MPH FROM THE WEST

0–100 R	101–450 R	451–2,500 R	2,501–5,000 R
5,001–10,000 R	10,001–20,000 R	> 20,000 R	

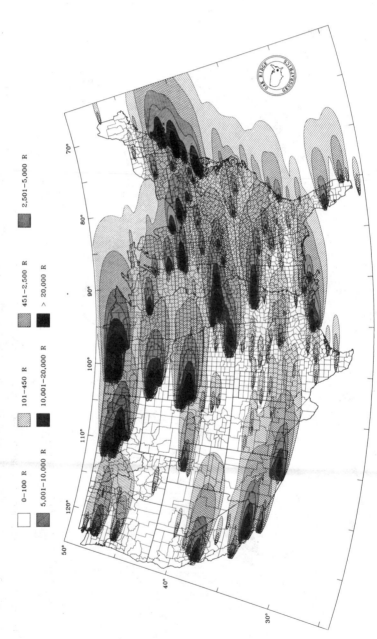

Figure 7.2 Dose contours for large-scale nuclear attack (in rems).
Source: Oak Ridge National Laboratory DWG 81-6307 supplied by Conrad Chester.
Notes: Contours for two-week accumulated dose in rems for a large-scale attack on the U.S., assuming an idealized 20 mph west wind. The attack assumed that 6,559 megatons were delivered, of which all but 17 percent are ground burst. The radiation doses

In the areas directly hit (the circled areas in the hypothetical attack in figure 7.1), there would be damage on a scale never before witnessed, except on a smaller scale at Hiroshima and Nagasaki. Most hospitals would have been destroyed. Medical attention and rescue efforts would be all but impossible because the streets would be filled with debris. It is doubtful that "outside" areas would be able to offer assistance or would want to buck the flood tide of evacuation. Smaller cities and towns would probably be spared direct bomb damage, but would be soon inundated with refugees. There would be tremendous confusion and panic, although some panic could be avoided if reliable information could be provided and if such information were believed.

The heaviest fallout from ground-burst weapons targeted on midwestern ICBM fields would begin arriving on the densely populated Boston to Norfolk corridor within twelve to thirty hours depending on the wind speed. (Fallout from other targets would arrive much sooner.) Hence, for survivors in much of the eastern United States, as well as other areas, life-and-death decisions such as whether to seek nearby shelter or to evacuate would need to be made in the first hours before wind-borne fallout arrives. Many people would not find adequate shelter and would die from radiation sickness. Others would flock to already overcrowded shelters. They would have to endure a number of life-threatening problems associated with inadequate water and food, and health problems made worse by inadequate sanitation, radiation exposure, and psychological reactions that might mimic radiation sickness. In the heaviest fallout areas, the shelter period could last up to a month, although in most areas it would be much less. (This is discussed in more detail in chapter 9.) During this shelter period some people might need to forage outside briefly for food or water. If the shelter was not equipped with radiation monitoring equipment, nor was there any communication with outside, there would be great uncertainty over when it was safe to leave the shelter. It is doubtful that most people would be sufficiently "rational" under such conditions to believe that symptoms mimicking radiation sickness were psychologically induced (although they might well be), even though the radiation meter indicated a safe level.

Survival in the rural areas and in small towns might be significantly easier than in other areas. The population there would have been spared the initial traumatic exposure to tremendous death and destruction. Additionally, such areas would be less crowded, and the more self-reliant rural population would be likely to have previously stored supplies on hand, enabling them to better survive the shelter period. Nevertheless, survival of appreciable numbers of people during the first weeks and months does not assure their long-term survival. Several very serious long-term threats to survivors are discussed in the next chapter.

WHAT ARE THE PROSPECTS FOR RECOVERY FOLLOWING A LARGE NUCLEAR ATTACK?

We shall now consider the question of the probability of eventual recovery in the event of a large nuclear attack and what differences might exist between the recovery ability of the United States and the Soviet Union. The question of the long-term, worldwide effects of a large nuclear war will be deferred to the next chapter.

Whether economic recovery of a society is possible following a large nuclear attack depends on the physical survival of enough people and resources and whether those survivors are able to organize themselves. Those studies cited in the OTA report and elsewhere indicate that, despite wide ranges in the estimated number of survivors, the survival of some nonnegligible fraction of the original population is quite probable. Moreover, the survivors would not be a cross section of the prewar society but would be considerably more rural, probably hardier, though also lacking some key industrial skills. Aside from medicine, initially there would be no essential commodity in short supply. For example, the amount of stored grain in the United States amounts to a supply of between several months and more than a year, given the present population.[11] The effect of the intense fallout radiation on growing crops depends both on the particular crops and on the time of year. Crops are most vulnerable during the months April through June, though even during this period between half and two-thirds of various crops would survive, barring a "nuclear winter" (see chapter 8). As seen by comparing table 7.1 with figure 7.2, the radiation levels needed to give a 50-percent reduction in crop yield would not be reached over many areas of the country.

It is also important to note that fallout is not taken up by crops through the soil to any significant degree and that fallout on the surface of surviving crops can be washed off with water. While most of the surface water would become contaminated with fallout, a homemade filtration system could be used to filter out 99 percent

Table 7.1   Estimated Radiation Doses Considered Lethal to Half the Exposed Crops (rads)

Peas	1,000
Rye	1,000– 2,000
Wheat	2,000– 4,000
Corn	2,000– 4,000
Cucumbers	2,000– 4,000
Cotton	6,000– 8,000
Melons	6,000– 8,000
Soybeans	8,000–12,000
Beets	8,000–12,000
Rice	12,000–16,000
Strawberries	12,000–16,000

Source: Office of Technology Assessment, Effects of Nuclear War, p. 88.

of the radioactivity. In addition, underground water supplies such as wells would not become contaminated to any significant extent. As noted earlier, livestock would perish to a much greater degree than crops, although poultry for which the LD-50 dose is 850 rads should survive in many areas.

Even though food stocks and most other essential goods would probably survive in sufficient amounts, restoring production would be extremely difficult. It cannot be said whether the surviving productive facilities would sustain recovery. However, the main problem probably would be an organizational one rather than an insufficient amount of people or material goods. For a society to function there must be some kind of division of labor. The first priority is physical security. Unless someone is maintaining order, people would be reluctant to go to work if they had no assurance that their family, home, and possessions would be safe until they returned. We can only speculate whether this security function might be performed by a strong central government maintaining martial law, by a local militia, or by armed gangs requiring tribute in return for protection from other armed gangs. Assuming physical security existed in some areas, travel over highways between such areas might be quite unsafe, as it was in the Middle Ages. Hijacking of trucks containing food or other supplies on highways by armed groups might become commonplace. Without a strong central government to control such disorder, the country could well break up into regions in conflict with one another. Considering the attitude that now exists between energy-producing and energy-consuming states, for example, it is hard to be sanguine that grain-rich states would be willing, without some compulsion at a national level, to give up their food surpluses for paper money that might be worthless or subject to hyperinflation. The nonexistence of a currency that people had confidence in could lead to a strictly barter economy which is extremely inefficient. In our society many people have highly sophisticated skills that can only be made use of in large organizations, thus they would have nothing to barter with unless they devoted their energies to more basic tasks for which they would be ill prepared.

The basic problem facing the survivors can be stated very simply: Would production be restored before existing assets ran out? If not, the race for survival would be lost and a downward spiral could set in that would return society to something like the Middle Ages. However, it should be noted that even medieval society had a fairly sophisticated economy, but one in which most people's present knowledge and skills would be of very little survival value.

The large number of unburied corpses, lack of sanitation, and lack of medical care following a nuclear attack would constitute an ideal environment for the expansion of the rodent and insect population, and the consequent spread of plague and other epidemic diseases. It has been estimated that 12 percent of survivors would be infected by plague and that half would die. According to some speculations, perhaps as many as a quarter of the survivors might contract some fatal epidemic disease.[12] Outbreaks of uncontrolled epidemics could further fragment society, both psychologically and physically.

An event in which the majority of survivors experienced either the death of close relatives, severe injury, or forced separation from family would have such a profound impact on society that anything might be possible: canibalism, total repudiation of any surviving government, bloody revolution, reconstruction of cities underground. Moreover, among the imponderables is whether the war would be over quickly or whether it might go on for a period of weeks or months. One can only imagine the survivors' feeling of hopelessness if, after making some modest recovery efforts, the country continued to be bombarded by missiles from surviving enemy nuclear submarines or other forces. Moreover, the presence of such continued military action might well divert resources needed for a recovery. In past major wars such as World War II, people have rallied behind the government and made sacrifices. In a large nuclear war it is impossible to predict what the attitude of survivors might be to the prospect of continued hostilities. Once a large nuclear war occurs, the unthinkable will have happened and nothing will ever be the same—particularly our attitudes.

HOW DO THE PROSPECTS FOR SURVIVAL IN THE UNITED STATES AND THE U.S.S.R. COMPARE?

Until now we have been considering the impact of a large Soviet nuclear attack on the United States. The OTA report also described the impact of a large U.S. nuclear attack on the Soviet Union. The U.S. attack is assumed in that report to be a retaliatory attack, and hence one involving only those strategic nuclear forces that are assumed to survive a Soviet first strike. These surviving forces would be capable of inflicting a devastating blow to the Soviet Union, destroying about 70 percent of its economy and resulting in millions of deaths. The fatality estimates according to the various studies mentioned in the OTA report lie in the range 20 to 40 percent if the population did not evacuate, or up to 13 percent if it did successfully evacuate.[13] These percentages are significantly lower than those given earlier for a Soviet attack on the United States, mainly for four reasons: (1) the Soviet Union has made more extensive civil defense preparations than the United States; (2) the Soviet arsenal has larger weapons that can cause more blast and fallout deaths; and (3) the Soviets are assumed to attack first, thereby destroying a sizable fraction of the U.S. nuclear arsenal.

The question of whether the Soviet Union could eventually recover from such an attack is unanswerable. Nevertheless, there are interesting differences between the relative likelihood of eventual recovery in the Soviet Union and the United States. We first consider those factors mentioned in the OTA report that suggest recovery would be less likely in the Soviet Union than in the United States. We also consider qualifying circumstances that might mitigate these Soviet disadvantages or perhaps turn them into advantages.

ALLEGED SOVIET DISADVANTAGES

1. *The Soviet Union reportedly has smaller existing grain stockpiles than the United States.* To compensate for this disadvantage, it should be noted that because Soviet agriculture is inadequate even in peacetime, the U.S.S.R. is quite experienced in handling shortages. Moreover, the probable much smaller radiation damage to Soviet crops (see next section) should not greatly affect the harvest. Finally, it should be noted that not all investigators believe that the Soviet Union has a small existing grain stockpile. According to Harriet Fast

Scott, a Washington-based consultant, the U.S.S.R. has a one-year strategic grain stockpile that is untouchable in peacetime.

2. *The Soviet economy has less "fat" than the American economy.* Offsetting this disadvantage is the fact that the Soviet citizenry has much more experience with real suffering and hardship than American citizens have. In fact, the difference in living conditions between Soviet cities and the countryside is considerably harsher than in the United States. Centuries of living in village poverty have made most Soviet country dwellers much more self-sufficient than their American counterparts.

3. *The Soviet Union has a more concentrated population than the United States.* The comparison between Soviet and American population densities is a complex one. As far as the urban population of each nation is concerned, Soviet cities are indeed more compact. The entire Soviet urban population lives within an area of less than 5000 square miles compared to 14,000 square miles for the U.S. population.[14] Nevertheless, in another sense the Soviet urban population is more dispersed than in the United States: Although half the U.S. population resides in 140 cities, the corresponding figure for the U.S.S.R. is 1000 cities. The existence of many more small- and medium-size cities in the Soviet Union than in the United States means that Soviet cities are more surrounded with vast open spaces, in principle allowing for easier evacuation. As far as the density of the two nations' rural populations are concerned, the comparison is also complex. Although the Soviet Union has a much larger area than the United States, its fraction of habitable land is much less. Overall, the rural population of each nation occupies roughly the same area. Thus all things considered, the population-density differences do not clearly favor either side (see figure 7.3).

4. *The Soviet Union's population lives closer to its industry.* This alleged fact would presumably be a Soviet disadvantage, since weapons targeted against industry would be more likely to kill population as well. However, not so clear that statistics actually favor the Soviet Union on this point. If, for example, we ask what fraction of the work force lives within 1.5 miles of its place of work, the figures show a greater degree of Soviet colocation of population and industry: 31 percent of Soviets as compared to 22 percent of Americans live closer than 1.5 miles. If, however, the home-to-work distance is 5.0 miles, the American degree of colocation is greater: 68 percent of Americans and 52 percent of Soviets live closer than 5.0 miles.[15]

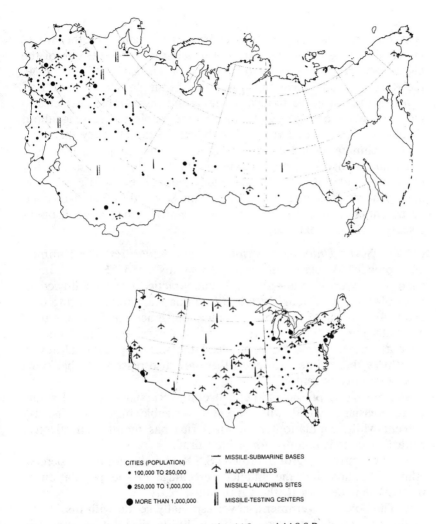

CITIES (POPULATION)
● 100,000 TO 250,000
● 250,000 TO 1,000,000
⬤ MORE THAN 1,000,000

— MISSILE-SUBMARINE BASES
↑ MAJOR AIRFIELDS
| MISSILE-LAUNCHING SITES
‖ MISSILE-TESTING CENTERS

Figure 7.3   Target concentrations in the U.S. and U.S.S.R.
Source: K. Lewis, "Prompt and Delayed Effects of Nuclear War," *Scientific American*, July 1971, pp. 44–45.
Note: Relative concentrations of population and military targets including missile submarine bases, major airfields, missile-launching sites, and testing centers in the U.S. and U.S.S.R.

Again, the claimed area of Soviet disadvantage, in fact, shows no clear edge for either nation.

5.   *The Soviet Union has a more severe climate than the United States.* The intense cold of the Russian winter (which in many areas

lasts half the year) would pose enormous problems for the Soviet Union following a nuclear war, and it perhaps represents one of the biggest Soviet disadvantages relative to the United States. Although the Russian people have coped with the harsh climate for centuries, it would present grave though probably not insuperable obstacles to recovery. These obstacles go far beyond the problem of digging fallout shelters in frozen dirt (which actually can be done). They include a host of climate-related difficulties ranging from impassable country roads during the wet spring and autumn to the increased susceptibility to disease epidemics of an inadequately fed and sheltered population during the subfreezing Soviet winter. This Soviet disadvantage would be accentuated if there were a severe global temperature drop as discussed in the next chapter.

6. *The Soviet Union is a nation of many minorities.* The common U.S. practice of using the terms "Russians" and "Soviets" interchangably is erroneous—although that practice is also followed in most places in this book. In fact, the ruling Russians constitute only about 48 percent of the Soviet population. Since the Russians preferentially live in the cities, their relative percentages would decline after a nuclear war. This could lead the minority nationalities to overthrow the regime. However, there are also reasons for believing this possibility is remote.

a. Even if the present 48-percent ethnic Russians declined somewhat, Russians would still represent a sizable minority. The 10-percent white population in South Africa has maintained effective control over that country for a long time.

b. The controlling group in the U.S.S.R. is really not the 48 percent ethnic Russians, but the smaller percentage of the population (6 percent) that belongs to the Communist party.

c. The Soviet government, never especially gentle with dissidents, might be expected to use all means at its disposal to maintain control—ways that an unarmed citizenry would be helpless to challenge.

d. The Soviet population, normally docile and used to following orders, is unlikely to become rebelious when their very survival would depend on information and orders given by the government.

7. *Postwar threats from other countries.* It is claimed that the Soviet Union would be more vulnerable than the United States following a large nuclear attack because of a continued threat of attack from NATO countries or China. This possibility would seem to require that Western Europe and China not be involved during the initial

U.S.-Soviet nuclear exchange. Although theoretically the English, French, and Chinese could opt to launch their own small independent strategic nuclear arsenals, it is not easy to fathom any motive they might have in attacking a "crazed, badly wounded bear," thereby insuring their own destruction. It should be remembered that even in peacetime a number of NATO governments have been reluctant to station U.S. missiles on their soil lest they become targets.

Only one of the preceding seven reasons for poorer Soviet recovery prospects, the more severe climate, appears to be a significant and unambiguous disadvantage.

We shall see that some of the reasons cited in the OTA report that favor the Soviet Union's recovery prospects may be more significant than those that favor the United States. These reasons are quite apart from the Soviet's smaller number of deaths and injuries if the U.S. attack on the Soviet Union is assumed to be a retaliatory one.

ALLEGED SOVIET ADVANTAGES

There are numerous reasons why the initial period following a large attack on the Soviet Union, as horrible as it would be, might not be quite as grim as a large attack on the United States. In the next we shall discuss Soviet civil defense efforts; such measures include evacuation plans, extensive shelter construction, hardening of industrial facilities against blast, and, perhaps most importantly, public education about nuclear-weapons effects and measures that would be required of survivors.

The Soviet Union also has an advantage over the United States by virtue of its much larger land area, although a smaller fraction of the land is habitable. Nevertheless, the Soviet Union could conceivably face average radiation levels up to one hundred times less than those in the United States under most favorable circumstances.[16] These lower radiation levels not only would produce far fewer fallout deaths, but they would also cause fewer health problems among survivors, less time in the shelters, and less crop and environmental damage.

Perhaps the greatest differences between the probabilities of eventual recovery in the Soviet Union and the United States arise from many socio-economic and political factors. These include:

- A population largely trained in first aid

- Medical dispensaries decentralized, unlike big-city hospital care in the United States which could become largely non-existent

- A high degree of government control over population mobility even in peacetime—a factor essential not only for evacuation, but for maintaining economic control in the recovery period

- A population more used to cramped quarters in shelters or in relocated host areas

- More engineers and technical people than in the United States, especially engineers skilled at improvising solutions when parts are unavailable

- A greater fraction of the population (one-third of the work force) involved in agriculture

- A system of agriculture that is not the high-technology (and thus more vulnerable) enterprise it is in the United States

- Fewer people involved in professions that would be useless following an attack, e.g., insurance salesmen, entertainers, real estate brokers, financial analysts, and lawyers

- A population used to making sacrifices

- A population used to following instructions without question

- A population that does not own guns (either to challenge government troops or to create civil disorder)

- Much less private ownership of material possessions, generally making it easier to share hardships without encountering ownership and legal questions

- Less dependence on the private automobile which would almost certainly become extinct

- Industrial production techniques much simpler than those in the United States, where many stages with highly specialized processes could create potential bottlenecks when a key production element is removed

- Larger military forces that could assist in recovery (the Soviet military has been trained to operate in a contaminated environment)

- Assistance in recovery from other countries such as that following World War II (the Soviets may be in a better position to compel such outside assistance than the United States, given their surviving nuclear and conventional forces)

- Extensive survival of the Communist-party apparatus in numerous city blast shelters would almost certainly result in some continuing Soviet government to coordinate recovery efforts[17]

- A greater capacity for organization and prioritization under a centrally planned system

The last two points cited are of particular importance in light of the comment made in the OTA report that "whether economic recovery would take place, and if so what form it would take, would depend both on the physical survival of enough people and resources to sustain recovery, *and on the question of whether these survivors could adequately organize themselves*" (emphasis added).[18]

Nearly all the factors cited in the previous discussion which would make eventual recovery in the Soviet Union either more likely or less likely than recovery in the United States were cited in the text of the OTA report. An objective reading of these two lists of factors might point to the conclusion that the two societies would face very different probabilities of eventual recovery. Surprisingly, however, the OTA report, after discussing the possibility of eventual recovery in the two societies, concludes: "nor is there any evidence that the Soviets face a lower risk [than the U.S.] of finding themselves unable to rebuild an industrial society at all." [19]

On the whole, many people consider the OTA report to be a relatively balanced description of the probable effects of a nuclear war, neither given to understatement nor overstatement. However, on the issue of relative survivability of the United States and U.S.S.R., the extensive discussion in the report may lead the objective reader to different conclusions from those reached by the reports' authors.

It is possible that the authors of this study did not want to encourage the belief that nuclear war might be survivable—especially the notion that it might be more survivable in the Soviet Union than in the United States. Such uncomfortable thoughts could possibly lead to the idea of a "winnable" nuclear war—an idea that might well make war more likely. However, it seems unwise to keep from the public objective factors that might make a nuclear war more survivable for the Soviet Union than for the United States, even on the basis of such a high-minded justification.

The leaders of both the United States and the U.S.S.R. have, on numerous occasions, said that they do not believe in winnable nuclear wars, but that the government of the adversary *does* appear to hold that belief. In addition, while denouncing the idea of a winnable nuclear war, high officials on each side have said that their country would "prevail" in a nuclear war, although it is not clear how prevailing and winning differ. In the absence of the event, the question of whether a nuclear war can be won—in the sense of one country having much better recovery prospects—seems unlikely to have a definitive answer. Certainly, there would be no winner in a nuclear war, in the sense that both countries would suffer very great levels of damage. Nevertheless, the Soviet Union does not need an OTA report for its leaders to come to the conclusion that in many respects a large nuclear war might be more survivable for their country than for the United States. It is possible they might even conclude that it is "winnable," while steadfastly maintaining the opposite. A chorus of U.S. spokesmen who continually proclaim that nuclear war is not winnable will not convince the Soviet leadership, if in fact there are objective reasons for them to believe otherwise. Therefore, it is essential for the U.S. public and its leaders to view facts objectively and to not delude ourselves into believing things we would wish were true, e.g., that no sane person could believe in a winnable nuclear war.

Regardless of the beliefs of political leaders, the military planners in the United States and the Soviet Union appear to have a different view of the winnability of nuclear war. When military planners speak about recovery following a nuclear war, they do not have in mind recovery to the prewar state of society. Rather, the planners are thinking of recovery of the ability to wage nuclear war. They see the most likely result of a nuclear war as a race to prepare for another one. If the military planners are right, then the threat of nuclear war would not end with Nuclear War I, and moreover the country with poorer recovery prospects might never recover. It is also possible, of course, that this fate could belong to both the "winner" and the "loser" in an all-out nuclear war, particularly if there should be a catastrophic worldwide impact—the subject of the next chapter.

STUDY QUESTIONS

1. What are some of the reasons it is difficult to determine the number of casualties that might result from a nuclear war?

2. To what extent do you think our political beliefs and psychological makeup predispose us to be "pessimists" or "optimists" about the question of survivability of a nuclear war?

3. What do studies indicate would be the effects of a nuclear war limited to counterforce targets? An all out nuclear attack? Do you believe the studies? Why?

4. What would conditions probably be like for survivors several days after an all-out nuclear attack? Several months? Several years?

5. In what respects would the Soviet Union be more likely or less likely than the United States to be able to recover from an all-out nuclear attack? In what respects might the United States be more likely to recover than the U.S.S.R.?

6. Is it a good idea to do studies on the survivability of a large nuclear war?

7. Do you believe that overall a large nuclear war would be more survivable for the Soviet Union or for the United States? Explain.

8. If studies indicate that in some ways a large nuclear war might be more survivable for the Soviet Union than for the United States, is it wise to admit this and make it known? Could such an admission have an adverse effect on prospects for peace? Should they influence U.S. defense and arms-control policies?

Eight _____

THE LONG-TERM
WORLDWIDE EFFECTS
OF A NUCLEAR WAR _____

WHAT ARE THE LIKELY WORLDWIDE EFFECTS OF A LARGE-SCALE NUCLEAR WAR?

The world's strategic and theatre nuclear arsenals include an estimated 13,000 megatons. One discovers many uncertainties in attempting to estimate the likely casualties that would result from the use of these arsenals, equivalent in total yield to one million Hiroshima bombs. If, for example, we assumed that a nuclear war involved not just the United States and U.S.S.R. but all NATO and Warsaw Pact countries as well, then the population directly at risk would double from 500 million to one billion persons. In addition, if we were to assume that China is attacked, then the population directly at risk would double again to include nearly half the world's population.

One study of the direct effects of a large-scale nuclear war, reported in the Swedish journal *Ambio,* assumed that the targets would include most cities in the Northern Hemisphere in addition to other economic and military targets.[1] The resulting direct casualties in the *Ambio* scenario would include 750 million fatalities and about 340 million seriously injured, or roughly a quarter of the world's

213

population. Other studies that make different assumptions about likely targets get different estimates that are usually lower than those of the *Ambio* scenario. At least one study, however, making very pessimistic targeting assumptions has reported twice the *Ambio* casualties.[2]

It is futile to argue that specific countries would or would not be targets in a large-scale nuclear war. There probably are various geopolitical reasons why the United States might, for example, not with to attack Eastern Europe or why the U.S.S.R. might wish to spare parts of Western Europe. Nevertheless, once a nuclear war begins, the psychology of those individuals controlling the arsenals may make such geopolitical considerations irrelevant. It is, therefore, impossible to dismiss as implausible scenarios that result in anywhere from several hundred million to two billion casualties, or even figures outside this range.

As horrible as the direct effects of a large-scale nuclear war might be, in this chapter our primary interest is with the delayed long-term effects and what they portend for the survival of those who do not perish in the initial days following a large-scale nuclear war. The delayed effects, in contrast to the direct effects, would have worldwide impact, therefore, they could threaten populations remote from the countries where nuclear detonations occur.

A number of scientific studies have been completed on the probable worldwide impact of a large-scale nuclear war. One such widely quoted study was conducted by the National Academy of Sciences (NAS) in 1975.[3] The NAS study described the worldwide impact as serious, but by no means catastrophic in areas remote from nuclear-weapons detonations; in fact, it concluded that the survival of the human race would not be in question following a large-scale nuclear war. More recent studies, however, have come to somewhat more pessimistic conclusions, based on the consideration of an effect on global climate that had been overlooked in the 1975 NAS study.

In 1982 Crutzen and Birks claimed that a large-scale nuclear war could create enough smoke to block out perhaps as much as 99 percent of ambient sunlight for an extended period of time—perhaps many months.[4] The extended period of blocked sunlight would result in a severe temperature drop at the earth's surface over much of the Northern Hemisphere. The prolonged period of darkness and cold referred to as a "nuclear winter" could have a devastating impact on surviving humans, plants, and animals.

Following the initial work of Crutzen and Birks, other studies by Turco et al.,[5] Covey, Thompson, and Schneider,[6] and Mac-Cracken,[7] have also found that it is likely there would be a severe climatic impact resulting from the dust and smoke created in a nuclear war.[8] The study by Turco et al., which has been given the acronym TTAPS after the first initials of its five authors, has perhaps received the most publicity. One rather grim summary of these findings was presented at a conference on the worldwide impact of nuclear war:

In the aftermath of a 5,000 Mt nuclear exchange, survivors would face extreme cold, water shortages, lack of food and fuel, heavy burdens of radiation and pollutants, diseases, and severe psychological stress—all in twilight or darkness.

It is clear that the ecosystem effects alone resulting from a large-scale thermonuclear war would be enough to destroy civilization as we know it in at least the Northern Hemisphere. These long-term effects, when combined with the direct casualties from the blast, suggest that eventually there might be no human survivors in the Northern Hemisphere. Human beings, other animals and plants in the Southern Hemisphere would also suffer profound consequences.

Even more ominously, the summary concludes that "the scenario described here is by no means the most severe that could be imagined with present world nuclear arsenals and those contemplated for the near future." [9]

Are these conclusions realistic? We are not so much interested in "what could be imagined," as in what might be expected to occur and with some estimate of its likelihood. It is understandable that we want to know the worst that is likely to happen. Nevertheless, if that worst case has a negligibly small likelihood, it may be more useful to worry about more probable occurrences. Alternatively, if we should find there is a significant likelihood of a climatic catastrophe of the magnitude some have suggested, then the indirect effects of a nuclear war would assume much greater importance than the direct effects, and the policy implications could be profound.

We shall focus mainly on the three primary, indirect long-term effects of a large-scale nuclear war: climatic change (nuclear winter), ozone-layer depletion, and radioactive fallout. We will need to ex-amine in each case both the magnitude of the effect and its probable impact on man and on the environment. It may be helpful to summarize the conclusions of our analysis at the outset of the discussion.

1. The authors of the TTAPS and other studies have performed a valuable service in alerting the scientific community and the public to the fact that the worldwide long-term impact of a nuclear war could be significantly more severe than had earlier been expected.

2. In correcting an earlier misconception, some scientists may have gone too far in the other direction and used tentative findings to imply that catastrophic ecological changes would be the likely outcome of any nuclear war, even a "small" one.

3. Much research remains to be done before we can have great confidence in the estimates of worldwide ecological damage resulting from a nuclear war. However, even after these additional studies are done, it is inevitable that considerable uncertainty will remain.

4. Even though more refined studies on the worldwide impact of a nuclear war may show somewhat different results, a discussion of the policy implications should not await more refined studies. In these findings there are possibly important implications for policy, not all of which are obvious.

WHAT CLIMATIC CHANGES WOULD A NUCLEAR WAR BRING ABOUT?

Catastrophic changes in the world's climate must be viewed with the greatest concern. There is evidence to suggest that the dinosaurs became extinct 65 million years ago due to a severe climatic change that occurred when a large meteorite collided with the earth and created a huge quantity of dust in the atmosphere, thereby blocking the sunlight for an extended period.[10] Moreover, even changes in average global climate on a relatively small scale can have a very large impact on a local or regional basis. A volcanic eruption in 1815 put enough dust into the atmosphere to lower the average global temperature by 1°C. This modest global drop was associated with very severe regional temperature drops. In fact in Europe and America, 1816 was known as "the year without a summer."

Although volcanic eruptions can have an effect on climate, the magnitude of that effect is now believed to be much less than would occur following a nuclear war. In the 1975 National Academy of Sciences study it had been thought that a large volcanic eruption could serve as a model for the climatic impact of a nuclear war, since the amount of dust thrown up would be approximately the same.[11] Nuclear explosions are, however, far more efficient in adding fine dust to the atmosphere than are volcanic eruptions. This result comes about partly because the nuclear dust is finer than volcanic dust, which makes it a better scatterer of light and allows it to block more sunlight for a longer time. A second reason that the volcano comparison is a poor indication of likely climatic change following a nuclear war is that it neglects to consider the large amount of smoke resulting from fires that might burn in cities, forests, and oil refineries for weeks following the war.

There is a very important difference between the effect expected from dust and that from smoke in the aftermath of a nuclear war, even though both result in a sunlight blockage and an associated temperature drop. The smoke would be expected to cause a relatively more severe temperature drop than the dust, but one that would not last as long. The reason for this difference is that the soot particles in smoke are, on average, smaller than dust particles and are much better absorbers of light, making them better able to block sunlight.[12] Smoke particles from fires, however, do not normally rise to as high an altitude as the dust, and therefore they are removed faster by precipitation scrubbing than the higher-altitude dust.

The relative amounts of smoke and dust that would occur in the aftermath of a nuclear war depends largely on what assumptions we make about the nature of the targets. Weapons air burst over cities would be expected to produce primarily smoke, while weapons ground burst on missile silos would produce primarily dust. Thus, the details of the predicted climatic change in the aftermath of a nuclear war depends on what scenario we assume. In order to make a detailed calculation of this kind it is necessary to assume specific-size weapons detonated at a specific altitude over a specific set of targets, and then to estimate the magnitude of the dust and smoke that would be created, and how long each would stay up before descending back to earth. The TTAPS study considered a whole range of different scenarios, four of which are shown in figure 8.1.

The four curves labelled A, B, C, and D in figure 8.1 show the predicted average land temperature drop in the Northern Hemisphere as a function of time after the nuclear war for each of four scenarios. It is quite clear from the large differences between some of these four curves that the climatic consequences of a nuclear war are highly dependent on the assumed scenario; therefore, it is important to understand what assumptions have been made in each case.

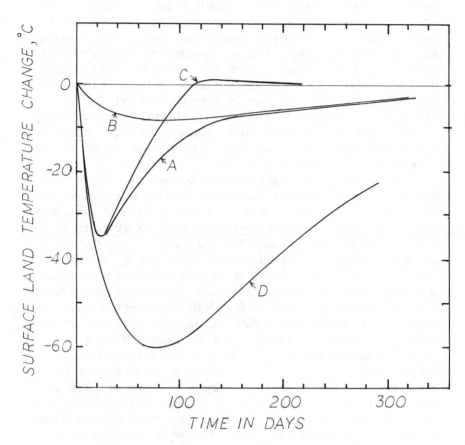

Figure 8.1   Temperature declines after nuclear war.
Source: C. Sagan, "Nuclear War and Climatic Catastrophe; Some Policy Implications," *Foreign Affairs,* Winter 1983–84.

Curve A—The baseline scenario. The baseline scenario corresponds to the use of 5000 megatons, 20 percent of which is directed
against urban and industrial targets and the rest against military
(counterforce) targets, especially missile silos. Many analysts might
consider this scenario to be a reasonably plausible large-scale nuclear
war. The use of less than half of the 13,000 megatons in the strategic
arsenals assumes that a significant fraction of one or both side's
arsenal is destroyed, rendered incapable of delivery, or held back as
a reserve force.

Curve B—The counterforce scenario. The counterforce scenario corresponds to the use of 3000 megatons directed against military targets only, primarily missile silos. The counterforce scenario would result in the smallest temperature drop of the four cases shown in figure 8.1.

Curve C—The small-nuclear-war scenario. The small-nuclear-war scenario corresponds to the use of 100 megatons directed exclusively against cities. A scenario of this type, according to most analysts, would probably be considered to be extremely implausible given the present size of the strategic arsenals and the fact that only cities are targeted. Its inclusion in the TTAPS study was solely for the purpose of making a very surprising point: the temperature drop associated with the 100-megaton war is nearly the same as that for the 5000-megaton baseline scenario (compare curves A and C).

Curve D—The 10,000-megaton "severe" scenario. The "severe" scenario corresponds to the use of 10,000 megatons against a wide range of urban, industrial, and military targets. The scenario is severe in the sense that a number of parameters used to calculate the temperature drop are assumed to have adverse, but not implausible, values. It would be misleading to call this a worst-case scenario, since we cannot rule out the possibility of a nuclear war having a still more adverse climatic impact. Nevertheless, curve D probably represents a scenario whose likelihood is very small, as will be seen when its underlying assumptions are examined.

On what basis can we understand the different temperature drops for these four scenarios, particularly the surprising result that a small nuclear war involving the use of only 0.8 percent of the strategic nuclear megatonnage would produce nearly the same temperature drop as the 5000-megaton baseline case? These four temperature variations can be easily understood by recalling the different behavior of smoke and dust. In the counterforce scenario (curve B), the nature of the targets (missile silos) is such that huge quantities of dust would be thrown up into the stratosphere from many large ground-burst weapons. Although there could be significant smoke emissions from forest fires during specific times of the year, these are more uncertain and have been ignored. In the small 100-megaton scenario (curve C), air-burst weapons directed against cities would produce a great amount of smoke from fires, but very little dust. Thus, the all-dust case (curve B) shows a less severe temperature drop that is very prolonged, due to the extended stratospheric residence time of the dust, and the all-smoke case (curve C) shows a more severe temperature drop that is less prolonged, due to the assumed rapid rainout of the soot.

In the 5000-megaton baseline scenario, both cities and counterforce targets are assumed to be hit. Therefore, curve A shows both a large temperature drop (due to the smoke), as well as a slow recovery back to ambient temperature (due to the dust). The reason that the temperature drop is no greater in the 5000-megaton scenario than for the 100-megaton scenario is that only 100 megatons are necessary to burn the targeted major urban areas.

Four percent of urban buildings might initially sustain a fire following a nuclear attack, and these fires could spread to eventually consume 50 percent of all buildings.[13] Based on this estimate the TTAPS authors have calculated that 100 megatons would be sufficient to burn most of the principal urban areas in all NATO and Warsaw Pact countries.[14] This estimate makes the 100-megaton scenario a kind of threshold level: a significantly smaller attack would produce less smoke and less of a temperature drop, while larger amounts of megatonnage could produce greater amounts of smoke, but not necessarily a correspondingly greater temperature drop. The threshold can also be considered in terms of the absolute smoke or dust production. The 100-megaton city attack would produce around 130 million tons of smoke, and the baseline scenario would produce around 220 million tons from burning cities and forests.[15] Since 130 million tons of smoke should be sufficient to cause a major global-scale climate perturbation, while a much smaller amount would not, 100 megatons can be considered a threshold. It must be stressed, however, that 100 megatons is only a threshold for a severe temperature drop under the restrictive assumption of many small (100 kiloton) weapons directed at many cities. There would be no such threshold if other targeting strategies were followed. There is no such threshold in the counterforce scenario, for example, since more megatonnage would produce more dust, and hence a greater temperature drop. The fact that the idea of a threshold is extremely dependent on the assumed scenario is best illustrated by the fact that the 3000-megaton counterforce attack (curve B) produces much less of a temperature drop than the 100-megaton case (curve C), even though the counterforce attack is thirty times in excess of the so-called threshold megatonnage.

Table 8.1   Magnitude and Duration of Temperature Drop for Four Scenarios

Scenario	Peak Temperature Drop	Time During Which Drop Exceeds 20° C
A. Baseline	−35° C (−63° F)	2 months
B. Counterforce	−8° C (−14° F)	—
C. 100-megaton small war	−35° C (−63° F)	2 months
D. 10,000-megaton severe war	−60° C (−108° F)	10 months

HOW LIKELY IS IT THAT THE TEMPERATURE DROP WOULD BE CATASTROPHIC?

All four scenarios depicted in figure 8.1 exhibit significant temperature drops. Even for the least severe case (the counterforce scenario), the maximum temperature drop of 8°C (14°F) would be significant, although perhaps too small to be termed nuclear winter. However, a very substantial difference exists between the least severe temperature drop (curve B) and the most severe drop (curve D). These differences can also be expressed in terms of the maximum temperature drop and the length of time that the drop exceeds 20°C (see table 8.1). The temperature drop indicated by curve D is truly catastrophic and would threaten the survival of all humans, plants, and animals in the Northern Hemisphere. The temperature drop associated with the baseline scenario (curve A) might also merit the adjective catastrophic, but its more limited duration would considerably lessen the threat to human and ecosystem survival.

What are the assumptions underlying the 10,000-megaton severe scenario, and how improbable are they?

1. *Megatonnage.* Although the megatonnage of the severe scenario is twice that of the baseline scenario, the severe scenario cannot be ruled out, considering that the estimated world strategic and theatre arsenals include still 30 percent more megatonnage.

2. *Firestorms.* In the baseline scenario fires were assumed to spread, eventually including 50 percent of all urban buildings, but the spread of fires was supposed to occur largely in the absence of firestorms. The assumed extent of firestorms is the most significant single difference between the baseline and 10,000-megaton severe scenarios. In the baseline scenario only 5 percent of urban areas are assumed to suffer firestorms, while in the severe case the figure is 30 percent.[16] The importance of this supposition lies in the fact that during the intense updrafts in a firestorm, some of the smoke can

be injected higher into the troposphere, where it tends to stay for a much longer time than smoke injected into the lower-lying atmosphere. Therefore, even if the amount of smoke produced in a firestorm were no more than that from ordinary fires, it would have a longer-lasting effect on climate.

Is the firestorm figure of 30 percent excessive? Given the density of combustible materials in most urban areas, firestorms should be relatively rare in the United States (see chapter 6), but it is difficult to set any kind of upper limit on what could be reasonably expected.

3. *Flammables.* The severe scenario assumes that the total mass of combustible material consumed in urban areas, forests, and oil refineries is two to three times as great as in the baseline case.[17]

4. *Fine dust.* The severe scenario assumes that the quantity of very fine dust per unit yield is greater by a factor of six over the baseline case.[18]

5. *Washout.* The severe scenario assumes that the washout of smoke particles from the atmosphere by precipitation is slower than in the baseline case.[19]

Any one of these five assumptions underlying the 10,000-megaton severe scenario cannot be regarded as overly pessimistic. The five assumptions taken together, however, would seem to be extremely pessimistic, and they constitute a scenario with rather low probability.[20] Unfortunately, the TTAPS authors note that they are unable to give any estimate of how low the probability of this severe scenario might be relative to the baseline case.[21]

While it is only natural for us to want to know what the worst climatic impact of a nuclear war is likely to be, it is difficult to know how to treat a prediction whose probability of occurrence is totally unknown. It would, for example, make a great deal of difference if the severe scenario is a billion times less likely or only ten times less likely than the baseline case. Such a difference might not directly translate into our degree of abhorence of nuclear war, but it certainly would be important in terms of the confidence limits we can place on the likely climatic consequences of a nuclear war.

The adverse assumptions used in the severe scenario indicate there are many parameters that have uncertain values that can greatly affect the calculated temperature drop. The TTAPS authors have used their best estimate for each of the many parameters in the baseline scenario, but these best estimates might or might not be correct. And there are many other uncertainties that apply to all the scenarios considered:

- Is it reasonable to expect 50 percent of all combustible material in cities to burn?

- Might the effects of the blast put out fires to some degree? [22]

- Would forest fires be likely to burn for many weeks?

- Would smoke be injected to very high altitudes, allowing it to stay up longer?

- Would all attempts at fire fighting to contain urban fires be futile? [23]

The calculated maximum temperature drop depends primarily on the amount of smoke and the altitude to which it is injected. The answers to the preceding questions (and many others), could therefore greatly affect the magnitude of the temperature drop for a given scenario. A nuclear war could, of course, involve any number of possible scenarios. As seen in figure 8.1, there is a sizable difference between, for example, the temperature drops for the counterforce scenario and the others. While many people might regard a strictly counterforce scenario as being implausible, other analysts might regard as implausible the premise of the baseline scenario—that every major city in all NATO and Warsaw Pact countries is targeted.

An additional category of uncertainties in the calculations of temperature declines arises from the mathematical model used by TTAPS and all other studies mentioned. The most extensive calculations are usually one-dimensional calculations in which the smoke and dust movement through the atmosphere is calculated only in the vertical direction. In one-dimensional calculations a highly artificial assumption is made that the smoke and dust rises all at once from every part of the earth's surface, even though the actual detonations and fires would in fact be highly localized. Correct three-dimensional calculations, however, are more complex and suffer from a variety of problems that makes precise calculations difficult.[24]

The authors of the TTAPS study estimate that a correct, three-dimensional calculation might result in land-surface temperature drops that might be 30 percent less for continental interiors or 70 percent less within a hundred miles of coastlines.[25] The much-less-severe temperature drops along coastlines would be due to the warming effect of the ocean, which has a much higher heat capacity than the land. Thus, when the sunlight is blocked for a prolonged period, air above land would cool much more quickly than air above water.

Soviet scientists have attempted a three-dimensional calculation that predicts an average maximum temperature drop of only 14°C, which is 60 percent less than that reported by TTAPS. In the Soviet calculation, however, the maximum temperature drop varies significantly from place to place over the earth's surface, ranging from 0°C to 56°C.[26]

Nevertheless, none of the calculations done to date adequately treat the possible rainout of soot that could conceivably reduce the temperature decline due to smoke to negligible proportions. Given all the uncertainties that exist, one cannot be definitive about the likely climatic consequences of a nuclear war. The temperature drop would possibly be serious, but whether it would be catastrophic depends on many unanswered and some unanswerable questions.

WHAT WOULD BE THE IMPACT OF A LARGE CLIMATIC CHANGE?

A large change in the global climate would have a severe impact on surviving humans, plants, and animals. The impact on plants would depend on the magnitude of the temperature drop, its duration, and on the time of year it occurred. A temperature drop of the magnitude and duration of the baseline scenario, occurring in the spring or summer, would damage virtually all crops in the Northern Hemisphere, and it would kill many. A nuclear war in the fall or winter would have a lesser impact on plants, as it would have occurred after the crops have been harvested. Moreover, if the recovery to ambient temperatures occurred at the rate indicated in the baseline scenario, it probably would be possible to plant crops in the spring, although the residual climatic effects could significantly inhibit plant growth. A nuclear war in the fall or winter would have a much greater impact on tropical vegetation, which is vulnerable to the onset of low temperatures any time of the year.

Many farm animals would die from the cold if the temperature drop was particularly severe. Wild animals would suffer not only from the cold, but also from the lack of food, if much vegetation died, as well as a lack of surface water, if temperatures dropped well below freezing. Human survivors without access to stored food would also starve.

Survivors in coastal areas would be better off since the coastal temperature drop would not be nearly so severe. In addition, marine life in the oceans could provide some sustenance to survivors without access to stored food. However, continual severe coastal storms driven by the very large land-sea temperature differential could make ocean-fishing expeditions extremely hazardous. Moreover, the marine food chain could be significantly disrupted by the lack of sunlight.

The aftermath of a nuclear war would not only be a period of depressed temperatures, but also of very low light levels approaching that of twilight. A large decrease in the light intensity would have an effect on plants that would be as serious as the cold. The magnitude of the light-reduction effect is even more scenario dependent than the temperature drop. The decrease in sunlight from its normal unperturbed value found in the TTAPS study is shown in figure 8.2 as a function of time. The four curves A, B, C, and D are for the scenarios previously discussed, and they give an average for the Northern Hemisphere.

Figure 8.2 also shows the three different light levels, one of which, the "compensation point," is of particular importance. The compensation point is the light level at which photosynthesis can barely keep pace with plant metabolism, however, the specific values are somewhat species-dependent. The baseline scenario (curve A) would cause the light level to briefly dip below the compensation point, which would not be fatal. In the case of the 10,000-megaton severe scenario (curve D), the amount of sunlight reaching plants in the Northern Hemisphere would be below the compensation point for two months; this would have a much more catastrophic effect, though one that is likely to show significant variation from place to place, and from plant species to species. The counterforce scenario (curve B) would result in a negligible effect on the average Northern Hemisphere light level.

All things considered, it is clear that the impact of a nuclear winter on prospects for survival would greatly depend on many factors, especially the time of year the war occurred and the particular scenario assumed. Thus, many survivors in a grain-rich country such as the United States could perhaps subsist on stored grain and animal feed, even if the war occurred at an unfavorable time of the year (spring or summer), assuming that the means and organization existed to bring the stored grain to the population. The success of such an undertaking would, as discussed in the previous chapter, depend on many unknowns, most importantly whether any surviving government existed and whether survivors would receive and heed the orders of such a government.

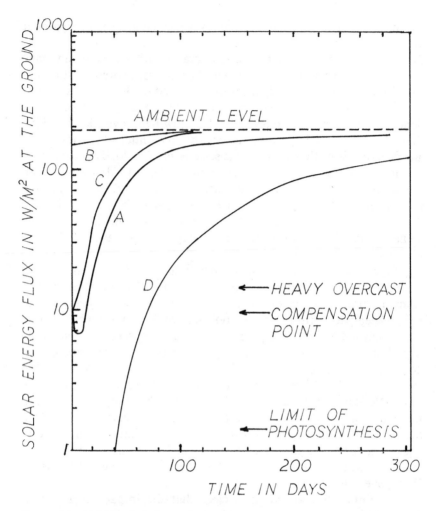

Figure 8.2   Light-level declines after nuclear war.
Source: Turco et al., "Nuclear Winter: Global Consequences of Multiple Nuclear Explosions," *Science,* 222 (1983), p. 1287.
Notes: Calculated declines in average light level in the Northern Hemisphere following a nuclear war given as a function of time. The four curves labelled A, B, C, D correspond to the four scenarios discussed in the text.

Survivors in Northern Hemisphere nations that now require large food imports would likely suffer an immediate cessation of such imports. These nations would be forced to turn to domestic agriculture, which might only be able to provide for a fraction of their population, even if there were no worldwide climatic catastrophe. Therefore, food-importing nations would probably suffer greatly, even if they were spared the direct effects of a nuclear war.

In summary, the effect of a nuclear winter could be extremely serious in most of the Northern Hemisphere, and it could be catastrophic if the climatic impact was as large as that assumed in the 10,000-megaton severe scenario—a highly unlikely occurrence. Many survivors would die from starvation if the attack occurred in spring or summer and if no stored grain were made available. The magnitude of the nuclear-winter effect is highly dependent on many of the assumptions underlying the calculation, especially on the particular scenario that is assumed. The uncertainties are so large that we cannot exclude the temperature drop being anything from "negligible" to "extremely severe." Even in the most severe case, however, it is unlikely that the temperature drop would be sufficiently long lasting to trigger another ice age, given the enormous heat capacity of the world's oceans.[27]

Severe changes in global climate are, of course, just one life-threatening hazard confronting survivors in the aftermath of a nuclear war. We now shall consider the two other principal long-term global dangers: destruction of the ozone layer and radioactive fallout.

WHAT WOULD BE THE IMPACT OF A DEPLETED OZONE LAYER?

The ozone layer shields living organisms from the sun's harmful ultraviolet radiation. In fact, it is believed that life on earth could not have evolved without an ozone layer. Threats to the ozone layer should be viewed, therefore, with great concern. Moreover, the existence of such a threat has only been recognized for the last dozen years or so, first in connection with the impact of supersonic transports, and then later with the impact of nuclear-weapons detonations.

When a nuclear weapon is detonated, a large quantity of oxides of nitrogen (NO_x) is injected into the atmosphere in the nuclear fireball. The altitude of injection depends on the cloud stabilization height. Weapons with less than a 500-kiloton yield inject NO_x into the troposphere, while higher-yield weapons inject it into the stratosphere. The nitrogen oxides, through a chain of photochemical reactions, cause the breakdown of ozone (O_3) molecules in the stratosphere. The magnitude of the effect is difficult to estimate accurately for several reasons. Firstly, the number of NO_x molecules injected is only poorly known: 0.4 to 1.5 x 10^{32} molecules per megaton of explosive. Secondly, the ozone-depletion effect is difficult to quantify because the relevant transport processes affecting recovery are poorly understood.

Attempts have been made to directly measure the amount of ozone depletion resulting from the atmospheric nuclear tests prior to the Limited Test Ban Treaty. No unambiguous evidence for any ozone depletion resulting from the nuclear tests was found. However, the ozone could have been depleted as much as 2 to 3 percent without it being noticed, due to the "noise," i.e., spontaneous fluctuations in the average level of ozone. Many calculations have been made since 1975 on the probable magnitude of ozone depletion that would follow a large-scale nuclear war.[28] These calculations typically show that in the Northern Hemisphere, the maximum depletion would be approximately 60 percent if the entire world's strategic nuclear stockpile were detonated, and perhaps 30 to 45 percent if only half that amount were detonated.[29] These reductions would only be temporary, since natural atmospheric processes would be expected to restore half of the depleted ozone in two to three years, and nearly all of the ozone layer would be restored in five to six years. The manner in which the ozone-depletion effect might be expected to vary with time is shown in figure 8.3.

These calculations depend not only on the total megatonnage but also on the size of weapons detonated. Weapons having yields of less than 0.5 megatons do not create a fireball that rises high enough into the ozone layer to cause it to decompose appreciably. Despite the continuing growth in the superpowers' arsenals, it appears that the potential threat to the ozone layer has actually declined during the last twenty years because of the move to smaller warheads. Consider, for example, the twenty-year period from 1962 to 1982. During that time the total megatonnage in the combined U.S.-U.S.S.R. strategic arsenals grew by 20 percent (while the U.S. figure alone actually declined by 50 percent).

The 20-percent growth in combined U.S.-U.S.S.R. megatonnage has increased the potential threat to the ozone layer far less than the move to smaller warheads during that period decreased it.

The depletion of the ozone layer to an estimated 50 percent of normal would have a serious impact on surviving humans, animals, and plants. Given the variation of ozone layer with latitude, a 50 percent depletion would correspond to that experienced in moving from mid-latitudes to the equator in peacetime. As a result of the 50 percent ozone layer depletion, ultraviolet radiation would reach the earth's surface at about three times its normal rate when the

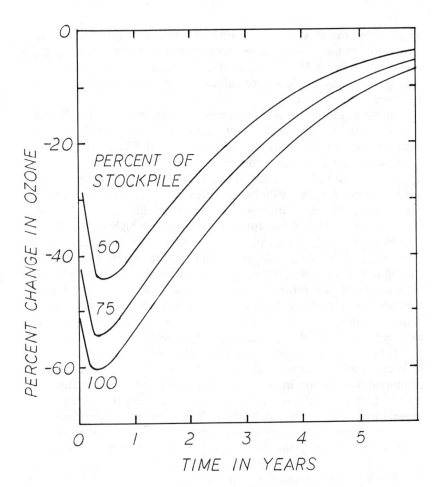

Figure 8.3   Ozone-layer depletion after nuclear war.
Source: Knox et al., "Program Report for Atmospheric and Geophysical Sciences," Lawrence Livermore Laboratory, p. 44.
Note: Calculated change in hemispheric mean total ozone versus time for various fractions of the combined U.S. and U.S.S.R. strategic nuclear stockpiles.

Table 8.2   Growth in Strategic Nuclear Megatonnage

	U.S	U.S.S.R.	Total
1962	8,650	1,600	10,250
1982	4,080	7,940	12,020

ozone depletion is at is maximum[30]. There are three principal ways ultraviolet radiation, or more specifically the short wavelength ultraviolet known as UV-B, is harmful to humans: (1) skin cancer and "aging" of the skin, (2) severe sunburn, and (3) eye problems (snow blindness and cataracts).

Much evidence links skin cancer with exposure to UV-B radiation in sunlight. The incidence of skin cancer increases dramatically with age, since it depends on the accumulated lifetime UV-B dose. This pronounced age dependence is clearly indicated in figure 8.4 by the skin cancer rates for white males living in three different areas. Figure 8.4 also clearly indicates a direct link between skin cancer incidence and latitude. For example, for all ages the skin cancer rates in Dallas are roughly 100 percent higher than for the two more northerly locations. There are two reasons for the dramatic increase in skin cancer that occurs nearer the equator: (1) the protecting ozone layer gets thinner as one moves to lower latitudes, and (2) less UV-B absorption takes place when the sun is more nearly overhead—a simple geometric effect. The correlation with latitude is quite pronounced since the normal UV-B dose is found to double for every 12° to 15° decrease in latitude between 20° and 60° latitude.

It has been estimated that the depletion of the ozone layer likely to occur from the detonation of 10,000 megatons would cause an estimated 10-percent increase in skin cancer at midlatitudes.[31] By way of comparison, this would be roughly a tenth the increase now experienced in spending one's life in Dallas instead of San Francisco.

The reason that the expected increase in skin cancer is as small as 10 percent, despite the fact that the expected UV-B peak-intensity increase is around 200 percent, is that it is the cumulative lifetime UV-B dose that is important, and the ozone layer would be largely restored in a relatively few years after the detonations.

Skin cancer should not be dismissed as a trivial problem just because it has a very high cure rate (99 percent in the United States for basal cell and squamous cancers). Nevertheless, the fact that skin cancers account for only 1.6 percent of all cancer deaths means that a 10 percent increase in skin cancer due to ozone-layer depletion would mean only a 0.16 percent rise in the cancer death rate generally, in those parts of the world where medical care continued to be available.

An effect potentially more serious than skin cancer would be the severe sunburn and blistering that exposure to UV-B would cause. In the Northern Hemisphere, the peak 200 percent increase in UV-B intensity associated with a 50 percent ozone-layer depletion

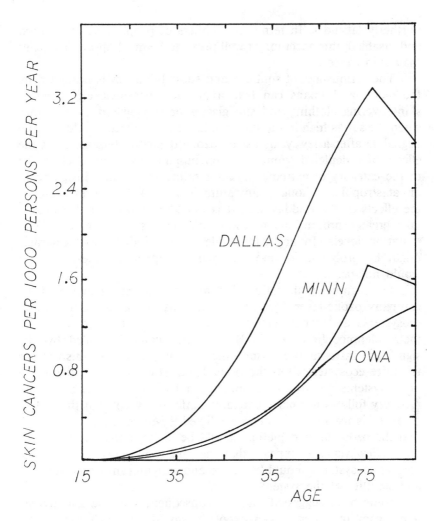

Figure 8.4   Incidence of nonmelanoma skin cancer.
Source: Long-Term Worldwide Effects of Multiple Nuclear-Weapons Detonations, National Academy of Sciences, 1975, p. 185.
Note: Figure shows age-specific incidence rates of nonmelanoma skin cancer for white males in several different geographic areas.

means that serious sunburn would be obtained in one-third the time. In the tropics for example, a severe sunburn that includes blistering is now experienced by exposed Caucasian skin after 180 minutes. A 50 percent ozone-layer reduction near the equator would lower the time to severe burn to 60 minutes, with longer times for more northerly latitudes. In terms of numbers of people severely burned and disabled, this effect might well prove to be much more significant than skin cancer.

The seriousness of sunburn and snow blindness is mitigated by the fact that humans can take avoidance measures, e.g., wearing skin-covering clothing and sun glasses or staying indoors at times when the sun is high in the sky. In addition, the effects would become negligible after a few years as the ozone depletion lessens. Thus the effects of a depleted ozone layer on humans are more likely to be in the category of extreme nuisance rather than either insignificant or catastrophic. Although many animals now take measures to escape the effects of the midday sun, it is not known whether they would take greater precautions to escape the effects of increased UV-B radiation levels. In any case while snow blindness and cataracts might be problems for most animals in upper latitudes, sunburn would not be.

The significant increase in ultraviolet radiation that would accompany ozone-layer depletion would also be a threat to natural ecosystems and agriculture. Some plant species may be now near their tolerance limit to UV-B, and they could be killed by any significant increase in exposure, thereby causing possible disruptions to entire ecosystems. On the other hand, studies on the disruption of ecosystems due to intense ionizing radiation exposures show that recovery follows normal predictable patterns, except that the rate of recovery is usually faster than predicted.[32] Moreover, given the fact that the ozone-layer depletion should be in large measure mitigated after a few years, it appears that the long-term effects of UV-B on natural ecosystems should be minor and insignificant to the survival and stability of the system.[33]

Some have suggested that the consequences for natural ecosystems from increased UV-B exposure would be much more catastrophic than described here. For example, Kosta Tsipis has claimed that the ozone-layer depletion following the use of only 10 percent of the world's nuclear arsenals could result in the blinding of most animals by ultraviolet radiation, and hence their probable extinction.[34] Such assertions would seem to be greatly exaggerated. It is known that exposure to UV-B can cause cataracts and also snow blindness, a painful but temporary ailment. However, the suggestion that all animals would be blinded is quite disproportionate to the actual exposure levels likely to occur—especially considering that unblinded animals now exist at equatorial latitudes.

WHAT IMPACT WOULD RADIOACTIVE FALLOUT HAVE ON HUMAN HEALTH?

Nations either directly attacked with ground-burst nuclear weapons or downwind of such detonations would experience the highest fallout levels. Lethal and near-lethal radiation levels would cover large areas in the attacked countries, as discussed in the previous chapter. In addition to such "local" fallout there would also be a global component. The global component would consist of fine radioactive dust particles thrown into the upper troposphere and stratosphere, where they would be carried around the earth by the winds and then descend back to earth in the ensuing weeks, months, and years.

Until recent years, calculations of the average Northern Hemisphere radiation dose received by survivors of a nuclear war appear to have been significantly underestimated. These earlier calculations were based on a simple scaling of the dose measured during the period of atmospheric testing. It is now known that the dose received is not proportional to the fission megatonnage detonated, since weapon size is very important.[35] The same shift to smaller warheads, which has made the ozone-layer depletion potentially less serious, has increased the magnitude of the problem of widespread fallout. Low-yield weapons do not throw the radioactive dust up so high as large-yield weapons; therefore, dust falling back to earth from low-yield weapons lands sooner and before its radioactivity has decayed as much as dust from weapons of higher yield. Thus low-yield weapons result in a larger cumulative radiation dose than high-yield weapons for a given total fission megatonnage.

An estimate of the average whole-body dose to humans in the Northern Hemisphere following a 5000-megaton nuclear war is 20 rems, most of which would be accumulated in the first few months following the war.[36] In addition to this whole-body dose received externally, survivors would also be exposed to roughly the same internal dose from eating contaminated food, drinking contaminated water, and breathing contaminated air.[37] Of the many radionuclides present in fallout, three important ones are iodine-131, strontium-90, and cesium-137. Although there are known ways to remove partially these radionuclides from food and water, it is unclear whether survivors would want to take the trouble.

The global deposition of fallout would depend on the season and on meteorological conditions, and it would tend to be highly nonuniform, with many "hotspots." The fallout in midaltitudes of the Northern Hemisphere (30°–70°N) might be considerably higher than the hemisphere average, since most of the likely targets are in midlatitudes and fallout spreads slowly to other latitudes, giving the radioactivity time to decay. It is likely that the Northern Hemisphere midlatitude average radiation dose might be two to three times the average for the entire hemisphere,[38] or about 50 rems whole-body dose, plus another 50 rems internal dose to specific organs. The 100 rem estimate for the average lifetime dose, however, neglects the important effects of weathering and sheltering, and is, therefore, almost certainly a significant overestimate. A total dose of 100 rems is well below the dose considered lethal, but it is extremely high by ordinary peacetime standards. A dose of 100 rems is equivalent to 10,000 chest x-rays or about twenty times the cumulative lifetime dose someone would receive from natural background radiation.

The effect of radiation on humans depends on both the dose received and the time interval in which it is received. Very high doses of radiation received over a short time would cause radiation sickness whose gruesome symptoms include nausea, hair loss, destruction of blood cells, and possibly the hemorrhaging of the intestines, leading to death. If the acute radiation dose exceeds 750 rems, death is almost certain to occur within two weeks. If the dose is 450 rems, there is a 50-percent chance of recovery; if it is less than 200 rems, recovery is almost certain. For doses below 150 rems the only symptom most persons experience is a lowering of the red-blood-cell count, with possible suppression of immunilogical responses. Below 25 rems no overt symptoms are observed.

In addition to these short-term radiation effects, there are important long-term hazards, especially an increased susceptibility to cancer. The uncontrolled process of cell division that we refer to as cancer is known to be linked to radiation, but in ways not fully understood. It is not known how radiation damage to single cells causes them to become cancerous. Nor is it understood why, in a given population exposed to a particular level of radiation, some individuals will develop cancer and die and others will not. All we have been able to do so far is observe what fraction of people will develop cancer for any particular level of radiation.

The most important single source of information on the effects of radiation on humans are the survivors of the Hiroshima and Nagasaki bombings who have been closely studied. Many of these survivors were exposed to relatively high radiation levels, i.e., usually exceeding 50 rems. At lower levels of radiation exposure, the health effects attributable to radiation are of sufficiently small magnitude compared to those found in the unexposed population that the effects cannot be directly measured. For the substantial radiation doses that concern us here, it has been found that a linear relationship exists between the size of the dose and the probability of getting cancer. Thus, for example, the percentage of excess cancers or cancer deaths among people who have been exposed to 200 rems is twice the percentage of those who have been exposed to 100 rems.

The validity of the linear relationship between radiation dose and the (age-adjusted) cancer death rate relies on the data for the Hiroshima and Nagasaki survivors shown in figure 8.5. The radiation dose that any particular survivor received had to be estimated based on his or her distance to ground zero, and it also included estimates of radiation shielding provided by buildings. Individuals were then grouped in seven different dose categories based on the estimated dose received. The size of each vertical error bar reflects the statistical uncertainty in the data, based on the number of individuals in each dose category. The dotted sloping lines indicate those straight lines that best fit the date for each city, and the lines indicate how the incidence of cancer death rates among survivors varies with the dose they received—the so-called dose-response curve. It is clear from the size of the vertical error bars on the data that there is considerable uncertainty over the slope of the dose-response curve. The Nagasaki data even appears to be consistent with a horizontal dose-response curve, i.e., no effect of radiation on the cancer death rate, up to near-lethal doses.

Why there is a sizable difference between the data from Hiroshima and Nagasaki survivors is not clear. The difference could be largely a result of statistical uncertainties. It is believed, however, that much of the difference between Hiroshima and Nagasaki disappears when better estimates are used for the dose received by individual survivors.

The most authoritative estimates of cancer risks due to radiation come from the International Commission on Radiological Protection (ICRP). According to the ICRP if a million people were exposed to 100 rems, 12,500 would subsequently die of cancer.[39] As noted earlier, 100 rems is the estimated lifetime experienced by survivors in Northern Hemisphere midlatitudes following a large-scale nuclear war. 12,500 cancer deaths per million persons corresponds to 7.8 percent of the naturally occurring cancer death rate.[40] The average loss in life expectancy resulting from a 100 rem dose would be around 0.2 years, compared to a loss of 6.0 years for those who

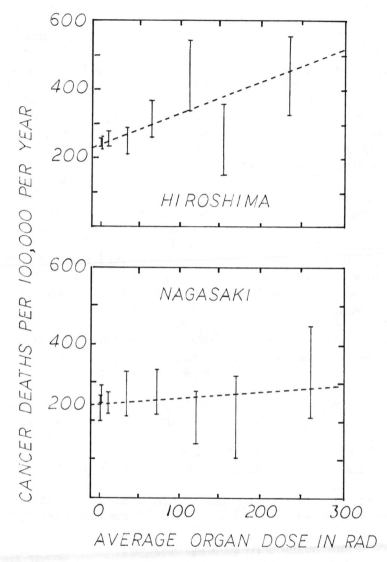

Figure 8.5   Cancer death rate among Hiroshima and Nagasaki survivors.
Source: Effects on Populations of Exposure to Low Levels of Ionizing Radiation, National Academy of Sciences, 1980.
Notes: Age-adjusted death rate (1955–74) for cancers except leukemia for Japanese A-bomb survivors as a function of the estimated average dose received. Dotted lines show the fitted linear regression dose-response curve for each city. Vertical error bars at each dose correspond to 80-percent confidence limit, based on statistics.

smoke cigarettes.[41] There is no intention to downplay the hazards of radiation by such a comparison. Those who choose to smoke do so voluntarily. Nevertheless, one cannot help but wonder what would be the average smoker's attitude toward cigarettes (and toward the cancer hazards of a nuclear war), if he or she learned of the best estimates of the two relative risks.

The impact of increased incidence of cancer following a large-scale nuclear war would be very different for different age groups. The human fetus, for example, is believed to be particularly sensitive to radiation, so it would be expected that those born in the year immediately following the nuclear war would suffer a somewhat higher incidence of cancer during their lifetime than other age groups. Those born after the first year would experience very much lower levels of radiation, and they would suffer little effects. Most cancers are believed to have a latency period of around twenty years. Therefore, many of those exposed to a radiation dose at ages above thirty-five would die from other causes before the increased incidence of cancer manifested itself in later years.

WHAT OTHER EFFECTS WOULD RADIOACTIVE FALLOUT HAVE?

The link between radiation exposure and incidence of cancer is well established. There is no such clearly established link between radiation exposure and the incidence of other diseases, despite extensive studies. An important source of information on the possibility of such a link is a study of the Japanese A-bomb survivors who later died of various diseases. The number of all noncancer deaths among Japanese survivors during the twenty-year period 1950–70 is listed in table 8.3 according to the estimated radiation dose received.[42] The third column of the table shows the ratio of the number of deaths observed to the number expected based on Japanese mortality statistics. The fact that the ratios for all five dose levels are less than 1.0 means that for all doses, survivors had lower incidences of fatal diseases apart from cancer than the Japanese people as a whole. Of course this finding does not constitute evidence that radiation has the beneficial effect of reducing the incidence of disease other than cancer. The lower incidence of noncancer deaths among the survivors might well be attributable to the fact that the A-bomb survivors tended to be among a hardier group of Japanese. If that hypothesis is correct, then the absolute values of the ratios in table

Table 8.3   Noncancer Japanese Deaths, 1950–70

Estimated Dose (rems)	Noncancer Deaths	Observed to Expected Ratio
0–9	8395	0.88
10–49	2234	0.86
50–99	616	0.88
100–199	414	0.95
200+	349	0.98

8.3 are of less importance than their trend with increasing radiation dose. There is, in fact, a small indication in the table of some increase in the ratios with increasing dose received. If, for example, we take the ratio of the numbers in the highest and lowest dose categories, the result is 1.12 ± 0.08, which would indicate a possible effect. However, the effect is one of marginal statistical significance. In addition, two other factors cast doubt on the existence of a clear link between radiation dose and noncancer fatal disease: (1) no trend is seen for the first three dose categories in table 8.1, which have the smallest statistical uncertainty, and (2) the slightly higher ratios for the two highest dose categories might well be attributable to nonradiation injuries these persons sustained because they were closer to ground zero. Although one researcher has claimed that these data do indicate a link between radiation exposure and fatal diseases other than cancer,[43] the general consensus is that no such link has been demonstrated to exist.

Many writers discuss the health effects of high radiation doses on human health in somewhat more catastrophic terms. For example, Edward Kennedy and Mark Hatfield in *Freeze!* write: "Cancer rates among the Hiroshima survivors soared over the ensuing decades to 5, 15, and 40 times the normal rates. So did mental retardation and chromosome damage." [44] However, it is only for rare leukemia, not cancer generally, and only for those Hiroshima victims in particular years after their exposure that one can obtain anything like such dramatic increases as those cited by Kennedy and Hatfield. Moreover, the implications that mental retardation and genetic damage appeared in correspondingly large increases among survivors' offspring is incorrect.

Although it is fair to say that the exact magnitude of the long-term impact of radiation on humans remains controversial, that fact alone indicates that even for extremely high doses, the effects, with the exception of leukemia, are not so large that their magnitude is clear (see figure 8.5). For low radiation doses, the statistical uncertainty makes it impossible to separate the small radiation-induced effects from other causes, and therefore, there is great uncertainty as to how the dose-response curve extrapolates to zero for very low doses.

In addition to its effect in increasing the incidence of cancer, radiation is also well known to increase the incidence of genetic birth defects. However, there is probably no area of nuclear-weapons effects in which a greater gap exists between public perceptions and informed scientific opinion than in the area of genetic effects. It is quite clear that a definite link exists between radiation exposure and genetic defects, as animal studies clearly demonstrate. Moreover, there is also no question that while spontaneous mutations are essential for the process of natural selection and the development of life on earth, fully 99 percent of all mutations are not beneficial. The discrepancy between public understanding and informed scientific opinion concerns the magnitude and character of radiation-induced mutations.

The results of an informal survey by this author of a group of university students offers an illustration of what is probably a commonly held view. A majority of a group of sixty students either agreed with the following statement or expressed uncertainty: "The great number of mutations caused by a nuclear war might well cause animals or people to develop into a new race of monsters." In another group of twenty-five university faculty, again a sizable majority did not know that this statement was grotesquely false.

At one time, the magnitude of radiation-induced genetic effects was a source of some controversy among geneticists. However, that controversy has largely subsided. Among Japanese A-bomb survivors, for example, no evidence has been found that shows genetic effects to be in excess of the rate of spontaneously occurring effects.[45] This is not to say that these survivors did not suffer any genetic damage, only that the rate of increase was such that, given limited statistics, no effect was seen.

It is often noted that even though the presence of excess genetic defects has not yet been observed among Japanese A-bomb survivors, that fact does not preclude the possibility of an effect later showing up among the descendants of survivors. However, even if the radiation damage is done to recessive rather than dominant genes, there is every reason to believe that the extent of genetic damage in later generations would be less than that in the first generation. It is only the rate of decrease in genetic defects from one generation to the next that would be affected by the damaged genes being recessive or dominant.

Had the increase in genetic defects among the A-bomb survivors been as great as a 1-percent increase in the rate of genetic defects per rad dose, it almost certainly would have been observed. Based on the data on Japanese survivors and other research, and exposure of 100 rems would be estimated to result in between 500 and 7,500 additional serious genetic defects per million live births in the first generation.[46] These additional genetic defects would represent, at most, a 7.5 percent increase in the 100,000 spontaneous genetic defects per million live births, thereby raising the rate of genetic defects from 10 percent to, at most, 10.75 percent of all births. Excess genetic defects would also occur in subsequent generations, but at a declining rate that reaches half the original increase after four generations.

While a 0.75 percent increase in the incidence of genetic defects might not seem enormous when expressed as a percentage, it would represent a large absolute number of people, and certainly no increase should be viewed as "acceptable." Nevertheless, it should be remembered that medical science, through its advances in keeping more people with genetic defects alive, has already doubled the percentage of genetic defects. Finally, it should be stressed that the nature of radiation-induced genetic defects is no different from spontaneous genetic defects, i.e., the defects are much more likely to be extra fingers or toes or dwarfism, rather than two-headed "monsters."

To what degree are the relatively small genetic effects cited here challenged by other studies? Some authors quote levels of genetic damage hundreds or thousands of times greater than those discussed here. For example, Fred Kaplan suggests that 5 rads would be enough to double the rate of spontaneous genetic defects.[47] In that event, Hiroshima and Nagasaki survivors, many of whom were exposed to 100 rads, should have experienced a twenty-fold increase in genetically defective offspring.[48]

In addition to carcinogenic and genetic defects, radiation is also well known to have an impact on human reproductivity. For a typical survivor in the Northern Hemisphere midlatitudes, the expected increase in early fetal mortality would be about 0.8 percent for all recognizable pregnancies.[49] (A large percentage of pregnancies miscarry before they are recognized as such.) An increase this small would have an insignificant effect on the ability of the human species to reproduce.

Permanent sterility would not be likely to occur in most people receiving sub-lethal doses. Sterility requires acute exposures to over 600 rems for men and 300 to 400 rems for women.[50] The ability of people to have children would, therefore, not be seriously impaired. Whether people would want to have children live such an extremely unpleasant existence is, of course, another matter.

No inference should be made that the quoted increases in the percentage of genetic defects and miscarriages are "acceptable." Any unnecessary increase in genetic defects would be tragic. Nevertheless, the magnitude of the human genetic effects, even in directly targeted countries, would be considerably less than is generally imagined by the general public. While there are many good reasons to avoid a nuclear war, a catastrophic impact on human genetics or reproductivity is not among them.

Radiation would also have potentially significant effects on plants and animals as well as people. In fact, plants show a considerable variation in their tolerance of radiation exposure—the lethal dose for the most sensitive and least sensitive species differs by a factor of 5000. For most species of plants, however, the lethal dose is considerably in excess of that for humans (see table 7.1 in chapter 7).

The genetic effects of radiation on crops is another potential cause for concern. The worldwide level of radiation would be such that the direct impact of genetic damage in areas far from the detonations would be small. The main worry is that indirect effects would cause mutations in plant pathogens, which would increase their virulence. A mutation for virulence could spread rapidly through a plant population much as plant diseases are spread today. Thus, it has been suggested that in plant communities subject to high radiation levels near the detonations, virulent strains might be created through mutations, and these strains could be transferred to distant lands. Such a spread of plant diseases could seriously affect agriculture, although the probability of such an occurrence is a matter of controversy.

Marine life would also suffer some impact from radioactive fallout. The worlds' oceans would accumulate radioactive fallout directly from the atmosphere and through runoff from the land. For persons consuming seafood, the fifty-year total body dose would be expected to be less than .05 rems and the thyroid dose 1.0 rems.[51] These exposures are less than 20 percent of the natural background radiation level. No observable effects would be anticipated either for humans or for most aquatic organisms.

Lest it be thought that the effects of radiation following a large-scale nuclear war have been presented here as too benign, it is appropriate to conclude this discussion of the effects of radioactive fallout on a more somber note. We have until now neglected the possibility that in a nuclear war, nuclear-power reactors and fuel-cycle installations would be attacked. If all the materials in these facilities were vaporized, their presence in fallout would significantly increase the hazard to survivors.

If all nuclear-power capabilities in the Northern Hemisphere were attacked, the dose contribution to survivors in the Northern Hemisphere midlatitudes might be as much as 300 rems.[52] "Hot spots" would of course encompass areas of much higher dose. The figure 300 rems represents an extreme worst case estimate, however, since it assumes: (1) an expanded nuclear industry by the year 2000 beyond what is now projected, (2) a scenario in which all reactors and storage facilities in the northern hemisphere are attacked, and (3) direct hits on all reactor cores which result in their complete vaporization.

There is an important distinction between the radiation from the radionuclides released from vaporized nuclear reactors and those present in ordinary fallout: the reactor nuclides decay at a much slower rate. This fact has three important implications: (1) the radiation will persist in the environment for a much longer time, posing a continuing hazard for many years, (2) the fact that the radiation exposure is experienced over an extended time, rather than in a few days or weeks, means that rad for rad it is less harmful than promptly delivered radiation, and (3) the fact that the radioactivity lasts so long means that its global effect will be proportionately more important than its local effect, as compared to ordinary fallout which decays much more quickly (a thousand-fold drop in intensity from one hour to two weeks).

The significance of this last point is that each side in a nuclear conflict may be deterred from attacking the other's nuclear reactors if each is cognizant of the potentially serious health problem that would be created for itself due to the large increase in global fallout. This, of course, may be wishful thinking, since each side may put a greater emphasis on the "bomb-making potential" of the other side's nuclear reactors, or they may give little thought to global environmental concerns once a nuclear war begins.

WOULD CIVILIZATION AS WE KNOW IT SURVIVE?

Until now we have been primarily concerned with the three primary worldwide effects of a large-scale nuclear war: climatic changes, ozone-layer destruction, and radioactive fallout. The likely magnitude of these effects on the Northern Hemisphere can be summarized as follows:

Climatic impact—possibly negligible, possibly very serious and potentially catastrophic, depending on many unknowns

Ozone-layer destruction—probably serious, but not catastrophic

Radioactive fallout—probably serious, and possibly very serious if all nuclear reactors and facilities are targeted

In an actual nuclear war these factors would, of course, not act singly, but in combination, and their synergistic whole might be greater than the sum of the parts. Thus, surviving humans made more susceptible to infection due to radiation might die from influenza due to exposure to reduced temperatures. Alternatively, crops might be killed by the combined effects of ultraviolet radiation, ionizing radiation, severe cold, and diminished light, even though each effect alone might not be lethal.

In asking whether civilization as we know it could survive, we are, in effect, asking whether potentially catastrophic effects would occur on a worldwide basis, or whether it is likely that at least some regions would survive with relatively minor damage. The majority of the world's population resides in the Northern Hemisphere, which would be certain to experience far worse devastation than the Southern Hemisphere. The Southern Hemisphere would certainly not escape unscathed, since the smoke and radioactive fallout initially generated in the Northern Hemisphere would eventually find its way to the Southern Hemisphere as well. The ozone layer would also experience some depletion in the Southern Hemisphere. Nevertheless, barring a major disturbance in the atmospheric circulation pattern, the magnitude of these effects on the Southern Hemisphere would be considerably less:[53]

- Temperature drops in the Southern Hemisphere due to smoke and dust would be expected to be around one-quarter as much as for the Northern Hemisphere.[54]

- Ozone-layer depletion in the Southern Hemisphere would be expected to be less than one-third as much as for the Northern Hemisphere.[55]

- Radioactive fallout in the Southern Hemisphere would be expected to be only 1/20 as much as for the Northern Hemisphere.[56]

Radioactive fallout in the Southern Hemisphere is more suppressed than the other two effects due to the radioactive decay during the time it would take fallout to drift from one hemisphere to the other.

In view of these much smaller effects, it seems almost certain that countries in the Southern Hemisphere would not suffer catastrophic impacts, and, therefore, that civilization would survive. The alternative possibility, of course, cannot be ruled out. It is conceivable that some madman would attack all cities in the Southern Hemisphere, even though according to conventional wisdom there are relatively few targets there. It is also possible that a major perturbation of the atmospheric circulation pattern could occur, thereby increasing the severity of the effects on the Southern Hemisphere, and moderating the effects on the Northern Hemisphere. Furthermore, it is also conceivable that our understanding of the effects of nuclear weapons is incomplete, and that some may be significantly worse than we believe them to be. Thus, all that can be said is that, based on the best evidence available, it seems likely that civilization would survive, at least in the Southern Hemisphere. The survival of civilization in the Northern Hemisphere would be more problematical and would depend on many unknowns, most importantly the exact magnitude of the climatic impact and the time of year the war occurred.

WHAT ABOUT POLITICAL AND PSYCHOLOGICAL FACTORS?

Although there may be great uncertainties in our knowledge of the likely physical effects of a large-scale nuclear war, questions relating to the economic, political, sociological, and psychological consequences are still more speculative. Nevertheless, they are worthwhile to consider, since for lands remote from nuclear detonations these factors may assume the greatest importance.

The political impact of a large-scale war is likely to be highly dependent on the way the war ends. For example, it is not inconceivable that one or both of the superpowers, though devastated, would still possess a large number of nuclear weapons at the end of the conflict. Might such arsenals be used to enslave other nations of the world, and to compel them to rebuild the victor's devastated society? If at the end of a large nuclear war the "winner" had just one nuclear submarine, it might be the most militarily powerful nation on earth. Alternatively, the crew of that one submarine, after establishing themselves on some remote island, might constitute the most powerful nation on earth. It is difficult to dismiss such possibilities, given the unprecedented power of nuclear weapons and the unknown psychology of the devastated countries. One might wish to believe that out of the ashes of a devastated world a more humane society with no need for nuclear weapons might emerge, but that might not be the case.

The psychological impact of a large-scale nuclear war might also be profound. What, for example, would be the psychological impact on people living in remote lands to the sudden annihilation of hundreds of millions of people? Might the have-not citizens of the Third World think that the industrialized world got what it deserved? Might they be relieved that most of the nuclear stockpiles were no longer around to threaten them? Would the people in many areas of the world be amazed that the unthinkable had actually happened and that the world hadn't come to an end—nor had they even suffered greatly in their region? Could they comprehend the magnitude of what had happened, or might their concern with the dead and dying in distant lands be a fleeting one—much as the concern in the West for the past tragedies of the Third World. While the number of deaths probably would make this catastrophe far greater than anything in recorded history, would a fleeting concern over several hundred million killed really be any harder to comprehend than the feelings in the West over two million Kampucheans (Cambodians) murdered under the Pol Pot regime? Other past tragedies have etched a more vivid imprint in our collective conscience, such as the Holocaust in which six million Jews were slaughtered by the Nazis. The difference in our reaction to these two tragedies seem to have little to do with the sheer numbers murdered. Rather, the greater impact of the Holocaust in our collective conscience is probably due to the fact that enough Jews survived. Not only did they make their horror stories known to the rest of the world, but they have not allowed the world to forget the horror, nor its own complicity. No comparable reminders of the Kampuchean genocide have been provided to the world by survivors of that more recent massacre.

In the event of a large nuclear war, there would be two important elements missing in comparison to the Jewish holocaust. First, those parts of the world that might emerge relatively unscathed would have little reason to feel any complicity in the annihilation of several hundred million people. Secondly, those in distant countries would probably shun contact with any survivors in the radioactively contaminated lands devastated in the nuclear exchange. It might be a long time before people in distant countries would learn firsthand of the magnitude of the catastrophe or hear the horror stories. There probably would not be on-the-scene TV coverage of the devastation for sometime afterwards. Nowadays, TV coverage is responsible more than any other media for literally bringing home the emotional impact of suffering in distant lands. After a large-scale nuclear war, without TV coverage, without anyone to tell the horror stories of the hundreds of millions killed in the industrialized world, and without any sense of complicity in the deed, might the rest of the world simply go on about its business of survival on an impoverished planet?

As another example of how our psychological attitude towards great tragedies is influenced primarily by factors other than the number of deaths, we should remember that the Soviet leaders often remark how the 20 million Soviet citizens killed in World War II make the Soviet people eager to avoid another major war. It is almost certainly true that most Soviet citizens fear another world war even more than their American counterparts, whose experience with war is primarily limited to the TV screen. However, it may also be worthwhile to remember that perhaps as many as 12 to 60 million Soviet citizens were killed by their own government during the Stalinist purges.[57] That event has important implications for future world peace, since it serves to remind us that for some Soviet leaders, political goals may be of much greater importance than the lives of vast numbers of the nation's citizens or considerations of global environmental damage. These two preceding examples underscore how past tragedies can carry very different implications for future world peace. They also illustrate how the lessons we draw from past tragedies, *and* which ones we choose to remember, can be greatly influenced by our political leanings.

Our tendency either to exaggerate or to downplay the magnitude of a potential catastrophe is also greatly influenced by our political beliefs. For example, it seems quite plausible that many of those who believe that a nuclear war would mean the end of the world are attracted to that position because it buttresses their belief that it is pointless to increase the U.S. nuclear arsenal (since the existing arsenals can supposedly destroy the world many times over). It seems probable that our view of the consequences of a nuclear war depends much less on the calculations and the uncertain estimates of scientists than on our politically determined predisposition.

Prodisarmament groups have for many years advocated reducing the nuclear arsenals to minimum-deterrent levels of 100 megatons or less. The assertion of the TTAPS study that there exists a 100-megaton threshold above which a nuclear war is likely to result in a global climatic catastrophe would seem to be tailor-made for the advocates of minimum deterrence. A careful reading of TTAPS and other studies reveals, however, that no such absolute threshold for global climatic disaster is claimed. Nevertheless, Carl Sagan one of the authors of TTAPS, has been vigorously promoting just such a caricature of this study's findings.[58] It is not impossible that scientists are just as influenced by their politically determined predispositions as anyone else.

Most people understand well the need not to understate the effects of a nuclear war. If it is believed that the impact of a nuclear war could be "tolerable," some officials could "justify" their idea that nuclear wars can be fought and won. Any rational person can see the danger in the false belief that a nuclear war would be "tolerable" or "acceptable." However, it is also dangerous for people to believe the inaccurate assumption that a nuclear war would necessarily have a catastrophic long-term worldwide impact, because questions relating to the nuclear balance of power or to vulnerabilities in the nuclear arsenal are then seen as irrelevant. In fact, however, such questions may have a significant impact on the probability that a nuclear war will occur and on the outcome of such a conflict.

STUDY QUESTIONS

1. What are the principal long-term worldwide effects of a large-scale nuclear war? Which effects are potentially the most serious and the least serious?

2. How likely is it that a large-scale nuclear war would lead to the extinction of life on earth? The end of civilization as we know it?

3. Which of the long-term worldwide effects are known with most certainty and which with the least certainty?

4. What are the uncertainties in the prediction of a "nuclear winter"? What would be the probable impact of a significant temperature drop?

5. What are all the probable effects resulting from an ozone-layer depletion? How serious are the effects likely to be?

6. What are all the worldwide effects of radioactive fallout? How serious are they likely to be?

7. What do you believe the political, economic, and psychological effects of a large-scale nuclear war might be in the targeted countries? Worldwide?

8. Do you believe that there are psychological and political factors that predispose people to consider the worldwide impact of a nuclear war to be more severe or less severe? Explain.

9. If it could be demonstrated that a large-scale nuclear war would probably lead to the extinction of life on earth, what impact would that fact have, if any, on your attitudes toward nuclear weapons, arms control, etc.

IV

POLICY OPTIONS AND OBJECTIVES

EFFECTIVENESS OF
CIVIL DEFENSE _____

WHY IS IT DIFFICULT TO EXAMINE CIVIL DEFENSE OBJECTIVELY?

The topic of civil defense, always controversial, has generally been regarded by the media as a matter for derision rather than as a topic for serious debate. Why should civil defense, which seems to be nothing but insurance in case deterrence fails, engender such hostility and ridicule? Perhaps civil defense comes less naturally to the United States than to a Soviet society that suffered 20 million dead in World War II and that knows what it means to have its land ravaged by war. Or perhaps some U.S. citizens view civil defense as the government's manipulative way of safeguarding key personnel, while pretending that nuclear war might not be so bad. Also civil defense is a ridiculed topic because of the many psychological associations with "kooky" people and survivalists, with thoughts of food rotting away in fallout shelters, or perhaps images from our childhood of diving under school desks or taking other such seemingly futile measures to avoid what could be near-total destruction.[1]

But civil defense needs to be evaluated for both its advantages and shortcomings in a relatively dispassionate way. As an example of the need to recognize the pros and cons of civil defense issues, let us consider the duck-and-cover drills of the early 1950s, which are now a subject of considerable ridicule. For many people these exercises may have represented a way to reassure young children that they could save themselves from the horror of a nuclear war by taking some simple action, and that no matter what happened the adult world could keep things under control. It is of some importance, however, to recognize also that a duck-and-cover action is not in the same category as a magic chant to keep the bombs away. Children in schools anywhere within the vicinity of a nuclear detonation most certainly could not escape being vaporized by ducking under their school desks. But for children in schools more distant from nuclear detonations, such protective action could make a considerable difference. The most common injury sustained by Hiroshima survivors was laceration from flying glass fragments. Moreover, in a nuclear war today, the danger from flying glass would exist over a much larger area than any other danger for people indoors who would have some protection against burns. A child who dives under a school desk and covers his or her face could significantly reduce the risk and severity of injury from flying glass. Although our image of death in a nuclear war is generally one of instantaneous annihilation, fully half of those killed at Hiroshima took more than six days to die as a result of the injuries they sustained at the time of detonation. Duck-and-cover drills were not as absurd as they might seem to be.

Given the well-documented high level of nuclear anxiety in today's school-age children, there is little danger that such drills, were they to be reinstituted, would be seen as reassurance that nuclear war would not be so bad. I am not arguing here for a return to duck-and-cover drills, only a recognition that they were not nearly as futile as civil defense opponents claim, especially at a time when the size of the nuclear arsenals were much smaller. Contrary to those who believe these drills were a form of false reassurance, I believe their effect today probably would be to further emphasize the horrors of nuclear war. This hypothesis is supported by a comparison of attitudes held by U.S. and Soviet children. Children in both societies overwhelmingly believe that they would not survive a nuclear war. This belief is held by a greater percentage of Soviet than American children, 97 versus 84 percent, despite the relatively larger amount of civil defense training to which Soviet children are exposed.[2] Some instruction of American children about nuclear weapons and their effects might not be such a bad idea if bias-free curricular materials could be developed.

One other civil defense measure that is the subject of considerable ridicule is the use of fallout shelters. Some people base their skepticism on a belief that a nuclear attack is likely to come with little or no warning. A further basis for skepticism for many is that given the destructiveness and number of weapons in the strategic arsenal of the Soviet Union, seeking protection in fallout shelters within public buildings in U.S. major cities would almost certainly be a futile measure against all but fairly limited nuclear-attack scenarios—scenarios such as the hypothesized counterforce attack on U.S. ICBM silos or the kind of attack the U.S.S.R. would have been capable of mounting during the early 1960s when its arsenal was very much smaller than today.

In order to have a chance of any significant impact today, civil defense would have to involve "crisis relocation" (evacuation) and sheltering of the populations of our major cities or much more costly blast shelters in cities. In addition, there would need to be protection against the threat of lethal fallout on a nationwide basis. There are numerous questions that have been raised about the wisdom of making such efforts. First we shall examine the feasibility of crisis relocation and sheltering, and later the option of blast shelters in cities.

COULD A CRISIS RELOCATION SAVE MANY LIVES UNDER FAVORABLE CIRCUMSTANCES?

Favorable circumstances here include, most importantly, ample warning time. The general public perception about an all-out nuclear war is that "we'd all be dead." But studies such as *The Effects of Nuclear War* made by the U.S. Congress, Office of Technology Assessment (OTA) indicate that despite the enormous unprecedented devastation, there would be many millions of survivors.[3] Moreover, under favorable circumstances, civil defense could make a very significant difference in the number of casualties. According to a 1978 CIA study on Soviet civil defense (see Table 9.1), crisis relocation of the population of Soviet cities could reduce the casualties from in excess of 50 percent of the population with only a few hours warning to roughly 10 percent (or "low tens of millions") with a warning period of up to a week or more. The effects of civil defense in reducing U.S. casualties could be similarly dramatic based on three independent estimates yielding 48 to 75 percent fatalities with no civil defense measures taken, versus 10 to 26 percent fatalities with relocation and sheltering.[4] The estimated percentages assume

---

Table 9.1 1978 CIA Report: Summary Findings on Soviet Civil Defense

---

- Under worst conditions for the U.S.S.R., with only a few hours or less to make final preparations, Soviet casualties would be well over 100 million, but a large percentage of the leadership would probably survive.
- The critical time for preparation appears to be two or three days, because only by evacuating could the Soviets hope to avert massive losses. With a few days for final preparations, casualties could be reduced by more than 50 percent; most of this reduction would be due to evacuation, the remainder to shelters.
- Under the most favorable conditions for the U.S.S.R., including a week or more to complete urban evacuation and to protect the evacuated population, Soviet civil defenses could reduce casualties to the low tens of millions.
- While many of the essential personnel sheltered at economic facilities would probably survive an attack, the Soviets could not prevent massive damage to their economy and the destruction of many of their most valued material accomplishments.

Source: "Soviet Civil Defense," Report to the Director of Central Intelligence, 1978.

that the bulk of the Soviet arsenal is used, that weapons are ground burst for maximum fallout, that fatalities resulting later from injuries sustained in the attack are counted, and that the relocated population following an evacuation has been retargeted by the U.S.S.R.—a worst-case attack scenario considered overly pessimistic by civil defense supporters.[5]

Such casualty estimates are generally dismissed by civil defense opponents as overly optimistic and based on unprovable assumptions. Nevertheless, some civil defense opponents do grant that under favorable circumstances civil defense could initially save tens of millions of lives. The reluctance of many civil defense opponents to come up with alternative calculations on casualties is based on the view that they would be making the same mistake they see civil defense proponents making, i.e., ignoring those factors that cannot be calculated and assuming that calculated estimates without these factors taken into account are meaningful.

One crucial assumption behind the calculations of crisis-relocation proponents is that there would probably exist a warning period of several days. The warning time would need to be a matter of days, since it has been estimated that the time needed to evacuate 85 percent of persons in high-risk areas would be forty-eight hours. While daily experience with rush hour traffic jams may engender skepticism of such estimates, experience with actual evacuations in the case of natural disasters offers some confirmation that large-scale evacuations can be accomplished. For example, during a hurricane in the Gulf Coast area, 750,000 people were moved up to three hundred miles within a day or two.[6] Civil defense opponents correctly point out that the probable degree of panic and confusion would almost certainly be much greater preceding a nuclear attack than a hurricane, but that does not necessarily mean that citizens would not follow instructions if some prior planning had been done. In the absence of any plan or public education efforts, however, many citizens would be likely to take the more cynical view that any ordered evacuation would be impossible and would not do any good.

Such public cynicism is also fed by overenthusiastic civil defense proponents such as T. K. Jones who concludes that the United States could fully recover from an all-out nuclear war with the Soviet Union in "two to four years . . . if there are enough shovels to go around." Jones's optimism does the cause of a realistic civil defense program little good. Considerable harm is also done by other loose administration statements that convey the impression to some people that the goal is to be better prepared to fight and win a nuclear war, rather than to save as many lives as possible if the worst should occur. Nevertheless, the anti-civil defense view ascribed to by the Physicians for Social Responsibility and many other groups—"There is no effective civil defense. The blast, thermal, and radiation effects would kill even those in shelters, and the fallout would reach those who had been evacuated."—is just as dogmatic and exaggerated as T. K. Jones's view that we can all be saved if there are enough shovels to go around. Of course there really is no way to prove the feasibility of a crisis relocation short of an actual evacuation conducted in time of extreme crisis. In the unlikely event that a practice evacuation of a major city were actually conducted and it went well, civil defense opponents might argue that the degree of panic in a real evacuation would make the test result inapplicable. If the test result went poorly, civil defense supporters could argue that in a real evacuation people would be much more motivated to get out and not treat the whole thing as a joke. A practice evacuation would be extremely costly and in the end might prove very little.

WHY COULD A CRISIS RELOCATION POTENTIALLY BE SO EFFECTIVE?

Civil defense has the potential to make a large difference because the total U.S. land area that might be devastated by primary nuclear-weapons effects (blast, heat, and fire) is estimated to be only 4 to 5 percent,[7] although a majority of the population normally resides in these areas.

Thus, in the unattainable limiting case in which people were uniformly dispersed over the entire U.S. land area, about 4 to 5 percent of the population would be in areas devastated by primary nuclear-weapons effects. In the event of a large-scale attack with many ground-burst weapons, fallout, of course, would be a life-threatening hazard for people without protection over most areas of the United States, even if a crisis relocation took place. However, the radiation levels for people in shelters, or even home basements, would not be lethal in most instances. For example, a fallout shelter with a three-foot thickness of earth overhead would provide a protection factor of 1000 (the radiation intensity inside equals one thousandth that outside), and a typical home basement, might provide a protection factor of 10 to 20.[8] Outside radiation intensity levels would be expected to decline rapidly with time, allowing shelter occupants to leave after a period that depended largely on how much fallout was deposited at any particular location.

The question of time spent in a shelter is sometimes glossed over by civil defense supporters who point out (correctly) that radiation levels are one-hundredth their initial level after two days and one-thousandth their initial level after two weeks. However, these facts may cause us to overlook the importance of cumulative radiation exposure after leaving a shelter. We must also keep in mind the possibility that continued nuclear bombardments would raise the radiation levels back to their original high levels, and the further possibility that nuclear reactors might be targeted, giving rise to a radiation-intensity component that declines very slowly with time.

OVER WHAT FRACTION OF THE UNITED STATES WOULD SURVIVAL IN SHELTERS BE FEASIBLE?

The idealized fallout-distribution map in figure 7.2 gives a rough idea of probable fallout levels following a large-scale nuclear attack in which most weapons were ground burst. In order to see the effects of realistic weather conditions, Leo Schmidt of the Institute for Defense Analyses has calculated probable fallout patterns for various months of the year using the known prevailing winds for each month. It would appear, based on Schmidt's calculations, that survival over most of the eastern half of the country would be possible following a large nuclear attack only if the population were sheltered. (Recall that the lethal whole-body dose is between 200R and 700R, with 450R being lethal to half those exposed.)

Using a total of twelve different prevailing-wind distributions, one for each month of the year, Schmidt has also calculated contours of likelihood of the dose being 500R or less (see figure 9.1). For the striped areas of figure 9.1, the likelihood of a dose less than 500R is 50 percent or less; for the crosshatched areas, there is only a 10 percent likelihood of the dose being less than 500R.

To get a better idea of how large an area of the country would be facing extremely serious fallout problems, we show in figure 9.2 the likelihood contours for the cumulative lifetime exposure being less than 2500R following an all-out attack. Approximately 90 percent of the U.S. land area would have a better than even chance of having radiation levels below this amount according to figure 9.2. For cumulative levels no higher than 2500R, a shelter or below-ground-basement with a protection factor of 20 would reduce the cumulative dose to 125R.

How long would a person need to stay in a shelter if the cumulative outside level was as high as 2500R? That would depend largely on how long it took the fallout to arrive initially. For a typical fallout arrival time of ten hours, a person leaving a shelter after one month would receive for the rest of his life 25 percent as much radiation as an initially unsheltered person. This means that after leaving the shelter, a person would receive 625R spread over the rest of his life, assuming he did not relocate. While 625R exceeds the mean lethal dose, the fact that it would be spread out over a very long time reduces its effect considerably. In the general case of a dose received at a constant rate over W weeks, the LD-50 dose may be expressed as: $345W^{1/4}$. Based on this formula, radiation received at very low intensities over a year is only one-third as harmful as the same dose received during a short time interval. Thus a dose of 625R spread over a year might be roughly equivalent to around 200R received in a short time. Moreover, long-term exposure would be further reduced because a person spends a fraction of his time indoors. Of course, for most people a dose of 200R, while sublethal, is an extremely high radiation dose that they would ordinarily want to avoid. Therefore, many people may want to emerge from their shelters for only short times initially, or else promptly relocate to a less contaminated area, if possible.

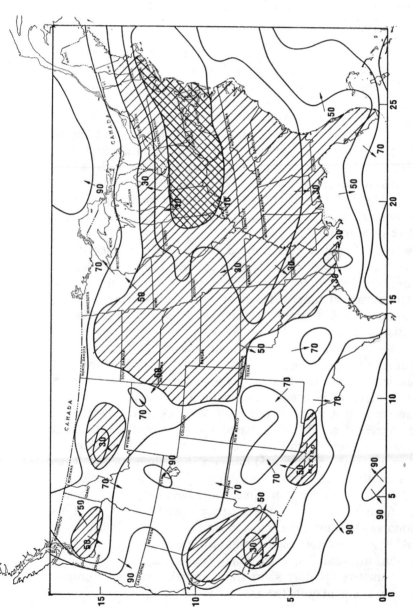

Figure 9.1 Likelihood contours of dose below 500 rads.
Source: L. Schmidt, "A Study of Twenty-four Nationwide Fallout Patterns from Twelve Winds," Institute for Defense Analyses, 1981.
Notes: Contours of likelihood of two-week dose being below 500 rads to unsheltered person for a large-scale nuclear attack (6,541 megatons), obtained by averaging over twelve monthly prevailing wind patterns. Striped areas have more than a 50 percent likelihood of the dose being about 500 rads. In crosshatched areas, the likelihood exceeds 90 percent. All weapons are assumed to have been burst for maximum fallout.

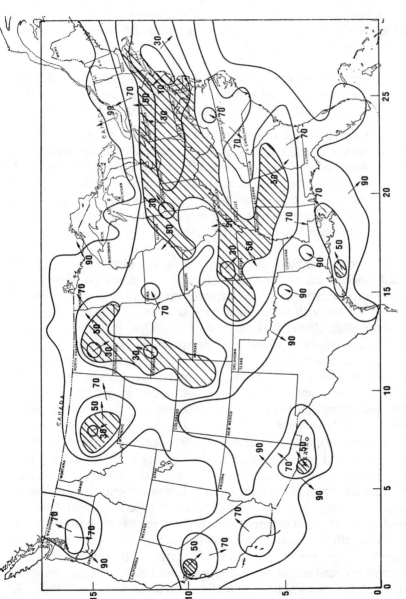

Figure 9.2 Likelihood contours of dose below 2500 rads.
Source: See figure 9.1.
Notes: Contours of likelihood of two-week dose being below 2500 rads to unsheltered person for a large-scale nuclear attack (6,541 megatons), obtained by averaging twelve monthly prevailing wind patterns. Striped areas have more than a 50 percent likelihood of the dose being above 2500 rads. All weapons are assumed to have been ground burst for maximum fallout.

It should be kept in mind that only 10 percent of the U.S. land area is likely to be covered by cumulative radiation levels as high as 2500R, even given the worst-case scenario of many ground-burst detonations, so the previous example is a very conservative one for most areas of the country. An optimistic assessment of the fallout problem and consequent sheltering needs after an all-out attack would look something like the following:

- Over 90 percent of the U.S. land area, the expected radiation levels would require stays in a shelter of less than a month, and in most areas less than a few days.

- Over parts of the remaining 10 percent of the land area, survival might still be possible, especially if the population were to relocate after emerging from shelter. (However, it must also be remembered that perhaps 4 to 5 percent of the U.S. land area would have been devastated by the direct bomb effects of blast and heat, and that a majority of the population resides in these areas.)

Until now, we have considered the fallout distribution from an all-out nuclear attack. Schmidt has also calculated patterns for a counterforce attack primarily targeted against missile silos. Figures 9.3 and 9.4 show the likelihood contours for a cumulative dose of less than 500R (figure 9.3) and less than 2500R (figure 9.4) for the counterforce attack. Clearly, the prospects for survival would be better in the eastern half of the country in the case of a counterforce attack versus an all-out attack. The preceding assessment of what sheltering could accomplish over most areas of the country may seem too optimistic. How is it that different observers come to such contradictory assessments of the effectiveness of civil defense?

Statements made by civil defense opponents and supporters often seem contradictory, since they do not indicate either the level of risk assumed or the outside radiation exposure assumed. Consider for example the assertion made by Edward Kennedy and Mark Hatfield in their book *Freeze!:* "shelter occupants would have to spend as much as 100 percent of the first month in shelter. In the second month they could spend perhaps 75 percent of their time in shelters." [9] The use of "as much as" in the statement should alert the cautious reader that the authors are assuming either a very high outside radiation level (corresponding to a small fraction of the U.S. area), or a very low level of risk. In fact, if we use average postulated

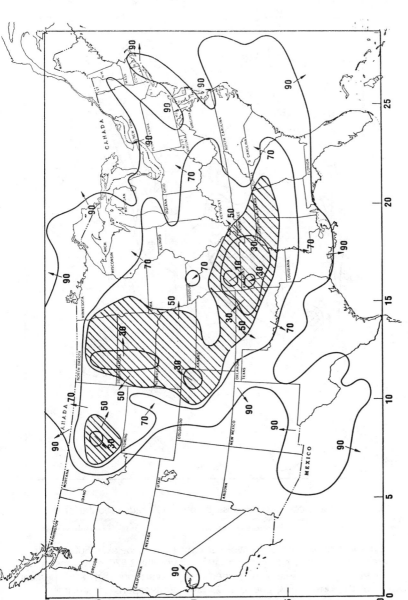

Figure 9.3 Likelihood contours of dose below 500 rads (counterforce attack).

Source: See figure 9.1.

Notes: Contours of likelihood of two-week dose being below 500 rads to unsheltered person for a counterforce nuclear attack involving 2,570 megatons delivered primarily against missile silos. Striped areas have a more than 50 percent likelihood of the dose being above 500 rads. All weapons are assumed to have been ground burst for maximum fallout.

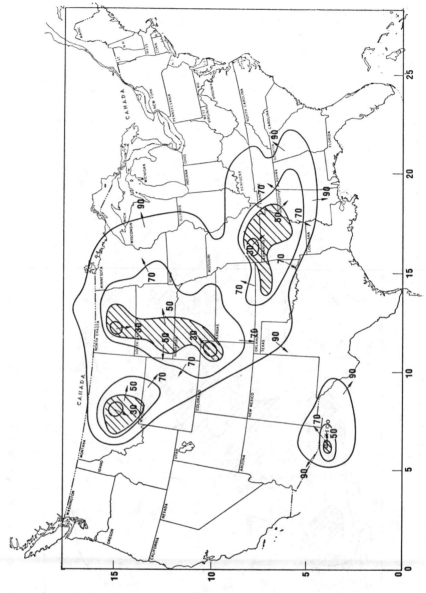

Figure 9.4   Likelihood contours of dose below 2500 rads (counterforce attack).
Source: See figure 9.1.
Notes: Contours of likelihood of two-week dose being below 2500 rads to unsheltered person for a counterforce attack involving 2,570 megatons delivered primarily against missile silos. Striped areas have more than a 50 percent likelihood of the dose being above 2500 rads. All weapons are assumed ground burst for maximum fallout.

radiation levels and higher-than-peacetime levels for an acceptable risk criterion, the picture changes drastically, especially if one assumes sheltering following a relocation.

The feasibility of a civil defense program based on a relocation of the population followed by sheltering depends on many other factors besides nonprohibitive time in a shelter. One frequently heard objection to such a plan is that the evacuated population could simply be retargeted by the aggressor. Of course, such would not be the case assuming that the evacuation took the form of a dispersal in which small groups are sent to a very large number of host areas. Moreover, a dispersal in which people brought some of their supplies with them might in part avoid the problems of an unfriendly host reception and an overload of available facilities.

The most difficult part of planning a crisis relocation is arranging the support in the host areas to shelter and sustain the evacuated population. Most of the plans under discussion involve lodging for evacuees in congregate care facilities such as churches and schools rather than private homes. Nevertheless, we should not necessarily expect that people now living in the countryside will welcome with open arms to share their shelter and food hordes of culturally and ethnically different evacuees from the cities. Nor will people living in the countryside welcome a civil defense program that may be perceived as making it more likely that the countryside as well as cities will become a target for nuclear destruction. However, the survival of many tens of millions of people should obviously call for some reassessment of our peacetime views concerning private property rights. Unfortunately, given the incidence of gun ownership in the United States, it is hard to be sanguine that such an urban relocation to the countryside would be accomplished without some violence, and without, for example, newly arrived evacuees wanting to keep later ones out. Nevertheless, no matter how many deaths might occur in such an evacuation, they would undoubtedly be much fewer than the lives lost had no evacuation taken place. Moreover, the panic and violence of an evacuation for which no plans have been made would almost certainly be greater than one for which planning had been done—although no one can imagine any evacuation would proceed smoothly according to plan.

In a very severe but prolonged crisis, perhaps involving the prior use of tactical nuclear weapons in Europe, or perhaps even following the start of Soviet evacuation of their cities, it is hard to imagine that large percentages of the U.S. urban population would resist the impulse to evacuate—particularly once a spontaneous evacuation began to get underway. At the Three Mile Island accident, for example, it is estimated that 40 percent of the nearby population evacuated spontaneously. The real choice a U.S. government would have during an extreme crisis would be between directing an evacuation based on some plan, or allowing a spontaneous evacuation to occur with all the chaos that is likely to entail.

HOW LIKELY IS IT THAT CIRCUMSTANCES WOULD BE SO FAVORABLE AS TO ALLOW A CRISIS RELOCATION TO TAKE PLACE?

Of the circumstances necessary for a crisis relocation to be successful, ample time is, as noted, the most important. Given the various events that could precipitate such a directive to evacuate, perhaps the most plausible one would be the Soviet evacuation of their cities. Given the extent of U.S.S.R. civil defense capabilities and the Soviet high regard for defensive measures generally, such an attempted evacuation of Soviet cities in an extreme crisis would not seem to be an improbable event. The evacuation might not signal their intention to strike first, rather it might reflect their judgment that a U.S. first strike was imminent. Such a Soviet evacuation would probably be quickly detected by spy satellites (assuming they are still working) or by other means, but what would the U.S. response be? The alternatives might include: (1) increasing the readiness of our nuclear forces, but not ordering an evacuation of U.S. cities (in that case, assuming the Soviet evacuation became public knowledge, the result might be mass turmoil and spontaneous evacuation of U.S cities); (2) making up a highly complex evacuation plan, disseminating and implementing it with no prior planning; (3) launching a suicidal first strike on the U.S.S.R. before their evacuation runs its course; (4) retargeting U.S. missiles at the Soviet evacuation centers, which would be counter to stated U.S. targeting objectives and which would only work in the unlikely event that the U.S.S.R. evacuation did not lead to a great deal of dispersal; (5) ordering a previously planned evacuation of U.S. cities and calling the Soviet leader on the hot line in an attempt to forestall the impending catastrophe.

While these alternatives may be neither exhaustive nor exclusive, number 5 would seem preferable to the others and to any other response I can think of to the question: What do we do if the Soviets begin evacuating their cities? The president could, of course, call the

Soviet leader without ordering a U.S. evacuation, possibly even threatening a first strike unless the U.S.S.R. ordered its "citizen-hostages" back to their cities. However, it is hard to imagine a Soviet leader complying with such a request when it was fear of an imminent U.S. attack that might have stimulated the order to evacuate in the first place.

An argument sometimes given against the need for a U.S. counterevacuation capability is that if the Soviets wished to attack, they would never reveal their intentions by evacuating their cities and thereby causing U.S. forces to go on alert. That suggestion is not implausible, in light of the great military advantage conferred by a surprise attack. We should not, however, consider only Soviet offensive strategic thinking. An evacuation might be ordered purely as a defensive move, or as a signal to the United States that the Soviets were deadly serious and prepared for the worst.

There are, of course, many scenarios in which a nuclear war might start without sufficient warning to permit an evacuation. These include (1) a surprise attack (with no detectable prior Soviet evacuation), (2) a very rapid escalation from a conventional war with the U.S.S.R., (3) by accident, or (4) by design—started by third parties seeking mutual U.S.-U.S.S.R. destruction. There are obviously many such situations for which a crisis relocation would be unfeasible, just as there are also many other scenarios for which it would be feasible. But most people do not refrain from buying life insurance just because they know that their policy will not pay off under certain circumstances, e.g., death during a nuclear war. The key factor in making such judgments would seem to be how likely are those circumstances that make a plan feasible and how likely are those that make it unfeasible. That question is not an easy one to answer, either for life insurance or civil defense.

Aside from having ample time, a successful evacuation of cities would also apparently require a "cooperative enemy" who would refrain from launching an attack while the evacuation is in progress. Otherwise, the casualties might be even greater than had no evacuation taken place.[10] Such restraint by the enemy need not result from any benign attitude, but rather from the deterrence stemming from the mutual destruction that each side could inflict on the other's fleeing evacuees. This mutual deterrence would, of course, be completely absent if only one side were to evacuate its cities. However, even more important than the deterrence acting to prevent targeting of fleeing populations, would be a deterrence of the impending war altogether. This deterrence would seem more assured if both sides are perceived as being capable of inflicting comparable damage on one another. If it is perceived that an effective Soviet evacuation might allow them to suffer only 10-percent casualties (the estimate in the C.I.A. study), while the U.S. might suffer as much as 75-percent fatalities with no evacuation or warning, there could conceivably be a significant U.S. temptation to strike while the Soviet evacuation was in progress. This is one way in which it might plausibly be argued that a U.S. civil defense program matching that of the U.S.S.R. might contribute to deterrence. There are other ways discussed in the next section in which it may be argued that such a plan would have the opposite effect.

HOW WOULD AN EXPANDED U.S. CIVIL DEFENSE EFFORT AFFECT THE STRATEGIC BALANCE?

The U.S.S.R. has had a civil defense program that has been expanding since the late 1950s. This program now involves over 100,000 full-time military and civilian personnel and perhaps sixteen million others.[11] It also includes a significant amount of public education on the subject of nuclear war and nuclear weapons. For example, training in civil defense is compulsory for all citizens and includes seven courses totaling 124 hours of training time. The program includes scholastic as well as practical training, including fallout shelter construction, medical self-help, and preparation for evacuation. Soviet civil defense planning includes both a crisis relocation of urban populations and blast shelters in cities for key personnel. In the early 1970s a shift was made toward providing shelter protection for the entire urban population considered to be at risk. The cumulative shelter construction to date has provided capacity for a large proportion of the population. Because the population is being trained in the construction of expedient shelters, the Soviets claim that everyone should be able to obtain protection in blast or fallout shelters within 72 hours of government announcement of a threatening situation.

Soviet expenditures on civil defense are estimated to be at least ten to twenty times U.S. expenditures.[12] Approximate expenditure comparisons like this involve much guesswork, and they are based on the estimated cost to replicate the Soviet program in the United States. Nevertheless, even if the estimates are very inexact, they do reveal a sizable difference in scope between U.S. and Soviet civil defense efforts. Although many Soviet citizens may treat Soviet civil defense as a joke, their attitude might change abruptly should a nuclear crisis arise. If the United States were to add to its civil defense effort, such a move would not disturb the strategic balance, but rather restore the balance now lacking. Whatever one's attitude about the relative U.S.-U.S.S.R. balance of offensive weapons, it is a very "stable" balance given the amount of destructive power possessed by each side; additions or cuts in the number of offensive weapons do not greatly affect each side's mutual assured destruction (MAD) capability. The same cannot be said about defensive measures. In particular, it may be argued that if one side has an effective civil defense system that might significantly reduce casualties or, equally important, the system is perceived that way, this potential is more destabilizing than if both sides have the capability. Much the same thing can be said about only one side having an extensive antiballistic missile system. Just the possibility that a defensive system might work, or that it could be quickly upgraded to the point where it would work at some future time, could be highly destabilizing. Ostensibly, it was for that reason that the U.S. and U.S.S.R. agreed in 1972 to limit ABM systems.

It is common among civil defense opponents to dismiss the effectiveness or importance of Soviet civil defense efforts by correctly pointing out the massive levels of destruction the Soviets would suffer even with their civil defense program. For example, even if Soviet casualties could be held to the "low tens of millions," [13] it is almost certainly true that their economy would be devastated in a retaliatory attack, since some have estimated that 70 percent of Soviet industry is capable of being destroyed with only 1300 U.S. warheads.[14] Nevertheless, this does not negate the fact that Soviet civil defense could be highly effective in that it could save many tens of millions of lives and probably safeguard the political leadership. Moreover, the great difficulties in implementing Soviet evacuation plans are often somewhat overstated by civil defense opponents. For example, John Weinstein claims that

> Soviet evacuation plans call for 17 million urban residents to walk 30 miles (1.5 miles for 20 hours), and then build expedient protection. How the very young, the very old, and the sick are to make such formidable progress (while carrying two weeks' worth of food, water, and supplies) is not clear.[15]

For many Americans, walking thirty miles in twenty hours might represent "formidable progress." However, particularly when they are fleeing for their lives, such a hike might seem less formidable to a Soviet populace that is far less dependent on automobiles than U.S. citizens.[16] Moreover, the fact that some of the old and sick might not be able to evacuate may not play much of a role in a Soviet defense planner's thinking regarding the feasibility of an evacuation whose purpose is to save as many of those who can be saved. Furthermore, many Soviet city dwellers would not need to walk to the countryside. Over 15,000 blast shelters have been built to house 20 million people.[17] In addition, a system of deep subway tunnels has been built in all cities whose population exceeds one million. In Moscow alone the subway tunnels would provide protection for a half-million people. Unlike subway tunnels in the United States, those in the Soviet Union are equipped with the necessary blast doors.

Many observers do not attribute any motivation to the Soviet civil defense effort beyond the desire to protect the population against any possibility, although some analysts would see the effort as evidence that the Soviets are planning to fight and win a nuclear war. Nevertheless, whether or not such Soviet motivation exists, the massive Soviet civil defense effort, without any comparable American effort, cannot help but affect Soviet and American thinking on the strategic balance and be one of many factors that in a crisis could precipitate disaster. It doesn't matter that many American civil defense opponents believe the Soviet civil defense plans cannot work. The important point is that given their investment, Soviet leaders appear to believe otherwise.

Civil defense opponents sometimes argue that a sizable U.S. civil defense effort would be destabilizing because it would prompt the U.S.S.R. to add still more weapons to its nuclear arsenal in order to ensure the capability to destroy the United States. However, there is no indication that the United States has found it necessary to build a larger arsenal in order to keep pace with the Soviet civil defense effort. Deterrence does not depend on one's ability to kill in retaliation as many of the enemy as he killed in the initial attack. The point is rather that if there is a great disparity in that regard, then this factor, along with others, e.g. the sizable advantage to the side that strikes the first blow, could significantly undermine deterrence and increase the probability of nuclear war. If one reason for a lack of concern that MAD is still "mutual" is that one U.S. option at present includes launching a first strike while a Soviet evacuation is in progress so as to inflict a comparable level of devastation, then it would seem desirable to remove the necessity for such a drastic option by having a comparable U.S. counterevacuation capability.

Asking whether an expanded U.S. civil defense effort would stabilize or destabilize the U.S.-U.S.S.R. strategic balance is, in effect, asking whether the action would increase or decrease the probability of nuclear war. Perhaps the most persuasive argument that has been advanced against civil defense is that it would allow people to conclude falsely that nuclear war might be survivable or winnable. While a nuclear war might be survivable in the technical sense of there being survivors, recovery in the affected countries would by no means be assured, as we have seen in previous chapters. An expanded civil defense effort would therefore need to be accompanied by a realistic portrayal of how terrible a nuclear war would really be. Unfortunately, past governmental public-education efforts have failed to show the consequences of a nuclear war and the extraordinary hardships survivors would undergo. However, ordinary citizens in the U.S.S.R. seem no more eager than U.S. citizens to have a nuclear war, despite their government's sizable civil defense effort. Therefore, it is hard to say why a U.S. civil defense effort accompanied by extensive public education would make nuclear war less abhorrent to U.S. citizens—in fact it might well become more abhorrent and thereby strengthen deterrence. Thus, instead of taking the position that we should work on methods to reduce the risk of nuclear war rather than methods to survive one (civil defense), we may alternatively take the position that we should simultaneously promote civil defense and other methods to reduce the risk of war.

Another argument presented against the need for a U.S. evacuation plan is that a U.S. evacuation of its cities after a Soviet evacuation took place might well trigger a Soviet first strike. That analysis is correct as far as it goes, but a crisis relocation plan would permit a U.S. evacuation while any Soviet evacuation is underway. After a Soviet evacuation has occurred with no corresponding U.S. evacuation in the interim, a mutual deterrence to strike might no longer exist, and the Soviets may well choose to strike first regardless of what the United States were to do. A government that orders an evacuation of its cities is taking an extreme and provocative act— one likely to be interpreted by the other side as a preparation for a preemptive strike. To react passively by not ordering a reciprocal evacuation in the face of such an extremely provocative act could well invite disaster. A Soviet military planner might well conclude that a brief "window of opportunity" had opened in which a preemptive first strike would inflict very much greater damage on the United States than the United States could inflict on the Soviet Union in retaliation. Alternatively, the Soviet military might be tempted to be much more aggressive in whatever military involvement prompted the Soviet evacuation, given the temporarily much greater U.S. vulnerability.

This temptation to engage in "brinksmanship" is exactly what some civil defense opponents say they want the U.S. military to avoid. The Soviets, however, already have a crisis relocation plan while the United States does not. As in the days of John Foster Dulles, brinksmanship is much more likely to arise when one side has a capability not matched by the other. It is true that adoption by the United States of a crisis relocation plan would expand the options of military planners. The options being expanded, however, are not those that would lead to risky military adventures, but rather those that would allow the United States to choose some action other than a preemptive first strike or inaction in the face of a Soviet evacuation. By itself, an effective civil defense program can hardly be viewed as an inducement to adventurism, given the devastation a nuclear war would inflict even with civil defense. Ship captains do not navigate more recklessly because their ship is equipped with lifeboats.

In fact, the CIA's 1978 study on Soviet civil defense concluded that "we do not believe that the Soviet's present civil defenses would embolden them to expose the U.S.S.R. to a higher risk of nuclear attack." [18] Since most U.S. civil defense opponents would probably agree with that statement, it is hard to understand why they view a U.S. crisis relocation plan in a much more sinister light, unless they distrust the motives of U.S. leaders more than those of the Soviet Union's leaders.

One indication of how the Soviets would view a greatly expanded U.S. civil defense program is supplied by the Soviet booklet: *Whence the Threat to Peace?* The first edition of this booklet was prepared by the Soviet Defense Ministry in response to the controversial 1981 U.S. Department of Defense booklet, *Soviet Military Power.* The earlier U.S. booklet described Soviet military might in stark terms, and it included a section of Soviet civil defense as well.[19] The Soviet booklet was more balanced in that it compared the two superpower's military arsenals and then proceeded to attack all the elements of the proposed U.S. buildup under President Reagan as undermining an alleged existing nuclear parity.[20] The one notable omission in the Soviet attack on the U.S. military buildup was any reference whatsoever to the proposed significant expansion of U.S. civil defense efforts. One may infer from this omission that the Soviets have found no fault with a U.S. program designed to save lives and that they do not view it as provocative or destabilizing. An alternate explanation of their silence on this one point might be that they would just as soon see the United States waste defense dollars on a useless undertaking. That interpretation, however, is implausible given the scope of the Soviet civil defense program and the fact that they now spend many times what the United States spends in this area.

It is even possible that the Soviets view U.S. inattention to civil defense in an ominous light. A Soviet defense planner might well regard a near-total U.S. neglect of civil defense as a strong indication that the first U.S. option of choice is a first strike or that we in the United States really have little appreciation for what war would be like on our own soil. Lacking such an appreciation, we might therefore react in panic in a military confrontation and thereby blunder into a full-scale nuclear war. Whether or not it may seem farfetched that the lack of a civil defense effort should have an ominous connotation, precisely that view has reportedly been voiced in conversations with individual Soviet citizens and officials.[21] The interpretation given to actions or inactions of one country by people in another country is not always easy to second guess—particularly when two countries harbor such deep suspicions of each other's intentions. Whatever the Soviet view of an expanded U.S. civil defense effort, Soviet officials seem eager to downplay the scope of their own effort.[22] Since there are many U.S. civil defense opponents who equate civil defense with preparation for a nuclear war, the Soviets do not wish to be seen holding that view, particularly when denouncing a U.S. administration on that score.

Much more important than dollar expenditures on civil defense is how the money is to be spent. If a U.S. civil defense program is going to accomplish anything, it is essential that past mistakes be corrected—particularly in producing educational information for the public that shows the real dimensions of a nuclear catastrophe. It is difficult for the public to be optimistic that officials charged with the mission of creating a civil defense plan really know what they are doing when one reads media accounts of administrative procedures for forwarding mail and collecting taxes following a nuclear war.[23]

HOW WOULD AN EXPANDED U.S. CIVIL DEFENSE EFFORT AFFECT THE PROSPECTS OF EVENTUAL RECOVERY?

Although it has been asserted that civil defense could, in fact, have a very significant short-term impact on casualties, its impact on the long-term recovery of the society is less clear. For example, even if the CIA assessment of Soviet civil defense capabilities is correct, and, in the most favorable circumstances, the U.S.S.R. were to suffer no more than 10-percent casualties following a U.S. retaliatory strike, the survival of the U.S.S.R. as a functioning society would be far from assured. As the physicist Henry Kendall notes, a second U.S. retaliatory strike would have devastating consequences on the U.S.S.R. economy and social structure, wiping out the bulk of its industry, oil refineries, military and political targets, and cities.[24] Moreover, given the scarcity of material goods and, more importantly, the destruction of an economy that makes production of new goods possible, a case can be made that the eventual recovery of a society is more likely if there are fewer initial survivors.[25]

However, the morality of this anti-civil defense argument is equivalent to that of taking just enough survivors into a lifeboat so that, given the limited provisions on board, all can be reasonably certain of surviving for some time, rather than taking as many as the boat can hold. Quite apart from the dubious morality of not making serious civil defense efforts that might save many tens of millions of lives since it might endanger long-term recovery, the truth of the asserted proposition is by no means self-evident. It may well be that to reconstruct a devastated society, the most important asset is not physical, but rather the accumulated skills and knowledge of its surviving individual citizens. It is possible that the great bulk of our accumulated knowledge adapted to a highly technological civilization would have little relevance to the utterly unprecedented situation in which the survivors would find themselves. However, it would seem equally absurd to think that the extremely difficult and perhaps impossible road back to a functioning society would necessarily be made more difficult by the presence of too many physicians, engineers, policemen, craftsmen, farmers, and people generally.

Moreover, civil defense supporters note that the situation for survivors might not be so different from the marginal existence in many parts of the world today or from the way everybody lived not long ago. Obviously extremely difficult, possibly insurmountable, problems would exist in restoring production of food and other essential goods, as well as equally important problems in distributing these goods. These problems are so serious that civil defense planning before the fact can only make things less miserable for the survivors and for the possible eventual reconstruction of society. Such planning cannot assure that there will be a government in charge to follow through on the plans, that people would receive and obey instructions of such a government, or that society would eventually recover.

It may well be that following an all out U.S.-U.S.S.R. nuclear exchange, the survivors would indeed envy the dead. Just as in World War II concentration camps, there would be many among the survivors who would give up all hope and would not bother to try to survive. There would also be those who would try to survive at the expense of others' lives. However, we should not prejudge these things and try to minimize such actions by minimizing the number of survivors.

Finally, even if we grant there is uncertainty over whether such a program would help the long-term recovery following an all-out nuclear war, there are other events for which a civil defense program would be of unquestionable benefit. Without indicating how probable such eventualities are relative to an all-out nuclear war, they include: (1) a limited nuclear war with the U.S.S.R., (2) a limited nuclear war initiated by a third party, (3) an accidentally fired U.S. missile hitting a U.S. target, (4) a nuclear terrorist attack, (5) a catastrophic nuclear reactor accident, and (6) other nonnuclear disasters. While in many of these cases there is unlikely to be much warning time before the event, much less warning would be needed. For example, suppose a nuclear war were intiated by a third party or by an accidental launch of a small number of Soviet missiles. Whether such actions would quickly lead to all-out war is impossible to say. While many untargeted cities hundreds of miles from the detonation would have zero warning before the blast itself, they would have ample warning of perhaps a day (depending on wind velocity) of the approaching radioactive cloud.

HOW EFFECTIVE ARE SHELTERS?

Our main focus so far has been on government civil defense efforts, particularly the idea of crisis relocation of the population. The neglect of other possible government programs such as shelter construction has, as already noted, been a matter of concern over cost rather than probable effectiveness. Individual citizens must also decide for themselves if individual civil defense efforts are worthwhile. Such precautions might range from plans to move now to Australia, to constructing a shelter or becoming familiar with what precautions would need to be taken so that these individual plans could be carried out during a period of severe international crisis. The book *Nuclear War Survival Skills* by Cresson Kearny, a physicist at Oak Ridge National Laboratory, favors this last approach.[26] One advantage of this approach is that it avoids developing a "survivalist" mentality through which an obsessive concentration on an expected doomsday can, in some perverse way, make one look forward to the catastrophe in order to test one's knowledge, skills, and equipment. The other main advantage to the approach is that it avoids the expense and possible embarrassment inherent in putting a shelter in one's back yard. Those who have built such shelters sometimes find themselves the object of ridicule sufficient to deter other people from such an undertaking. However, the conventional wisdom of what is "crazy" and what is "normal" might change abruptly in a severe crisis. People in other countries, particularly the Swiss and the Chinese, do not find such precautions crazy.

The Swiss, for example, who have not fought a war in 150 years, currently have a shelter beneath every home, apartment building, hotel, and factory. All but unnoticed by the rest of the world, the Swiss have gone underground. The Swiss expect to finish their long-term effort, now more than half complete, by 1990, at which point there will be a nuclear-shelter space for every citizen. Their massive civil defense effort, costing on a per capita basis fifty-seven times that of the U.S. effort, has so far placed underground three hundred hospitals, five hundred large community shelters, a thousand command, communications, and medical-aid posts, as well as shelter spaces for the majority of the population. The Swiss are convinced, on the basis of their research, that their extensive shelter system will allow the vast majority of their population to survive a nuclear attack after a stay in shelters ranging from a few hours to two weeks at the most. The strenuous Swiss civil defense effort is certainly not typical of other nations, but neither is the relative U.S. lack of effort. Of the countries of Western Europe, only France spends less on civil defense on a per capita basis than does the United States.

Shelters come in two basic varieties: those designed to protect against fallout and those designed to protect against blast as well. Occupants in a well-constructed blast shelter capable of withstanding overpressures of 50 psi could survive the blast 0.84 miles or more from a one-megaton ground-burst bomb, whereas survival outside a blast shelter closer than 2.8 miles would not be likely. In the case of a bomb air burst at the "optimum" altitude, survival from the initial blast would actually be possible in a blast shelter located at ground zero (directly beneath the explosion), where the overpressure would be around 30 psi. Using figures such as these, what can we conclude about the efficacy of blast shelters?

It is necessary to distinguish three types of shelters for which there will be somewhat different answers:

- Blast shelters for key government leaders

- Blast shelters for citizens in high-risk areas

- Blast shelters for citizens outside high-risk areas

Key government leaders have several advantages over ordinary citizens, most notably that (1) no expense would be spared in building a blast shelter for them, and (2) depending on which side strikes first, they might have advance notice of the nuclear attack. There are also two big disadvantages that government leaders have: they are likely to be primary targets of the enemy, and hence they would be targeted at the onset of an attack. Moreover, even if they did have enough warning time to reach a shelter, the location of that shelter might well be known to the enemy and would probably be a prime target. The likelihood of keeping secret the location of shelters for top government officials is not easy to guess. Possibly construction for such shelters might not be detected by spy satellites. Moreover, given the differences between Soviet and American societies, it seems likely that the location of shelters for key government officials might be kept secret much easier in the Soviet Union. But even if the location of shelters for key government people should become known, it is still possible that the shelters could be effective even if they are directly targeted—for example, if the shelters are at the bottom of a deep mine, some of which are more than a mile underground. (By way of contrast, the crater depth would be 250 feet for a one-megaton ground-burst weapon and 800 feet for a 20-megaton weapon.)

Ordinary citizens do not need to worry about bombs directly targeted on their shelter. For residents of a major city, some idea of the chances of survival in a blast shelter may be conveyed by comparing the area subject to 50 psi or more overpressure from the blast to the total area of a major city. For example, a one-megaton ground-burst bomb would produce 50-psi overpressures over an area equal to only 0.7 percent the area of New York City. While the chances of survival in a city blast shelter might seem reasonable based on this one statistic, there are many other factors lowering the odds of survival. In a large city likely to be struck by many bombs, the high levels of radiation could require prohibitively long stays in shelters (many months). In addition, in a city there is a greater probability of a firestorm compared to the suburbs, greater chance of shelter-ventilation problems due to fires, and greater depth of rubble preventing egress from a shelter. The suburban resident would have a considerably greater probability of surviving in a blast shelter than the city dweller, given that less than 0.5 percent of the area of the U.S. would experience overpressures as high as 50 psi, even if the entire Soviet nuclear arsenal were ground burst.

To summarize, the probable effectiveness of blast shelters would greatly depend on the circumstances. Key government leaders in the country that initiated the conflict would almost certainly have ample time to reach blast shelters. These shelters would offer their occupants an excellent chance of survival if either their location were kept secret to prevent targeting or if they were put in impregnable locations such as very deep mines. Key government leaders in the attacked country would survive only if they evacuated prior to the attack, possibly during a period of mounting crisis. Ordinary citizens who were able to reach blast shelters prior to the attack would have a very good chance of surviving the initial phase of the attack outside major cities. Inside major cities, survival from blast would still be possible, but many other factors might lower the chances of long-term survival, depending on the nature of the attack. In outlying areas not subject to direct bomb effects, blast shelters would not be necessary; fallout shelters would be sufficient to substantially improve chances of survival.

If you believe that civil defense is worthwhile, but, for whatever reason, you are not interested in building a shelter, Cresson Kearney's approach is still open: learn what precautions need to be taken and hope that there is enough time in a severe crisis to implement them. The main disadvantage of Kearney's approach is that it requires sufficient warning. He estimates that construction of an expedient fallout shelter (described in his book) that would also give some protection against blast could be accomplished in forty-eight hours using hand tools. As discussed in Appendix B, families living in homes with below ground basements outside high risk areas might actually be better off in their basement rather than in a shelter.

There are numerous ethical questions that have been raised concerning individual shelters. People who have built shelters for their family's use might find it necessary to turn away friends and neighbors—perhaps at the point of a gun. The fine ethical distinctions in our ordinary peacetime existence would undoubtedly be radically transformed following a nuclear attack or immediately preceding one. Your decision on whether civil defense makes sense ultimately needs to be based on whether you would want to survive in a world that is likely to be more primitive ethically and morally, as well as physically. However, it is impossible to know beforehand what kinds of horrible moral choices survivors may need to make. Perhaps the most honest response to your neighbor's question, "Would you shoot me to keep me from sharing your shelter? " might be, "I really don't know what either of us might do under such difficult circumstances, but why don't you let me help you build your own shelter so that the situation will not arise? "

This book is not intended to be a nuclear-war survival manual, although Appendix B discusses measures the individual can take to increase the chances of survival following a nuclear war. Before you examine specific ways that might increase your chances of survival following a nuclear attack, however, you must first make the most fundamental choice of all: Do you really *want* to survive a nuclear war? There may be many readers who, while granting that civil defense can save lives, nevertheless believe that death would be preferable to survival following a nuclear war. However, it is also possible that the commonly heard "I want to be the first to go" may be a reflexive reaction that would bear little relation to how people actually would act.

"INSURMOUNTABLE" OBSTACLES TO AN EFFECTIVE CIVIL DEFENSE

We conclude this chapter by examining four very significant obstacles to an effective civil defense and consider the extent to which they might prove insurmountable.

Climatic Catastrophe

If a nuclear war were to result in catastrophic climatic or ecological changes of the magnitude some scientists have suggested, then the long-range prospects of human survival would indeed be bleak. It must be remembered, however, that there is considerable uncertainty in these predictions and that it is not possible to estimate the probability of a climatic catastrophe. Moreover, to the extent that the governments of the United States and Soviet Union believe predictions of climatic catastrophe, they may be moved to actions that mitigate against that possibility. Such actions might include a further move to smaller weapons, a change in targeting strategy (avoiding cities and nuclear reactors), or a mutual reduction in the size of the arsenals.

The magnitude of the climatic effect termed "nuclear winter" is a key issue for civil defense. Although a catastrophic temperature decline might make all but the most heroic civil defense efforts futile, the likelihood is that a temperature decline would be of less-than-catastrophic proportions, and that would make certain civil defense measures potentially very important, e.g., having large individual and national stored food reserves.

Enemy Targeting Strategy

It is possible to construct hypothetical war scenarios that would negate any civil defense preparations. One can, for example, imagine an attack against the relocated population using many ground-burst weapons to maximize fallout. If the population were dispersed, however, such an attack would require a very large number of nuclear weapons—even more than both sides are believed to possess. Many strategists, moreover, regard such an attack as unlikely. From the attacker's point of view, the primary targets in a nuclear war would almost certainly be the enemy's strategic nuclear forces and his command, control, and communication structure. Secondary targets would probably include economic and industrial centers that could serve in a future warmaking capacity. It is believed to be neither U.S. nor Soviet policy to target population per se. It is, therefore, thought by some that directing nuclear weapons at the relocated population (away from industrial targets) would be rejected as a "wasteful" use of weapons that could be used to better effect against other targets. That assessment is probably correct only as far as the initial stages of a nuclear war are concerned. Once a major war begins, one can well imagine all sorts of possibilities, especially including a desire to kill as many of the enemy as possible in an attempt to achieve the total destruction of his country. If the primary goal is vengeance and a desire to impede recovery to the maximum extent possible, there will probably be continued nuclear attacks over an extended period of time. Nuclear submarines with their cargo of ballistic missiles can stay submerged for months. Continued attacks against the civilian population would greatly impede recovery and indeed make life terrible for survivors, but this possibility would not make civil defense efforts futile.

Public Opinion

Public-opinion surveys show that the U.S. public is divided on the issue of civil defense. Many citizens, particularly those who know of the magnitude of the Soviet civil defense program, believe that the government should be doing something to save lives in the event of nuclear attack. At the same time, however, most citizens are pessimistic about the chances of their own survival, even with civil defense, and they believe that it might be better to be the first to die rather than to try to survive. Short of a crisis such as the 1962 Cuban missile crisis, it seems likely that the relative apathy of most of the U.S. public toward civil defense will prevent a massive civil defense effort from gaining large public support. The extent of public apathy towards civil defense is probably enhanced by media portrayals of life after nuclear war, whether or not these portrayals are realistic. In addition, there is an active lobby against civil defense by groups who see it as worse than useless, since they believe it makes nuclear war more likely. In view of the opposition of these groups, the apathy of much of the public, and the lack of any significant pro-civil defense lobby, it seems unlikely that a massive civil defense program would receive much political support in the absence of a severe crisis. When President Kennedy tried to push such a massive effort in the early 1960s, it created a great deal of fear and panic and was subsequently abandoned. With that experience in mind, national leaders today tend to be cautious in their approach toward civil defense. Even conservative presidents who support civil defense may be reluctant to take a strong leadership position on the issue, lest the public view them as reckless warmongers or possibly kooky survivalists. U.S. public opinion has proven volatile on defense matters generally. It is not easy to say whether public attitudes on civil defense are ever likely to shift sufficiently to make a massive civil defense effort a high-priority national goal in peacetime.

Societal Disintegration

A commonly held view is that a nuclear war would so disrupt the fabric of society that recovery as an organized country might not be possible for many years, or even forever. Those who believe this assessment to be unduly pessimistic cite the following two kinds of evidence for their belief:

1. A study of major wartime disasters, including, for example, Hiroshima and Nagasaki, shows that there was little or no overt panic. It is difficult to say to what extent that may reflect the particular cultural traits of stoicism and repression more common in Japanese than in Americans. Certainly, the levels of destruction in a major nuclear conflict today would dwarf the Japanese experience, and there might be no help of any kind from the outside world, making the Japanese experience a poor guide.

2. No past experiences with major natural disasters, including fires, floods, earthquakes, or epidemics, support the societal-disintegration hypothesis. Of course, such catastrophes would be dwarfed by the devastation of a major nuclear war and, hence, also may be very poor models from which to draw any parallels.

Our beliefs as to what would happen to the "social fabric" in a major nuclear war basically relate to our view of human nature. Some observers look at the nihilism in much of twentieth-century life and imagine a complete disintegration once our highly complex and artificial society is smashed. Others note that man is a social animal and that, as such, he has a desire to band together and survive in a social group. These observers believe that such a need might be just as strong, if not stronger, than the urge to disintegrate. Whichever view is correct, there can be little question that the world after all-out nuclear war would bear little resemblance to today's world, civil defense or not.

While there are major obstacles to survival following a nuclear war, it is by no means clear that these obstacles are insurmountable. In the nuclear age the goal of preventing nuclear war must, of course, take priority over surviving one. Nevertheless, because a nuclear war could occur despite our best efforts at prevention, prudence requires that some attention be devoted to the problem of survival.

STUDY QUESTIONS

1. What accounts for the negative reactions some people have towards the idea of civil defense?

2. What are the arguments for and against an expanded U.S. civil defense effort, particularly a crisis relocation plan?

3. Could civil defense make a nuclear war more survivable in the short term? In the long term?

4. In what ways would an expanded civil defense effort make nuclear war more likely? Less likely?

5. If you don't think civil defense is a good idea, what would you think an appropriate U.S. response would be to a Soviet evacuation of their cities? Is that something worth thinking about? Explain.

6. To what extent do you think that government plans to expand civil defense are directed towards saving lives rather than towards matching the Soviet civil defense effort?

7. Does the size of the Soviet civil defense effort worry you? Explain.

8. What are the moral and ethical questions concerned with expanding the U.S. government's civil defense program? With not expanding the program?

9. Do you plan to do anything by way of civil defense? Explain.

Ten _____

ARMS CONTROL AND
DISARMAMENT _____

WHAT HAS BEEN THE HISTORY OF EFFORTS TO CONTROL
NUCLEAR WEAPONS?

The history of attempts to control nuclear weapons, as old as the
nuclear age itself, is not one filled with shining achievements. In
one of the first efforts, the U.S. government put forth the Baruch
Plan at the end of World War II. This plan, which would have
placed all nuclear-weapons production capability under United Nations' control, collapsed owing to an impasse over whether America's
small nuclear stockpile should be destroyed before or after the
agreement went into effect. Efforts to achieve general and complete
disarmament continued during the 1950s. Many would characterize
these early U.S.-Soviet wranglings as insincere posturing in which
each side put forth plans it knew would be unacceptable to the other.
Gradually, the idea of arms control began to replace that of disarmament which became a distant goal. Advocates of arms control
basically accepted the arms race as a given; they tried to restrain
and manage it, so as to achieve a stable balance between the two
sides. (See Table 10.1 for a list of nuclear-arms-control-agreements.)

The first major arms-control agreement was the 1963 Limited
Test Ban Treaty which prohibited atmospheric nuclear testing by all
signatories. That treaty did have some beneficial effects on human

---

Table 10.1   Multilateral and Bilateral Nuclear-Arms-Control Agreements

---

1. Restrictions on Weapons Testing
   - *Partial Test Ban Treaty* bans tests in the atmosphere, outer space, or under water.
   - *Threshold Test Ban Treaty* bans underground tests in excess of 150 kilotons.
   - *Peaceful Nuclear Explosions Treaty* bans underground peaceful nuclear explosions in excess of 150 kilotons.
2. Strategic Arms Limitations
   - *SALT I* froze for five years the numbers of missile launchers and forbade a conversion of light to heavy ICBMs.
   - *ABM Treaty,* a part of SALT I, limits ABM systems to two areas (later reduced to one).
   - *SALT II* would have placed ceilings on the number of missiles of various types (see table 10.2).
3. Nonproliferation of Nuclear Weapons
   - *Non-Proliferation Treaty* prohibits nonnuclear signatories from acquiring nuclear weapons and requires weapon states to render peaceful nuclear assistance and to work towards disarmament.
   - *Security Guarantee* (U.N. Security Council Resolution) provides for immediate assistance by the United Kingdom, United States, and U.S.S.R. to any nonweapon state attacked with nuclear weapons while party to the Non-Proliferation Treaty.
4. Nuclear-Free Areas
   - There are treaties banning nuclear weapons from Antarctica, Latin America, outer space, and the seabed.
5. War Prevention
   - *Hot-Line Agreement* provides for an emergency communications link between the United States and U.S.S.R.
   - *Nuclear Accidents Agreement* provides for notification of accidental missile launches and advance notification of missile launches.
   - *Nuclear War Prevention Agreement* provides for urgent consultations between the United States and U.S.S.R. if there is a conflict in which there is a threat of nuclear war.

---

health and the environment. However, the effect of the Limited Test Ban Treaty on slowing the arms race has probably been negligible. The superpowers simply moved testing underground, and the new members of the nuclear club—France, China, and India—were non-signatories, and hence not bound by the treaty's provisions. Subsequent efforts by the superpowers to stop weapons tests altogether have not borne fruit. A Threshold Test Ban Treaty (TTB) which limits underground tests to weapons with yields of 150 kilotons was signed between the United States and Soviet Union in 1974. The TTB Treaty, however, has not been ratified by the U.S. Senate, although both the United States and the Soviet Union claim to be abiding by its provisions. Negotiations on a Comprehensive Test Ban Treaty (CTB) were discontinued in 1980. On the U.S. side, concern over verification issues has been cited as a major problem in regard to both the TTB and CTB treaties. Most seismologists, however, now believe that ample means exist to detect and distinguish from earthquakes all but very-low-yield underground nuclear explosions. It seems likely that coolness to these treaties on the part of conservatives stems less from verification issues than a belief that continued weapons testing is necessary for military reasons.

The SALT I arms agreement between the United States and Soviet Union, concluded in 1972, was the first successful attempt to place limits on each side's offensive and defensive (ABM) systems. Many supporters of the treaty believed that it helped to slow the offensive arms race and promoted stability by limiting antiballistic missile systems. The SALT II treaty negotiated under three different U.S. administrations would have put additional limits on the arsenals, but that treaty was never ratified by the U.S. Senate. SALT II was in trouble in the U.S. Senate prior to the Soviet invasion of Afghanistan, and that action merely sealed its fate. Nevertheless, the treaty continues to be informally observed by the United States and Soviet Union, despite its having been labelled "fatally flawed" by 1980 Presidential Candidate Ronald Reagan.

As a result of a long history of little progress, both supporters and critics of traditional arms control have become increasingly disenchanted with the process. Many long-time supporters of arms control have found the process, in retrospect, to be nothing more than a legitimization of the arms race in the guise of restraint. They might well agree with then Vice-President Walter Mondale's 1975 observation that SALT appeared to be nothing more than a stapling together of the defense programs of the two sides. Indeed, many have noted that the SALT process has often stimulated the arms race by encouraging each side to develop new weapons as bargaining chips and by building numbers of weapons right up to the treaty limits. The close linkage between arms control and arms acquisition is further exemplified by the history of the MX missile. President Carter was pressured to support the MX in order to gain conservative support for SALT II, while President Reagan was pressured to support the "build down" arms-control plan in order to rescue the MX. It seems that under liberal administrations missiles are needed to rescue arms control treaties, and under conservative administrations treaties are needed to rescue missiles.

For those whose goal has been disarmament, the process of arms control was bound to produce disappointment. Not only does arms control have a very different goal from disarmament, but the process has diverted public attention from what those favoring disarmament would consider the main problem—reducing or eliminating the nuclear arsenals. There has always been a considerable tension between arms controllers and disarmers, not fully appreciated by much of the public. Arms controllers reject the notion that the arms race itself is the source of tension between the superpowers. However, for arms controllers there is much to fear in an uncontrolled arms race in which a real or perceived temporary advantage could fuel fears and possibly lead to war through miscalculation. Many arms controllers would see no inherent conflict between the pursuit of arms control and construction of new weapons—indeed they are two aspects of the same process. In fact, a conservative criticism of the arms control process is that in the past it has not been linked closely enough to U.S. defense planning. In the words of Senator Sam Nunn, "U.S. military planners must have a greater input in shaping our arms control objectives so that arms control measures can also be treated as viable instruments for attaining required security objectives." [1] According to some conservative critics, the arms control process has been pursued as an end in itself without any real sense of purpose or direction. More importantly, according to the critics the process has caused the United States to neglect its defenses while it sought agreements for their own sake.

WHAT IS THE BASIC PURPOSE OF ARMS CONTROL?

Most people would probably reply that the basic purpose of arms control is to halt or moderate the arms race. However, it is obvious that the basic purpose should be to reduce the risk of nuclear war. These two purposes are not identical, and it is at least conceivable that measures that would promote one would not promote the other. Is it possible that the reason many people focus on reversing the arms race rather than on reducing the risk of nuclear war is because progress in the former case can be measured in quantitative terms? We can easily count the number of warheads, missiles, bombers, and submarines. It is much less easy, however, to determine the risk of nuclear war at any given time. How much weight should be given, for example, to bellicose statements by U.S. and Soviet leaders, superpower involvement in Third World conflicts, and numbers of nuclear weapons in the arsenals? Anyone who pretends to be able to measure "the distance to the brink" or the "time before midnight" based on such factors is simply advancing a particular hypothesis that is completely untestable in the real world. Which is not to say that the risk of nuclear war is independent of such factors, only that the nature of the dependence cannot be known with any degree of confidence. Moreover, the actual risk of nuclear war may not be closely related to the level of public concern. In our nuclear age the perception of security (or danger) may have little relation to the reality of security (or danger). We could feel very secure perhaps by simply ignoring our nuclear dilemma, as most people have done until recent years. Conversely, coming out of our slumber, we may overreact and believe the world to be in imminent peril of a nuclear holocaust that could be triggered by any minor conflict.

Our views on arms control are intimately bound up with our views on the relationship between the superpowers and between nations generally. Henry Kissinger has characterized the way many liberals and conservatives view foreign policy as being "psychiatric" and "theological," respectively.[2] In the psychiatric view, relations between states are equated to relations between individuals, therefore, great importance is placed on trust and unilateral gestures of good will. In contrast, according to the theological view held by some conservatives, relations between nations are part of the eternal struggle between good and evil.

In the theological view of foreign policy there are no good arms-control agreements, since anything the Kremlin would be willing to agree to could not be in U.S. interests. The theologians remain leery of arms control as a Soviet ploy to constrain U.S. forces. The fact that setting verifiable limits on both superpowers' arsenals could, in some cases, enhance mutual security seems to escape the theologians.

Those ascribing to the psychiatric view of foreign policy put great stress on the relaxation of tensions and the creation of a favorable political climate. In this view it is virtually impossible to have a bad arms-control agreement, since any agreement would involve communication and cooperation between the parties, and hence result in a more favorable political climate. Moreover, according to the "psychiatrists," nuclear-policy statements made by the United States and Soviet Union can also have a significant impact on building levels of trust and reducing the risk of war. For example, according to Richard Barnet:

A joint [Soviet-American] official statement about nuclear war would discourage irresponsible statements about nuclear "victory" and "survival" through absurd, provocative evacuation plans and create a channel for providing mutual reassurance. U.S. experts on the U.S.S.R. would no longer have to carry on a sterile debate in American journals about what the Soviets think.[3]

In other words, once the U.S. and Soviet leaders "officially" eschew the concept of victory or survival in a nuclear war, that should largely settle the matter and eliminate doubts anyone might have about the adversary's intentions. In reality, of course, such a joint Soviet-American statement would accomplish no such thing. The leaders of each side must, of necessity, give emphasis to the capabilities of the other side as well as its stated intentions. As long as the Soviet Union has extensive air defense and civil defense capabilities and an offensive arsenal suited for war fighting rather than for deterrence, then suspicions will persist among some in the United States that the Soviets may believe that victory and survival are possible in a nuclear war. The increasing emphasis on U.S. war-fighting strategies and weapons may, of course, fuel similar Soviet concerns.

According to the psychiatric view of foreign policy, suspicion and hatred between nations is the basic cause of war. Therefore, by reducing these destructive emotions it should be possible to eliminate war and the need for nuclear weapons. This analysis overlooks the fact that suspicions and hatreds rarely arise spontaneously, but often occur as a result of conflicting interests between nations. In addition the psychiatric view fails to reckon with the basic element of opportunism that underlies much of the dealings between nation states. There are any number of examples in history of nations taking advantage of opportunities that momentarily presented themselves. While it is perhaps not likely, it is nevertheless possible that the Soviet Union (or the United States?) would initiate a nuclear war—not because of hatred of the enemy, but simply because an opportunity seemed momentarily to present itself to forever eliminate its rival for world power. In the words of Herman Kahn, "The missile attack is a problem in engineering and physics in a way that no other military action ever has been. It is so calculable that if we let our guard drop it is quite possible that the other side might exploit a temporary weakness in the coldest of cold-blooded manner." [4] While Kahn may have considerably overstated the calculability of a nuclear missile attack, he reminds us that wars can result from calculations of military advantage as well as from other causes.

Thus, arms-control agreements that place real limits on both sides' arsenals and prevent military advantages or "temporary weaknesses" from arising serve to reduce the risk of nuclear war. On the other hand, arms-control agreements that prevent one side from remedying a temporary weakness in its nuclear arsenal may increase the risk of nuclear war, even if they seem to generate a favorable political climate.

Opponents of new U.S. weapons programs generally believe that any attempt by one side to unilaterally improve its security by building new weapons will invariably be offset by the other side, resulting in less security in the end. However, that analysis overlooks the possibility that if the United States and Soviet Union both deploy new weapons that are less vulnerable to a preemptive counterforce attack, this action could increase security for both sides and reduce the risk of nuclear war. If our basic objective is to reduce the risk of nuclear war, then both arms control and arms acquisition can under certain circumstances achieve that goal. Similarly, the wrong kind of arms-control agreement and the wrong kind of new weapons system may serve to increase the risk of war. There are many examples one could cite for the wrong kind of weapons system— perhaps the worst would be highly MIRVed and highly accurate missiles deployed in a vulnerable basing mode. There are also many examples of undesirable arms-control agreements, including those that

- are of questionable verifiability,

- stimulate the arms race,

- prevent vulnerabilities from being remedied,

- impose unequal limits on the parties,

- divert attention from better ways to reduce the risk of war.

What accounts for the great disillusionment now felt by many long-term arms-control advocates? Many would agree with Bernard Feld's assessment that

the rule until now seems to be that only those weapons or activities can be eliminated or banned that are of no interest to any substantial fraction of the military in the United States or the Soviet Union. Why after 30 years of intensive

efforts in this direction are we nowhere? Indeed we are even
behind where we started.[5]

Feld, whose goal really is disarmament rather than arms control is
probably correct in his assessment of the reason that no progress
has been made towards disarmament. However, if the arms-control
efforts of the last thirty years are viewed in terms of ways that the
risk of nuclear war may have been reduced, then Feld's judgment
is too harsh. Without any arms-control efforts, might the United
States and Soviet Union have already built costly, ineffective, and
highly destabilizing ABM systems? Would fear and miscalculation
possibly even have resulted in war? No one knows. But the progress
of arms control needs to be measured by the disagreeable things
that did not happen as well as by the good. While Feld's appraisal
of the lack of progress of arms control may be overly pessimistic,
it is probably shared by much of the general public. This perception
of little or no progress in traditional arms control has almost certainly
been a major factor in the reemergence of the nuclear-arms issue as
a central topic on the national agenda.

     Many other reasons also account for the nuclear debate surfacing
rather suddenly as a topic of great concern to the general public.
Certainly a major reason would be the rising fears of many Americans
of a nuclear holocaust, fears caused in part by careless public statements and actions by the Reagan administration and, perhaps of
equal importance, by the way such statements have been portrayed
by the media and opposition politicians. It is very frightening to
many people to read statements by high officials such as Eugene
Rostow, former head of the Arms Control and Disarmament Agency,
who said in testimony to the Senate that following a nuclear exchange
between the United States and the Soviet Union "there would be
10 million dead on one side and 100 million on the other, but that
is not the whole population. Japan after all not only survived but
flourished after the nuclear attack." [6] Rostow's parallel between an
all-out nuclear war today and the attack on Japan using two much-
lower-yield weapons certainly gives rise to questions about whether
he understands what an all-out nuclear holocaust would mean. Moreover, many people would find the inference in Rostow's statement
that nuclear war is survivable and perhaps winnable to be only a
short step from the belief that nuclear war is manageable and not
to be greatly feared. Indeed, many journalists seem to believe it is
their responsibility to fill in that step, whether or not it is warranted
based on the context in which the statement was made. Careless

administration statements can only give ammunition to those who misperceive the nuclear debate as being between those who want to fight and win a nuclear war and those who want to disarm and prevent one.

The magnitude of the public reaction on the nuclear issue has been a surprise to most observers, and it has undoubtedly been a source of pressure driving the political pendulum back to the center. Nevertheless, it may be noted that public anxieties that can be aroused by careless administration statements can also be quieted by soothing ones, all without any fundamental change in policy. Apparently, after several years of unnecessarily provocative rhetoric, the Reagan administration learned that its prodefense political coalition could best be held together by cooling the level of rhetoric. That political necessity was in a sense the mirror image of the one facing those who favor disarmament. Even those favoring unilateral disarmament realize that in order to gain widespread public support for an arms-control proposal, it would have to be seen as not being to the United States's military disadvantage.

HOW DOES THE PUBLIC VIEW THE NUCLEAR-FREEZE PROPOSAL?

The idea of a freeze on the production and deployment of nuclear weapons can be traced back to a proposal made by President Lyndon Johnson. At that time, of course, the United States was vastly superior to the Soviet Union in nuclear weapons and the proposal was quickly rejected by the U.S.S.R. Moreover, the Johnson years (1963–68) were a period in which a sizable increase in the number of Soviet nuclear warheads accompanied a sizable decrease in the number of U.S. warheads—a state of affairs the Soviets found preferable to a freeze.

A more recent version of the nuclear-freeze proposal is the one included in a U.S. Senate resolution (S.J. Res. 163) introduced by Senators Kennedy and Hatfield. The proposal contains these two nonbinding resolutions:

1. As an immediate strategic-arms-control objective, the United States and the Soviet Union should: *(a)* pursue a complete halt to the nuclear-arms race; *(b)* decide when and how to achieve a mutual and verifiable halt to testing, production, and future deployment of nuclear warheads, missiles, and other delivery systems; and *(c)* give special attention to destabilizing weapons

whose deployment would make such a freeze more difficult to achieve.

2. Proceeding from this freeze, the United States and the Soviet Union should pursue major, mutual and verifiable reduction in nuclear warheads, missiles, and other delivery systems through annual percentages or equally effective means, in a manner that enhances stability.

The genesis of the nuclear-freeze idea is attributed to a 1979 proposal made by Randall Forsberg. Forsberg's version of the freeze is an attempt to freeze present technology, and it would allow for replacement of existing weapons with current versions. This version of the freeze explicitly recognizes that the increased danger we face is primarily from the kinds of weapons being built, rather than from sheer numbers.

Since 1980, the growth in the nuclear-freeze movement has occurred at a rate that astounded even its most ardent supporters. There are many reasons for this phenomenal growth in support, some of which have already been discussed: rising fear of nuclear war, nonprogress in traditional arms control, careless administration statements and policies, and media treatment of these issues. Another factor is the simplicity of the nuclear-freeze in contrast to many earlier proposals. The SALT II Treaty, for example, was much more complex, and its terms were probably known only to a tiny fraction of the American public. In selling either politicians or soap to the American people, it is well understood that simplicity is a great virtue. Nevertheless, while simplicity may make it easier to get political support for an idea, it may not make for good arms control. While one can understand the impatience of some over the seemingly interminable wranglings needed to hammer out a complex arms-control agreement, those wranglings are not solely due to the insincerity of the bargainers.

The idea of a nuclear freeze appears to enjoy wide public support. In one public opinion poll, the U.S. public has backed the idea of an immediate bilateral freeze on the production and deployment of nuclear weapons by a margin of 75 to 25 percent.[8] This three-to-one margin of support is particularly striking in view of the fact that according to the same poll, the public believes that the Soviets are ahead in nuclear weaponry and that they would try to cheat on any freeze agreement. Eighty percent of those polled thought the Soviets would try to cheat, and only 29 percent thought the freeze would not give the Soviets an advantage. How then can we understand the sizable margin of support for the freeze in view of these seemingly contradictory beliefs? The reason that the large public support for the freeze persists, despite a belief that the Soviets would gain from it, is probably twofold. Firstly, the public appears to accept the basic thesis of mutual assured destruction. By a 79 to 16 percent margin, those surveyed agreed that it doesn't matter who is ahead in nuclear weapons since both sides have enough to destroy each other no matter who attacks first. Secondly, the public sees more risk of nuclear war resulting from the continued buildup of nuclear weapons than from any advantage they believe the Soviets to have. This belief was supported in the survey by a 55 to 30 percent margin.

In earlier chapters we have expressed the view that in an age of counterforce weapons, the question of who's ahead may be an important one in presenting temptations to one side or the other to strike first in a crisis. The public acceptance of the thesis underlying MAD—that it doesn't matter who's ahead or who strikes first, since in any nuclear war both societies will be destroyed—shows that either the public is unaware of the counterforce scenarios new weapons make possible or it does not believe them. However, the belief that deterrence can continue to prevent war independent of any nuclear advantages one side may have, could in the end prove as fatal as the contrary belief that we must strive for clearcut nuclear superiority no matter how provocative or costly that might be.

The public belief that the risks associated with a nuclear freeze are less than those associated with a continuation of the arms race brings us to the heart of the nuclear debate. Nuclear-freeze supporters often portray the debate as being between those who believe that a nuclear war can be fought and won and those who wish to avoid a war by freezing nuclear weapons at their present levels. Of course, what the debate is really about is whether a nuclear freeze or some other action is the best way to reduce the risk of nuclear war.

IS OVERKILL UNDESIRABLE?

Freeze supporters generally acknowledge that the freeze is only a beginning. In the words of Senators Edward Kennedy and Mark Hatfield, "In reality, it is a first but essential step back from the nuclear precipice; it can stop the arms race from rushing over the edge of that precipice, and subsequent reductions can truly move us back to a safer place, further from the brink." [9] The question of why the "distance to the brink" should be inversely proportional to the number of the nuclear weapons is an issue deserving of more attention. In contrast to Kennedy and Hatfield who speak of the "absurdity and danger of overkill," [10] some observers take the opposite point of view that overkill is precisely what is needed to help insure the invulnerability of each side's deterrent, regardless of who strikes first. Just because more weapons have not brought us more security, it does not logically follow that less weapons will bring us more security. While less weapons might bring some people more perceived security, i.e., more piece of mind, the effect on the actual risk of nuclear war might be quite different.

The position that massive overkill is a good thing may strike some readers as terribly bloodthirsty, and holders of that view would seem to be far to the right of those conservatives who have embraced the concept of deep cuts in the nuclear arsenals. However, it must be remembered that the whole point of massive overkill is not to be able to better fight a nuclear war, but rather to better deter one by convincing the adversary that it would be hopeless to try to eliminate enough of the victim's arsenal in a surprise attack to avoid a devastating retaliatory blow. President Reagan, in making proposals for deep cuts in the arsenals, was following a long tradition of American presidents who have found that political support for their defense policies can best be obtained by convincing the American public that they are dedicated peacemakers at heart. No American president can afford to tell the public some hard realities it apparently would prefer not to face.

1. *The "good old days" of mutual assured destruction in which numbers of weapons didn't matter are no more.* Despite assertions that a small fraction of the presently invulnerable U.S. submarine-based warheads is sufficient to destroy all major Soviet cities and 70 percent of its industry, the fact is that we really have no idea what level of destruction is needed to deter a Soviet preemptive attack. Moreover, while the U.S. submarine fleet does contain half of the warheads in the arsenal, it is also true that half the ships on patrol at one time contain only 5 percent of the total U.S. megatonnage, given the smaller size of most SLBM warheads. Despite the potency of even that 5 percent of U.S. megatonnage, it is by no means clear that the U.S.S.R. would refrain from a surprise first strike that it believed could eliminate most of the rest of the U.S. arsenal—*particularly* if a United States armed with first-strike weapons posed a similar threat to the Soviet Union. First strike weapons

greatly undermine MAD, since they offer a significant military advantage to the attacker. But even before first strike weapons existed, MAD may have been, in part, a matter of wishful thinking. As Richard Pipes has observed, "MAD was a way of telling ourselves that nuclear war won't happen; it can't happen. No sane person would pull the nuclear trigger . . . the unthinkable simply won't come to pass, so why think about it? " [11]

2. *The total elimination of nuclear weapons is not possible to verify, nor will it ever be possible to verify.* If we cannot verify the elimination of nuclear weapons, cries of "ban the bomb" become nothing more than naive yearnings for a world that cannot be. Mankind will never be able to eliminate totally the risk of nuclear war. We must learn to live with each other and also to live with our weapons of mass destruction which, like an inoperable cancer, cannot regrettably be excised.

3. *As long as we cannot eliminate nuclear weapons, we may be safer with more rather than less.* Massive overkill cannot guarantee that one side will not conclude that it can accomplish a disarming first strike. However, possession of only a minimum deterrent makes it much more likely that sooner or later a reckless military planner will contemplate starting a winnable nuclear war—particularly if one side may have secretly supplemented its minimum deterrent over a period of time.

The main argument favoring drastic reductions in the nuclear arsenals is that if a nuclear war should occur, it is very probable that the level of global destruction would be greater in proportion to the size of the arsenals. On the other hand, as we have seen in chapter 8, some scientists have claimed that even a small nuclear war would result in a global climatic catastrophe, and further that such a worldwide disaster would occur even if a nuclear attack went unanswered.[12] Neither of these claims, however, have received general scientific acceptance, and neither is likely to convince a prudent policy maker to reduce the arsenals to subthreshold levels in order to make the world safe for nuclear war. Until the nations of the world learn to live in harmony nuclear overkill may make us safer by reducing the probability of a nuclear war.

There are many who desperately wish to believe that there is a permanent solution to the nuclear dilemma that will totally eliminate the risk of nuclear war and who view disarmament as the way to achieve that goal. No American president is about to dash those hopes, even if he knows them to be naïve, futile, and dangerous.

WOULD A NUCLEAR FREEZE RAISE OR LOWER THE RISK OF NUCLEAR WAR?

If the total elimination of nuclear weapons is only a dream, and if drastic cuts in the arsenals to minimum-deterrent levels would leave us less safe than at present, then what is the point of a nuclear freeze as a first step? Perhaps the strongest argument for a nuclear freeze is that the new weapons the United States is adding to its arsenal may be particularly destabilizing owing to their capability to threaten Soviet land-based missiles. It is possible that the United States would be better off finding ways to remedy the vulnerability in its land-based ICBMs that did not simultaneously threaten Soviet ICBMs and deploying only those new weapons, e.g., cruise missiles, that did not have a first-strike potential. However, none of these initiatives could be accomplished under a freeze which would freeze in certain U.S. vulnerabilities. But those favoring a nuclear freeze are possibly correct that new U.S. counterforce weapons will put a "hair-trigger" on the Soviet arsenal. However, freeze advocates ignore the fact that freezing in a vulnerability in the U.S. arsenal might some day force U.S. military planners to compensate by adopting risky strategies such as a launch-on-warning policy. Similarly, by freezing in Soviet superiority in intermediate-range missiles in Europe, the United States may be commiting itself to the possibly more risky strategy of defending Europe with the U.S. strategic arsenal. This policy carries the two-sided risk that: (1) the United States would in fact be drawn into an all-out nuclear war to "save" Europe, or more likely (2) the tattered U.S. nuclear umbrella will be seen for the bluff that it is and will not deter the Soviets from conventional aggression in Europe.

Another problem with a nuclear freeze at a time when U.S. vulnerability to Soviet counterforce weapons greatly exceeds a similar Soviet vulnerability is that the freeze reduces any incentive for the Soviets to negotiate reductions in these particularly destabilizing weapons. The very early Soviet warmth toward the nuclear-freeze proposal may not solely be due to their desire for peace, but may reflect more pragmatic considerations. This certainly would not be the first time that one or the other of the superpowers embraced arms-control proposals that it believed would give them a military advantage. Nor would this be the first time that many in the West would be willing to support an arms-control proposal, even though they believe it would result in a Soviet military advantage—so great is the public yearning for peace. If only the public in the Soviet Union had a corresponding ability to moderate their leader's opinions and induce them to support proposals made by the West—even those proposals that might pose risks for the Soviet Union—there would then be no difficulty in reaching an arms agreement fair to both sides.

Freeze advocates often note that the U.S. nuclear arsenal cannot be inferior to that of the Soviet Union since no one in authority would be willing to trade nuclear arsenals with the Soviets. However, the issue is less one of superiority or inferiority as it is one of survivability and an assured second-strike deterrent. The U.S. arsenal has so far been primarily structured with a second-strike retaliatory mission in mind, and accordingly it has a more diversified force among all three legs of the triad, thereby making for greater survivability. It is because of that diversity well suited to the U.S. second-strike mission that the United States would not trade forces with the Soviet Union. The Soviet arsenal, though more menacing in terms of megatonnage and counterforce capability, would be less survivable if the United States were to develop its counterforce capability.

Many nuclear-freeze advocates in fact believe that the Reagan administration has been specifically trying to put the United States into a position where it could launch a preemptive first strike against the Soviet Union. One cannot deny that the capability the Reagan administration has sought to develop may well be viewed by the Soviets as a serious first-strike threat, and that such a capability could be highly destabilizing in a crisis. Nevertheless, the view that this U.S. capability is being developed with the intention of actually using it to carry out a preemptive first strike seems somewhat farfetched. According to Henry Kissinger, at no time during the postwar era did the United States even come close to using nuclear weapons.[13] Moreover, even during the height of the cold war, when the United States had vast nuclear superiority and could have destroyed the Soviet Union in one blow with relatively little damage in retaliation, it refrained from any such action. It therefore seems infinitely less likely that the United States would willingly undertake such a rash action as a preemptive first strike now that it could no longer escape a much more devastating retaliation—expanded civil defense or not.

The nonuse of U.S. nuclear weapons during the period of U.S. nuclear monopoly and the much longer period of vast U.S. nuclear superiority serves as an interesting example of the intrinsic ambiguity of lessons drawn from history. For example, according to Richard Barnet, a strong advocate of nuclear disarmament, "The conclusion one should draw from such a history is that nuclear superiority cannot be translated into power during a crisis without communicating a specific threat that involves unacceptable moral and political costs." [14] This view, however, overlooks the fact that nuclear superiority in the hands of a power more ruthless than the United States might not be restrained owing to "unacceptable moral and political costs." Would the Soviet Union have exerted similar restraint if it possessed a nuclear monopoly? For that matter would the United States again be so restrained, if history could be replayed, given the knowledge that someday the U.S.S.R. would reach or surpass the U.S. level of nuclear weaponry? There were, after all, at least twenty occasions since 1945 during which responsible officials of the U.S. government formally considered the use of nuclear weapons.

As already noted, the nonuse of nuclear weapons during a period when the United States had vast nuclear superiority casts some doubt on assertions that the United States would want to launch a deliberate preemptive nuclear attack in the present era when it could not escape devastating retaliation. However, the great danger of a large increase in U.S. counterforce capability is precisely that it does not matter whether U.S. intentions are sinister or benign. From the Soviet point of view, a growing U.S. first-strike capability cannot be seen as anything other than an extremely threatening development—even an inducement to the Soviets to strike first in a crisis. Thus, the Reagan-administration decision to proceed with counterforce weapons has been a very big gamble. On the one hand, it could give both sides a big incentive to agree to eliminate such weapons, or at least to take unilateral measures to reduce the vulnerability of their own weapons. On the other hand, it might lead either to risky strategies, e.g. launch on warning, or even to war through miscalculation or through a premeditated act.

It is not surprising that the Reagan administration's reaction to the proposal for a nuclear freeze was negative, since it would prevent the modernization of U.S. nuclear forces that the Administration has proposed. In addition, the freeze proposal would have taken the initiative on arms control away from Reagan who, after a very slow start, had come up with his own plan for the reduction of nuclear weapons.

WHAT HAS BEEN THE REAGAN ADMINISTRATION'S APPROACH TO ARMS CONTROL?

The Reagan administration's strategic arms proposals have focused primarily on the most destabilizing weapons in the nuclear arsenals—the land-based ICBMs capable of launching a surprise first strike. Reagan's initial proposal would have reduced total U.S. and Soviet warheads by one-third and limited the fraction of warheads on ICBMs to 50 percent. For the Soviets, who now have 70 percent of their warheads on ICBMs, the one-third reduction in warheads would need to come almost entirely from ICBMs. The United States, which has only 25 percent of its warheads on ICBMs, would be able to make the one-third cut from any part of its arsenal. President Reagan's plan, according to some critics, was designed as a fig leaf to cover the anticipated expansion in U.S. nuclear forces that would not be constrained by the plan, at a time when the Soviets were expected to cut the same kinds of weapons the United States was building. Not surprisingly, the initial Moscow reaction to the Reagan plan was negative.

A more favorable view of the plan is that it would have resulted in a more stable balance of terror by leading to a smaller vulnerable fraction of each side's nuclear arsenal. If the United States does add the counterforce weapon systems of MX and Trident II, then as much as 70 percent of the Soviet arsenal on ICBMs will become vulnerable, whereas under the Reagan plan 50 percent at most would be vulnerable. For the United States, a sizable cut in Soviet ICBM warheads would result in less vulnerable U.S. nuclear forces. On the other hand, it is also true that if the United States were to take the one-third cut in warheads from its less vulnerable SLBMs and bombers, the U.S. arsenal would become more vulnerable. It must be remembered, however, that the majority of U.S. SLBM warheads are fairly small, so that a 50-percent cut in number of SLBM warheads might not greatly reduce U.S. retaliatory capacity measured in equivalent megatonnage. It may be recalled that ten U.S. SLBM warheads of 40-kiloton yield would be needed to inflict the same level of damage on a large city as one average-yield Soviet warhead of one megaton (see figures 3.1 and 3.2). It may well be that a good part of Moscow's negative reaction to the Reagan plan is that Moscow has little interest in trading one-megaton warheads for U.S. SLBM warheads that are twenty-five times smaller in yield.

Was the Reagan plan one-sided? It was in the sense of requiring only the Soviets to cut their ICBM force, while the United States could take the one-third cut in any area. However, the end result (arsenals smaller by a third with no more than 50 percent of warheads on ICBMs) would be the same for both sides. Moreover, the trading of small U.S. warheads for big Soviet warheads would not be unreasonable if one takes at face value assertions by those claiming U.S.-Soviet nuclear parity that it is only the number of warheads that really counts, not their yield. The Soviets, however, are unlikely to want to give up their three-to-one advantage in megatonnage and their advantage in counterforce capability, while the United States would be free to add to its arsenal in both these areas.

Supporters of the Reagan plan note that even if the plan was one-sided, it is a good negotiating tactic to make an initial offer favoring the United States, since any Soviet counteroffer is bound to be tilted at least as heavily in the Soviet direction. According to many critics of the earlier SALT negotiations, the United States could have gotten a fairer final treaty if it had not followed the practice of coming in with initial offers judged likely to be acceptable to the Soviets.

It is hard to find fault with an active public debate on the nuclear dilemma that puts pressure on U.S. political leaders to come to terms with the Soviet Union. Nevertheless, if an impatient U.S. public exerts too much pressure, unaccompanied by any corresponding pressure from the Soviet public, this situation could easily lead to an agreement not in U.S. interests. As in any negotiating process, if one side is too eager to reach an agreement then it may not reach an equitable one.

WAS SALT II A SOUND TREATY?

Some observers, noting the probable long road ahead in reaching an arms agreement, have suggested that the U.S. Senate should in the interim ratify the SALT II Treaty—a treaty that President Reagan has characterized as "fatally flawed." (See table 10.2 for a summary of provisions of SALT II.) Some find it odd that Reagan has con-

Table 10.2   Some Terms of the SALT II Treaty[a]

Limits on numbers of launchers (defined to include ICBMs, SLBMs, heavy bombers, and air-to-surface missiles [ASBMs] with ranges exceeding 600 km)
2,400—to be later lowered to 2,250, of which no more than 1,320 are in the categories of MIRVed ICBM, SLBM, or ASBM, and airplanes equipped with long-range cruise missiles, and of which no more than 1,200 launchers are in the first three of the preceding four categories, and no more than 820 launchers are in the first two categories

Fractionation limits
10 RVs per ICBM, 14 RVs per SLBM, and an average of 28 cruise missiles per bomber

Ceilings on throw weight
No new missiles whose throw weight exceeds each side's heaviest existing missiles

Bans on new systems
Only one new type of ICBM may be tested and deployed
No new fixed ICBM launchers
No conversion of light ICBM launchers to heavy ones
No heavy mobile ICBMS, SLBMs, or ASBMs

Verification by national technical means
No interference with such means of verification or deliberate concealment, e.g., encoding relevant missile test data

[a] A protocol to the treaty which would have remained in force only until 1981 would have banned deployment (but not testing) of mobile ICBMs, long-range cruise missiles, and ASBMs. The treaty itself would have remained in force until 1985.

sidered it in the U.S. interest to abide by the terms of this "fatally flawed" treaty as long as the Soviets do likewise. The probable reason for Reagan's abiding by SALT II is that the treaty would prevent the Soviets from greatly expanding the number of MIRVed warheads on their large ICBMs—an expansion the United States could not hope to match in a comparable time. There are other advantages SALT II would have for the United States if it were ratified. The treaty calls for a ceiling of 2,250 missile launchers plus bombers, which would mean that the Soviets would have to dismantle 250 missiles or bombers while the United States, already under the ceiling, would not need to dismantle any. Finally, not a single weapons system in President Reagan's five-year defense plan is forbidden by SALT II. In fact, it could be said that Reagan's defense plan had been designed with SALT II in mind.

The question of whether SALT II is a balanced treaty is complex. The SALT II Treaty does have some military disadvantages for the United States. For example, it does not count Soviet backfire bombers in the 2,250 ceiling. These planes are capable of round-trip strategic missions against the United States with midair refueling or one-way missions without refueling. Nevertheless, overall, the SALT II Treaty was reasonably equitable in the constraints on both sides' arsenals. Those areas of Soviet advantage not covered by the SALT II treaty, e.g. backfire bombers, could be roughly offset by some American advantages, such as nuclear allies. There are nevertheless, varying points of view on what factors make for a balanced treaty. Any asymmetries in a treaty invariably creates opposition among conservative critics. Treaty proponents can argue that the asymmetry may be due to the historical forces that shaped each side's arsenal and that they are offset by other asymmetries that favor the United States. Nevertheless, the suspicion will persist among critics that the eagerness of the U.S. public for arms control will invariably result in the United States getting the worst of the bargain when the treaty terms are not identical on each side.

The suspicion of treaties with different constraints on each side is further fueled by the Soviet insistence that a balanced treaty must be one that provides for "equal security" for each nation. Thus, the fact that the Soviet Union has no nuclear allies, potentially hostile neighbors, and little access to the sea, supposedly must all be taken into account in arriving at equitable (but not equal) limits on each side's arsenal. The Soviet Union, however, has shown no desire to include other factors under the equal-security criterion, factors that could be used to argue for higher limits on the U.S. arsenal. Thus, for example, the fact that the Soviet Union has more extensive air, civil, and ABM defenses could justify the need for larger U.S. offensive forces in a treaty that was based on equal security or, more properly, "equal jeopardy." The idea of equal security, if taken seriously, would require some mutually agreed way of measuring various threats. Is, for example, the Soviet lack of nuclear allies more or less of a disadvantage than the relative American lack of civil defense? Equal security would also require that as one factor in the overall equation changed, there would need to be a compensating change allowed on the other side. It is hard to imagine the Soviet Union agreeing to a treaty that, for example, permitted the United States to have a higher limit on the number of its missiles at a point when China ceased to become a hostile neighbor to the Soviets or when the U.S.S.R. expanded its civil defense system. Equal security may be useful to the U.S.S.R. in pressing for advantages in an asymmetrical treaty, but it would be impossible to implement in a literal sense.

Many of those who support the idea of a nuclear freeze are unlikely to approve of SALT II, which is the classic mold of controlling rather than halting or reversing the arms race. Conversely, many conservative critics of SALT II blame the "SALT syndrome" for deficiencies in the U.S. arsenal that occurred during the 1970s while the United States was mesmerized by the arms-control process. However, Henry Kissinger is probably correct in noting that whatever nuclear deficiencies or imbalances that may have occurred during the last decade came about as a result of voluntary decisions by successive U.S. administrations over what constituted nuclear sufficiency, not as a result of the SALT process.

HOW VERIFIABLE SHOULD ARMS-CONTROL AGREEMENTS BE?

One aspect of the SALT II Treaty, the nuclear-freeze proposal, or indeed any arms-control proposal that merits particular attention, is the question of verifiability. An otherwise equitable treaty that has problems with verification would indeed be "fatally flawed." Proponents of any arms-control proposal will invariably give assurances based on the testimony of experts that the proposal is verifiable to a high degree. However, upon closer inspection, it sometimes turns out that the degree of verifiability is not as great as claimed by proponents. An example in this regard may be instructive. Congressman Les Aspin, a strong supporter of SALT II, has carefully studied all the ways the Soviets could cheat under SALT II and has found the odds against Soviet cheating to be "extremely high." [15] In a 1979 article on verification of the SALT II Treaty, Aspin finds that "the U.S. has at its disposal ample 'national technical means' [spy satellites] to detect any attempt by the U.S.S.R. to gain a significant military advantage by violating a new arms pact." [16] However, it seems that Aspin's conclusion of "extremely high" odds against successful Soviet cheating is open to question. For example, Aspin noted in his article that the Soviets could at some point greatly expand their arsenal by developing a transferable warhead for their missiles, allowing them to replace single warheads on missiles with highly MIRVed warheads. Moreover, according to Aspin, the United States would not be able to detect this activity. Aspin justifies his overall conclusion on the "extremely high" odds against successful cheating on the grounds that, in his judgment, nearly all the many other ways the Soviets could cheat would not escape detection by the United States, and also on the grounds that the Soviets probably would not develop a transferable MIRVed warhead until the mid-

1980s. However, the idea that successful cheating is extremely unlikely because nearly all methods of cheating could not escape detection sounds similar to the proposition that a bucket 99-percent free of holes would be unlikely to leak. A party wanting to cheat on a treaty can be expected to carefully seek out the few ways that undetected cheating is possible in an otherwise foolproof treaty.

Aspin's judgment on the unlikelihood of undetectable Soviet cheating becomes further suspect when he discusses the lack of any Soviet motive to cheat: "There could be no political gain unless the Russians made their transgressions public. No one is intimidated by weapons that are not known to exist. Yet if the Russians did make public the fact of their cheating there would be enormous political repercussions." [17] Should the Russians ever develop in secret a new major weapons system, no doubt they might wish to keep it undercover until a time of their own choosing, when its sudden revelation might have some political or military value. Moreover, while nuclear weapons may be of value in political intimidation, they also are not without a military purpose. Should the Soviets ever secretly build an arsenal capable of a disarming first strike, they might conceivably use it for more than just political intimidation. Exactly the same could be said for the United States, except that the possibility of secretly building such an arsenal in the United States seems somewhat remote.

The nuclear-freeze proposal presents different problems in verification than the SALT II Treaty. A nuclear freeze would constitute a ban on the testing, production, and development of nuclear weapons and their delivery systems. The most difficult aspect of the freeze to verify would probably be the production phase. It is quite possible that weapons such as cruise missiles could be produced in and deployed secret. In fact, Averell Harriman has noted that cruise missiles are "unverifiable [and they] will make existing agreements to reduce the numbers of nuclear arms obsolete and future agreements impossible." [18] Harriman has used this assertion as an argument for agreeing not to produce cruise missiles, which by his own admission would be an unverifiable agreement. Other freeze advocates, Senators Kennedy and Hatfield, have tried to provide reassurance on the verifiability of cruise missiles and other "hard" cases by noting that "these methods [of verification] continue to improve over time, and what may appear difficult to verify now may well become verifiable in the future." [19] In other words, while verification of cruise-missile production may not be possible right now, improved future methods of verification may make them verifiable later on, so we should not be too concerned about this large loophole in the nuclear-freeze proposal. In fairness to Kennedy and Hatfield, their Senate resolution specifically called for a verifable freeze—one in which what cannot be verified would not be frozen. Nevertheless, it is hard to know how such a requirement would actually be interpreted. For example, suppose that the United States found it could secretly produce cruise missiles or some other weapon without detection by the Soviets. Would that finding put the weapon in the unverifiable category and therefore not subject to the freeze?

Freeze advocates are perhaps correct that a total ban on production of nuclear weapons would be easier to verify than a partial ban. They may also be correct in asserting that a large degree of cheating would probably not escape detection. However, that is not something that can be known with great confidence. It may be true that much is now known in the United States about Soviet weapons programs, despite Soviet attempts at secrecy. However, that should not lead to the conclusion that there are no significant Soviet programs that are not now known about, nor should we conclude that a determined effort to keep a weapons program secret would necessarily have a low probability of success in the future.

The Soviets, in fact, have a KGB chief directorate for "strategic deception" charged with conveying misinformation about Soviet strategic nuclear assets, according to a high ranking Soviet military defector.[20] At one time when they were far behind, the Soviets found it advantageous to create the impression that they were actually far ahead of the United States in ABM technology. This feat was accomplished by constructing monumental ABM stations that were actually facades.[21] It seems possible that the Soviets might now take the opposite approach of trying to camouflage a portion of their arsenal at a time when there are numerous voices in the United States claiming Soviet nuclear superiority.

There is simply no way to know how much we do not know about Soviet weapons programs. Moreover, even if it were correct that only a small amount of cheating could escape detection, a small amount could in some cases have a large impact, e.g., secretly replacing single-warhead ICBMs by ones that are highly MIRVed. More importantly, if a freeze is just a first step to significant reductions in nuclear arms, a small degree of undetected cheating, leading over time to large secret stockpiles, could offer significant temptations to a first strike when stockpiles are very much smaller than today's levels.

Cheating is often very difficult to establish conclusively despite good information-gathering capabilities. In 1984 the Reagan Administration accused the Soviets of "probable" cheating on a number of arms agreements, most importantly the 1972 ABM Treaty which severely restricts radar systems for ABM purposes. While clearcut violations of an important treaty might justify great caution before seeking to reach agreement on further treaties with the violator, it is difficult to know how to deal with "probable" violations. The ambiguity in this case arises out of the language of the ABM Treaty which restricts phased array radars for ABM purposes but not for other purposes such as tracking spacecraft, the use claimed by the Soviets. Whether or not this "probable" violation does represent a violation of the ABM Treaty, it serves to remind us that the temptations to engage in deployments that violate a treaty may be especially great in areas where ambiguities in the treaty permit alternative interpretations.

We shall return to the question of treaty verifiability again in connection with a discussion of complete disarmament. We conclude this discussion on verification by stressing the importance of only agreeing to limit those things that can truly be verified. When supporters of a particular arms-control proposal speak about possibly improved verification techniques in the future, the need to agree to ban weapons that can be produced without detection (even though such an agreement is by definition unverifiable), and the lack of Soviet motives to cheat, it is clear that their belief in the need for the proposal is so strong that they are not overly troubled by its unverifiable aspects.

One area of the U.S.-Soviet arms competition that has great significance for the verifiability of arms-control treaties is the development of antisatellite (ASAT) weapons. Both the United States and U.S.S.R. have been working on ASAT systems since the early 1960s. The United States eventually discontinued its early efforts in the hope that the U.S.S.R. would do likewise. This U.S. restraint was motivated by a recognition of its greater dependence than the U.S.S.R. on satellites for surveillance and communications. By the late 1970s, however, the United States altered its approach and resumed work on ASAT systems, while continuing to seek to limit them by treaty. The earlier U.S. unilateral restraint on ASAT had not been followed by the Soviet Union which had conducted some twenty ASAT tests and fielded an operational system believed capable of attacking satellites in low-altitude earth orbits up to around 1400 miles. Under the Reagan administration the United States altered its stance on ASAT once again. The U.S. interest in a treaty banning ASAT seems to have faded, just at the point when the Soviets appeared very interested. The timing of the proposed Soviet ASAT treaty was viewed with suspicion, coming when the U.S.S.R. already had an operational ASAT system and the United States was about to begin testing its own.

Advocates of an ASAT treaty argue that the Soviet system is only a primitive one not yet capable of posing a serious threat to most U.S. satellites which are in very high earth orbits—particularly those satellites that would warn of a nuclear attack. They also note that it is better to have the Soviet Union forgo ASAT work and thereby prevent a threat to U.S. satellites than for the United States to try to develop a threat to Soviet satellites. Skeptics, however, note that while satellites are essential for purposes of surveillance and verification of arms-control treaties, a treaty banning ASAT would itself have serious verification problems. The skeptics also worry about the possibility of "breakout," that is, the rapid development of an ASAT capability by the Soviet Union in violation of any treaty. The development of full-fledged ASAT capabilities on each side would indeed raise troublesome possibilities. Attempts to forestall that eventually would seem to be worthwhile, although we may have already come too far to prevent that possibility by treaty.

DISARMAMENT AND WORLD GOVERNMENT — A FEASIBLE LONG-RANGE SOLUTION?

There are two sharply contrasting views on the feasibility of total nuclear disarmament. There are many people who see nuclear disarmament as the only way mankind will eventually become free of the risk of nuclear war. Others, including many freeze supporters, would agree with Senator Alan Cranston's remark: "We'll never know if nuclear weapons have been eliminated. The threat of nuclear war will be with mankind forever." [22] The belief that the risk of nuclear war can be eliminated through nuclear disarmament is attractive to many well-meaning idealists. It is possible, however, that the path of total nuclear disarmament may be the surest road to nuclear war.

We simply do not have the means to determine whether a nuclear armed power has secretly stored away a large quantity of nuclear weapons. Despite the assurances of disarmers such as Paul

Ehrlich that "many ingenious systems for vitually cheatproof nuclear disarmament have already been invented," [23] we unfortunately have no such ingenious systems, either now or in the foreseeable future. In fact, even now probably neither the United States nor the Soviets have any idea how many nuclear weapons the other side has stored away that do not show up on the official "census." It is only deployed weapons, i.e., those in missile silos, submarines, and bombers that can be counted with any confidence. There is no way to use a nuclear weapon's radioactivity or other means to "sniff out" all the nuclear bombs a nation may have hidden away.

Moreover, in the eventuality that nuclear disarmament were agreed to, the United States or the Soviet Union would need to keep only a tiny fraction of its existing arsenal to give itself a war-winning advantage over its adversary, providing the other country kept its word and destroyed all its weapons. The notion that the leaders of both the United States and U.S.S.R. would not try to hide some nuclear weapons away "just in case" betrays a profound ignorance of human nature. On what basis would a nation's leader reject the advice of his military advisors to secretly store some nuclear weapons just in case the adversary does not destroy all of his weapons? Are U.S. and Soviet leaders too moral to consider such a reprehensible act? Would they be concerned about the moral approbation of world opinion if they got caught, knowing that the chances of getting caught would be infinitesimal? It seems much more likely that both countries would secretly store away a large quantity of nuclear weapons just in case the other side attempted nuclear blackmail or the actual use of its nuclear arsenal.

Not only would a secret cache of nuclear weapons be virtually undetectable, but perhaps a secret underground weapons laboratory would possibly escape detection as well—almost certainly in the Soviet Union. On-site inspection cannot reveal very much about sites whose existence is not known.

Finally, even if by some miracle all countries did destroy all their nuclear stockpiles, and even if the United States and the Soviet Union became good friends, on what basis should we assume that "everyone lives happily ever after"? Given that the knowledge of how to make nuclear weapons cannot be destroyed, it seems likely that at some time in the future, a country or a subnational group would build a nuclear arsenal. Are we to believe that once nuclear weapons are destroyed, evil or opportunistic people will never again be in positions of power or that countries will never again feel hostility towards one another?

Advocates of disarmament often recognize these possibilities, but they are likely to view them as acceptable risks because of their belief that nuclear war is certain if the nuclear arms race continues. The author favors the sharply opposing view that an attempt at nuclear disarmament is the sure path to nuclear disaster and that our best chance of avoiding the holocaust lies in keeping our nuclear arsenals. Living under the dangling nuclear sword is acceptable only because the other alternative—attempted nuclear disarmament—is much more likely to lead to nuclear war. This admission may prompt the thought: Why not at least try to devise a really foolproof technical means of verifying whether nuclear weapons have in fact been destroyed? That approach is a bit like failing to face the reality of our energy problem by encouraging people to solve it by experimenting with devices that would violate the first or second law of thermodynamics. No successful device would in fact be built. However, a clever charlatan could invent a device that seemed to work and could fool enough people who desperately wanted to believe.

In this respect, a considerable similarity can be found between those who advocate complete disarmament and those, often on the other end of the political spectrum, who advocate a ballistic-missile defense of the population. Both positions consider it unacceptable that mankind should live forever under the threat of nuclear annihilation. The two "solutions" (disarmament and ballistic-missile defense) appeal to a naïve American belief that there are no limits to the possible and that all obstacles can be overcome with either good will or Yankee ingenuity. The two "solutions" are equally misguided, and both, if implemented, could be a sure prescription for World War III.

Disarmers often point to the lessons of history to show why the nuclear arms race must end in catastrophe. It may be true that arms races in the past have led to war. However, we may also ask which war was avoided by disarmament following an arms race? The lesson from the period preceding World War II certainly does not support the view that the Western democracies' desire for disarmament was a force promoting peace. The lessons of history may give better support to the ancient Roman motto that if you want peace, prepare for war.

History also contains ambiguous lessons regarding the use of especially terrifying weapons. Many weapons were originally thought to be too terrifying to use, including the crossbow and dynamite, which at the time of its invention by Nobel was thought to put an end to all future wars due to its destructive force. While in retrospect we can see the naïvité of such views, most people believe that nuclear weapons really are fundamentally different, since their destructive force is so many orders of magnitude greater than anything in history. It is conceivable, however, that survivors of some future nuclear war will view our present belief that nuclear weapons make war obsolete with the same sad wonderment that we now hold towards the older, quaint beliefs about crossbows and TNT.

The only thing of comparable repugnance to nuclear weapons would be biological and chemical weapons. Following extensive use of chemical weapons in the First World War, these weapons with some exceptions have not been used in sixty years. Even during World War II, despite the existence of huge stockpiles of deadly CB agents, they were not used (with a few rare exceptions, one of which involved Japanese tests of biological agents on Chinese and American POWs). Some have cited the 1925 Geneva Protocol, which banned first use of such weapons, as being the main factor accounting for their almost nonuse in World War II. However, can we seriously believe that Adolph Hitler would have refrained from using CB agents solely because of the 1925 Geneva Protocol, if the Allied nations did not also possess large stockpiles? It seems much more plausible that the relative nonuse of CB weapons in World War II can be attributed to the deterrent value of huge stockpiles on each side. That belief is given additional support by the fact that nearly all the uses of CB agents that have occurred since 1925 have been in cases where only one side in the conflict possessed such weapons and the means to deliver them: the Italians in Ethiopia (1935–36), the Nationalists in China (1937–45), the Egyptians in Yemen (1963–67), the Americans in Indochina (1963–73), and the Soviets in Afghanistan (1980–   ). It seems likely that mutual deterrence, rather than moral pressures to observe a treaty, plays a much larger role in determining whether a particularly terrifying weapon will remain unused. The nonuse of CB agents during World War II also may contain another lesson: Even during an all-out conflict, nations may be deterred from using every weapon in their arsenals if the enemy also has large stockpiles. Hence, the possession of large nuclear arsenals does not necessarily mean they would be used even if war should occur.

Many advocates of nuclear disarmament suggest that the only way to achieve that goal is through the abolition of nation-states and the formation of a world government. That proposition is probably partly correct. As long as nation-states exist, they will insist on being ultimately responsible for their own security, and they will not relinquish the means for their own defense. However, it is by no means clear that if a world government were formed, the risk of nuclear war would be eliminated or even reduced. It is not, for example, exactly unheard of for a civil war to occur within a country after it has been united. Why should joining all the nations of the world into one country eliminate war? Quite aside from the nearly insurmountable political obstacles to the formation of a world government, its accomplishment would not of itself cure our nuclear problem which is, of course, rooted in the human condition. Total nuclear disarmament and world government should best wait until that day when human beings evolve to learn a new way of dealing with each other. However, even if that blissful day should ever come, it is possible there would still be a few unenlightened Neanderthals left. It seems likely that these few remaining unrepentant sinners might find themselves attracted to the profession of politics, where such scoundrels would be in a position to do great harm in a totally disarmed world.

WHAT ARE SOME ALTERNATIVES TO TRADITIONAL ARMS CONTROL?

There are numerous problems with the traditional arms-control process, some of which have already been discussed. In this concluding section, we review some of these problems and consider alternatives to the traditional approach.

Traditional arms-control efforts have often stimulated the arms race by leading both sides to develop weapons as bargaining chips. The bargaining-chip syndrome sometimes leads to the development of weapons of little military value; at other times it leads to the development of weapons that, because of their highly destabilizing character, a country would be better off without them. The bargaining-chip idea also can result in a nation keeping obsolete weapons in its arsenal strictly for trading purposes at some future date.

Another problem with the arms-control process is that it may be seen by some people as making a strong defense unnecessary. Arms-control negotiations sometimes seem to have a tranquilizing effect. Many people would regard efforts to modernize U.S. nuclear forces while arms-control negotiations are underway as both provocative and unnecessary. Attempts to negotiate arms-control agreements while continuing to build nuclear weapons are in this view characterized as "voodoo arms control." For those who make no distinction between arms control and disarmament, progress in arms control is in fact not possible if the United States continues to add to its arsenal. The view of the desirability of unilateral U.S. restraint in weapons building as a gesture of goodwill to induce reciprocal Soviet restraint is often steadfastly adhered to without the slightest evidence that unilateral U.S. restraint will induce Soviet restraint. As Harold Brown, former secretary of defense has noted: "We have found that when we build weapons, they build; when we stop they nevertheless continue to build." [24]

The Soviets apparently have a more realistic view of the arms-control process than many in the West. Many Western defense analysts believe that for the Soviets, the arms-control process is primarily a way of confirming an existing balance of forces. In addition, the Soviets appear to see the arms-control process as a way of manipulating Western public opinion, so that the United States will unilaterally constrain its nuclear forces. The Soviets do not have any sizable pro-Moscow constituency in the West to accomplish this feat, but they don't need one. It is enough that there is a large fraction of the U.S. public who oppose new U.S. nuclear weapons systems while they are generally silent about, and often uninformed about, Soviet weapons programs. Moreover, the Soviet leaders, having no significant domestic public-opinion pressure with which to contend, can continue to develop a massive arsenal without any domestic voices cautioning that some of its new weapons "built strictly for defensive purposes" may be extremely threatening to the West.

There are further important consequences resulting from the differences between Soviet and American society. For example, the Soviets will always know much more about U.S. weapons programs than we know about theirs. In addition, the massive antinuclear movement in the West, with no counterpart in communist countries, could have a profound effect on the U.S.-Soviet arms negotiating process. Soviet leaders know that there is considerable public pressure on U.S. leaders to reach an agreement before the next election. Moreover, if U.S. public opinion polls are to be believed, the public support for arms control is so great that the public is not overly concerned that an agreement could give the Soviets a military advantage. Thus, if the Soviets find themselves negotiating with a U.S. administration that is not sufficiently forthcoming, they can easily afford to outwait their American counterparts and perhaps count on a more reasonable administration which a U.S. public seeking to end the arms race might install.

A closely related problem for the United States with the arms-control process is the increasing degree of polarization in the debate over defense, nuclear war, and arms control. During liberal administrations the conservative opposition tends to attack arms-control proposals as either being tilted against U.S. interests or not being sufficiently verifiable. During conservative administrations the liberal opposition tends to seize on nonprogress in arms control as evidence that the administration is not sincere and is only putting forth proposals it knows the U.S.S.R. will not accept. Both of these tendencies make it very difficult to keep domestic politics out of the arms-control process. Even when an arms-control treaty has bipartisan support, as was the case during part of the SALT negotiations, ratification of the final treaty may prove extremely difficult. Conservative critics of a particular arms-control treaty are often able to block it in the U.S. Senate where a two-thirds vote is needed for ratification. With such a high degree of polarization it is difficult to sustain any degree of continuity, either in defense policies or in arms-control negotiations, since each administration is likely to reject the approach of its predecessor.

In addition to all the political pitfalls facing the United States in the traditional arms control process, there are also a number of major technical problems that may make arms control, as we have known it, obsolete. Until now, the problem of verification has been relatively manageable. However, we are now entering an era when we can no longer count certain weapons with any degree of assurance. The two technical developments that present the greatest challenge for verification are the cruise missile and interchangeable MIRV warheads. Interchangeable warheads could allow a very sizable clandestine expansion in number of warheads, particularly for the Soviet Union, whose much larger ICBMs are capable of a much larger degree of fractionation. It makes no sense to ban such developments, as some nuclear freeze advocates have suggested, if the ban itself is unverifiable. Moreover, the possibility of undetectable expansions in numbers of warheads in such areas as cruise missiles raises questions about the importance of striving to put limits on numbers of warheads in those areas that are verifiable.

Moreover, even areas now considered verifiable may be less verifiable than we think. For example, consider the question of the number of reentry vehicles (RVs) carried by a given type of ICBM—a matter of no small importance. The traditional (SALT II) approach on the number of RVs per missile has been to assume that all missiles of a given type have a number of RVs equal to the number that type was observed to have by eavesdroppers on missile tests. That assumption may be without justification. For example, the Soviets, given their large throw-weight ICBMs, might design a new ICBM carrying thirty RVs, but test it by only firing ten randomly selected RVs. Existing ICBM warheads could then be replaced with the new ones, resulting in a sizable expansion of Soviet warheads that might well escape detection.

Another technical problem faced by traditional arms control is the increasingly blurred dividing line between strategic, theatre, and tactical nuclear weapons. ICBMs based in the United States or the Soviet Union can generally be unambiguously identified according to their mission. For example, the Soviet SS-20s intended for use against West European targets can be distinguished, based on the number of rocket stages, from the longer-range ICBMs. However, the range of cruise missiles is much less obvious from their external appearance, and the same can be said for bombers. Moreover, even short-range aircraft can have a strategic mission, as in the case of U.S. forward-based planes around the periphery of the Soviet Union. These dual-mission or "gray-area" systems greatly complicate each side's assessment of the other side's nuclear strength since weapons capable of both strategic and theatre missions tend to be counted twice. The increasing number of these gray-area systems underlines the importance of linkage between nuclear-arms-control talks at all three levels: tactical, theatre, and strategic.

A further problem for the future of arms control is that we may not know which weapons are "stabilizing" and which are "destabilizing." For example, the cruise missile, according to some, is highly destabilizing because its small size makes it difficult for each side to verify how many the other side has produced and deployed. However, others would point to the cruise missile's relatively slow speed which makes it, unlike the ICBM, not as useful for a surprise first strike, and hence a stabilizing weapon. Even the most destabilizing weapon of all, the highly accurate MIRVed ICBM, capable of a counterforce mission against the other side's missile silos, could conceivably be a force for stability. This could transpire either through unilateral action, i.e., each side taking steps to make its ICBM force less vulnerable through mobility, or through mutually agreed reductions in the number of such weapons.

Many of the examples in the preceding discussion illustrate how the pace of technological change in weapons development often outpaces the progress in arms-control negotiations. What may have been verifiable at one time becomes much less verifiable at a later time when, for example, cruise missile and interchangeable warheads enter the picture. In their frustration at having the pace of arms-control efforts continually outstripped by technology, it is little wonder that some in the arms-control community want to freeze nuclear technology in its tracks. Quite apart from whether such a total freeze would be verifiable, there is also the question of whether it is the best way to reduce the risk of nuclear war. Calling a halt to the arms race and reducing the risk of nuclear war are, of course, two different goals that may, in some cases, call for different actions. It may be that the best way to reduce the risk of nuclear war is through the proper mix of arms control, unilateral restraint (in some cases), and modernizing U.S. nuclear forces (in other cases). Moreover, we need to interpret arms control more broadly than formal negotiations and treaties. The quiet removal of U.S. forward-based missiles from Turkey following the forced Soviet withdrawal of its missiles from Cuba in 1962 was certainly an example of arms control, whether or not it was based on an explicit agreement. Similarly a U.S. decision to refrain from building the MX missile in return for the Soviet dismantling of its SS-18 first-strike missiles would also be an example of arms control promoting stability. Regrettably, it is probably true that such a trade could not occur as long as the Soviets believe they have other ways of stopping the MX missile. In any case, such tacit agreements may hold as much promise in constraining the arms race in the future as more formal agreements.

The most important criticism of the traditional arms-control process is well enunciated by Senator Gary Hart. According to Hart, arms control has focused too narrowly on controlling numbers of weapons; instead "we must refocus the negotiations specifically on measures to achieve stability and prevent the use of nuclear weapons. Preventing the use of nuclear weapons must be the organizing principle for future arms control talks. It is the clearest definition of the problem we face and it is consistent with a strong national defense." [25] Measures to prevent the use of nuclear weapons would encompass avoidance of nuclear war by accident or miscalculation, avoidance of nuclear proliferation to nonnuclear states, and the reduction of the vulnerability of both sides' retaliatory forces to surprise attack.

Many of those who have lost patience with the slow progress of the arms-control process remind us of the need to keep in mind the big picture, which can often be lost sight of in endless detailed discussions. It has been observed that just as the medieval scholastics

11. Would SALT II be verifiable? How about a nuclear freeze?

12. Should the U.S. deploy ASAT systems or should we seek an agreement to ban them? Why?

13. What are the problems associated with total disarmament?

14. What are the problems faced by the traditional arms-control process? What are some alternative approaches?

Eleven

NUCLEAR-WEAPONS
PROLIFERATION

WHO ARE THE PROLIFERATORS?

About 98 percent of the world's nuclear weapons are in the arsenals of the United States and the Soviet Union. That one fact explains our strong emphasis on the threat posed by U.S.-U.S.S.R. nuclear arsenals. However, aside from the growth of the superpowers' arsenals, known as "vertical" proliferation, there are an increasing number of nuclear-armed nations, a trend known as "horizontal" proliferation. In fact, some people suspect that the probability of a nuclear war involving one or more Third World countries exceeds that of a war directly involving the superpowers. Lest we find any relief in such an assessment, we must realize that a small nuclear war could possibly ignite World War III.[1]

There are now six known members of the nuclear club. The dates these six countries detonated their first nuclear device are: United States, 1945; U.S.S.R., 1949; Great Britain, 1952; France, 1960; China, 1964; and India, 1974. India, however, has not acknowledged that its 1974 nuclear detonation was a bomb, preferring instead to call it a peaceful nuclear explosion. In addition to these six states, there are two others widely suspected of having secretly developed the bomb, namely Israel and South Africa, raising the number of probable nuclear-weapon states to eight.[2]

Table 11.1   Near-Nuclear Nations

NPT Signatories	Belgium	Germany, W.	Netherlands
	Bulgaria	Hungary	Philippines
	Canada	Italy	Rumania
	Czechoslovakia	Japan	Sweden
	Finland	Korea, S.	Switzerland
	Germany, E.	Mexico	Yugoslavia
NPT Nonsignatories	Argentina	Cuba	Spain
	Brazil	Pakistan	Taiwan

Note: "Near-nuclear" nations do not include those nations suspected of already acquiring nuclear weapons (South Africa and Israel). The twenty-four listed are projected to have a cumulative total of around 400 metric tons of plutonium in spent fuel from their commercial reactors by 1990.

Also generally acknowledged is the fact that there are at least six additional nations with the capability to build the bomb if they were to decide to do so: Canada, Italy, Japan, Sweden, Switzerland, and West Germany. All six of these countries have, however, by their ratification of the Non-Proliferation Treaty (NPT), renounced any such intention. Most lists of possible future nuclear-weapon states include these six advanced industrial nations plus the other eighteen nations listed in table 11.1, of whom six have not signed the NPT. There are reasons, however, why many observers regard some of the less-developed near-nuclear nations with greater concern than the advanced industrial nations. Some of the less-developed near-nuclear countries are considered to have relatively unstable regimes, while others are believed likely to become involved in regional conflicts. In addition, it is possible that weapons built by such nations would be technically unreliable and, therefore, likely to trigger a nuclear war by accident. However, Western suggestions that nuclear weapons in the hands of developing nations are especially dangerous would ring hollow to these nations themselves, in light of the vertical proliferation of the superpowers' arsenals.

Beyond the near-nuclear countries listed in table 11.1, there are over fifty nations that have nuclear reactors and therefore, may be considered to have taken the first steps that could eventually lead to a nuclear-weapons capability. About half of this larger group has or plans to acquire a spent-fuel reprocessing plant which would allow them to extract plutonium, the material from which fission bombs can be made.

In virtually all cases, the nuclear technology, materials, and knowledge has been supplied to these nations by advanced industrial countries, especially the United States. Some observers view the continuing dissemination of nuclear technology as directly responsible for the problem of nuclear-weapons proliferation, while others believe these technology transfers serve as a way of keeping things under control. According to the latter viewpoint, a judicious combination of incentives and disincentives tailored to the specific circumstances of each nation is a better way to avoid proliferation than a denial of nuclear technology. Many of the developing nations, for example, lack an adequate energy supply and have associated balance-of-payments problems. Although some in the United States may believe that there are far better energy alternatives for Third World countries than nuclear energy, the leaders of these countries may feel differently. Quite apart from the prestige value of a nuclear plant, Third World nations may prefer this option to imported oil or coal.

For most nations the main obstacle to building a bomb is the problem of acquiring the necessary raw materials rather than a lack of knowledge about bomb design. Any nation with enough of a technological base to justify an engineering school probably would be able to design and build a bomb. The only real obstacle to building the bomb, for most nations, is the political decision to go ahead. In recognition of that unpleasant reality, many people believe that a U.S. policy of denying nuclear technology to developing countries would not prevent those nations from acquiring nuclear weapons. In this view, the long-term solution to the proliferation problem requires (1) creation of economic and political disincentives to build nuclear weapons, (2) implementation of technical and other measures to guard against diversion of nuclear technology, and (3) creation and enhancement of international norms that regard nuclear weapons as undesirable. This third approach of creating a self-organized, self-policed behavioral system in which nuclear-weapons acquisition is deplored has often been referred to as a nonproliferation regime.

The split between the advocates of denying nuclear technology and those favoring its dissemination under strict control parallels the split between the advocates of disarmament and arms control. The first side in each dispute believes that those who speak of control are simply deluding themselves, in light of the amount of proliferation, both horizontal and vertical, that has already occurred. The second side, however, the controllers, believe that a policy of denial and secrecy might well have led to even more proliferation.

HOW SERIOUS IS THE PROBLEM?

Most observers believe that the potential for future proliferation is greater than ever before. The number of countries that have the beginnings of a nuclear-weapons capability is now very large. In addition, the increasing number of nations supplying peaceful nuclear technology also aggravates the proliferation problem. While the United States was at one time the only nuclear supplier, that is no longer the case. Among the other nuclear-supplier nations, many have very different views from the United States on the necessary technical safeguards to prevent diversion and on the political reliability and stability of nations seeking nuclear technology for commercial purposes.

A further reason that proliferation may accelerate is the large increase in the world's supply of plutonium. Altogether, 219 tons of plutonium have been produced by commercial power reactors in the noncommunist world through 1982.[3] The bulk of this plutonium is in the form of highly radioactive spent fuel, but 20 percent (44 tons) had been reprocessed and, in principle, could be used to make bombs.[4] The amount of plutonium needed for one Nagasaki-size bomb is approximately 15 pounds, making the spent-fuel stockpile equivalent to 25,700 potential nuclear weapons.[5] Although most of the reprocessed plutonium can be found in nations that already possess nuclear weapons, that situation appears to be on the verge of changing as more nations begin to acquire reprocessing plants.

Moreover, in view of the risks of "subnational" terrorist acts we should not regard large plutonium stockpiles in nuclear-weapon states as not dangerous. Even though nuclear terrorism is not normally regarded as proliferation per se, it is a serious danger that increases with the number of reprocessing sites and the amount of plutonium reprocessed. There are many possibilities for diversion of nuclear material besides physical assaults on such plants. For example, in any reprocessing system there are inevitably small quantities of plutonium that are unaccounted for, and this could mask a gradual but systematic diversion of material by employees at the facility.

Some people believe that while the potential for nuclear terrorism is a matter for serious concern, it is less serious that the problem of horizontal proliferation. Numerous reasons are cited for this belief. For example, safeguards, including physical security, can be implemented to greatly diminish the likelihood of a successful terrorist attempt to steal nuclear materials. Moreover, while the subject of bomb design is no longer secret, the successful construction of a bomb is quite another matter. A terrorist group would need a collection of highly trained persons with a wide range of specialized skills. In view of the sizable technical obstacles and the possibility that the bomb fabricators might lethally contaminate themselves, terrorists might instead try to steal a bomb from a nuclear-weapons stockpile. They would, in this case, face obstacles in the form of physical security far more severe than those denying them access to nuclear materials at a nuclear power plant or reprocessing facility.

An additional reason that the risks of nuclear terrorist actions are thought to be overstated is that there are many far easier, cheaper, and less risky ways for terrorists to kill or hold hostage large numbers of people, such as poisoning a large city's water supply. That view may fail to reckon with the reasons behind terrorist actions. Most terrorists, much like those in charge of selecting targets for strategic nuclear weapons, are not interested in killing people simply for the sake of killing. A fanatical group may be especially attracted to the use of nuclear weapons in order to make a political statement. The group may reason that even if it is forced to carry out its threatened use of a weapon against innocent civilians, a larger political good would be served, namely a popular groundswell demanding the abolition of all nuclear weapons. Although only a tiny fraction of antinuclear activists might contemplate such an action, the large size of the antinuclear movement means that there could well be thousands of fanatics willing to undertake such a mission. Thus, the fact that terrorists may have far easier means of wreaking havoc than nuclear weapons should not blind us to the special appeal such weapons might hold for a fanatical antinuclear group. It has, in fact, been reported that the Defense Nuclear Agency "has seen evidence in Europe that terrorist groups and members of organizations opposed to nuclear weapons had begun to join forces with the theft of a nuclear weapon in mind." [6]

There is still another reason for regarding the possibility of nuclear terrorism with at least as much concern as nuclear proliferation: A nuclear terrorist group that acquires a nuclear weapon is very likely to use it. In contrast, a nation that acquires a nuclear-weapon capability may simply test its weapon and be satisfied that it had demonstrated to the world that it is now a power with which to be reckoned. Moreover, a nuclear weapon detonated by terrorists might carry the greater potential for changing the course of world history. There can be little doubt that the magnitude of the impact on the U.S. and the world would be far different given these two hypothetical headlines: "White House and Congress Annihilated by Nuclear Terrorists," or alternatively "Argentina Drops Bomb on Brazil." The latter event might shock the world, but the former might ignite World War III.

The preceding comments about the catastrophic impact of potential nuclear terrorist actions are not intended to downplay the seriousness of the risks associated with nuclear proliferation. However, it must be remembered that the key question regarding nuclear proliferation is: How does the risk of nuclear war depend on the number of nations armed with nuclear weapons? It is commonly supposed that there is a link between these two factors, but the nature of that link is by no means obvious.

Some people have argued that nuclear proliferation may not be such a serious problem, i.e., that the risk of nuclear war, particularly a large nuclear war, is not significantly increased because of proliferation. Those who hold this view usually anticipate that further nuclear proliferation will not take place at a rapid rate. They note that the pace of nuclear proliferation to date has been far slower than many feared it would be twenty to thirty years ago. There are, however, several reasons for questioning this optimistic projection of past trends. The reprocessing facilities in the twenty or so near-nuclear countries will soon give them sizable plutonium stockpiles. In addition, there could well be a domino effect in which one nation's decision to acquire nuclear weapons is influenced by that of a regional rival. Alternatively, the twenty countries that are all very close to developing nuclear weapons may reason that once one or two take the fateful step, there will be little moral approbation or actual political sanctions directed against nations three through twenty. If the remaining countries delay in taking the final step, however, the world community could resolve to impose sanctions on further proliferators, so the most opportune time to act might be immediately after the first one or two have done so. If the domino theory of proliferation is correct, then the future spread of nuclear-weapon states may be very rapid. Moreover, rapid changes in the relative military capabilities of nations are more likely to give rise to instabilities and lead to war.

HOW GREAT IS THE NUCLEAR-WEAPONS-NUCLEAR-POWER CONNECTION?

Many questions have been raised about the desirability of nuclear power for generating electricity, but what sets nuclear power apart from all other energy sources is its potential for nuclear-weapons proliferation. The link is clear: any of the methods for using nuclear reactors to produce electricity involve the use or the production of fissionable materials such as uranium or plutonium.[7] The key point, however, is to examine the likelihood of further nuclear proliferation both with nuclear power and without it, so as to determine if the power-weapons connection is tenuous or dangerous.[8]

The arguments on each side are not always clear-cut. For example, while a switch from nuclear energy to alternative sources might result in less raw material for nuclear weapons, it could also cause an increase in the international competition for imported oil. This situation would raise the already vital stake many nations have in ensuring that the oil flow from oil-exporting countries is not terminated by hostile powers. Thus, the elimination of nuclear power, particularly by a large oil-importing country such as the United States, could put severe strains on the international market for oil, exacerbate world tensions, and provide incentives for other nations to build nuclear power plants, if not weapons. Nuclear-power opponents believe this argument is overdrawn since in most countries not much oil is used to generate electricity. In the United States, for example, only 10 percent of U.S. electric power comes from oil. That rebuttal, however, overlooks the fact that countries wishing to provide for growth in their energy supply may find that an increasing reliance on nuclear energy is essential if domestic oil or coal reserves are unavailable.

There are many different types of commercial nuclear reactors, the main one being the light-water reactor (LWR). "Light" water in this context is water in which the hydrogen is in its normal isotopic form, in contrast to "heavy" water in which the hydrogen nucleus contains an extra neutron. The water in a light-water reactor serves the dual purpose of carrying heat away from the reactor core and moderating or slowing the neutrons from the fission reactions. Three other common types of reactors in commercial use include the graphite-moderated gas-cooled (MAGNOX) reactor, the heavy-water (CANDU) reactor, and the liquid-metal fast-breeder (LMFBR) reactor. These three, together with light-water reactors, account for over 95 percent of the total power output of commercial reactors in the Western world.

The process by which nuclear fuel is obtained, prepared, used, and disposed of is known as the nuclear fuel cycle. When it is mined, uranium ore contains primarily the isotope ^{238}U. The isotope ^{235}U is present in uranium ore at a concentration of only 0.7 percent. In all the reactor types mentioned except the CANDU reactor, the concentration of the isotope ^{235}U must be enriched to 2 to 4 percent before the uranium can be used in the reactor. This enrichment process is a complex technological feat in view of the fact that the different uranium isotopes are chemically identical. The isotope separation (enrichment) process must rely on the small mass differences between the two uranium isotopes.

Uranium that has been slightly enriched to the level of 2 to 4 percent for use in a nuclear reactor cannot be used in making a bomb. In a bomb the ^{235}U isotope must be present at a level of at least 20 percent (90 percent for a military-grade weapon). However, the same technology that can enrich uranium to 2 to 4 percent can also enrich it to 90 percent. Enrichment must, therefore, clearly be regarded as a "sensitive" technology because it allows the production of weapons-grade material from naturally occurring uranium. There are a number of countries besides the United States and the U.S.S.R. that have or plan to acquire enrichment facilities, including Britain, France, China, South Africa, Brazil, Japan, and Australia.

Even though the enrichment technology is sensitive, the nature of that technology represents one impediment to nuclear-weapons proliferation. One method of uranium enrichment known as gaseous diffusion is extremely costly and probably beyond the means of any but the most advanced industrialized states. Two other methods, including gas centrifugation and laser isotope separation, are much cheaper and suited to a small-scale operation, but they are not capable of producing highly enriched uranium at a significant rate.

While one sensitive technology (enrichment) involves the processing of fuel before it goes into a nuclear reactor, the other sensitive technology involves processing (or reprocessing) the depleted fuel once it is removed from the reactor. During the course of its operation, a reactor burns up the fissionable isotope ^{235}U. Neutrons emitted from the fission of one ^{235}U nucleus cause other ^{235}U nuclei to fission in a chain-reaction manner. The ^{238}U nuclei in the fuel are also affected by the emitted neutrons, but in a different way. Rather than undergoing fission, some of the ^{238}U present in a light-water reactor is transmuted, by neutron absorption, into other isotopes such as ^{239}Pu, which are themselves capable of undergoing fission. Isotopes such as ^{238}U, which are not fissionable but can be transformed into a fissionable isotope in a reactor, are said to be "fertile."

After a reactor has burned up most of the fissionable ^{235}U, its spent fuel will, therefore, contain significant quantities of newly created fissionable isotopes such as ^{239}Pu created from the fertile ^{238}U. The extraction of the plutonium isotope ^{239}Pu can allow it to be recycled as an economic supplement to the reactor fuel. Reprocessing is clearly as sensitive a technology as enrichment, since ^{239}Pu is a fissionable plutonium isotope usable for constructing bombs. Unfortunately, unlike the case of enrichment, the technology for reprocessing appears to be much more accessible to a large number of nations. In fact, many of the near-nuclear countries in table 11.1 now have, or expect to soon acquire, reprocessing facilities. In the United States the only reprocessing that is done, at present, is for military not commercial purposes.

Many questions have been raised about reprocessing, including whether it should be done at all. The alternatives to reprocessing include disposing of the highly radioactive spent fuel ("waste") without first extracting the plutonium or, alternatively, allowing the spent fuel to accumulate in holding tanks until a decision on reprocessing is made. Although the United States has decided to forgo commercial reprocessing for now, other countries have concluded that it is an economically viable option.

Another motivation for reprocessing, besides economics, is that the presence of plutonium in the radioactive waste complicates the precautions needed for its safe disposal. The 24,000 year half-life of ^{239}Pu means that it must be kept isolated from the environment for thousands of years.

Although in the case of the light-water reactor reprocessing is optional and can provide waste-extracted plutonium as a fuel supplement, reprocessing is mandatory in the case of the breeder reactor. A breeder reactor accomplishes the implausible-sounding trick of breeding more fuel than it consumes. The breeder reactor is fueled with a mixture of ^{239}Pu and ^{238}U. As the fissionable ^{239}Pu fuel is burned up, the fertile ^{238}U is converted to more ^{239}Pu than was consumed. The spent fuel can then be reprocessed and the ^{239}Pu produced can be extracted and used to refuel the reactor together with a new supply of ^{238}U. The process is, in principle, much more efficient than the once-through cycle of the light-water reactor, since all the ^{238}U eventually gets converted to fissionable material, not just the 0.7 percent ^{235}U. This special benefit of the breeder is also the source of its special danger. Once reprocessing becomes mandatory, the level of risk is raised for nuclear proliferation and terrorist diversion of plutonium.

Although the breeder has been surrounded by controversy in the United States, other advanced industrialized countries appear to be more committed to its development. Many of these other nations, which lack the vast uranium reserves of the United States, apparently believe that at some point in the future a scarce uranium supply and escalating fuel costs will no longer permit the luxury of a once-through fuel cycle. The future status of breeders, however, is far from certain. While breeders offer the advantage of an assured fuel supply, they also have the disadvantage of much higher capital construction costs. In recent years high interest rates have driven construction costs up, while the economic slowdown and lack of new reactor construction have kept uranium prices from rising. These short-term factors have acted to diminish the breeder's primary advantage (assured low-cost fuel supply) and enhanced its primary economic disadvantage (high construction costs).

While breeder reactors may pose a special proliferation risk because of mandatory reprocessing, all nuclear power reactors pose potential proliferation dangers in at least three respects:

- They offer the possibility of diversion of material by terrorist groups. (This concern is particularly serious if reprocessing is done to extract plutonium.)

- They provide a nation with a legitimate cover for undertaking a secret weapons program.

- They develop a nation's technological infrastructure in the form of trained people, equipment, and raw materials that could be later used in a weapons program.

How valid are each of these links between power and weapons? Although the potential for nuclear terrorism must be taken seriously, there are ways that a nation can greatly reduce the risks. Nations can, for example, follow the U.S. lead and forgo commercial reprocessing so as to avoid sizable plutonium stockpiles. Terrorists, however, may not respect national boundaries and may simply steal their plutonium elsewhere. There are other precautions of a technical nature that could alleviate the problem, precautions such as "spiking" the reprocessed plutonium with various radioactive isotopes so as to make it unusable for bombs.

The second of the three links between nuclear power and nuclear-weapons proliferation is the "cover" scenario. Some nations may accept commercial nuclear technology with the intent of secretly developing a weapons capability. To date there are no known examples of a nuclear-weapons program that was developed as a spin-off from a commercial nuclear-power program. Nevertheless, there are two nations, India and China, whose first nuclear device was built using technology provided by other nations who thought the technology was to be used only for peaceful purposes. It is doubtful if such assistance would have been provided to India (by the United States and Canada) or to China (by the U.S.S.R.) if the supplier nations were aware of the recipients' eventual purpose.

The political need for a cover to keep secret a nation's nuclear ambitions may depend on its circumstances. Nations with powerful nuclear-armed neighbors may find it expedient to develop a bomb secretly and reveal it only at the time of their first nuclear test—or perhaps not even then. The plausibility of the cover scenario is often challenged on a number of grounds. It is sometimes noted, for example, that the political value of nuclear weapons depends on their existence being known, or at least suspected, as in Israel's case. Nevertheless, it may be politically and militarily hazardous to prematurely reveal one's intent to acquire nuclear weapons, as Iraq, for example, learned when Israel bombed its suspicious reactor. In addition, a secret nuclear arsenal can give a nation a big political and military advantage if it should ever be militarily challenged by a nonnuclear neighbor.

The cover argument for a power-weapons connection is sometimes also challenged on the grounds that civilian power reactors are not a particularly good way for a nation to develop a nuclear-weapons capability. It is suggested, for example, that civilian nuclear reactors, under strict international safeguards, offer less opportunities for diversion of plutonium than would a secret research or plutonium production reactor located in some remote area. In addition it has been claimed that the spent fuel from commercial reactors cannot be used to make good nuclear weapons, because the spent fuel contains too much of the wrong plutonium isotopes.[9]

Neither of the two preceding arguments against the cover scenario appears very strong. International safeguards against the diversion of plutonium, in practice, are not nearly as effective as commonly supposed, and they might have little deterrent value for a nation determined to build a bomb. Admittedly, the presence of the wrong plutonium isotopes in commercial-reactor spent fuel does make the weapons produced from such fuel not quite as good as those from a dedicated research or production reactor.[10] However, the amount of plutonium produced in the commercial reactor is far greater than what a small secret research reactor could produce. A power reactor could produce enough plutonium for perhaps twenty to fifty bombs per year, while a small research reactor might produce only enough for a few. That large difference in quantity would seem to overwhelm considerations of bomb quality.

A nation seeking a nuclear-weapons capability could attempt a program without the cover of a commercial nuclear-power program, but it might have more problems in that case. The nation's technical job is certainly made easier if it gets technological assistance from abroad. In addition, it might have domestic and international political programs that would make secrecy an important objective. A purely domestic weapons program might be harder to keep secret than a weapons program conducted under the guise of a nuclear-power program.

A nation opting for nuclear weapons could build a sizable plutonium stockpile from its commercial program and secretly build all the other bomb components. If the nation refrains from assembling the components, it will appear to be in strict compliance with any obligations it might have under the Non-Proliferation Treaty and yet be only days away from possession of a sizable nuclear arsenal. Under this scenario, even if the safeguards against the diversion of plutonium worked exactly as planned, they would work too late to do any good. The nation's true intentions would have been revealed only after it had diverted the plutonium and constructed a nuclear arsenal. For this reason some observers now believe that the crucial step a nation takes in demonstrating its intent to build the bomb is its decision to acquire a reprocessing plant to extract plutonium from spent reactor fuel. In this view, the commercial justification for reprocessing is sufficiently questionable that it is likely a nation has other motives.

Another way in which nuclear power can lead to nuclear-weapons proliferation is through nuclear power's role as an "attractive nuisance." A nation that initially has no intention of acquiring nuclear weapons may one day reassess its decision, particularly if the presence of nuclear technology supplied by others greatly simplifies its task. A large stockpile of weapons-grade plutonium convertable into weapons in a matter of days or weeks may present an irresistable temptation to a government under seige or to a guerilla group seeking the government's overthrow.

In conclusion, the connection between nuclear power and nuclear-weapons proliferation is not a tenuous one. It is a link greatly strengthened by spent-fuel reprocessing, but it is present even in the absence of reprocessing. The recognition of such a link, however, does not necessarily mean that the problem of nuclear proliferation can be either solved or ameliorated by denying nuclear technology to countries that profess to want it for peaceful purposes. We shall see that a wide range of methods have been tried to stem the tide of nuclear proliferation during the post-World War II era; none of them can claim unambiguous success or failure.

WHAT HAS BEEN THE HISTORY OF EFFORTS TO CONTROL PROLIFERATION?

The United States had recognized at the outset of the nuclear age that many nations would eventually acquire nuclear weapons. America hoped to forestall that eventuality by putting forth a plan for the international control of nuclear energy. Under this Acheson-Lilienthal plan, presented to the United Nations by financeer Bernard Baruch in 1946, no individual nation would be allowed direct access to materials from which bombs could be made. The Baruch Plan (as it came to be called) was rejected by the Soviet Union which insisted that the United States first destroy its nuclear stockpile before the international control of nuclear technology was established. The United States refused and the plan collapsed. It is not clear if the plan could have indefinitely kept bombs out of the hands of nations that wanted them, and no one can know what post–World War II history would have been like had the plan been adopted. However, many observers believe that the world missed its only chance to prevent widespread proliferation in 1946 with the Baruch Plan.

Following the collapse of the Baruch Plan, the U.S. Congress created a five-person Atomic Energy Commission (AEC) to oversee the development of nuclear energy in the United States. The mission of the AEC dealt with all facets of nuclear energy, both military and civilian. Although the United States realized that its nuclear monopoly was only temporary, it hoped to delay the acquisition of nuclear weapons by other nations through a strict policy of secrecy.

Accordingly, one function of the AEC was to place strict limits on the dissemination of all information about nuclear technology.

By 1953 it had become clear to U.S. leaders that the strict policy of secrecy and denial of technology was not working. Two nations, the U.S.S.R. and Great Britain, had already developed the bomb, and three more—Canada, France, and Norway—had built reactors and seemed well on their way to weapons acquisition. In 1953 President Eisenhower, in a sharp reversal of the former policy, launched his Atoms-for-Peace Plan. Eisenhower hoped to slow the process of nuclear-weapons proliferation by creating a more favorable international climate in which nations could have free access to the peaceful benefits of nuclear energy if they agreed to forgo its military applications.

The legislation resulting from Eisenhower's initiative was the Atomic Energy Act passed by Congress in 1954. This legislation removed AEC authority over the dissemination of unclassified nuclear information and permitted bilateral agreements through which other nations could receive nuclear technology and materials. Nations receiving such assistance were required to offer guarantees of no diversion to weapons applications, but no inspection was mandated by Congress to certify compliance.

The about-face in U.S. policy under the Atoms-for-Peace Plan led to the beginning of an era of expanded international nuclear cooperation. A typical early U.S. bilateral agreement involved the transfer of low enriched uranium to another country for research purposes. The recipient nation was required to transfer the spent fuel in the same form (no reprocessing) and was required to agree to U.S. inspection "from time to time." The U.S. policy on inspections to verify compliance grew steadily stricter, at least in theory. The post-1956 agreements, for example, called for broad rights of inspection through "access to all places." Stricter verification was considered important as the magnitude of fuel transfers increased, particularly after 1958 when the United States also permitted reprocessing of its fuel by other nations.

In the 1950s, the United States helped to create the International Atomic Energy Agency (IAEA), which it hoped would oversee and implement safeguards on nuclear transfers made under bilateral agreements. The United States at first believed that an international agency was the best way to establish standardized safeguards and that such an agency would give greater credibility to the verification process. Being the only supplier initially, the United States was able to play the dominant role in the development of IAEA safeguards.

Considerable controversy existed over the issue of safeguards, with the supplier nations within the IAEA pushing for stricter safeguards than many of the recipient nations wanted. Most recipient nations probably wanted looser safeguards to avoid unnecessary restrictions on their national sovereignty, not because they were interested in creating a system that could be easily circumvented.

The role of the IAEA in implementing safeguards was initially somewhat haphazard. U.S. bilateral agreements, for example, were only under IAEA safeguards if that was specifically called for under the agreement. After 1961 the United States required that all its bilateral agreements be subject to IAEA safeguards and inspections. Up until that time, the United States was surprised to find that most recipient nations preferred to be subject to U.S. inspections and safeguards rather than those of the IAEA.

During the 1960s there was a growing consensus among many nations over the dangers of nuclear proliferation and the need to provide nations access to peaceful nuclear applications under adequate safeguards. These twin concerns culminated in the Non-Proliferation Treaty of 1968. (As of May, 1983, 118 countries have signed the NPT.) Unlike any treaty before or since, the NPT is inherently discriminatory in its recognition of two distinct classes of nations: those who possessed nuclear weapons (before 1968), and those who did not. The treaty, in effect, represents a bargain in which the nonweapon states agree to refrain from developing weapons, and in return the weapon states agree to provide assistance on peaceful nuclear applications and to work towards reducing their own nuclear arsenals.

One very important feature of the NPT is that it extended IAEA safeguards over all the peaceful nuclear activities of the states that signed the treaty. Thus, a signatory nation is bound by IAEA safeguards, even if it receives no nuclear-technology transfers from oth*the* The NPT was never concevied of as a permanent solution *s to* proliferation problem, and there have been recurring dou*t with* how well it has lived up to its original promise. One pr*ve not* the NPT is that too many of the near-nuclear count*r powers* signed it (see table 11.1). In addition, two of the *gave rise to* (France and China) are nonsignatories.

The international consensus on proliferatio*t of a number* the NPT began to weaken in the early 1970s *India's "peaceful* of separate developments, the most significa*a non-NPT sig-* nuclear explosion" (PNE) in 1974. Altho*as the first time a* natory, violated no treaty by her acti nation had detonated a nuclear device using technology supplied by others specifically for peaceful purposes. India had obtained a nuclear reactor from Canada and heavy water from the United States under early agreements that required no inspection of facilities. These early agreements also contained another flaw: while they forbade construction of nuclear weapons they did not specifically rule out peaceful nuclear devices. The distinction is not quite as absurd as it may seem now, and PNEs are even mentioned in the NPT.

At the time the NPT was negotiated some scientists raised hopes of using nuclear explosives for large-scale construction projects such as the digging of harbors, the diversion of rivers, and even prospecting for minerals. The non-nuclear-weapon states did not wish to be deprived of the economic benefits PNEs might bring forth, although unfortunately there have been no such benefits to date.

Four years before India detonated its peaceful nuclear explosion it inquired whether its nuclear suppliers, the United States and Canada, would recognize the distinction between a PNE and a nuclear-weapon test. India received a negative answer, but was not dissuaded from working towards its goal, nor did India's inquiry deter continued nuclear assistance from its suppliers. Even after India's 1974 peaceful nuclear explosion, it suffered very few economic or political consequences as a result of this act. There were not many countries that took a public stand in condemning India's action. Aside from India's rival, Pakistan, only Canada, Japan, and Sweden publicly deplored India's PNE. The United States, while chagrined that its nuclear assistance may have played some role, did not wish to get involved in a public dispute with India. America probably also understood that its own enormous nuclear arsenal did not allow it to deliver moral rebukes to others who might choose to develop nuclear weapons. Most of the nations of the Third World took a ꞏnign view of India's PNE. In fact, most of the Third World actually cꞌ ꞉ratulated India on its achievement. One of their own had demon꞉ted that it could master the technology that previously only the ꞌ꞉nced, industrialized nations possessed.

a nucꞌdid India, the birthplace of Mahatma Gandhi, seek to build on a meꞌvice? Apart from the supposed clout that is conferred concerns. ꞉f the nuclear club, India did have some major security India felt ꞉ing on nuclear-armed China and unfriendly Pakistan, adversaries ꞌ꞉ demonstrating its nuclear capability, potential India probablꞌ꞉ave a reason to be more cautious. In addition, would be levellꞌ꞉ that no serious economic or political sanctions ꞉ the country, and if so, its guess was correct.

Finally, India was still able to preserve a self-image as a nation of peace. While other nations might regard India's nuclear detonation as a kind of coming of age, India had a very different view. In India's eyes, it had demonstrated peaceful intentions by not constructing a nuclear arsenal, after having shown the world that it was capable of doing so. India argued, not implausibly, that to refrain from building a nuclear arsenal when one has shown that one can do it, is a highly moral posture. Unfortunately, India's moral claims may be somewhat undercut by a 1983 IAEA finding that India has begun accumulating sizable stockpiles of separated plutonium that would permit it to build twenty nuclear weapons per year, should a decision be made to do so.

Although India's characterization of its 1974 nuclear detonation as "peaceful" may be specious and self-serving, some observers believe it best not to challenge that assertion, especially since unlike other weapon states, India has, in fact, conducted no further known nuclear tests. According to this view, proliferation should not be thought of in terms of one irreversible act. Rather, we should allow for the possibility that nations may wish to demonstrate their prowess in one nuclear test, and we should do everything possible to encourage restraint once they have committed that symbolic act.

India's 1974 PNE was a major reason for the increasing concerns over proliferation in the 1970s, but it was not the only reason. This decade was also a period in which the potential for nuclear terrorism became more apparent and in which transfers of nuclear technology to developing countries with less stable regimes accelerated. Moreover, this was also a period in which an expanded number of supplier nations led to competition for customers between the United States and its allies. Recipient nations, who regarded safeguards as a nuisance at best, found themselves shopping for the most favorable economic package with the loosest safeguards.

In this increasingly worrisome climate the nuclear-supplier nations held a series of secret meetings in London between 1975 and 1977. Nearly all the supplier countries attended, including the Soviet Union. Among the positive developments of these meetings was the development of an agreed-upon "trigger list" of specific items whose export would only be allowed under IAEA safeguards. A further major development was the inclusion of France, a non-NPT signatory, in the consensus. The London group also agreed on improved measures for physical security of nuclear facilities and materials, and they agreed not to transfer assistance for peaceful nuclear explosions—an omission in the NPT.

One major topic not resolved by the secret London meetings was the export of reprocessing facilities, which the United States viewed with particular concern. Nevertheless, the London group did agree that nuclear suppliers should exercise "restraint" in this area, in effect leaving the matter up to each nation's good judgment.

The United States first began to have serious concerns about reprocessing under the Ford administration. Until that period it was assumed that the nuclear technology supplied to recipient nations would eventually include the breeder reactor, for which reprocessing is mandatory. Gerald Ford, in the first presidential initiative since Eisenhower's Atoms-for-Peace Plan, directed that commercial reprocessing in the United States be held in abeyance until the implications for proliferation were clarified.

Reprocessing was an area that warranted careful study for President Ford; for his successor, it was an area of grave concern. President Carter, who made nonproliferation a high-priority goal, decided to defer reprocessing indefinitely and to try to find an alternative to the breeder reactor and its "plutonium economy." Carter believed that even if reprocessing should prove economically feasible, the dangers of national and subnational diversion of plutonium were so great that these considerations should override economics.

President Carter hoped that by taking a step in which the United States put principle ahead of economics, it might demonstrate its sincerity to the world and get others to follow its example. Other nations were not so sure that the United States had put its principles ahead of economics. They noted that the United States, with ample coal and uranium reserves, had far less need for reprocessing than other countries. These other nations also pointed out that were other countries to follow the U.S. lead, the vast American uranium supply—36 percent of the non-communist-world total—would become much more valuable. The basis of this suggestion is that other nations would have a greater need for uranium if they did not recycle reprocessed fuel, and this increasing demand for uranium would drive up its price.

The Carter administration's concern over the problem of proliferation led to the Non-Proliferation Act passed by Congress in 1978. This act directed that the United States undertake a variety of negotiations and seek cooperative initiatives with other nations to accomplish a number of objectives:

- Develop approaches to provide for the world's energy needs, including an international stockpile of uranium, so as to reduce incentives for reprocessing

- Renegotiate all existing agreements for nuclear cooperation, so as to strengthen safeguards

- Seek agreements with other supplier nations to adhere to certain policies and restrictions

- Strengthen the IAEA and its safeguards

- Negotiate the establishment of sanctions for nations that violate the NPT

- Cooperate with other nations in developing alternative energy sources

Some of these policy initiatives have continued under the Reagan administration which has had a very different approach toward proliferation than its predecessor. Reagan considered Carter to be too preoccupied with the problem of reprocessing and the plutonium fuel cycle. He also believed Carter had adopted moralistic positions that other nations could not be expected to follow. Carter had, of course, understood that unilateral U.S. actions on reprocessing could only have a limited effect on other countries. He had hoped, however, that reprocessing could be sharply limited, perhaps only to those countries with breeder reactors. Reagan was also aware of the dangers of reprocessing, but he felt that it could best be limited by the more ad hoc approach of limiting U.S. transfers of reprocessing technology to nations it considered trustworthy. The Reagan departure from the Carter proliferation policies marked something of a return to the policies relied on by prior administrations in which nuclear cooperation under strict safeguards was regarded as a more fruitful way of slowing proliferation than denial of nuclear technology.

HOW TO BEST REDUCE THE RISK OF PROLIFERATION?

The two basic approaches to reduce the risks of proliferation attempt to influence the means and the motivation for proliferation. Those who advocate primary attention to the means of proliferation often favor denial of sensitive technologies to other countries, arguing that safeguards can have only limited value. Those who favor relying instead on reducing a nation's motivation to proliferate argue that there is now no real technologically feasible alternative for any country that wants the bomb. Moreover, they argue that the explicit bargain of the nonproliferation treaty between weapon states and nonweapon states was that assistance in the area of peaceful nuclear energy would be provided in return for nonacquisition of weapons.

Unfortunately, the inclusion of reprocessing facilities as part of the transferred nuclear technology has, in a sense, blurred the line between civilian and military applications. Unlike the loophole in the NPT concerning peaceful nuclear explosions, reprocessing is not an area about which there is likely to be any consensus. A nation that acquires a reprocessing plant can create a sizable plutonium stockpile, leaving it days or weeks away from fabricating a nuclear arsenal. Therefore, nonweapon states can be in strict compliance with the NPT, receive all the economic benefits associated with reprocessing, and know that if the need should ever arise they could break their treaty commitment and quickly amass a nuclear arsenal. It seems unlikely that nonweapon states would willingly give up such a comfortable position.

Even the strictest safeguards mean nothing in terms of preventing a nation from carrying out the diversion of nuclear material. Safeguards can only detect and report the violation, generally some time after the act has occurred. Sanctions refer to those measures that may be taken in reprisal if a nation violates its commitments and builds nuclear weapons. Sanctions may mean as little as safeguards to the nation that wishes only to keep open the option of building nuclear weapons. A country might believe that some extreme threat to its security could require it to amass a nuclear arsenal at some future time, and it might not care greatly about sanctions under such circumstances, even in the unlikely event that sanctions were actually imposed.

Given the preceding arguments, a nation that willingly accepts strict safeguards is, therefore, not necessarily one that has no intention to forego the nuclear-weapons option under any and all circumstances. Similarly, a nation that bridles at strong safeguards may have no intention of every building nuclear weapons, but instead may resent interference with its national sovereignty. On-site inspections carried out by the IAEA may not seem like a major infringement of sovereignty, but this practice represents the first time nations have agreed, as part of a treaty provision, to allow inspections conducted by an international agency.

The significance of safeguards becomes even more questionable when we consider how they have worked in practice. Some safeguards seem to have been devised to make cheating as convenient as possible:

- The NPT specifies that all of a nation's nuclear facilities should be open to IAEA inspection. However, IAEA inspectors are not authorized to search for clandestine facilities, and they may only inspect nuclear material that a nation has "declared" to the IAEA.

- A nation must allow its nuclear facilities to be open to inspection at all times. However, IAEA inspectors must announce their visits weeks in advance—ample time for a country to get rid of all signs of bomb-making activity.

- In between infrequent inspections, compliance is verified using technical means such as cameras. According to one IAEA report, these surveillance methods are completely inadequate.[11]

Even IAEA inspectors themselves have reported that they probably would not have detected any bomb-making activity if it were being conducted. According to one IAEA inspector, Roger Richter, testifying before a congressional committee: "You try to forget that you have just been party to a very misleading process."[12]

It should not be particularly surprising that IAEA safeguards have become little more than a stamp of approval. Under the U.N. system of one man, one vote, the rules on safeguards are being decided by the recipients of nuclear technology who have every incentive to make them as loose as possible.

Some nations, cognizant of the ineffectiveness of international safeguards to prevent proliferation may feel compelled to take direct action when they feel their security is at stake. On 7 June 1981, Israel bombed an Iraqi nuclear reactor that Israel claimed was a bomb factory. The Israeli action was widely criticized in the world press, and it was noted that the IAEA had certified that the Iraqi reactor was in compliance with all safeguards. Nevertheless, based on suspicious design features and the expressed intentions of Iraqi leaders, Israeli intelligence indicated otherwise.

In light of what is now known about the enforcement of IAEA safeguards, the validity of Israeli suspicions may have been well founded. It is debatable whether these Israeli concerns justified the bombing raid. Nevertheless, it cannot be denied that this action appears to have been effective in slowing proliferation—certainly more effective than the IAEA safeguards on the Iraqi reactor. The Israeli bombing also underscored the international community's inattention to the ineffectiveness of safeguards. The Israeli act was an exercise of national self-interest, carried out in an international climate often filled with hypocrisy and pretense. A cynic might, in fact, characterize the present "nonproliferation regime" as nothing but a sham in which the nuclear-weapon states pretend that they are seriously working toward disarmament and the nonnuclear-weapon states pretend to have no interest in nuclear weapons.

The belief that a nonproliferation regime actually exists may be attributing too much significance to a marriage of convenience between the nuclear-weapon states and the nonweapon states. Events such as India's 1974 peaceful nuclear explosion, the benign world reaction to that event, and the Israeli bombing of the Iraqi reactor all remind us that the world consensus against proliferation may be, in part, wishful thinking.

All nations have a strong incentive to reduce the risk of nuclear war. No nation, however, is likely to believe that because it demonstrates the capability to detonate a nuclear device, this risk is significantly increased. While the superpowers might believe that the world is safer when only "responsible" countries possess nuclear weapons, no nation is likely to consider itself irresponsible. Most developing nations are likely to consider the superpowers to be the most irresponsible nations of all, due to their enormous arsenals and their lack of progress on disarmament as mandated by the NPT.

The preceding analysis may suggest the pessimistic view that national self-intererst will inevitably lead to the increasing spread of nuclear weapons. A less pessimistic alternative conclusion, however, is that in attempting to slow proliferation we need to appeal to national self-interest rather than to supposedly universal goals that may, in fact, not be shared. Many nations, for example, have a strong interest in maintaining an assured energy supply. They would, therefore, have disincentives to divert nuclear technology for weapons purposes if the suppliers were willing to enforce strong sanctions in case of violations. However, as we have already noted, such sanctions will mean little to countries that want the option of a nuclear-weapons capability to deal with grave threats to their security. Many nations will seek such a capability as long as an anarchic system of nation-states exists. Some nations that demonstrate a weapons capability may be satisfied with a token display of their nuclear prowess in detonating one nuclear device. Such restraint would be admirable, but it is unlikely to be the rule. It seems more likely that many will choose to follow India's example of amassing a plutonium stockpile in case it should ever be needed to fabricate weapons.

The United States, like any other nation, operates on the basis of self-interest, although sometimes it may pretend otherwise. U.S. policies advocated under the guise of morality may be seen as little more than self-righteous rhetoric by other nations, as may have been the case with the U.S. attempt to set a "good example" by foregoing reprocessing. The Reagan-administration approach of giving only "reliable" countries sensitive technology is certain to be resented by countries not considered reliable. However, such a policy may better reflect the political reality that some countries are greater risks than others, while better meeting Western security interests.

Although there are limits to what the United States can do unilaterally in slowing proliferation, efforts conducted with the aid of other nuclear suppliers may be effective, as the London meetings demonstrated. Such efforts will not be popular with recipient nations who have different self-interests than the suppliers. However, it makes little sense to paper over such differences and pretend that an international agency such as the IAEA, now dominated by the recipient nations, has the proliferation problem under control.

The problems of horizontal and vertical proliferation are probably susceptible to limited international control. In fact these two kinds of proliferation may be linked in ways we do not fully understand. For example, it is likely that horizontal proliferation has not been any worse precisely because of the great (vertical) expansion of the superpower arsenals. An idealist might attribute the connection to the realization on the part of many nations that the U.S. and Soviet arsenals are such a menace to world peace that there was no point in making a bad situation worse. A less idealistic way of explaining the inverse relationship between the two kinds of proliferation is that many nations, despairing of the superpowers' enormous lead in weaponry, believed that a small arsenal would have no strategic value and would only make them targets in any future war.

The likelihood of further horizontal and vertical proliferation appears very great. By the year 2000 it is expected that there will be enough plutonium in the spent fuel of the world's commercial reactors to produce 88,000 Nagasaki-size nuclear weapons.[13] A non-negligible fraction of this total will be in some of the twenty-four near-nuclear countries that have reprocessing plants to extract this plutonium. No one can say whether the international system can evolve in time to allow large numbers of nuclear-armed states to resolve their conflicts without war. Efforts to slow proliferation cannot keep nuclear weapons out of the hands of nations that want them; such efforts can only buy time. That should not be a cause for pessimism, however, since if the world has enough time, the nations of the world may yet learn to live with one another.

A rapprochement between the rich industrialized nations and those of the Third World will probably be extremely difficult, but it is essential for long-term stability. Over the shorter term, the most vital need is for an accommodation between the United States and the Soviet Union that does not require either nation to give up its own way of life. The Soviet Union is a great and powerful country about which most Americans know virtually nothing. The Soviet system has many positive features as well as a sinister side—often the only side some Americans hear about. Education and cultural exchanges, bilateral trade, increased coverage of Soviet society by the media, and people-to-people contacts are all ways that the two nations can build better relations. At one time this process was referred to as détente or peaceful coexistence. These phrases in some eyes now have a negative connotation, since many Americans have become concerned that détente was really used as a cover for a massive Soviet military buildup. During the period of détente many Americans felt that matching increases in military strength were either unnecessary or harmful to good U.S.-Soviet relations. Poor relations between the superpowers, however, are not caused by their nuclear arsenals. Rather, each feels a need for its arsenal because of the suspicion and hostility it has toward the other. These negative feelings can be dissipated over time if we establish a new kind of relationship with the Soviet Union that might be called hard-headed détente. Reducing or eliminating nuclear weapons is neither a necessary nor sufficient condition to establish better relations and to reduce the risk of war.

STUDY QUESTIONS

1. Do you believe the potential for further weapons proliferation is increasing? Why?

2. Which do you consider the more serious threat—nuclear terrorism or nuclear proliferation? Why?

3. Do you believe the nuclear-power–nuclear-weapons connection is tenuous or dangerous? Why?

4. Why are enrichment and reprocessing especially "sensitive" technologies?

5. What are the advantages and disadvantages of the breeder reactor?

6. How valid is the argument that nations may find it convenient to conduct a secret nuclear-weapons program under the guise of a commercial-power program?

7. Why did Eisenhower launch his Atoms-for-Peace Plan in 1953?

8. What was the basic bargain in the Non-Proliferation Treaty of 1968?

9. Why did India detonate its "peaceful" nuclear explosion in 1974? Why did the world express so little condemnation?

10. What factors other than India's PNE increased many nations' concern that the "nonproliferation regime" was weakening in the 1970s?

11. How did the Carter-administration approach to proliferation differ from that of its predecessors? How about the Reagan-administration approach?

12. How well have international (IAEA) safeguards worked in practice? Why can safeguards and sanctions have only limited value even if they work perfectly?

13. What is the best course of action to minimize the extent of further proliferation?

14. How great a connection exists between the extent of proliferation and the risks of nuclear war? How greatly does that connection depend on the rate of proliferation? Do you consider a domino theory of proliferation to be valid?

Appendix A _____

THE PHYSICAL PRINCIPLES OF NUCLEAR ENERGY AND RADIATION _____

WHAT IS NUCLEAR ENERGY?

Before this century mankind had no awareness of the enormous power contained in the atom. How did this awesome amount of power get there in the first place, and why did humanity take so long to learn of its existence let alone the secret of how to unleash it?

In the strict sense, we have been unleashing the power of the atom even since the discovery of fire. The chemical reactions that take place during combustion result in the shifting of the configuration of atoms as they combine to form various molecules. When changes of atomic structure occur, the internal energy content of the atoms is reduced and an exactly equal amount of energy is said to be "liberated" in the form of heat and light. This example is one of the most basic principles of physics—the law of conservation of energy, according to which energy cannot be created nor destroyed, but only converted from one form to another. If the atoms in a lump of coal or other type of fuel possess excess stored energy that can be liberated during combustion, that internal energy often has resulted from some past energy-conversion process. In the case of fossil fuels, the energy of sunlight and the heat and pressures under the earth cause chemical changes in buried decaying organic matter; this process converts the matter into energy-rich coal, oil, and gas over periods of millions of years. This same kind of energy storage occurs on a much shorter time scale in the case of renewable fuel such as wood. In this case, the energy of sunlight is converted via photosynthesis into stored chemical energy that can be liberated during combustion.

Although ordinary energy-liberating chemical reactions, including combustion, are in the strict sense releases of "atomic energy," the common usage of this term refers to a different kind of reaction, i.e., one involving the very small nucleus of the atom. For such reactions the term nuclear energy is preferable to atomic energy. Many people think of the atom as kind of a miniature solar system with electrons in orbit around the nucleus corresponding to the planets orbiting the sun. Like the sun in the solar system, it is the central nucleus that contains the great bulk of the mass of the atom— an astonishing 99.95 percent—even though the diameter of the nucleus is only 1/100,000 of the atom. This in effect means that most of the atom and indeed most of ordinary matter is actually empty space. Unlike the solar system, the electrons in orbit about the nucleus are bound to it through an electrostatic force instead of the gravitational force that keeps the planets in orbit about the sun. While the gravitational force always causes matter to be attracted to other matter, the electrostatic force can give rise to either attraction or repulsion. Thus, it is due to the opposite-sign of the electric charges (negative for the electron and positive for the nucleus) that electrons are attracted to the nucleus. Two charges of the same sign, say two electrons, would repel rather than attract one another electrically.

Although the miniature-solar-system model of the atom may form an attractive mental picture, it fails miserably when we attempt to use it to explain many of the known facts about atoms and their interactions. Without going into the more current view of the atom as it is described by quantum mechanics, we may simply imagine that when a chemical reaction such as combustion takes place, two or more atoms combine and their electron orbits are rearranged. If the electrons jump to lower energy orbits, then we would find that energy has been liberated by whatever amount the atoms' energy has been reduced. Similarly, if the internal atomic changes result in a state of higher energy, then we would find that outside energy has been consumed. Some energy-liberating reactions can take place spontaneously, but energy-consuming reactions cannot take place unless energy is supplied in the form of light, heat, or some other kind of energy.

All ordinary chemical and physical processes only involve changes in the electron orbits of the atom, not in its nuclear structure. The incredibly tiny dense speck of matter that we call the atomic nucleus is totally unaffected by the puny energies involved in ordinary chemical reactions. In order to make things happen inside the atomic nucleus, it is necessary to subject matter to extraordinarily high temperatures in excess of several millions of degrees. It is only at such temperatures that nuclei will collide with enough energy to overcome their mutual repulsion and make contact. Mankind was unaware of the existence of the atomic nucleus and nuclear reactions because until this century such temperatures (or such energetic atomic collisions) only occurred on a large scale inside the sun and other stars.

Most of the atoms of which our world and solar system are made were once part of some now defunct star which was initially mostly hydrogen. The light elements, starting with hydrogen, were cooked up in that star's interior during the energy-liberating reactions that fueled the star. The heavy elements (heavier than iron) could only be created during the energy-consuming reactions that occurred when our sun's ancestor ended its days in a blaze of glory that we call a supernova. The abundance of our solar system's heavy elements, which could not have been produced during the time of our sun's existence, is the reason we know that our sun cannot be a "first-generation" star, but rather was formed from the debris of some other star.

The supernova explosion from that star must have taken place over 4.5 billions of years ago, since that is the known age of the earth and solar system. Following that cataclysmic explosion, the residual dust and gases coalesced due to their mutual gravitional attraction to form the sun and solar system; in much the same manner this process is going on in the other regions of the galaxy today.

WHAT IS RADIOACTIVITY?

Of the atoms cooked up inside our sun's parent, some had nuclei that were stable, others had nuclei that were unstable. The atoms possessing unstable nuclei are responsible for the phenomenon known as radioactivity which consists of an emission of high-energy particles or electromagnetic radiation that we call gamma rays. Gamma rays are similar in many respects to the form of electromagnetic radiation we refer to as light. An atom can emit light when its electronic structure changes, but it emits a gamma ray only when its nuclear structure changes. Changes in the structure of the nucleus involve much greater energies than changes in the electronic structure of the atom. Therefore, the gamma rays liberated during changes in nuclear structure have a much higher energy than light and have a much greater penetrating power.

Many other forms of electromagnetic radiation besides light and gamma rays are known to exist, including radio waves, microwaves, ultraviolet radiation (UV), and X rays. All of these forms are referred to as electromagnetic radiation and all are present in nature, but the term radiation, or the more technically correct term "ionizing radiation," refers to that kind of radiation capable of causing biological damage by virtue of its very high energy. When ionizing radiation such as a gamma ray passes through matter it knocks electrons out of the atoms, a process referred to as ionization. Other non-ionizing forms of electromagnetic radiation such as microwaves, ultraviolet radiation, or even light can also be biologically harmful if the exposure is sufficiently intense. It is, however, important to keep in mind the distinction between the intensity of a radiation exposure (the number of particles or rays that would strike a unit area per unit time) and the energy of individual particles or "rays." Obviously, a very intense hail of marshmallows would have a very different effect on someone than a low-intensity exposure to a single very-high-energy rifle bullet.

In addition to electromagnetic radiation in the form of gamma rays, unstable atomic nuclei may also emit various types of particles such as alpha particles, beta particles, neutrons, and neutrinos. All of these particles (except neutrinos) are, like gamma rays and X rays, capable of creating a trail of ionization when passing through matter and, therefore, carry the potential for causing more biological damage than non-ionizing radiation. One important characteristic for assessing the potential for biological damage is the penetrating power of the particular form of radiation. Although alpha particles (identical to the nucleus of the atom helium) cause a great deal of ionization, they usually have little penetrating power unless their initial energy is very high. This is because they lose energy very rapidly in passing through solid matter, or even air. Beta particles (identical to the electron or its "antiparticle," the positron), also normally have little penetrating power, though somewhat more than alpha particles of the same energy.

During external radiation exposure, the most biologically damaging of the kinds of ionizing radiation so far considered are X rays, gamma rays, and particularly neutrons. Strictly speaking it is not the penetrating power of ionizing radiation that is responsible for its biological and physical damage, but rather the extent of the ionization trail it leaves, and whether that ionization trail is confined to the outer layers of skin (alpha and beta particles) or is deposited in the interior of the body (gamma rays, X rays, and neutrons). Radioactive alpha and beta emitters can, of course, be very harmful if taken internally.

The most penetrating form of radiation known, the neutrino, is capable of passing through a thickness of lead measured in light years, and yet it causes virtually no ionization and so is totally harmless. Even though there are at this very moment millions of neutrinos from the sun passing through each person's body and the entire earth, almost none of them will interact with atoms of the body (and the earth) and leave an ionization trail. The transparency of virtually everything to neutrinos has nothing to do with their size, but rather with the fact that they are only capable of reacting with other particles through a very weak force known simply as the "weak force."

HOW CAN PROTECTION AGAINST RADIATION BE ACHIEVED?

One way to protect yourself against harmful ionizing radiation is to place a sufficient thickness of material between the source of radiation and yourself to absorb a certain fraction of the particles or rays. Nature fortunately has provided us with just such a protective blanket in the earth's atmosphere, which absorbs a large fraction of the incoming particle radiation known as cosmic rays. Cosmic rays continually bombard the earth from all directions in space, but their origin is unknown. The extent of the reduction in cosmic-ray radiation intensity obviously depends on the thickness of the absorbing atmospheric layer, which is why people living at higher altitudes such as Denver, Colorado are subject to significantly higher background-radiation exposures than people living at sea level, perhaps even two to three times higher.

An absorbing layer of material is sometimes used in providing protection against man-made radioactivity, such as the use of a lead-lined apron worn by x-ray technicians. The thickness of the absorbing layer needed to reduce the radiation intensity to a safe level depends on a number of factors including:

1. The particular kind of radiation (neutrons being particularly harmful)

2. The radiation intensity and the exposure time

3. The energy of the radiation

4. The density of the absorbing material (high density such as lead is most effective in the case of anything but neutrons)

5. The particular areas of the body one is attempting to protect (reproductive organs, for example are particularly sensitive)

6. The level of radiation intensity considered "safe"

There are some who might take the point of view that no level of radiation may be considered "safe." However, the question of the extent of biological harm resulting from radiation exposure will be taken up at greater length elsewhere.

A second rather obvious way to protect yourself from radiation is to put some distance between you and the radioactive source. This, of course, is not possible in the case of the omnipresent cosmic rays, but it is quite effective in the case of a localized source of radiation such as a small commercial radioactive source. If the size of the source is small compared to your distance from it, then the intensity varies inversely in proportion to the square of the distance from the source. For example, if you double your distance you reduce the intensity of your exposure by $(1/2)^2 = 1/4$; if you triple your distance you reduce it by $(1/3)^2 = 1/9$, etc. This simple inverse-square rule only applies in the case of a point source. In the case of a nuclear explosion, each radioactive dust particle in the bomb's fallout acts as a separate point source.

A third manner in which the biologically harmful effects of radiation can in some cases be mitigated is through the passage of time. When a particular unstable (radioactive) nucleus emits a particle, it has transformed itself into a different nuclear species that may be either stable or unstable depending on the identity of the original nucleus. For simplicity, let us first consider the case in which the resulting nucleus, the so-called daughter, is stable or nonradioactive. In this case, a radioactive sample of material loses its radio-activity over time as more and more unstable nuclei emit radiation or "decay." The reason radioactivity is lost is that the strength of the radioactive source (its "hotness") depends on the number of unstable nuclei that emit radiation per second, and this number decreases with time as the number of undecayed nuclei declines. Which particular unstable nuclei in the sample will decay in any given time interval cannot be predicted based on any measurements made prior to the decay. However, the number of nuclei in the sample which decay in a given time interval follows a simple math-ematical law that states that the number of decays, per unit time, and hence the radiation intensity at a given distance from the source, is proportional to the number of unstable nuclei present.

While different radioactive species, known as nuclides or iso-topes,* lose their radioactivity at different rates, each isotope may be characterized by a particular time known as its half-life. For a nuclide that decays into a stable daughter, half the radioactive nuclei will decay and thereby become nonradioactive during a time equal to one half-life (by definition of the half-life). Similarly, the intensity of radiation also drops in half during that time. After a second half-life elapses the radiation intensity would again be halved. Thus, after a time equal to N half-lives the fraction of the original radiation intensity is equal to $\frac{1}{2}$ raised to the Nth power.

Different radioactive isotopes may have vastly different half-lives ranging from less than a billionth of a second to more than a billion years. The shortness of the half-life is a measure of the degree of instability of that particular isotope. Thus, completely stable nuclei would have an infinite half-life and never decay. Among the atoms of which our world is made, only those radioactive isotopes cooked up in a star billions of years ago, which have very long half-lives (comparable to billions of years), would have survived in appreciable amounts to the present day. Thus, for example, uranium 238 with a half-life of 4.5 billion years is found to exist in nature, but strontium 90 with a half-life of twenty-eight years is not found to exist in nature in detectible amounts. If there are radioactive isotopes with half-lives much longer than the age of our solar system, it is possible

---

* (Technically a nuclide is *any* atomic nucleus specified by its atomic number, atomic mass, and energy state, whereas an isotope refers to one of two or more atoms, the nuclei of which have the same number of protons or same atomic number, but a different number of neutrons or different atomic weights.)

that their radioactivity might go unnoticed and that they would be considered stable isotopes.

The point just made about the nonexistence in nature of short-lived radioactive isotopes only applies to the case of a radioactive isotope decaying into a nonradioactive daughter. Thus, some short half-lived radioactive isotopes actually do occur in nature if they are the daughters (or granddaughters) of other long-lived isotopes. Another way that such short-lived radioactive isotopes are found in nature is if they are made radioactive through a nuclear reaction induced by one of the high-energy cosmic ray particles. For example, this is the origin of the carbon 14 isotope used in radioactive carbon dating. Apart from the two natural mechanisms just discussed, short half-lived isotopes can also be created artificially by various means such as exposing a nonradioactive sample to the particle beam of a nuclear reactor or a particle accelerator, i.e., "irradiating the material," or alternatively, creating a nuclear explosion.

Regrettably, the opposite process of exposing a radioactive sample to the beam of a nuclear reactor to make it nonradioactive is probably not possible because in a radioactive sample of material only a fraction of the atomic nuclei (usually a very tiny fraction) are unstable or radioactive. The particular nuclei that are radioactive are randomly located through the material, and there is no way of aiming a beam of particles precisely enough to hit those particular nuclei without also hitting the other more numerous nonradioactive nuclei, thus possibly making them radioactive as well. Moreover, this problem does not appear to be one that can conceivably be overcome using some clever technology.

Whether or not something is made radioactive by being exposed to radiation depends entirely on the kind of radiation and its energy. High doses of certain kinds of radiation have been used to kill bacteria in food without causing the slightest harm to the food. It is important to understand that being exposed to radiation is not the same as becoming "contaminated," which means that some of the radioactive particles either get on one's skin and clothing or become ingested, a potentially serious problem, depending on the radiation intensity and half-life. The process of decontamination involves the removal of radioactive particles on the skin by washing with water. There is no antidote for ingested radioactive isotopes, but in the case of I^{131} a medicine can be taken that prevents absorption by the thyroid gland. The harm done by ingested radioactivity depends on the amount of ingested, the half-life, the type of radiation, and how long the material remains in the body, i.e., the biological half-life.

WHERE DOES THE ENERGY LIBERATED IN NUCLEAR REACTIONS COME FROM?

The vast amount of energy liberated in nuclear reactions results from the conversion of mass into energy. This process is based on Albert Einstein's famous relation $E = mc^2$ which gives the energy equivalent (E) of an amount of mass (m), with c^2 being a numerical conversion factor equal to the square of the speed of light. However, it is not just nuclear reactions, but all energy-liberating reactions, including chemical combustion, in which the energy released results from the conversion of mass into energy. Similarly, all energy-consuming reactions involve the conversion of energy into mass. The fact that mass-energy conversion is readily noticeable only for nuclear reactions and not for other reactions is due to the huge size of the number c^2 which requires that only an enormous amount of energy liberation (or consumption) will result in an observable change in mass: $m = E/c^2$. Thus, until this century scientists falsely believed in a law of conservation of mass in all reactions. However, if you were able to measure mass with sufficient accuracy, you would find that the mass of a piece of coal prior to burning plus the mass of oxygen consumed in burning actually exceeds that of the ashes and exhaust gases by the very tiny amount: E/c^2, where E is the liberated energy of combustion.

Those nuclear reactions in which one nucleus splits apart into several smaller nuclei are known as fission reactions, while reactions in which several smaller nuclei join together are known as fusion reactions. It has been found that the fission of very heavy nuclei and the fusion of very light nuclei are both energy-liberating reactions. Conversely, the fusion of heavy nuclei and the fission of light nuclei are both energy-consuming reactions. These facts can be understood in terms of the relation $E = mc^2$ since the products of the reaction are found to have less mass than the initial reactants when energy is released, and the products have more mass than the reactants when energy is consumed. However, this explanation needs to be carried a step further if we are to understand why mass is lost when heavy nuclei fission or light nuclei fuse. This in turn requires an understanding of the force that holds the nuclear constituents, the protons and neutrons, together.

WHAT IS THE STRUCTURE OF THE ATOMIC NUCLEUS?

All nuclei may be characterized by the number of neutrons *(N)* and protons *(Z)* they contain. Neutrons and protons are collectively referred to as nucleons. The number of protons *(Z)* and nucleons *(N + Z)* a nucleus contains are referred to as its atomic number and atomic weight, respectively. The number of protons (atomic number) determines the positive charge of the nucleus, or, for a neutral atom, the number of electrons surrounding the nucleus, and hence the chemical identity of the element. Two atoms having the same atomic number but different atomic weights will be chemically identical since they will have the same electronic structure. However, such a pair of atoms will have drastically different nuclear properties, with one possibly being stable and the other radioactive.

Stable nuclei, if they are not too large (less than about 40 neutrons plus protons), tend to have roughly equal numbers of neutrons and protons, and they tend to have more neutrons than protons if they are somewhat heavier. For example, the helium nucleus has two protons and two neutrons, while the most common isotope of uranium has 92 protons and 146 neutrons. These two nuclei would be symbolically identified as $^4_2$He and $^{238}_{92}$U, where the lower number is the number of protons (the atomic number), and the upper number the total of neutrons plus protons (the atomic weight). The presence of two or more protons in a nucleus means that these positively charged particles must mutually repel one another owing to the electrostatic force between them. The fact that the particles of a stable nucleus do not fly apart further implies that there must be another stronger attractive force between the nuclear constituents that overcomes the electrostatic repulsion. This is the so-called strong force which, together with the three forces previously mentioned (electromagnetic, gravitational, and "weak"), constitute the four fundamental forces in nature. They are fundamental in the sense that all specific forces, for example, the force of friction, the chemical bond, the contact force of one body against another, are examples of one of the four (electromagnetism in this instance).

The strong force, also known as the nuclear force, is such a short-range force that it only acts between neutrons and protons that are nearest neighbors inside the nucleus. We may think of the nucleus as a collection of neutrons and protons in contact and having some overall shape, perhaps that of a sphere. Those nucleons on the surface of the nucleus clearly have fewer nearest neighbors than those inside, and they are therefore less strongly bound than those inside. A medium-size nucleus has a smaller proportion of its nucleons on the surface than a small one, and therefore the nucleons of a medium-sized nucleus are more strongly bound on the average. We can make this more quantitative using the binding energy E_b, which is defined as the energy required to pull a nucleon free from its nucleus.

The mass of a nucleus is not the same as the sum of the masses of its constituent nucleons, but it is less by an amount related to the binding energy. We may define the average mass of a nucleon bound in a nucleus as equal to the nuclear mass divided by the number of nucleons. It then follows from Einstein's relation, $E = mc^2$, that the mass of a nucleon in a nucleus is less than that of a free nucleon by E_b/c^2, where E_b is the energy needed to free the nucleon. The nucleons in a heavy nucleus are ligther than those in very light nucleus because they are more strongly bound. As a result, mass is lost when two light nuclei fuse, and energy is therefore liberated.

UNDER WHAT CONDITIONS DO NUCLEAR FUSION AND FISSION OCCUR?

Fusion is referred to as a *thermo*nuclear process since the nuclear reaction will not take place in a lump of matter unless the matter is first heated to temperatures exceeding tens of millions of degrees. At lower temperatures the electrostatic repulsion between colliding, positively charged nuclei keeps them too far apart to feel the short-range nuclear attractive force. Thus, the "kindling temperature" of nuclear fuel is very much higher than for ordinary chemical combustion. In the hydrogen bomb these temperatures are achieved by initially detonating a fission bomb—the "match" that initiates the fusion reaction.

From the discussion so far it might be falsely concluded that the fusion reaction is always an energy-liberating process independent of nuclear size. However, that would ignore the role of the electrostatic repulsive force between protons that acts to reduce the average binding energy of nucleons inside the nucleus. In small nuclei the repulsive electrostatic forces between protons is overwhelmed by the much stronger attractive nuclear force. In very large nuclei, however, the electrostatic repulsion between protons becomes increasingly important. Unlike the short-range attractive nuclear force that only acts between nearest neighbors, the long range electrostatic force causes each proton to repel every other proton in the nucleus. As a result, nucleons in a very heavy nucleus tend to be less strongly bound than those in a moderate-size nucleus. The constituent nucleons in a very heavy nucleus therefore also have a larger mass than those in a more moderate-size nucleus based on the relationship between mass and binding energy. When a very heavy nucleus undergoes fission, the process is, therefore, one in which constituent nucleons have a decrease in their mass and a concurrent liberation of energy in accordance with Einstein's relation.

In speaking of the enormous energy liberated in fusing of two light nuclei or in fission of heavy nuclei, we are comparing these quantities of energy to the quantities liberated in a typical chemical reaction between two atoms such as in the process $C + O_2$ becoming CO_2, which could occur when coal is burned. Nuclear processes typically liberate around a million times more energy per atom than do chemical ones. However, the actual amount of energy involved in nuclear reactions is not large compared to everyday energy quantities unless a very large number of nuclei undergo such reactions.

UNDER WHAT CONDITIONS DOES A CHAIN REACTION OCCUR?

Uranium and plutonium are two elements that have particular isotopes capable of undergoing fission and producing a so-called chain reaction. In nature, the fissionable isotopes usually have a very small abundance, and they are thoroughly mixed in with other chemically identical isotopes. In order to produce bomb material, the fraction of the fissionable isotope must be enriched using one of a number of very difficult and expensive enrichment methods.

Suppose we consider the case of a piece of uranium enriched in its content of the relatively rare isotope $^{235}_{92}U$. Individual $^{235}_{92}U$ nuclei will undergo spontaneous fission on a random basis. In such a spontaneous fission, an average of around two neutrons are emitted, along with a significant amount of energy. If a neutron from one such fission is absorbed by another $^{235}_{92}U$ nucleus in the piece, it creates the nucleus $^{236}_{92}U$ which is highly unstable and promptly undergoes a "second-generation" fission. This nucleus then emits still more neutrons which promptly induce third-generation fissions, and so on. The key to such a chain reaction is to have a large enough lump of matter, i.e. in excess of the so-called critical mass, so that enough neutrons will induce fissions each generation rather than escape through the surface of the lump and the number of fissions each generation will multiply. In this case the number of fissions increases in each generation, resulting in an exceedingly rapid buildup of energy release.

Thus, in much the same way that a population explosion can result if each generation gives birth to an average of more than two children who survive to bring more children into the world, so also a nuclear explosion can result if each fission generation gives birth to an average of more than one neutron that survives to induce other fissions (rather than escape through the surface). The critical number of neutrons for a chain reaction is one since only one neutron from a parent nucleus is needed to produce one other fission reaction. In the case of ^{235}U, on the average of 2.5 neutrons are actually produced in each fission. Suppose that in each generation an average of 0.5 neutrons are lost and don't react to cause the next generation of nuclei to fission. This occurrence would result in a doubling of the number of fissions each generation (which lasts roughly 10^{-8} seconds) . Starting from one spontaneous fission it would take only 58 generations (58 doublings), or a time of 0.58 millionths of a second, to produce enough fission energy equivalent to 100,000 tons or 100 kilotons of TNT.

The chain reaction in a nuclear weapon accounts for the explosive character of the energy release. In a nuclear reactor, where a chain reaction also occurs, there is no such explosion. What accounts for the difference? The nuclear reactor, under normal operation, is kept just at the critical point where there is enough production of neutrons to sustain the chain reaction. A reactor can be kept at the critical point using so-called control rods that are inserted just far enough into the reactor core to absorb enough neutrons to accomplish this process. Inserting the neutron-absorbing control rods further into the core tends to damp out the reaction, making the reactor "subcritical," while removing the control rods beyond the critical point would cause a rapid increase in the reaction rate.

The heat from the fission reaction is normally carried away by the surrounding water that cools the reactor core. If for some reason water fails to cover the hot reactor core, a meltdown may occur, in which the fuel elements melt. A meltdown could result in a large pool of molten fuel at the bottom of the reactor vessel which could possibly exceed the critical mass, thereby causing a chain reaction. However, in this case the resulting explosion would be a thermal, not a nuclear, explosion. The fissionable material would be blown apart by the thermal pressure long before the chain reaction could proceed for enough generations for a nuclear explosion to occur. The worst conceivable reactor accident would involve a core melt-down followed by a rupture of the containment vessel, and the consequent release of radioactive gases into the environment on a large scale. As disastrous as such a worst-case accident might be, studies show that it would release far less radioactivity into the environment than would one average-size ground-burst nuclear weapon.

Why is a nuclear reactor incapable of a nuclear explosion, and what must be done to create one? The reason a nuclear explosion cannot occur in the case of a core meltdown in a reactor is that shortly after the chain reaction begins, so much heat is generated that the material blows itself apart before a very large number of generations can proceed. Because of the exponential growth in the previously considered example, 50 percent of the energy is released in the very last of the 58 generations and 99.9 percent of the energy in the last 7 of the 58 generations. Thus stopping the reaction at the end of 51 generations instead of 58 would produce 0.1 percent as much energy.

It is only in a nuclear bomb, which is deliberately designed to keep the fissionable material together long enough for enough gen-erations, that a nuclear explosion can be achieved. The assemblage of the fissionable material into a critical mass is usually achieved through a very carefully timed implosion in which conventional explosives cause an arrangement of spherically symmetric pieces of material to converge and be compressed. An alternative method, used in the bomb dropped on Nagasaki, employed a gun-type device in which one subcritical hemisphere is fired at high speed toward another to form a sphere in excess of the critical mass.

Why is the fusion (hydrogen) bomb so much more powerful than the fission (atomic) bomb? There are two important reasons. In the case of fission, there is a limit to how much fissionable material one can assemble in one place (the critical mass) before it blows itself apart; in the case of fusion there is no limit because, unlike fission, fusion is not a self-initiating process. In addition, the detailed way in which binding energy per nucleon varies with atomic weight results in a bigger mass loss per nucleon when light nuclei fuse than when heavy nuclei fission. Pound for pound the fusion bomb is much more powerful than the fission bomb.

Mastering the technical details of bomb building was an immense challenge to the scientists involved in the construction of the first atomic bomb during World War II. Nowadays, enough has been published in the open literature to make the design of a low-yield fission bomb a moderately interesting challenge to a bright undergraduate who has taken some physics courses. Fortunately there are more serious obstacles to the construction of a nuclear bomb than being able to design one. One such obstacle would be the need to obtain enough weapons-grade plutonium or uranium to implement the design.

The thermonuclear fusion bomb (or hydrogen bomb) is significantly more difficult to design or construct than the fission bomb. We will not address here the question of whether secrets still remain in the construction of such devices. The fact that these weapons exist has removed the most important uncertainty of all facing a prospective bomb builder, i.e., whether it is possible to make one. Once that is known, given the incentive to make such a bomb, the necessary financial resources, and a certain level of technology, it is not a question of whether a nation can make one, but only how long a time would be needed. However, our aim here has not been to discuss the technical complexities facing the bomb builder, but rather to look at the basic physical principles of nuclear energy, nuclear weapons, and nuclear radiation.

HOW IS RADIATION MEASURED?

The subject of radiation units can prove extremely confusing to the uninitiated. Here we define a few of the commonly used terms.

Curie. A curie is a measure of the strength or activity of a radioactive source corresponding to 37 billion disintegrations per second. After a time equal to one half-life, a one-curie source would have an activity of 0.5 curies.

Roentgen. When ionizing radiation passes through matter, the amount of ionization left in its wake serves as a way to measure the amount of radiation. A roentgen is the amount of radiation it takes to create one esu of elective charge per cubic centimeter of dry air.

Rad. A rad is a unit of radiation dose equal to the absorption of one hundred ergs of energy. An exposure to one roentgen would result in a dose of one rad.

Rem. Different forms of radiation cause different degrees of damage when humans are exposed to them. Thus, for example a one-rad exposure to neutrons may be ten times more harmful than a one-rad exposure to gamma rays. The rem unit incorporates such numerical factors so that a one-rem exposure to any form of radiation causes the same degree of damage, by definition. For gamma rays: 1 rem = 1 rad.

Rems/hour. In evaluating radiation exposure we need to be primarily concerned with the total dose received (in rems) over some period of time. The dose rate (in rems/hour) may also be of importance for prolonged exposures. For the case of a constant radiation intensity, total dose = dose rate × time.

If the radiation intensity varies in time, computation of the total dose from the dose rate becomes more difficult. Different types of radiation meters exist to measure either total dose or dose rate.

STUDY QUESTIONS

1. Why does the presence of heavy elements mean that our sun is not a "first-generation" star?

2. Why are very high temperatures needed to initiate nuclear reactions?

3. How do you distinguish between the intensity of a beam of particles and their energy?

4. Why does the extremely penetrating neutrino cause no biological damage?

5. In what three ways can one get protection against radiation?

6. Under what conditions can very short-lived radioactive isotopes be found in nature?

7. Exactly what does the equation $E = mc^2$ mean?

8. Under what conditions is fusion an energy-liberating reaction? How about fission?

9. How does the nuclear force differ from the electrostatic force?

10. Why do light nuclei liberate energy when fusing?

11. Why do heavy nuclei liberate energy when undergoing fission?

12. Why is a critical mass necessary for a chain reaction?

13. Why can't a nuclear reactor explode like a nuclear bomb?

14. Why is no critical mass necessary for a fusion reaction?

Appendix B _____

SURVIVAL AFTER
NUCLEAR WAR _____

1. *Decide if you really want to survive a nuclear war.* There may
be considerable truth to the notion that the survivors of a nuclear
war would envy the dead. Nevertheless, the ghastliness of life after
nuclear war might well depend on many unknowns, including your
distance to the detonations and what preparations you have made.

2. *Move away from potential targets.* Moving away from potential targets may not be practical for some Americans whose employment restricts their place of residence. However, in many cases
living thirty miles from a city and commuting to work is no less
feasible than living in the city. Cities, of course, are just one type
of potential target. Other probable targets include airports with run-
ways longer than 7000 feet, military bases, communication centers,
major industrial sites, oil refineries, power plants, and suburban
population concentrations. Ideally, you should try to live at least
forty miles from a highest risk area such as the center of a major
city and at least twenty miles from an average city or other potential
target. The Federal Emergency Management Agency publishes maps
showing suspected high risk areas in each state.

3. *Learn the types of warnings of an impending attack.* Most
Americans expect a nuclear attack to be a bolt out of the blue.
However, it is not unlikely that we would have "strategic warning"
of an attack some days in advance based on the international
situation. Strategic warning might include, for example, the outbreak

363

of a large-scale conventional war in Europe, a confrontation with the Soviet Union in the Persian Gulf, or another Cuban missile crisis. Should such a crisis occur, there will be a great temptation to refuse to believe that it will actually lead to a holocaust. The few days of warning time such a crisis could give might make the difference in your survival if the warning is heeded.

"Tactical warning" of an attack would be based on information from satellites or other sources that an attack on the United States is underway. In the missile age with Soviet ICBMs capable of reaching the United States, a thirty-minute tactical warning may not be feasible, considering the amount of time needed to detect the attack, transmit the information to government leaders, evaluate the information, and transmit the warnings to all communities. The third type of warning would be furnished by the attack itself which would probably occur in several stages. Probably the first missiles to arrive would be submarine-launched missiles whose flight times are only seven to fifteen minutes. These missiles would be targeted mainly at bomber bases and military command, control, and communication facilities in order to minimize any U.S. retaliation. These first explosions, probably occurring fifteen to twenty minutes before the ICBMs arrive, would be visible all over the United States, but they would not kill or injure a large fraction of the population. These explosions could be a life-saving "take-cover" warning to millions of Americans outside highest risk areas if they are properly informed.

4. *Decide whether or not to evacuate.* The three main questions concerning evacuation are when, whether, and where. The "when" has already been addressed. You should evacuate when you decide that you have evidence of a strategic warning. Obviously if you wait until an evacuation is ordered, the chaos and confusion may considerably reduce the probability of your reaching your destination. Moreover, an attack could occur before any evacuation order is issued. The decision whether to evacuate rather than try to build a shelter depends on many factors. For example, factors favorable to a decision to evacuate include:

- Living in a high-risk area

- Having a car, enough gasoline, and open roads to a lower-risk area

- Being in fairly good health or evacuating with someone who can look after you

- Having a planned destination

- Not having employment of the kind that would be vitally needed by your community

- Having tools to build or improve a fallout shelter as well as other supplies—especially food, water containers, clothing, etc.—needed for life in the area to which you would go

If you should evacuate before any warning, it might be best to leave the country or visit with relatives or friends in a low-risk area. If you wish to evacuate, a checklist of items to take is quite important. Some of the items you would need, particularly a fallout meter, are not owned by many Americans, although such a meter can be purchased for as little as one hundred dollars.

5. *Know how to improvise a fallout shelter.* In a low-risk area it may be sufficient to simply upgrade your below-ground basement by piling dirt up around the foundation, and even that might not be necessary. In an area in which very heavy fallout is expected or if you don't have a basement, it would be necessary to build an expedient shelter. This involves a lot more than digging a hole, but it can be done in forty-eight hours, given tools, detailed instructions, enough motivation, and some able-bodied workers. However, survival in a shelter will depend on your attention to a large number of very important details including ventilation, water, food, sanitation, radiation monitoring, etc. all of which are discussed at length in Cresson Kearny's *Nuclear War Survival Skills.*

It is possible that upgrading an existing home basement into a shelter may be far preferable to digging an expedient fallout shelter. In fact, the extra protection offered by a fallout shelter with a protection factor of 1000 over a basement with a typical protection factor of 20 may mean very little if you are able to stay sheltered much longer in the basement, given better ventilation, available water (in your hot-water-heater tank), and enough space to better manage sanitation and avoid claustrophobia. Moreover, without the need to dig a shelter, your time following a strategic warning of an attack could be much better spent in trying to obtain food supplies, building a radiation meter, etc. However, there are two important contingencies that could make the construction of an expedient shelter a good insurance policy: *(a)* to guard against the possibility of very high fallout levels, and *(b)* to guard against the possibility of your house being destroyed by blast or fire.

6. *Keep a number of items around the house.* Whether you plan to evacuate or improvise shelter you should keep the following around the house:

- Plans, tools, and materials needed to build a shelter
- Shelter-ventilating pump or plans to make one
- Fallout meter or plans to make one
- At least a two-week supply of food
- First-aid kit, antibiotic ointment, and pain-killing medication
- Flashlight with extra batteries
- A few large batteries
- Portable radio with extra batteries and a metal box or aluminum foil to protect it from EMP
- Other items on the evacuation checklist (see Kearny's book)

7. *Acquire long-term survival skills.* If you should survive all the horror of a nuclear war and its aftermath including famine, disease, assault by other survivors, etc., you would be living in a world in which very different skills are needed for survival than our present civilization. Your long-term chances of survival would be much greater if you have some knowledge of such things as first aid, medical self-help, self-defense, sewing, home construction, car repair, and low-technology agriculture.

8. *Know what to expect.* Those who survive may undergo the most terrifying experience imaginable. Fear can be a life-saving emotion and increase our ability to accomplish things. Extreme terror, however, can lead to irrationality and can paralyze our ability to act. The more you know about what a nuclear attack would be like, the less likely you would be paralyzed by terror. Moreover, the more you know what a nuclear war would be like, the more determined you will become to see that one does not come about—by whatever means that you believe that such a goal can best be accomplished.

NOTES

Chapter 2

1. It happens that those with their fingers on the red button in the United States and the Soviet Union currently are all male. Readers may have differing opinions as to whether the risks of nuclear war would be lessened if this were not the case.
2. Soviet and American citizens may be equally mystified about the real workings about one another's system. Nevertheless, the education of Soviet citizens concerning American literature, geography, history, and politics is far more extensive than what is taught in U.S. schools about the U.S.S.R. See, for example, E. McGrath, "Wanted More Kremlinologists," *Time,* 29 November 1982, p. 98.
3. J. Barron, "The KGB's Magical War for 'Peace'," *Readers Digest,* October 1982.
4. E. Kennedy and M. Hatfield, *Freeze! How You Can Prevent Nuclear War* (New York: Bantam Books, 1982), p. 94.
5. NBC-TV news lead item, 31 May 1982.
6. E. Diamond, S. Bates, and J. Boyer, "The Turning of TV News," *TV-Guide,* 7 August 1982, pp. 4–8.
7. John McMahon, deputy director of the CIA, quoted in congressional testimony to the House Select Committee on Intelligence, December 1982.
8. M. Mowlan, "Peace Groups and Politics," *Bulletin of the Atomic Scientists,* November 1983, p. 28.
9. U.S. Department of Defense, *Soviet Military Power* (Washington, D.C.: GPO, 1981).
10. U.S.S.R. Ministry of Defense, *Whence the Threat to Peace?* (Moscow: 1982).
11. Four Continent Book Corporation, New York; Imported Publications, Inc., Chicago; Victor Kamkin, Inc., Rockville, Maryland.
12. Edward O'Malley, assistant director of intelligence of the FBI, quoted in the *New York Times,* 10 December 1982.

13. The English translation of Khrushchev's famed remark apparently was "We will see you buried," which carries a distinctly different connotation from "We will bury you."
14. "A Dark Tunnel of Fear," *Newsweek*, 18 October 1982, p. 48.
15. H. Smith, *The Russians* (New York: Ballantine Books, 1976), p. 679.
16. G. Gallup, *The Gallup Poll: Public Opinion 1981* (Wilmington: Scholarly Resources, Inc., 1982), pp. 134–36.
17. J. Kalven, "A Talk with Louis Harris," *Bulletin of the Atomic Scientists*, August/September 1982, pp. 3–5.
18. E. Hastings and P. Hastings, eds., *Index to International Public Opinion 1979–1980*, (Westport: Greenwood, 1981), p. 124.

Chapter 3

1. Quoted from F. Kaplan, *Dubious Specter: A Skeptical Look at the Soviet Nuclear Threat* (Washington, D.C.: Institute for Policy Studies, 1980), p. 3.
2. Quoted from *Annual Report of the Department of Defense, FY 81* (Washington, D.C.: Government Printing Office, 1980), p. 66.
3. A one-megaton bomb has the explosive force of one million tons of TNT. One megaton (Mt) equals one thousand kilotons (kt).
4. Quoted in an article in the *Washington Post*, 27 December 1982.
5. J. Wit, "Progress in Antisubmarine Warfare," *Scientific American*, February 1981, p. 31.
6. *Washington Post*, 27 December 1982.
7. U.S. Congress, Office of Technology Assessment, *The Effects of Nuclear War* (Washington, D.C.: Government Printing Office, 1979), pp. 27–45.
8. "Soviet Acquisition of Western Technology," Central Intelligence Agency report, April 1982, p. 1.
9. *Jane's Military Review* (London: Janes, 1983).
10. Hearings Before the Subcommittee on Strategic and Theater Nuclear Forces of the Senate Committee on Armed Services, 26 October through 13 November 1981, pp. 124–25.
11. The effects of fallout are proportional to megatonnage rather than equivalent megatonnage. The Soviet lead is bigger in the former than the latter category.
12. Kennedy and Hatfield, *Freeze*, p. 147.
13. S. Talbott, *Time*, 29 March 1982, p. 19.
14. N. Kruschev, *For Victory in Peaceful Competition with Capitalism* (New York: E. P. Dutton, 1960), p. xv.

Chapter 4

1. Q. Wright, *A Study of War* (Chicago: University of Chicago Press, 1965), pp. 690–91.
2. Wright, *Study of War,* p. 1562.
3. L. Richardson, *Arms and Insecurity* (New York: Times Books, 1960).
4. P. Schrodt, "Microcomputers in the Study of Politics," *BYTE Magazine,* July 1982, p. 112.
5. Ibid., pp. 112–13.
6. Quoted in Ground Zero, *Nuclear War: What's in It for You?* (New York: Pocket Books, 1982), p. 101.
7. S. Zuckerman, *Nuclear Illusion and Reality,* (New York: Viking Press), p. 85.
8. B. Schemmer, "Reagan Okays M-X," *Armed Forces Journal,* November 1981, p. 28.
9. Quoted in Kaplan, *Dubious Specter,* p. 46.
10. K. Mshalenko, "Constant Combat Readiness Is a Strategic Category," FPD trans. 0087/69, *Voyennaya Mysl',* 1969, no. 1: p. 14.
11. B. Byely et al., "Marxism-Leninism on War and Army: A Soviet View," trans. U.S. Air Force, *Soviet Military Thought,* no. 2 (Washington, D.C.: GPO, 1974), p. 217.
12. C. von Clausewitz, *On War,* ed. and trans. by M. Howard and P. Paret (Princeton: Princeton University Press, 1976, p. 92.
13. Kaplan, *Dubious Specter,* p. 16.
14. B. Russett and B. Blair, eds., *Progress in Arms Control?,* (San Francisco: W.H. Freeman and Co., 1979), p. 114.
15. W. Knaus, *Washington Post,* 15 October 1982.
16. T. Powers, "Choosing a Strategy for World War III," *The Atlantic Monthly,* November 1982, p. 13.
17. H. Scoville, *MX: Prescription for Disaster,* (Cambridge: MIT Press, 1981), p. 87.
18. Quoted in B. Schneider, "Invitation to a Nuclear Beheading," *Across the Board,* 20, (July/August 1983), p. 14.
19. Quoted in Schneider, "Nuclear Beheading", p. 16.
20. Scoville, *MX,* p. 16.
21. J. Douglass, Jr., "What Happens if Deterrence Fails?," *Air University Review,* November/December 1982, p. 5.
22. *Washington Post,* 27 December 1982.
23. J. Anderson, "U.S. May Have Plans for a First Strike," *Washington Post,* 19 May 1983. ("Favorable assumptions" include no Soviet launch on warning or launch under attack.)
24. Scientist's Institute for Public Information, "Interview with Richard Garwin—Part 2," *SIPIscope,* 10 (September—October 1982), p. 12.
25. R. Garwin, "Ballistic Missile Defense: Silos and Space," Paper presented to the American Physical Society, 10 March 1982.

26. *Washington Post,* 27 March 1983.
27. *Washington Post,* 3 April 1983.
28. Ibid.
29. H. Brown, Speech to the Arms Control Association, 26 May, 1982.
30. Zuckerman, *Nuclear Illusion and Reality,* p. 132.
31. Quoted in S. Talbott, "The Risks of Taking Up Shields," *Time,* 4 April 1983.

Chapter 5

1. October 1981 Presidential Press Conference.
2. Quoted in P. Zimmerman and A. Greb, "How No First Use Can Work," *Bulletin of the Atomic Scientists,* December 1983, p. 48.
3. Gallup poll reported in *Newsweek,* 5 October 1981.
4. E. Hastings and P. Hastings, *Index to International Public Opinion 1980–1981,* (Westport: Greenwood, 1982), p. 257.
5. E. Hastings and P. Hastings, *Index to International Public Opinion 1979–1980,* (Westport: Greenwood, 1981), p. 145.
6. Ibid., p. 330.
7. Ibid., p. 331.
8. C. deBoer, "The Polls: Our Commitment to World War III," *Public Opinion Quarterly* 45 (1981), pp. 126–34.
9. U.S.S.R. Ministry of Defense, *Whence The Threat to Peace?* (Moscow, 1982), pp. 63–70.
10. A. Cordesman, "NATO's Estimate of the Ballance," *Armed Forces Journal,* August 1982, p. 48.
11. K. Dunn, "Mysteries about the Soviet Union," *Orbis,* Summer 1982, pp. 361–79.
12. Quoted in R. Garthoff, "The Threat to Europe," *Arms Control Today,* 12, March 1982, p. 9.
13. H. Kissinger, *Nuclear Weapons and Foreign Policy,* (New York: Doubleday, 1958), p. 124.
14. H. Kissinger, *The Necessity for Choice* (London: Chatto, 1960).
15. Kissinger, *Nuclear Weapons,* p. 142.
16. F. Kaplan, "Enhanced Radiation Weapons," *Scientific American,* May 1978, p. 48.
17. V. Ye Savkin, "Basic Principles of Operational Art and Tactics: A Soviet View," *Soviet Military Thought,* no. 4 (Washington, D.C.: GPO, 1974).
18. N. Vasendin and N. Kuznetsov, "Modern Warfare and Surprise Attack," FPB trans. 0005/69, *Voyennaya Mysl',* 1968, no. 6: p. 46.
19. Zuckerman, *Nuclear Illusion and Reality,* pp. x–xi.
20. I. Kristol, "Exorcising the Nuclear Nightmare," *Washington Post,* 12 March 1982.

21. G. LaRocque, *U.S. Military Force, 1980: An Evaluation*, (Washington, D.C.: Center for Defense Information, 1980).
22. Kennedy and Hatfield, *Freeze!*, pp. 137–38.
23. L. Beilenson, *Survival and Peace in the Nuclear Age*, (Chicago: Regnery/ Gateway Inc., 1980), p. 114.
24. P. Zimmerman and A. Greb, "The Bottom Rung of the Ladder: Battlefield Nuclear Weapons in Europe," *The Naval War College Review*, November/December 1982, pp. 35–51.
25. Ibid., p. 47.

Chapter 6

1. S. Glasstone and P. Dolan, *The Effects of Nuclear Weapons*, U.S. Department of Defense and the Energy Research and Development Administration (Washington, D.C.: GPO, 1977).
2. Office of Technology Assessment, *Effects of Nuclear War*, (Washington, D.C.: GPO, 1979).
3. Ibid., p. 21.
4. Conrad Chester of Oak Ridge National Laboratory, in an informal communication on January 1, 1983, noted that portable AM radio with ferrite bar antennas have survived threat-level EMP electric fields experimentally. FM radios, with or without the antenna extended, were found to have been rendered inoperable in the same experiments.
5. *Washington Post*, 5 December 1982.
6. H. Jack Geiger, "Short and Long-Term Health Effects on the Surviving Population of a Nuclear War," Testimony before the Senate Committee on Labor and Human Resources, Subcommittee on Health and Scientific Research, 96th Congress, 19 June 1980, p. 27.
7. K. Earp, "Deaths from Fire in Large Scale Attack—With Special Reference to the Hamburg Firestorm," British Home Office, London, Scientific Adviser's Branch, April 1953, CD/SA 28.
8. Office of Technology Assessment, *Effects of Nuclear War*, p. 22.
9. The Soviet Union is not believed to have any warheads with yields as large as 20 megatons, despite having once tested a 55 megaton device.
10. J. Schell, *The Fate of the Earth* (New York: Knopf, 1982), p. 51.

Chapter 7

1. Interview with Senator Alan Cranston as reported in *Time*, 29 March 1982, p. 16.
2. Schell, *Fate of the Earth*, p. 95.
3. Office of Technology Assessment, *Effects of Nuclear War*, p. 3.

4. Schell, *Fate of the Earth,* p. 65.
5. Gallup poll reported in *Newsweek,* 5 October 1981, p. 24.
6. L. Beres, "Relocation is Not Possible," Paper delivered to the Twenty-third Convention of International Studies, 1982.
7. S. Drell and F. von Hippel, "Limited Nuclear War," *Scientific American,* November 1976, p. 27.
8. Office of Technology Assessment, *Effects of Nuclear War,* p. 87.
9. Ibid., p. 88.
10. Ibid., p. 91.
11. Oak Ridge National Laboratory, "Survival of the Relocated Population of the U.S. after a Nuclear Attack," report ORNL-5041, 1976, p. 7.
12. Kennedy and Hatfield, *Freeze!,* p. 62.
13. Office of Technology Assessment, *Effects of Nuclear War,* p. 100.
14. United States Arms Control and Disarmament Agency, "An Analysis of Civil Defense in Nuclear War," (Washington, D.C., 1978), p. 3.
15. Ibid., p. 6.
16. In the most favorable scenario from the Soviet perspective, all U.S. land-based missiles, bombers, and submarines in port are destroyed in a surprise attack. The U.S. submarines at sea with half the warheads in the American arsenal would contain 200 megatons, equivalent to about 2.5 percent of the total Soviet megatonnage. The Soviet land area is 2.4 times that of the U.S., so that the megatonnage delivered per unit area against the U.S.S.R. in this extreme scenario would be one hundredth that delivered against the United States.
17. See discussion of blast shelters in chapter 9.
18. Office of Technology Assessment, *Effects of Nuclear War,* p. 97.
19. Ibid., p. 106.

Chapter 8

1. These analyses were reported as a collection of articles published in *Ambio* 11 (1982), p. 76; reprinted as *The Aftermath: The Human and Ecological Consequences of Nuclear War,* ed. J. Peterson (New York: Pantheon, 1983).
2. S. Bergstrom et al., "Effects of a Nuclear War on Health and Health Services," World Health Organization publication A36.12, 1983.
3. National Academy of Sciences, *Long-Term Worldwide Effects of Multiple Nuclear-Weapons Detonations,* (Washington, D.C., 1975).
4. P. J. Crutzen and J. W. Birks, *Ambio* 11 (1982), p. 114.
5. R. P. Turco et al., "Nuclear Winter: Global Consequences of Multiple Nuclear Explosions," *Science,* 222 (1983), pp. 1283–92.
6. C. Covey, S. Thompson, and S. Schneider, "Global Atmospheric Effects of Massive Smoke Injections from a Nuclear War: Results from General Circulation Model Simulation," *Nature,* 308 (1984), pp. 21–25.

7. M. C. MacCracken, "Nuclear War: Preliminary Estimates of the Climatic Effects of a Nuclear Exchange," UCRL-89770 Reprint, Lawrence Livermore Laboratory, October 1983.

8. The three studies show approximate agreement in the predicted magnitude and duration of the temperature drop.

9. This paragraph appeared in "Summary of Conference Findings" prepared for the World After Nuclear War Conference, 31 October—1 November, 1983, Washington, D.C. The conference proceedings have been reprinted in book form: P. Ehrlich, et al., *The Cold and The Dark*, (New York: W. W. Norton, 1984).

10. L. W. Alvarez, et al., "Extraterrestrial Cause for the Cretaceous-Tertiary Extinction" *Science* 208 (1980), p. 1095.

11. National Academy of Sciences, *Effects of Nuclear Weapons Detonations*, p. 6.

12. It might seem that larger particles would better block sunlight, but that is not the case unless the particles are much smaller than the wavelength of light.

13. Civil Defense Preparedness Agency, *DCPA Attack Environment Manual*, Chapter 3 (Washington, D.C.: GPO, 1972), p. 24.

14. Turco et al., "Nuclear Winter," p. 1285.

15. Ibid.

16. Informal conversation between the author and R. P. Turco on January 6, 1984.

17. Ibid.

18. Ibid.

19. Ibid.

20. Ibid.

21. Ibid.

22. The evidence is unclear, but the *DCPA Attack Environment Manual* (note 13) indicates that such an effect might occur.

23. In a large nuclear attack fire-fighting would seem hopeless. However, in a 100-megaton attack, involving the detonation of one 100 kt weapon over each city, fire-fighting might be feasible.

24. The Turco et al. calculation (note 5) is one-dimensional. The other studies (notes 6 and 7) include both one-, two-, and three-dimensional results.

25. Turco et al., "Nuclear Winter," p. 1286.

26. V. V. Aleksandrov and G. L. Stenchikov, "On the Modelling of the Climatic Consequences of the Nuclear War" (Moscow: U.S.S.R. Academy of Sciences, 1983).

27. Turco et al., "Nuclear Winter," p. 1290.

28. A list of studies on ozone depletion is given in J. B. Knox et al., "Program Report for FY 1982 Atmospheric and Geophysical Sciences Division of the Physics Department," UCRL-51444–82, Lawrence Livermore Laboratory.

29. Turco et al., "Nuclear Winter," p. 1289; Knox et al., "Program Report," p. 44.

30. Based on an informal conversation with Joseph Knox on January 6, 1984, the six-fold UV-B increase given in the National Academy of Sciences, Long-Term Worldwide Effects, p. 177 overstates the increase by a factor of two.

31. National Academy of Sciences, Long-Term Worldwide Effects, p. 14.

32. National Academy of Sciences, Long-Term Worldwide Effects, p. 73.

33. Ibid.

34. K. Tsipis, Arsenal: Understanding Weapons in the Nuclear Age, (New York: Simon and Schuster, 1983) p. 100; The Final Epidemic, a film made by the Physicians for Social Responsibility.

35. J. B. Knox, "Global Scale Deposition of Radioactivity from a Large Scale Nuclear Exchange," UCRL-89907, Lawrence Livermore Laboratory, 1983, p. 4.

36. Turco et al., "Nuclear Winter," p. 1289; Knox, "Global Scale Deposition," p. 2.

37. Ibid.

38. Ibid.

39. International Commission on Radiological Protection Recommendations, ICRP No. 26, cited in J. Leaning and L. Keyes, eds., The Counterfeit Ark—Crisis Relocation for Nuclear War, (Cambridge: Ballinger, 1984), p. 214.

40. Committee on the Biological Effects of Ionizing Radiations, The Effects on Populations of Exposure to Low Levels of Ionizing Radiation: 1980 (Washington, D.C.: National Academy Press, 1980), p. 3.

41. The 0.2 year loss in life expectancy is obtained by assuming that the average cancer death occurs at age 55, and corresponds to a life expectancy loss of 20 years. The average loss for the entire population is then found by multiplying 20 years by the 7.9 percentage increase in cancer deaths, and the 12.5 percent rate of naturally occurring deaths, i.e., (20 yrs.) (.078) (.125) = 0.2 yrs.

42. B. Cohen, Nuclear Science and Society (Garden City: Anchor, 1974), p. 64.

43. A. Steward, Epidimiology and Community Health, June 1982.

44. Kennedy and Hatfield, Freeze!, p. 46.

45. Committee on the Biological Effects of Ionizing Radiation, The Effects on Populations, p. 4.

46. Ibid., p. 5.

47. F. Kaplan, "Enhanced Radiation Weapons," Scientific American, May 1978, p. 50.

48. The general consensus is that no excess genetic defects have been observed among Hiroshima and Nagasaki survivors (see note 40). A doubling of the spontaneous rate almost certainly would have been detectible, let alone a factor of twenty increase.

49. National Academy of Sciences, *Long-Term Effects*, p. 16 cites an increase of .04 percent for a dose of 5 rems.

50. Committee on the Biological Effects of Ionizing Radiation, *The Effects on Populations*, pp. 497–98.

51. National Academy of Sciences, *Long-Term Effects*, p. 12 cites values of .005 rem and .1 rem based on a whole-body dose estimate of 5 rem. Therefore, the listed internal exposures have been increased by a factor of ten to correspond to a 50 rem external dose.

52. Knox, "Global Scale Deposition," p. 16.

53. Preliminary results from three-dimensional model calculations indicate that a major disturbance in the atmospheric circulation could occur (see, for example, Covey, "Global Atmospheric Effects," pp. 21–5). A major disturbance in the atmospheric circulation could increase the severity of effects in the Southern Hemisphere and moderate those in the Northern Hemisphere.

54. Turco et al., "Nuclear Winter," p. 1287.

55. National Academy of Sciences, *Long-Term Effects*, p. 44.

56. Knox, "Global Scale Deposition," p. 9.

57. A reliable number is difficult to ascertain. Alexander Solzhenitsyn uses a figure as high as 60 million; many Western analysts consider that figure to be a significant exaggeration, putting the figure instead at no more than 12 million. Understandably, Soviet authorities deride all such estimates as propaganda.

58. In an article in the *Washington Post* 30, October, 1983, Carl Sagan notes that "Even small nuclear wars can have devastating climatic impacts . . . enough to generate an epoch of cold and dark." Sagan fails to note, however, that the "small" (100 megaton) nuclear war would need to involve an extremely implausible scenario: one thousand "small" weapons each delivered against a different city, all of which burn extensively.

Chapter 9

1. Precautions such as school children diving under desks to protect themselves against flying glass were not so futile in the early 1960's, when the much smaller Soviet nuclear arsenal meant that many buildings even in large cities might be far enough from detonations to escape collapse due to blast.

2. M. Yudkin, "When Kids Think the Unthinkable," *Psychology Today*, April 1984, p. 20.

3. Office of Technology Assessment, *Effects of Nuclear War*, p. 10.

4. Ibid., pp. 94–5.

5. Reportedly, targeting civilians per se is not a part of U.S. or Soviet stated targeting policy.

6. S. Lens, *The Day After Doomsday*, (Boston: Beacon Press, 1977), p. 151.
7. The estimate of 4 to 5 percent is based on a calculation described in Chapter 3.
8. Typical residential basements have protection factors in the range 10 to 20, according to Glasstone and Dolan, *The Effects of Nuclear Weapons*, p. 441. Upgrading the radiation protection by shoveling six inches of dirt against the above ground portion of the exterior walls could triple the protection factor.
9. Kennedy and Hatfield, *Freeze!*, pp. 95–6.
10. This point is contestible, since even if only a few hours notice were available a fraction of the evacuating population might have a much better chance of survival.
11. Central Intelligence Agency, "Soviet Civil Defense," (Washington, D.C.: 1978), p. 8.
12. Ibid., p. 3.
13. Ibid., p. 4.
14. Arms Control and Disarmament Agency, "Civil Defense in Nuclear War," p. 5.
15. J. Weinstein, "Soviet Civil Defense: The Mine Shaft Gap Revisited," *Arms Control Today*, July/August 1982, p. 2.
16. Soviet cities have excellent public transportation systems even though citizens have far fewer private automobiles.
17. *Der Spiegel*, 28 August 1982.
18. Central Intelligence Agency, "Soviet Civil Defense," p. 4.
19. U.S. Department of Defense, *Soviet Military Power*, pp. 68–9.
20. U.S.S.R. Ministry of Defense, *Whence the Threat to Peace?*
21. Private communication on November 23, 1982 between the author and Leo Hecht, a scholar in the field of Russion studies and a frequent visitor to the U.S.S.R.
22. *Oregonian*, 13 October 1982.
23. This credibility problem is due to a lack of sophistication on the part of both administration spokesmen and the media. Moreover, the problem is compounded by politicians who want to make civil defense appear as absurd as possible in order to kill the program.
24. H. Kendall, "Second Strike," *Bulletin of the Atomic Scientists*, September 1979, p. 32.
25. H. Kendall, "Testimony on Civil Defense," prepared in connection with 8 January 1979 hearings before the U.S. Senate Committee on Banking, Housing, and Urban Affairs.
26. C. Kearny, *Nuclear War Survival Skills*, (Naperville: Caroline House, 1980).

Chapter 10

1. S. Nunn, "Arms Control: What We Should Do," *Washington Post,* 12 November 1981.
2. H. Kissinger, *Years of Upheaval* (Boston, Little Brown, 1982), reprinted in *Time,* 15, March 1982, p. 34.
3. R. Barnet, "Arms Control and Real Security," *Arms Control Today,* June 1982, p. 6.
4. Quoted in T. Martin Jr. and D. Latham, *Strategy for Survival* (Tuscon: University of Arizona Press, 1963), p. 138.
5. Quoted in Lens, *The Day Before Doomsday,* pp. 216–17.
6. Quoted in L. Wieseltier, *Nuclear War, Nuclear Peace* (New York: Holt, Rinehart and Winston, 1983), p. 43.
7. Forsberg's proposal was made in a 1979 speech to the Mobilization for Survival peace group meeting in Louisville.
8. ABC News Poll reported in the *Washington Post,* 29 April 1982.
9. Kennedy and Hatfield, *Freeze!,* p. 142.
10. Ibid.
11. Interview with R. Pipes reported in the *Washington Post,* 11 April 1982.
12. C. Sagan, "Nuclear War and Climatic Catastrophe: Some Policy Implications," *Foreign Affairs, Winter 1983/84,* p. 292.
13. Kissinger, *Years of Upheaval,* reprinted in *Time,* p. 34.
14. Barnet, "Arms Control and Real Security," p. 3.
15. Kennedy and Hatfield, *Freeze!,* p. 101.
16. L. Aspin, "The Verification of the SALT II Agreement," *Scientific American,* February 1979, p. 38.
17. Ibid., p. 45.
18. A. Harriman, "The Window of Opportunity," *Washington Post,* 4 November 1981.
19. Kennedy and Hatfield, *Freeze!,* p. 154.
20. P. Morrisroe, "Soviet Sleight of Hand," *Psychology Today,* June 1983, p. 7.
21. Ibid.
22. Interview reported in *Time,* 29 March 1982, p. 16.
23. P. Ehrlich, "Disarmament: The Lesser Risk," *Bulletin of the Atomic Scientists,* August/September 1982, pp. 7–8.
24. Quoted in H. Kissinger, *Years of Upheaval,* reprinted in *Time,* p. 34.
25. G. Hart, "Arms Control: Towards a Redefinition," *Arms Control Today,* May 1982, p. 1.

Chapter 11

1. That assessment is also a matter of speculation. It is equally possible that a small nuclear war could have an extremely sobering effect on the rest of the world and bring about positive political changes that could reduce the risk of worldwide holocaust.
2. Some intelligence reports indicate that Israel and South Africa may have collaborated on a project to build the bomb. Such speculation may not be entirely implausible in light of the similar world status of these two pariah states and the fact that each possesses what the other would need: Israel has the technological knowledge and South Africa has the uranium.
3. Nuclear Control Institute, "World Inventories of Civilian Plutonium and the Spread of Nuclear Weapons," (Washington, D.C., 1983).
4. Ibid., p. 1.
5. Ibid., p. 8.
6. *New York Times,* 24 October 1982.
7. Nuclear fusion reactors, which will not be feasible until the next century, do not use fissionable material.
8. Arguments in support of the "dangerous" and "tenuous" connection are presented in a booklet "Nuclear Energy, Nuclear Weapons Proliferation, and the Arms Race," published in 1982 by the American Association of Physics Teachers.
9. ^{240}Pu is a particularly unsuitable isotope because it undergoes spontaneous fission; in sufficient concentrations it causes a premature release of neutrons which result in a less predictable and less effective detonation.
10. The penalty for using commercial-reactor spent fuel to produce plutonium for weapons cannot be too serious, since at one time the U.S. government was considering that option.
11. J. Miller, "The Peaceful Atom Bases Its Teeth," *Readers Digest,* June 1983, p. 95.
12. Ibid.

BIBLIOGRAPHY _____

PERIODICALS AND YEARBOOKS

Annual Report of the Department of Defense by the Secretary of Defense, Superintendent of Documents, U.S. Government Printing Office, Washington, D.C. 20402. Annual.

Armed Forces Journal, 1414 22nd St., N.W., Washington, D.C. 20037. Monthly.

Arms Control Impact Sttement by the Arms Control and Disarmament Agency, Superintendent of Documents, U.S. Government Printing Office, Washington, D.C. 20402. Annual.

Arms Control Today, Arms Control Association, 11 Dupont Circle, N.W., Washington, D.C. 20036. Monthly.

Atlas-World Press Review, Box 915, Farmingdale, N.Y. 11737. Monthly.

Aviation Week and Space Technology, P.O. Box 430, Hightstown, N.J. 08520. Weekly.

Bulletin of the Atomic Scientists, 1020–24 E. 58th St., Chicago, Ill. 60637. Ten issues per year.

Bulletin of Peace Proposals, International Peace Research Institute, Radhusgt 4, Oslo 1, Norway. Quarterly.

Coevolution Quarterly, Point Foundation, Box 428, Sausalito, Calif. 94965. Quarterly.

Current News and the Friday Review of Defense Literature, Department of the Air Force, Washington, D.C. 20330. Weekly. By exchange agreement only.

Current Research on Peace and Violence, Tampere Peace Research Institute, Hamenkatu 13b A, 33100, Tampere 10, Finland. Quarterly.

Defense Monitor, Center for Defense Information, 122 Maryland Ave. N.E., Washington, D.C. 20002. Ten issues per year.

Disarmament Times, Room 7B, 777 United Nations Plaza, New York, N.Y. 10017. Eight issues per year.

Federation of American Scientists Public Interest Report, FAS, 307 Massachusetts Ave., N.E., Washington, D.C. 20002. Monthly.

Foreign Policy by the Carnegie Endowment for International Peace, 11 Dupont Circle, N.W., Washington, D.C. 20036.

International Security by the Program for Science and International Affairs of Harvard University, 79 Boylston St., Cambridge, Ma. 02138.

Jane's Weapons Systems, R. T. Petty and H. R. Archer, Jane's Yearbooks, London, England.

Journal of Civil Defense, P.O. Box 910, Starke, Fl. 32091. Monthly.

The Military Balance, International Institute for Strategic Studies, London, England. Annual.

Military and Social Expenditures, World Priorities, Box 1003, Leesburg, Va. 22075. Annual.

Military Posture Statement by the organization of the Joint Chiefs of Staff, Superintendent of Documents, U.S. Government Printing Office, Washington, D.C. 20402. Annual.

Scientific American, 415 Madison Avenue, New York, N.Y. 10017. Monthly.

Strategic Review, U.S. Strategic Institute of Washington.

Strategic Survey, International Institute for Strategic Studies, London, England, Annual.

Survival, International Institute for Strategic Studies, London, England. Bimonthly.

World Armaments and Disarmament, Swedish International Peace Research Institute, MIT Press, Cambridge, Ma. 02142. Annual.

BIBLIOGRAPHIES AND GENERAL BOOKS

Arkin, William. *Research Guide to Current Military and Strategic Affairs.* Washington, D.C.: Institute for Policy Studies, 1981.

Burns, R. D. *Arms Control and Disarmament: A Bibliography.* Santa Barbara, Calif.: ABC-Clio, 1977.

Cochran, T. B., Arkin, W. M., and Hoenig, M. M., *Nuclear Weapons Databook,* Cambridge, Ma.: Ballinger, 1984.

Dowling, J. *War, Peace Film Guide.* Chicago, Ill.: World Without War Publications, 1980.

Kincade, W. J. and Jeffrey D. Porro. *Negotiating Security: An Arms Control Reader.* Washington, D.C.: Carnegie Endowment for International Peace, 1979.

Labrie, R. P., ed. *SALT Handbook: Key Documents and Issues, 1972-1979.* Washington, D.C.: American Enterprise Institute, 1979.

Progress in Arms Control? A Reader. Readings from *Scientific American.* San Francisco: W. H. Freeeman, 1979.

U.S. Congress, House Committee on International Relations and Senate Committee on Government Affairs. *Bibliography: Nuclear Proliferation.* Washington, D.C.: Government Printing Office, 1978.

York, H., ed. *Arms Control: Readings from Scientific American.* San Francisco: W. H. Freeman, 1973.

INDEX